Integrated Reporting

Cristiano Busco • Mark L. Frigo
Angelo Riccaboni • Paolo Quattrone
Editors

Integrated Reporting

Concepts and Cases that Redefine
Corporate Accountability

Foreword by Sabina Ratti

 Springer

Editors
Cristiano Busco
J.E. Cairnes School of Business
 & Economics
National University of Ireland
Galway
Ireland

Angelo Riccaboni
University of Siena
Siena
Italy

Mark L. Frigo
Kellstadt Graduate School of Business
DePaul University
Chicago
Illinois
USA

Paolo Quattrone
The University of Edinburgh
Edinburgh
United Kingdom

This publication was grant-aided by the Publications Fund of National University of Ireland Galway / Rinneadh maoiniú ar an bhfoilseachán seo trí Chiste Foilseachán Ollscoil na hÉireann, Gaillimh

ISBN 978-3-319-34895-7   ISBN 978-3-319-02168-3 (eBook)
DOI 10.1007/978-3-319-02168-3
Springer Cham Heidelberg New York Dordrecht London

Springer is part of Springer Science+Business Media (www.springer.com)

Foreword

Integrated Reporting is arguably the current frontier of corporate reporting. The demands on corporate reports are growing rapidly in parallel with stakeholder engagement of a greater in-depth understanding of the companies they have an interest in. In this context, the recent establishment of the International Integrated Reporting Council by a number of leading organizations represented an additional, perhaps decisive, move towards the definition of a globally accepted reporting framework. Such a framework aims to bring together financial, environmental, social and governance information to enable stakeholders understand the true ability of a company to deliver sustainable value and to educate investors to overcome short-termism in their investment decisions. This, in turn, would further enhance a company's ability to make sustainable choices.

The definition of such a framework is everything but easy, though. This is because corporate numbers and information are quite meaningless without a proper and full understanding of the complex context which generates them. Let me draw a comparison with the act of watching a movie. If you watch the last 10 min of a movie you most likely know how the movie ends, you are aware of its final outcomes. If this is a romantic movie, you know if the two are still together or not; while, in the case of an action movie, you most likely end up discovering who the killer was. But, unfortunately, although you do get to see the final outcomes of the movie, you still miss a lot to make sense of it. You miss a full appreciation of the themes of the movie, its significant passage points and the unique and possibly complex story that has led to this specific final outcome. When you approach most of contemporary corporate reports, the feeling is similar to the one described above: it is difficult to fully understand how a number of different, and often stand alone, indicators have contributed to value creation; it is difficult to appreciate the complexity hidden behind the numbers. Ultimately, in most of the cases it is difficult to infer how sustainable value creation can be maintained and further developed in the future. Integrated Reporting aims to do that!

Because the efforts around Integrated Reporting are still in their early stages, I really do welcome this edited collection on the topic. When I have read the contents of this book, this has brought me back to my early days at Eni where, although my background is molecular biology, I was leading a project tailored to develop an early form of environmental accounting, as well as to identify a control system for evaluating the impact of business operations on the environment. I was working with an interdisciplinary team in search of metrics, solutions and data that would have eventually allowed the company to perform more efficiently in environmental protection, make savings and better understand its business. This experience has been extremely important for us at Eni. It allowed us to practice collaboration across disciplines and integrated thinking. This first step was mainly an internal effort, though. When, later on, we succeeded in incorporating the results of the dialogue with our external stakeholders, environmental and social reporting at Eni moved to the next level.

Stakeholders engagement has been of paramount importance in the evolution of corporate reporting. Systematic engagement with key stakeholders has enabled corporations to question, and then challenge, a number of things that possibly had been taken for granted before that. At Eni, after having issued a series of Environmental and then Sustainability Reports we realized that, although the numbers were allowing a true and fair review of the company's performance, operations and management, they were not necessarily relevant to the stakeholders or able to hint the sustainability of the business. Neither was the simple act of reporting data relevant per se. What was missing was a broader process of analysis and communication able to put performance in context, able to represent the strategic leverages the company was using to build and maintain its ability to produce value in the long term. Stakeholders' demands for greater transparency have, in time, been coupled with an internal reflection on what the company considered its strategic drivers: nowadays, our integrated reporting aims to respond to this challenge.

A cultural shift is, though, required to support such a process. A shift of paradigm rooted on the reorganization of systems, processes and practices in search of Sustainable Value creation and representation. In this respect, joining the Pilot Programme of the International Integrated Reporting Council back in 2011 was very useful to us. Integrated Reporting offers an opportunity to combine Sustainability and profitability in a single process, in a single document and, ultimately, in a single story. It is a promising powerful tool to increase the internal and external awareness, especially among investors, on the way in which the integrated management of the business is currently practiced.

Significantly, Integrated Reporting aims at offering a long-term view. It is a dynamic observatory designed and implemented to offer a space where organizational strategies, objectives, results and outcomes can be illustrated and interpreted in a combined fashion. The objective is not so much to unpack complexity, rather to make the users appreciate how the constitutive elements of a complex organization in a complex environment contribute to Sustainable Value creation over the short, medium and long term. In doing so, the numbers and information provided in the Integrated Report aim at representing the way in which Sustainability's objectives and multiple perspectives are fully embedded within the Company's business model and decision-making processes.

For the above-mentioned reasons, I do welcome the publication of this book. Integrated Reporting is in its early stages, and any effort to illustrate, discuss and eventually question its contents, elements and principles is a much needed and useful exercise. Integrated Reporting is currently a lively and engaging theme, worthwhile to be further explored both theoretically and practically around the globe. Along this line, the usefulness of this book is twofold. First, it provides a number of insightful chapters attempting to deepen our understanding on specific concepts and principles. Second, this book offers a collection of best practices attempting to describe and, in some cases, discuss how a number of companies, large and small, private or public, are approaching Integrated Reporting in practice.

The trajectory of Integrated Reporting is about to mark an important milestone. Soon, in December, the International Integrated Reporting Council will release the first version of its framework. The journey has just recently begun, but Integrated Reporting is about to enter in a critical phase where its rationale as well as its concept will be tested, challenged and advanced.

This book is very timely and prepares all of us to do that. I trust you will enjoy and benefit from reading it.

Sabina Ratti
Eni
Sustainability Senior Vice President

Introduction

What is Integrated Reporting? Who is driving the agenda? What are the building blocks and best practices to date? This book aims to address these questions by illustrating and debating the rise of and the challenges ahead for this new form of reporting. The purpose is to participate to the current debate on Integrated Reporting (IR) by reflecting both on the key concepts, elements and principles that underpin its adoption and on a collection of cases that describe how a number of companies, large and small, private and public, are approaching IR in practice.

What is Integrated Reporting? IR is a process that results in communicating—through the annual integrated report—value creation over time. According to the International Integrated Reporting Council (IIRC), an integrated report is a concise communication about how an organization's strategy, governance, performance and prospects, in the context of its external environment, lead to the creation of value over the short, medium and long term. Although providers of financial capital are the primary intended IR users, an integrated report should be designed to benefit all stakeholders—including employees, customers, suppliers, business partners, local communities, regulators and policy makers—interested in an organization's ability to create value over time. The key objective of IR is to enhance accountability and stewardship with respect to the broad base of six kinds of capital, or "capitals" (financial, manufactured, intellectual, human, social and relationship and natural), and promote understanding of their interdependencies. In doing this, IR is designed to support integrated thinking, decision making and actions that focus on sustainable value creation for stakeholders.

Who is driving the agenda? Although the journey of IR has started much earlier than that, 3 years have now gone by since a number of leading organizations, including the Prince's Accounting for Sustainability Project and the Global Reporting Initiative, announced the formation of the International Integrated Reporting Council (IIRC). During these years the IIRC, a global coalition of regulators, investors, companies, standards setters, the accounting profession and nongovernmental organizations, has actively operated to redesign the landscape of corporate reporting. In April 2013, the IIRC released a Consultation Draft (CD) of the first Integrated Reporting Framework. The CD focuses on how to prepare and present an integrated report and what to include in it. The CD was developed based on an analysis of the responses to the 2011 Discussion Paper "Towards Integrated Reporting—Communicating Value in the 21st Century", the publication of a draft outline in July 2012, and a Prototype Framework in November 2012. Importantly, the first version of its IR Framework is expected to be released by the IIRC in December 2013.

What are the building blocks and best practices to date? The CD released by the IIRC introduces and discusses a number of fundamental concepts, content elements and guiding principles for the implementation of IR. The fundamental concepts of IR are represented by the capitals that an organization uses and affects, the organization's business model and the creation of value over time. The business model is the vehicle through which an organization creates value. That value is embodied in the capitals—sometimes also referred to as resources and relationships—that the organization uses and affects. The assessment of an organization's ability to create value in the short, medium and long term depends on an understanding of the connectivity between its business model and a wide range of internal and external factors.

These factors represent the content elements of the integrated report. An integrated report is built around seven elements that define its content and communicate the organization's unique value-creation story. According to the CD these elements are organizational overview and external environment, governance, opportunities and risks, strategy and resource allocation, business model, performance and future outlook. By linking contents across these elements, an integrated report can build the story of the business from a basic description of the business model through the external factors affecting the business and management's strategy for dealing with them and developing the business. This provides a foundation from which to discuss the performance, prospects and governance of the business in a way that focuses on its most important aspects.

Because its intention is to offer an appropriate balance between flexibility and prescription, the IR Framework is principles based rather than being founded on a more rigid, rules-based approach. The idea is to recognize the wide variation in individual circumstances of different organizations yet, at the same time, to enable a sufficient degree of comparability across organizations to meet relevant information needs. For this reason, the IR Framework doesn't focus on rules for measurement, disclosure of individual matters or even the identification of specific key performance indicators. Rather, the framework is driven by integrated thinking, which, as illustrated in the CD, should lead to integrated decision making and execution towards the creation of value. The purpose of this approach is to stimulate the active consideration by organizations of the relationships between their various operating and functional units and the kinds of capital that they use and have an effect on. The CD introduces and recommends six guiding principles, which underpin the preparation of an IR, inform its content and affect how information is presented. The six principles are strategic focus and future orientation, connectivity of information, stakeholder responsiveness, materiality and conciseness, reliability and completeness, consistency and comparability.

Part one of the book includes a series of chapters reflecting on some of the key concepts, elements and principles that underpin IR adoption and that are introduced in more details in Chap. 1. In particular, after having reviewed the concept of sustainability (Chap. 2) and the recent trends in corporate reporting (Chap. 3), a number of guiding principles are then explored in the following chapters. These principles are connectivity of information (Chap. 4), materiality (Chap. 5) and stakeholder engagement (Chap. 6). Next, the book further analyse some of the most significant content elements of IR. In particular, Chap. 7 focuses on the interplay between strategy and the business model, Chap. 8 on performance measurement and the capitals, Chap. 9 on value creation and cost management, and Chap. 10 integrated risk management. Finally, Chap. 11 introduces a proposal of value added calculation within the context of multinational enterprises, and Chap. 12 offers some reflections concerning the adoption of IR in the Public Sector.

Part two of the book presents a collection of cases that describe how a number of companies, large and small, private and public, are approaching IR in practice. There is no particular reason that justifies the sequence of the chapters. Cases are focused on the following Companies: Eni (Chap. 13), Enel (Chap. 14), Vodacom Group (Chap. 15), Smithfield (Chap. 16), Monnalisa (Chap. 17), Eskom (Chap. 18), HERA (Chap. 19) and finally, the Auditor General of South Africa (Chap. 20). Although the adoption of IR (or similar form of reporting) by these companies is not comparable since each one of them has its own story, motivation and trajectory, all of these companies represent examples of organizations that are currently questioning traditional form of reporting to move towards an integrated way to communicate the story of sustainable value creation.

We would like to thank all the authors of the book chapters: without your enthusiasm and commitment this book simply would have not been possible. Our gratitude also goes to Dr. Sabina Ratti, Sustainability Senior Vice President at Eni, who has been so kind to take care of the foreword of this book.

Finally, we wish to acknowledge the precious support of Elena Giovannoni, Loredana Smaldore and Fabrizio Granà, who have contributed to the editing process of the book.

We trust you will enjoy the reading!

August 2013

Cristiano Busco
Mark L. Frigo
Paolo Quattrone
Angelo Riccaboni

Contents

Part III   Towards Integrated Reporting: Cases and Best Practices

Part I
Introduction

Towards Integrated Reporting: Concepts, Elements and Principles

Cristiano Busco, Mark L. Frigo, Paolo Quattrone, and Angelo Riccaboni

Abstract

Integrated Reporting is a process that results in communicating—through the annual *integrated report*—value creation over time. The purpose of this chapter is to introduce the idea and the logic underpinning Integrated Reporting, shed light on the reasons that enabled the debate on Integrated Reporting to gain relevance over the recent years, and illustrate the features of the Consultation Draft released by the International Integrated Reporting Council on April 2013. In doing so, we focus our attention on a brief review of the fundamental concepts, content elements and guiding principles proposed within the Consultation Draft. We end the chapter with some reflections on the challenges ahead for Integrated Reporting, and on the potential impact of its adoption on the role of the management accounting function.

C. Busco (✉)
School of Business and Economics, National University of Ireland, Galway, Ireland
e-mail: cristiano.busco@nuigalway.ie

M.L. Frigo
Kellstadt Graduate School of Business & Driehaus College of Business, DePaul University, Chicago, IL, USA
e-mail: mfrigo@depaul.edu

P. Quattrone
University of Edinburgh Business School, Edinburgh, UK
e-mail: Paolo.Quattrone@ed.ac.uk

A. Riccaboni
Department of Business Studies and Law, University of Siena, Siena, Italy
e-mail: riccaboni@unisi.it

C. Busco et al. (eds.), *Integrated Reporting*, DOI 10.1007/978-3-319-02168-3_1,
© Springer International Publishing Switzerland 2013

Introduction

The principles, concepts and elements that characterize the way organizations report their annual performances are currently being questioned, debated, and redesigned throughout the world[1]. This is happening as key notions such as capital employed, value creation, and accountability are redefined in practice. What should companies report? What are the types of capital that an organization uses and affects? To whom are organizations accountable? And again, can we currently measure, manage and communicate social and environmental impact? Is it really possible to capture and represent how value is created and sustained over time? The answers to these questions are almost certainly bedeviling a substantial number of interested managers, executives, consultants, academics, regulators and additional stakeholders everywhere around the world.

A possible response to these critical questions is offered by Integrated Reporting (IR), a process that results in communicating—through an annual integrated report—how organizations create value over time, and their impact from an economic, social and environmental point of view. According to the International Integrated Reporting Council (IIRC), the IR process has the potential to shed light on these critical issues as it "brings together material information about an organization's strategy, governance, performance and prospects in a way that reflects the commercial, social and environmental context within which it operates. It provides a clear and concise representation of how an organization demonstrates stewardship and how it creates and sustains value"[2]. For these reasons, the IIRC encourages and promotes the adoption of the IR as an organization's primary reporting vehicle.

Three years have gone by since the Prince's Accounting for Sustainability Project (A4S) and the Global Reporting Initiative (GRI) announced the formation of the IIRC. During these years the IIRC, a global coalition of regulators, investors, companies, standards setters, the accounting profession, and nongovernmental organizations, has actively operated to redesign the landscape of corporate reporting. In April 2013, the IIRC released a Consultation Draft (CD) of the first Integrated Reporting Framework. The CD focuses on how to prepare and present an integrated report, and what to include in it. The CD was developed based on an analysis of the responses to the 2011 Discussion Paper "Towards Integrated Reporting—Communicating Value in the 21st Century," the publication of a draft outline in July 2012, and a Prototype Framework in November 2012.

The purpose of this chapter is to introduce the idea and the logic underpinning IR, shed light on the reasons that enabled the debate on IR to gain relevance over the recent years, and illustrate the features of the CD released by the IIRC. In doing so,

---

[1] The contents of this chapter draw on and extend the article by Busco et al. (2013), "Redefining Corporate Accountability through Integrated Reporting", in *Strategic Finance*, n.8, August, pp. 33–41.

[2] Visit http://www.theiirc.org/, accessed on 28 June 2013.

after having introduced some of the issues that are leading towards a re-definition of themes such as accountability or corporate reporting, we focus our attention on a brief review of the fundamental concepts, content elements and guiding principles proposed within the CD. The chapter ends with some reflections on the challenges ahead for IR, and on the potential impact of its adoption on the role of the management accounting function.

1.2   Redefining Corporate Reporting as *Values* Meet *Value* Creation

In the aftermath of the recent financial crisis and corporate scandals, many people increasingly perceive the global economic system as busted, and they view business as one of the major causes of social, environmental, and economic problems. Issues such as huge national and individual debts, large unemployment rates, growing disparity across societies, persistent fraud and unethical behavior in managing public and private organizations, and increasing concerns for the environment have left large segments of contemporary society frustrated with the existing social and economic order, particularly with the logic, principles, and practices currently in place. Among others, the notion and functioning of capitalism, the ultimate purpose of the business, as well as personal and collective *values* systems and the concept of corporate *value* creation have been questioned and placed under the spotlight[3] (see Mackey et al. 2013; Porter and Kramer 2011; Mourkogiannis 2008).

In this context, the pressure on the private sector to consider the social, environmental, and economic impact of its conduct has grown tremendously as corporate leaders and entrepreneurs are urged to take the lead in bringing business and society back together. *Values* (broadly defined as principles, beliefs, standards, and ideals that shape our feelings and emotions and help us decide how to act) help to shape perceptions of how value is created, distributed, and reported. Societal perceptions of value also help shape individual perceptions of value. Therefore, it isn't surprising to see a number of entrepreneurs, corporate leaders, and organizations moving toward the hybrid ideal (Battilana et al. 2012) where the *values* embraced (economic, social, and environmental) influence and are influenced by the way in which *value* creation and distribution are accounted for and communicated within a company's annual report.

This makes the values embraced and the value created fundamental concepts around which contemporary corporate reporting can be routed. Unfortunately, however, the logic, principles, and practices of corporate reporting currently in place have been transforming annual reports in complex, compliance-driven documents that mainly are useful for accounting experts only. Much of the

---

[3] See, for example, the emergence and recent popularization of concepts such as "Conscious Capitalism" or "Shared Value".

information included in current corporate reports is not designed to offer forward-looking information about strategy, performance, and risk. There's an increasing sense among stakeholders—investors, customers, citizens, and the community—that existing corporate reporting, which is characterized by a strong focus on financial performance and a lack of information on corporate strategy and nonfinancial performance, is becoming gradually less fit for the purpose. Businesses are facing capital constraint from a broader range of resources than just finance. This needs to be accounted for, and communicated to, an expanding series of stakeholders who are eager to be informed about both values embraced and the value created.

To close this gap, over the last decade a large number of companies have voluntarily offered reports focused on sustainability and on corporate social responsibility. Also, a number of coalitions (like the IIRC), councils and nongovernmental organizations focused on improving and broadening the contents of corporate reporting have emerged. Here we focus on IR as an example of contemporary managerial innovation where a number of initiatives, organizations, and individuals began to converge in response to the need for a consistent, collaborative, and internationally accepted approach to redesigning corporate accountability (Eccles and Saltzman 2011).

1.3   The Road Towards Integrated Reporting

On the 2nd of August 2010, The Prince's Accounting for Sustainability Project (A4S) and the Global Reporting Initiative (GRI) announced the formation of the IIRC. The IIRC's mission is "to create a globally accepted integrated reporting framework which brings together financial, environmental, social and governance information in a clear, concise, consistent and comparable format" in order to "help business to take more sustainable decisions and enable investors and other stakeholders to understand how an organization is really performing"[4].

In September 2011, the IIRC released a Discussion Paper titled "Towards Integrated Reporting—Communicating Value in the 21st Century". Following an analysis of the responses to the 2011 Discussion Paper, the IIRC released the Draft Outline of the Integrated Reporting Framework on the 11 July 2012. According to the IIRC, this Outline was important to establish, for the first time, the basic structure of the Framework and was intended to keep stakeholders informed as the Framework developed. Then, the Draft Outline has been superseded by the Prototype IR Framework that was released in November 2012.

The Prototype Framework was a working document released to keep stakeholders informed of progress on the development of the Framework following the release of a draft outline in July 2012. The IIRC considered the release of the Prototype Framework as an interim step intended to demonstrate progress towards defining key concepts and principles that underpin IR, and support organizations'

---

[4] Visit http://www.theiirc.org/about/, accessed on 28 June 2013.

ability to produce an integrated report. During the development of the IR Framework, the Technical Task Force of the IIRC established Technical Collaboration Groups (TCGs) to prepare Background Papers for IR. The TCGs were coordinated by lead organizations with input from participants from a range of disciplines and countries. A number of Background Papers were produced ranging from the principles of materiality and connectivity, to the concepts of business model, capital(s) and value[5]. Finally, on the 16 April 2013, the IIRC released a Consultation Draft of the first Integrated Reporting Framework. Following that, for the 90 days leading up to 15 July, the IIRC called on all the potential stakeholders to analyze, challenge and critique the CD.

Since 2011, the IIRC has established a Pilot Programme that underpins the development of the International Integrated Reporting Framework. According to the IIRC, the group of organizations participating in the Pilot Programme has the opportunity to contribute to the development of the Framework and to demonstrate global leadership in this emerging field of corporate reporting. As highlighted by Paul Druckman, CEO of the IIRC, "We call the Pilot Programme our "innovation hub"—made up of people who want to push the boundaries just a little bit further, to challenge, or at least question orthodox thinking, and to acknowledge the importance of reporting to the way our organizations think and behave'[6]. Through the Pilot Programme the principles, content and practical application of IR are being developed, tried and tested by businesses and investors. The Pilot Programme will run until September 2014, thereby allowing participants time to test the Framework during their following reporting cycle. According to the IIRC, the Pilot Programme comprises "the Business Network", with over 90 businesses across the globe from multinational corporations to public sector bodies, and "the Investor Network", with over 30 investors organizations.

Interestingly, on the IIRC web site it is possible to consult the emerging integrated reporting database[7]. This database brings together extracts of reports chosen from publicly available documents (including those produced by the IIRC's Pilot Programme organizations), which illustrate emerging practices in the Guiding Principles and Content Elements.

1.4   Integrated Reporting: Concepts, Elements and Principles

IR is a process that results in communicating—through the annual *integrated report*—value creation over time. According to the CD realised by the IIRC, an integrated report is a concise communication about how an organization's strategy,

---

[5] A Comprehensive list of Background Papers produced by the Technical Collaboration Groups of the IIRC is included in the references.

[6] Visit http://www.theiirc.org/companies-and-investors/, accessed on 30 July 2013.

[7] Visit http://www.theiirc.org/resources-2/other-publications/emerging-integrated-reporting-database/, accessed on 30 July 2013.

governance, performance, and prospects, in the context of its external environment, lead to the creation of value over the short, medium, and long term (see p. 8 of the CD). Although providers of financial capital are the primary intended IR users, an integrated report should be designed to benefit all stakeholders—including employees, customers, suppliers, business partners, local communities, regulators, and policy makers -interested in an organization's ability to create value over time. The key objective of IR is to enhance accountability and stewardship with respect to the broad base of six kinds of capital, or "capitals" (financial, manufactured, intellectual, human, social and relationship, and natural), and promote understanding of their interdependencies[8]. In doing this, IR is designed to support integrated thinking, decision making, and actions that focus on sustainable value creation for stakeholders.

The International IR Framework is being developed to assist organizations with the IR process. In particular, the purpose of the Framework is to establish fundamental concepts, guiding principles, and content elements that govern the overall content of an integrated report. This will help organizations determine how best to express their unique value-creation story in a meaningful and transparent way. Significantly, the IR Framework doesn't intend to set benchmarks for such things as the quality of an organization's strategy or the level of its performance. The intended report users will do these assessments based on the information in an organization's integrated report.

Next, we begin our journey within the IR Framework as illustrated in the CD. Our analysis starts with the fundamental concepts proposed within the document.

1.4.1   The Fundamental Concepts of Integrated Reporting

The CD developed by the IIRC recognizes that value is not generated by or within an organization alone, but is *influenced* by the external environment (including economic conditions, technological change, societal issues and environmental challenges), which provides the context within which the organization operates; *created* through relationships with others; and, finally, *dependent* on the availability, affordability, quality and management of various resources (p. 10 of the CD). For these reasons, IR aims to provide insights about the external environment that affects an organization, the resources and relationships used and affected by the organization (which in the IR framework are referred to as the capitals), as well as about the way in which the organization interacts with the external environment and the capitals to create value over the short, medium and long term (p. 10 of the CD). Therefore, according to the CD, the overall purpose of the IR is to communicate and illustrate a broader understanding of the organizational performance compared to traditional reporting by describing, and measuring, where practicable, the material

---

[8] The CD refers to "capitals" instead of "capital," so we continue that use here.

elements of value creation, the different type of capitals employed and affected, and the intertwined relationships between them.

The fundamental concepts of IR are represented by (1) the capitals that an organization uses and affects, (2) the organization's business model, and (3) the creation of value over time. The business model is the vehicle through which an organization creates value[9]. That value is embodied in the capitals—sometimes also referred to as resources and relationships—that the organization uses and affects. The assessment of an organization's ability to create value in the short, medium, and long term depends on an understanding of the connectivity between its business model and a wide range of internal and external factors (these factors represent the content elements of the integrated report, and will be discussed later in the chapter).

As illustrated by the CD, organizations depend on different types of capitals, which are stores of value that, in one form or another, become inputs to an organization's business model (p. 11 of the CD). The six capitals identified within the IR Framework developed by the IIRC are: *financial, manufactured, intellectual, human, social and relationship, and natural*. However, it is important to note that the IR Framework does not require organizations to strictly adopt the six categories listed above. Rather, irrespectively of how an organization categorizes capitals for its own purposes, the types identified above are to be used as a benchmark to ensure the organization does not overlook a capital that it uses or affects.

The recognition that value is not created by or within an organization alone is supported by (Frigo and Ramaswamy 2009) in their work on co-creating strategic risk-return management: "Companies no longer create value and wealth just by themselves. Customers suppliers, investors, and others play an active role in this process"[10]. The concept of the need for a broad spectrum of capitals is reflected in how they proposed redefining capital and investors: "Defining an investor solely as someone who provides financial capital underscores the complex mosaic of the roles in Value Co-creation."[11]

The CD defines the business model as a chosen system of inputs, business activities, outputs and outcomes that aims to create value over the short, medium and long term (p. 14 of the CD). As illustrated above, the six types of capitals portrayed by the IR Framework are stores of value that become *inputs* to a company's business model (see Fig. 2). However, these capitals, and their value do change over time, as they are increased, decreased or transformed through the activities and *outputs* of the organization. It's also important to understand how the outputs affect *outcomes*, which represent the ultimate results of the outputs.

Finally, the fundamental concept that lies at the very heart of IR is value creation. According to the CD, an organization can create and maximize value by

---

[9] See the IIRC report (2013b) "Business Model—Background Paper for IR" for a review on this concept.

[10] See Frigo and Ramaswamy (2009), pp. 3–11.

[11] See Frigo and Ramaswamy (2009), p. 7.

serving the interests of, and working with, all its key stakeholders, such as employees, customers, suppliers, business partners, local communities, legislators, regulators, and policy-makers (p. 16 of the CD). In this way, the CD of the IIRC emphasizes how value created manifests itself not only in financial returns to providers of financial capital but also in positive or negative effects on other capitals and other stakeholders. In particular, since the types of capitals represent stores of value, the creation of value for an organization and its stakeholders results from the increase, decrease or transformation of the capitals caused by the organization's activities and outputs. Significantly, value is created over different time horizons and for different stakeholders through different capitals, and it is unlikely to be created through the maximization of one capital while disregarding the others (p. 16 of the CD).

In the following section our journey within the IR Framework developed by the IIRC continues as we describe the key content elements included within the CD.

1.4.2   The Content Elements of Integrated Reporting

An integrated report is built around seven elements that define its content and communicate the organization's unique value-creation story. According to the CD these elements are organizational overview and external environment, governance, opportunities and risks, strategy and resource allocation, business model, performance, and future outlook (see Exhibit 1.1). By linking contents across these elements, an integrated report can build the story of the business from a basic description of the business model through the external factors affecting the business and management's strategy for dealing with them and developing the business. This provides a foundation from which to discuss the performance, prospects, and governance of the business in a way that focuses on its most important aspects.

> **Exhibit 1.1. The Content Elements of Integrated Reporting.**
> **Organizational overview and external environment:**
>   What does the organization do, and what are the circumstances under which it operates?
> **Governance:**
>   How does the organization's governance structure support its ability to create value in the short, medium, and long term?
> **Opportunities and risks:**
>   What are the specific opportunities and risks that affect the organization's ability to create value over the short, medium, and long term, and how is the organization dealing with them?
>
> (continued)

Exhibit 1.1 (continued)

Strategy and resource allocation:

Where does the organization want to go, and how does it intend to get there?

Business model:

What is the organization's business model, and to what extent is it resilient?

Performance:

To what extent has the organization achieved its strategic objectives, and what are its outcomes in terms of effects on the capitals?

Future outlook:

What challenges and uncertainties is the organization likely to encounter in pursuing its strategy, and what are the potential implications for its business model and its future performance?

Source: "Consultation Draft of the International Integrated Reporting Framework," the International Integrated Reporting Council, April 2013, p. 7).

According to the CD, as for the content element *Organizational overview and external environment*, IR shall describe what an organization does and the circumstances it operates under. This includes the organization's culture, ethics and values; ownership and operating structure; principal markets; products and activities; and the competitive landscape and market positioning. Data on workforce, revenue, and geographical reach would be included as well, and factors that affect the external environment would be analyzed, including legal, commercial, social, environmental, and political factors (pp. 24–25 of the CD). In terms of *Governance*, an IR shall provide insight on how an organization's governance structure supports its ability to create value in the short, medium, and long term. This is likely to include, among others, the leadership structure; the strategic direction and approach to risk management; how culture, ethics, and values affect capitals; and how remuneration is linked to value creation (p. 25 of the CD).

As for *Opportunities and risks* content element, an IR shall explore the opportunities and risks that affect an organization's ability to create value over the short, medium, and long term, and how the company is dealing with them. To fulfill these expectations, IR shall identify the source of internal and external risks, assess on the likelihood the opportunity or risk will come to realization and its potential magnitude, and illustrate the steps that are being taken to mitigate risks (p. 26 of the CD). In terms of *Strategy and resource allocation*, an IR shall describe where the organization wants to go, and how it intends to get there. In order to do that, the IR report shall identify the organization's short, medium and long term strategic objectives; the strategies it has in place, or intends to implement, to achieve those strategic objectives; the resource allocation plans it has in place, or intends to put in place, to implement its strategy; how it will measure achievements and target outcomes for the short, medium and long term (p. 26 of the CD).

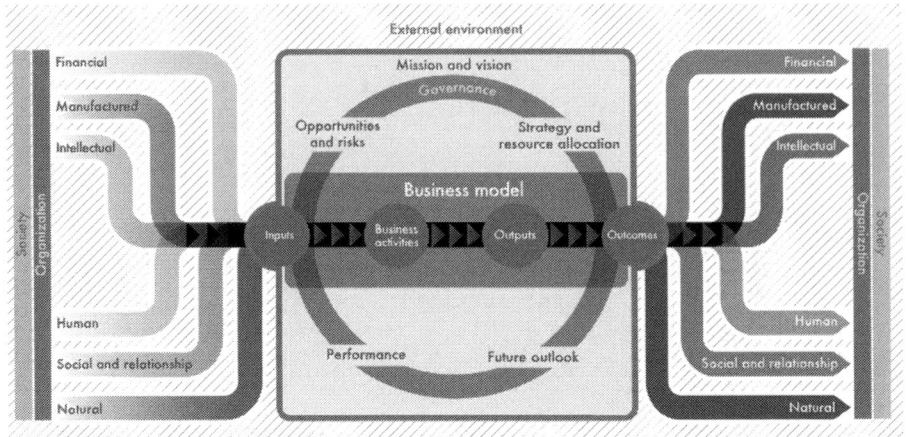

Exhibit 1.2 The intertwined relationship between the content elements and the fundamental concepts of the IIRC framework (*source*: CD, IIRC 2013a, p. 11)

In terms of representing the *Business model*, IR shall illustrate the characteristics of the key inputs and how they relate to the capitals from which they were derived. Additionally, the report shall also describe the fundamental business activities, such as how the organization differentiates itself in the market, how the need to innovate is managed in the company, and how the business model has been designed to adjust to possible change (p. 27 of the CD). Through the content *Performance* an IR shall describe the extent to which the organization has achieved its objectives, and how its outcomes have affected the capitals. The state of key stakeholder relationships shall be described, and links between past, current, and anticipated future performance need to be reported in the IR. Finally, as for the *Future outlook*, the challenges and uncertainties that the organization is likely to encounter need to be illustrated in the report. The possible effects of these challenges on the business model and future performance shall be disclosed in the IR as it describes how the organization is equipped to respond to difficulties it may face.

Exhibit 1.2 offers a representation on the intertwined relationship between the content elements and the fundamental concepts of the IIRC framework.

1.4.3 The Guiding Principles of Integrated Reporting

Because its intention is to offer an appropriate balance between flexibility and prescription, the IR Framework is principles based rather than being founded on a more rigid, rules-based approach. The idea is to recognize the wide variation in individual circumstances of different organizations yet, at the same time, to enable a sufficient degree of comparability across organizations to meet relevant information needs. For this reason, the IR Framework doesn't focus on rules for measurement, disclosure of individual matters, or even the identification of specific key performance indicators. Rather, the Framework is driven by integrated thinking, which, as illustrated in the CD, should lead to integrated decision making and execution toward the creation of value. The purpose of this approach is to stimulate the active consideration by organizations of the relationships between their various operating and functional units and the kinds of capital that they use and have an effect on. Through the integrated thinking promoted by the IR Framework, organizations are stimulated to focus on the connectivity and interdependencies among a range of factors that have a material effect on their ability to create value over time (see Exhibit 1.3).

Exhibit 1.3. The Guiding Principles of Integrated Reporting.

Strategic focus and future orientation. An integrated report should provide insight into the organization's strategy and how that strategy relates to the organization's ability to create value in the short, medium, and long term and its use of and effects on its capitals.

Connectivity of information. An integrated report should show, as a comprehensive value-creation story, the combination, interrelatedness, and dependencies between the components that are material to the organization's ability to create value over time.

Stakeholder responsiveness. An integrated report should provide insight into the quality of the organization's relationships with its key stakeholders and how and to what extent the organization understands, takes into account, and responds to their legitimate needs, interests, and expectations.

Materiality and conciseness. An integrated report should provide concise information that is material to assessing the organization's ability to create value in the short, medium, and long term.

Reliability and completeness. An integrated report should include all material matters, both positive and negative, in a balanced way and without material error.

Consistency and comparability. The information in an integrated report should be presented on a basis that is consistent over time and in a way that enables comparison with other organizations to the extent it is material to the organization's own value creation story.

Source: "Consultation Draft of the International Integrated Reporting Framework," the International Integrated Reporting Council, April 2013, p. 6.

As illustrated in Exhibit 1.3, the CD introduces and recommends six Guiding Principles, which underpin the preparation of an IR, inform its content and affect how information is presented. The six Guiding Principles are: strategic focus and future orientation, connectivity of information, stakeholder responsiveness, materiality and conciseness, reliability and completeness, consistency and comparability.

As for *strategic focus and future orientation*, the CD highlights how the execution of this principle is not necessary limited to the content elements Strategy and resource allocation and Future outlook. It is also integrated with the presentation of other contents such as, for example, the opportunities, risks and dependencies flowing from the organization's market position and business model; the relationship between past and future performance, and the factors that may change that relationship; the balance among short, medium and long term interests and perspectives. Significantly, the CD also stress the importance of an accurate implementation of the strategic focus and future orientation principles enable an IR to articulate how the availability, quality and affordability of significant capitals contribute to the organization's ability to achieve its strategic objectives in the future and thereby create value (p. 18 of the CD). Additionally, although the CD acknowledges that future-oriented information is by nature more uncertain and, therefore, less precise than historical information, it suggested that uncertainty is not a reason in itself to exclude such information, provide that the nature and extent of that uncertainty is accounted for.

Moving to the *connectivity of information*, this principle is crucial to ensuring that an IR focuses on the broad picture of the organization's unique value creation story; supports the intended report users' understanding of the different factors that affect the future of the organization and how they interact; helps to break down established silos in accessing, measuring, managing and disclosing information, and to extend the focus of reporting beyond the traditional focus primarily on financial and historical matters; facilitates the intended report users' ability to drill down and interlink information in other documents (p. 18 of the CD). According to the CD, connectivity of information is strictly associated to integrated thinking: the more integrated thinking underlies the organization's unique value creation story by being embedded into its activities, the more naturally will the connectivity of information flow into management reporting, analysis and decision making, and consequently into IR. Ultimately, it is only by connecting the content elements and the fundamental concepts of the Framework that the IR will be able to communicate the organization's value creation story.

Stakeholder responsiveness is the principle that emphasizes the importance of ongoing, positive relationships with the organization's key stakeholders because, as the CD maintains, value is not created by or within an organization alone, but is created through relationships with others (p. 19 of the CD). Engagement with stakeholders enables the organization to understand what matters and what is important to them. According to the CD dialogue with stakeholders shall assist organizations to understand how stakeholders perceive value; identify future trends that may not yet have come to general attention but which are rising in significance; identify material matters, including opportunities and risks; develop and evaluate strategy; manage risks; as well as, implement activities, including strategic and accountable responses to material matters.

Materiality (*and conciseness*) is a critical principle for IR. A matter (an event, issue, opportunity, amount, or even a statement by the organization) is material if, in the view of senior management and those charged with governance, it is of such relevance and importance (both in terms of nature and magnitude) that it could substantively influence the assessments of the primary intended report users with regard to the organization's ability to create value (p. 21 of the CD). According to the CD, in determining whether a matter is material, senior management and those charged with governance need to consider whether the matter substantively affects, or has the potential to substantively affect, the organization's strategy, its business model, or one or more of the capitals the organization uses or affects in the short, medium or long term. The CD shed light on the materiality determination process suggesting how it applies to both positive and negative matters (e.g., opportunities and risks, and favorable and unfavorable results or prospects for the future), and to financial and other information (p. 21 of the CD). Interestingly, the CD summarizes how determining materiality for the purpose of preparing an integrated report involves at least three steps: identifying relevant matters (i.e., those matters that have had a past effect, have a present effect, or could have a future effect on the organization's ability to create value over time); assessing the importance of those matters in terms of their known or potential effect on value creation; and, finally, prioritizing the matters identified based on their importance in terms of known or potential effect on value creation. Finally, in search of *conciseness*, an integrated report avoids redundant information, and be linked to additional detailed information to be provided separately.[12]

The *reliability and completeness* of information is arguably one of the most important principles for IR. Reliability, in particular, is enhanced by mechanisms such as strong internal reporting systems, appropriate stakeholder engagement, and independent, external assurance (p. 21 of the CD). According to the CD, senior management and those charged with governance generally exercise judgment in deciding whether information is sufficiently reliable to be included in an integrated report. As for completeness, the CD suggests that a complete integrated report shall include all material information, both positive and negative, being able to illustrate a company's unique value creation story.

Finally, *consistency and comparability*. According to the CD, although the specific information released through an integrated report will necessarily vary from one organization to another, they should be presented on a basis that is consistent over time and in a way that enables comparison with other organizations (p. 23 of the CD).

---

[12] See the IIRC report (2013c), "Materiality Background Paper for IR" for a review on this concept.

1.5 The Challenges Ahead for Integrated Reporting and the Possible Impact on the Management Accounting Function

The journey toward IR has just begun. It is a fascinating journey that unavoidably is likely to face a number of challenges as the first version of the IIRC framework is about to get finalized and realised. Additionally, it is very likely that the adoption of IR will require some adjustments of the processes and functions of those organizations that will choose to issue an Integrated Report. Among others, it will be interesting to explore how traditional accounting realms, such as Financial vs. Managerial accounting, will cope with this innovation in corporate reporting.

The fundamental concepts and contents elements of IR seem to imply a reassessment of the internal processes supporting corporate reporting. Within this reassessment, an interesting question to address, among many others, is: what is the role of management accountants within IR? In June 2013, IMA (the Institute of Management Accountants in the US) sent a response letter to the IIRC about the Framework CD, saying "management accountants are not 'just technical accountants', they are broad-based business thinkers who serve as trusted advisors inside organizations. Management accountants are 'at the table' on all issues involving strategy and sustainable value creation". For these reasons, concepts and contents such as capitals, business models, future outlook, risks, financial and nonfinancial key performance indicators, to name a few, call for the active participation and engagement of management accountants within IR.

What could the role of management accountants be as values meet with value creation within new forms of corporate reporting? The demands placed on management accountants have grown significantly in recognition of social and environmental challenges. These demands require a rich supply of information that's capable of informing corporate managers of the impacts of their decisions and enabling them to act. For these reasons, the linkages across the principles, concepts, and elements of IR seem to call for management accountants to master their knowledge regarding the organization's business model to identify and leverage the key drivers of business value.

Through their expertise, management accountants (at all levels) have the opportunity to actively integrate the operational, environmental, social, and governance aspects in place with the financial performance of their organizations. But rather than simply prescribing specific indicators or measurement methods to be used in the annual report, management accountants can lead the process of communication and reporting by designing innovative documents that can capture the interest and attention of diverse stakeholders. We mean innovative reports where values and capitals integrate with strategy and business models to generate and distribute added value in the short, medium, and long term. The innovation, learning, and growth needed in the continuing development of IR can benefit greatly from the active participation of management accountants.

Besides the consequences of the adoption of IR for the accounting function, it is important to highlight how the CD (and, before that, the IIRC paper in 2011) have offered a number of potential stakeholders the opportunity to analyze, challenge and critique the Framework of the IIRC. In 2011, for example, with a response letter to the IIRC paper "Towards Integrated Reporting: Communication Value in the 21st Century," IMA welcomed the development of the IR Framework as "an opportunity to modernize corporate reporting and corporate culture, unlock data from corporate silos and restrictive presentation formats, link operational, environmental, social and governance practices to financial performance, and make information relevant, meaningful and reliable for management and all stakeholders". Yet, although the IR Framework represents a major development in the area of disclosures to better inform investors and other stakeholders as to the sustainable value-creation capacity and capability of the enterprise, the design of corporate reports where the values embraced are blended with the process of value creation still presents a number of challenges.

As highlighted within the IMA response letter to the CD, there are several issues and concerns that deserve further consideration in the development of the IR Framework. Among others, the compelling market need for a single integrated report from investors and other market stakeholders, as well as the cost/benefit of the process, aren't described or articulated in the CD. Second, in light of the increasingly complex, turbulent, and competitive global marketplace we are currently experiencing, it's questionable whether investors and other market stakeholders would want management teams to disclose (potentially) competitively sensitive information about their sustainable business model. Third, and of great importance, there's a real danger, especially in the early stages of IR development, that overregulation will stifle innovation, learning, and growth. Mandatory reporting standards for IR could hamper the development of the framework and, most importantly, could be inadequate. Are regulators really in the best position to determine the best metrics to measure and disclose sustainable value creation in contemporary, highly diversified global markets? The need to face a number of challenges characterizes every innovative journey. IR is no exception in this respect, also because, although extremely solid and concrete, the journey has just begun.

Conclusions

Within this chapter we have tried to illustrate the rationale underpinning IR, shed light on the reasons that enabled the debate on IR to gain relevance over the recent years, and illustrate the features of the CD released by the IIRC on April 2013. We opened the chapter questioning whether we can currently measure, manage and communicate social and environmental impact. We wondered if it is really possible to capture and represent how value is created and sustained over time. We suggested that the possible answers to these questions are almost certainly bedeviling a substantial number of interested managers, executives, consultants, academics, regulators and additional stakeholders everywhere around the world.

We emphasised how a possible response to these critical questions is offered by IR, a process that results in communicating—through an annual integrated report—how organizations create value over time, and their impact from an economic, social and environmental point of view. In doing so, after having introduced some of the issues that are leading towards a re-definition of themes such as accountability or corporate reporting, we have focused our attention on a brief review of the fundamental concepts, content elements and guiding principles proposed within the CD. Finally, we have concluded the chapter with some final reflections on the challenges ahead for IR, as well as advocating the potential role of management accountants for its design and adoption.

Could BP's Deepwater Horizon disaster, the discovery of horsemeat in Tesco's burgers or even the Parmalat financial scandal be avoided with the adoption of IR? The answer is no, probably. However, since what a company reports externally is likely to shape over the long term how its employees behave internally, as well as the quality of the processes in place, there are definitely reasons for hoping that tools such as IR will contribute to diffusion and adoption of a business culture where sustainability is fully engrained in the process of value creation.

References

Battilana J, Lee M, Walker J, Dorsey C (2012) In search of the hybrid ideal. Stanf Soc Innov Rev 10:49–55

Busco C, Frigo ML, Quattrone P, Riccaboni A (2013) Redefining corporate accountability through integrated reporting. Strat Finance 8(August):33–41

Eccles RG, Saltzman D (2011) Achieving sustainability through integrated reporting. Stanf Soc Innov Rev Summer:56–61

Frigo ML, Ramaswamy V (2009) Co-creating strategic risk-return management. Strat Finance 5 (May):3–11

IIRC (2013a) Consultation draft of the international <IR> framework. http://www.theiirc.org/consultationdraft2013. Accessed 10 Jul 2013

IIRC (2013b) Business model - background paper for <IR>. http://www.theiirc.org/wp-content/uploads/2013/03/Business_Model.pdf. Accessed 10 Jul 2013

IIRC (2013c) Materiality - background paper for <IR>. http://www.theiirc.org/wp-content/uploads/2013/03/IR-Background-Paper-Materiality.pdf. Accessed 10 Jul 2013

Mackey J, Sisodia RS, George B (2013) Conscious capitalism: liberating the heroic spirit of business. Harvard Business, Boston, MA, pp 1–368

Mourkogiannis N (2008) Purpose–The starting point of great companies. Palgrave Macmillan, New York, NY

Porter ME, Kramer MR (2011) The big idea: creating shared value. Harv Bus Rev 89(1/2):62–77

Part II

Review of Key Principles, Concepts and Elements for Integrated Reporting

What Is Sustainability? A Review of the Concept and Its Applications

2

Elena Giovannoni and Giacomo Fabietti

Abstract

Whereas the concept of sustainability is broadly acknowledged as being multi-dimensional, its various dimensions have brought to light different discourses over time and have often been treated separately. In some cases, this separation has limited the actual implementation of sustainability to its mere rhetoric. By relying upon a review of the relevant literature which addresses the notion of sustainability (or of sustainable development), the present chapter aims to explore this notion by identifying its key dimensions and the intertwining relationships between them. In so doing, the challenges and opportunities brought out by an integrated approach towards sustainability are also emphasised, together with the role played by governance structures, business models, management, measurement and reporting systems in implementing 'integrated sustainability' within organizations. In this context, the contribution of integrated reporting is explored.

2.1 Introduction

In recent years, the growing concerns for environmental and climate change, together with issues of poverty, increasing disparity between societies and the tensions brought by social inequalities, have placed sustainable development under the spotlight. National and international institutions, policy makers and cross-country initiatives (see, for instance, the *Sustainable Development Solutions Network*—SDSN—of the United Nations launched in 2012), as well as practitioners (see, for instance, KPMG 2011) and academics (see, among others, Joseph 2012), have increased the attention given to social and environmental sustainability worldwide. As emphasised by Gray (2010), whereas everyone

E. Giovannoni (✉) • G. Fabietti
Department of Business and Law, University of Siena, Siena, Italy
e-mail: elena.giovannoni@unisi.it; giacomo.fabietti@unisi.it

C. Busco et al. (eds.), *Integrated Reporting*, DOI 10.1007/978-3-319-02168-3_2,
© Springer International Publishing Switzerland 2013

seems to agree on the importance of sustainable development, its very nature and meaning is rarely discussed and analysed in an explicit way[1]. As a result, the actual implementation of sustainability risks to be limited by the vagueness and ubiquity of its definition (Dixon and Fallon 1989). For instance, due to the ubiquity of the notion of sustainability, different discourses have emerged over time, thereby associating this concept with social responsibility, environmental management, or business sustainability, which are often treated in separated ways. These different discourses have also revealed their appeal over corporations, whose role and responsibility for sustainable development have been questioned.

In response to the increasing pressures coming from national and international regulations, and from society in general, corporations are gradually pushed towards the adoption of principles of both social and environmental responsibility within their strategies, structures and management systems (Werbach 2009). In this context, a sort of 'sustainability rhetoric' is emerging in mission statements, internal codes and external reporting systems. As argued by Gond et al. (2012), in some cases, this rhetoric was used in the attempt to reconstruct the eroded legitimacy of companies and did not necessarily involve the actual implementation of (or participation in) sustainable development. Otherwise, such active implementation and participation would require organizations to alter their existing practices and to allow a concrete strategic move towards sustainability (Hopwood 2009).

In the attempt to move beyond the sustainability rhetoric and to pursue an actual search for sustainable development, a clear definition of this concept and of its key dimensions is needed, together with the adoption of an integrated approach towards the notion of sustainability. This need has been advocated by both academics (see Gray 2010) and cross-country initiatives (such as the *SDSN*) to overcome the limits resulting from the separation between social, environmental, and financial concerns, as well as from an individualistic approach to sustainability. In fact, sustainable development cannot be achieved through isolated initiatives, but rather requires an integrated effort at various levels, comprising social, environmental and financial aspects. As addressed by recent studies on the very nature of sustainability, "*any foreseeable sustainable state will be the result of interactions between organizations, individuals, societies and states*" (Gray 2010, p. 57). From this point of view, an integrated approach towards sustainability would require realising the potentials of its key (financial, social and environmental) dimensions simultaneously, as well as managing the tensions, trade-offs and synergies between these dimensions (we will define this approach as 'integrated sustainability'). More importantly, in managing the tensions of sustainability, a key role can be played by *ad hoc* governance structures, business models, management, measurement and reporting systems, which could be purposefully designed according to an integrated

---

[1] In line with Gray (2010), in this chapter we will use the expressions 'sustainability' and 'sustainable development' as two analogues. In so doing, we also acknowledge a slight difference between the two expressions, in which 'sustainability' refers to a state, while 'sustainable development' refers to the process for achieving this state (see Gray 2010).

approach. In this context, the recent debate on integrated reporting is likely to play a relevant role.

By relying on the previous premises, this chapter aims to explore the concept of sustainability by identifying its key dimensions and the intertwining relationships between them. The aim is to identify the challenges and opportunities arising from an integrated approach towards sustainability, and the role of this approach in enabling organizations to actually implement sustainability beyond its mere rhetoric. In so doing, particular attention will be given to the perspective of companies and to management systems, practices and processes which could help integrate social and environmental concerns with the more commercial and financial needs of the business. As we will see subsequently, whereas these (social, environmental and financial) dimensions are all part of a broader and integrated notion of sustainability, their co-existence implies tensions and challenges which need to be addressed and managed in an attempt to actually implement sustainability.

In order to achieve the goal described above, this chapter relies upon the analysis of the relevant literature which has addressed the concept of sustainability from the perspective of companies. By reconstructing the evolution of this debate over time (see Sect. 2.2), the evolving discourses on sustainability are drawn upon in Sect. 2.3 to identify the key dimensions of this concept and the need for an integrated approach. Next, in Sect. 2.4, the synergies and tensions between these dimensions are discussed to outline the challenges and opportunities resulting from integration. In this context, the potential roles of governance structures, business models, management, measurement and reporting systems in implementing sustainability are suggested in Sect. 2.5. In particular, the contribution of integrated reporting is explored. The main messages of this chapter are then summarised in Sect. 2.6[2].

2.2 Changing Discourses on Sustainability: Insights from the Literature

As emphasised by Kidd (1992), the concept of sustainability is not new, it has a rather long history and it has evolved over time. Importantly, this evolution has been affected by different *"intellectual and political streams of thought that have molded concepts of sustainability"* (Kidd 1992, p. 3). In this section we will rely upon the relevant literature which has addressed the concept of sustainability according to different streams of thoughts. The review of these studies permits the identification of three main discourses that have shaped and characterised the

---

[2] Although this chapter is the result of the joint efforts and collaboration of the two authors, Elena Giovannoni is the author of Sects. 2.1, 2.4, 2.5 and 2.6; Giacomo Fabietti is the author of Sects. 2.2 and 2.3. This chapter is based on the outcomes of a broader research project entitled "From governance and risk management rules to performance: roles, tools and enabling conditions in Italian firms". The authors gratefully acknowledge the financial support of this research project provided by national funding within PRIN 2009.

evolving debate on sustainability[3]. We will label these as 'environmental', 'social' and 'business' discourses.

2.2.1 The Environmental Discourse

One of the prevailing discourses regarding the concept of sustainability has referred this concept to the relationships between men and nature (we will label this discourse as the 'environmental discourse'). Although the multidimensionality of sustainability has never been neglected, over the past 30 years it has been often compartmentalized as an environmental issue (Drexhage and Murphy 2010). In particular, during the 1970s, the term sustainability began to be widely used in relation to environmental problems. As shown by Kidd (1992), a number of books addressing issues of sustainability from an environmental point of view were published during that period (see, e.g., Meadows et al. 1972). In this context, growing concern on global environmental problems, and scepticism about the possibility for reducing industrial pollution significantly, pushed the United Nations (UN) to address these problems as a *"barrier to development"* (Kidd 1992, p. 16).

One of the key steps in this direction was the UN Conference on Human Environment, which took place in Stockholm in 1972. The conference led to the development of 26 principles, most of which addressed environmental concerns; in particular, by relying on the concept of *carrying capacity* (see e.g. Riddell 1981; WRI/IIED 1986), the third principle stated that *"the capacity of the Earth to produce vital renewable resources must be maintained and, wherever practicable, restored or improved"* (UN 1972, p. 4). The Stockholm conference acted as a vehicle for the creation of the UN Environmental Programme (UNEP), as well as for the creation of a number of national environmental protection agencies. Within UNEP the term sustainability appeared for the first time in the context of the UN (Kidd 1992). Since its foundation, in 1972, one of the most important aims of UNEP was the promotion of cooperation and strong leadership in the care of the environment. In this context, UNEP also stressed the importance of *eco-development* (Sachs 1984), defined as the *yield* of renewable resources and the simultaneous monitoring of the depletion of non-renewables. UNEP retrieved the concept of *sustainable yield* (Tivy and O'Hare 1982) in its definition of eco-development.

In 1980, the International Union for Conservation of Nature (IUCN), World Wildlife Fund (WWF) and UNEP set up the World Conservation Strategy (WCS).

---

[3] Given the numerous theoretical streams which have approached the concept of sustainability from different perspectives, it would be impossible to provide a comprehensive review of the literature which has addressed this notion in only one chapter. More generally, as argued by Kidd (1992, p. 3) *"the literature relating to sustainability is so voluminous that full analysis were not practical. And if it were practical it would probably not be worth the effort"*. Far from attempting to provide an exhaustive review, in this section we draw on some key studies which have addressed the concept of sustainability from different perspectives in order to outline some of the key discourses which have informed the debate regarding this concept.

The WCS referred to *'development that is sustainable'* in terms of both improvements in human life and conservation of natural resources. The primary aim of the WCS was to promote sustainable development through the identification of priority *conservation issues* (Drexhage and Murphy 2010). In this context, the term *conservation* stands for *"management of human use of the biosphere so that it may yield the greatest sustainable benefit to present generations while maintaining its potential to meet the needs and aspirations of future generations"* (IUCN, WWF and UNEP 1980, introduction). In 1987 the final report of the World Commission on Environment and Development (WCED), titled *Our Common Future*[4], provided an overview on the state of the environment, as well as the most popular definition of *Sustainable development*, as *"development that meets the needs of the present without compromising the ability of future generations to meet their own needs"* (p. 45). The report of WCED represented the *"momentum for the landmark 1992 Rio Summit"* (Drexhage and Murphy 2010, p. 8). Importantly, the UN Conference on Environment and Development (UNCED) in 1992, referred to as the Rio Earth Summit, produced a global action plan for sustainable development. Its outputs were the *Rio Declaration*, *Agenda 21* and the *Commission on Sustainable Development*. Particularly, *Agenda 21* provided advice and good practices for the achievement of sustainable development, by posing major emphasis on environmental aspects (Drexhage and Murphy 2010). Nevertheless, during the subsequent Kyoto Conference on Climate change in 1997, the poor progress in the achievement of *Agenda 21 goals* emerged.

The debate described above was not ignored by corporations. As argued by Berry and Rondinelli (1998), in the 1960s and 1970s, corporations acted in a 'reactive' way when faced with environmental issues, waiting for environmental crises to occur and then trying to mitigate their evil effects. During the 1980s, given the growing regulation on environmental protection, in many cases corporations limited their efforts to the mere compliance with laws and requirements. In the 1990s corporations began to adopt a more 'proactive' approach, through which they started to try to anticipate the environmental effects of their operations and to obtain a business advantage from the management of environmental performance. Since then, corporations have gradually attempted to embed environmental issues into their business culture and management processes by introducing Environmental Management Systems (EMSs). According to Melnyk et al. (2003, p. 332) an EMS is *"a system and database which integrates procedures and processes for training of personnel, monitoring, summarizing, and reporting of specialized environmental performance information to internal and external stakeholders of a firm"*. EMSs are conceived as important for complying with regulations and for waste reduction. Among these systems, the voluntary environmental management tool (labeled *Eco-Management and Audit Scheme - EMAS*), developed by the European Commission in 1993, embraced a broad range of indicators, including energy efficiency, material efficiency, biodiversity, emissions, water consumption and waste.

---

[4] This report is also known as the Brundtland Report.

As illustrated above, from the 1970s to the 1990s, sustainability has been primarily related to environmental concerns. In parallel, as we will see in the following sections, the social discourse was also emerging.

2.2.2 The Social Discourse

Whereas the environmental discourse was developing within the sustainable development debate, social aspects were not neglected. For example, the WCED's definition of Sustainable Development (WCED 1987) focuses on the reconciliation of the needs of present and future generations. According to Dempsey et al. (2011), the attention given to *inter-generational equity* by the WCED definition stresses social aspects, and particularly the key determinants of social equity, such as social justice, distributive justice and equality of conditions. In this context, exclusion from participation in the social, economic and political life of a community was considered to be at the core of the concept of social equity, since it could lead to racism and discrimination (e.g. Pierson 2002; Ratcliffe 2000).

In addition to this debate, the social discourse has also developed in the context of corporations and has been particularly associated with the notion of social responsibility. Already in 1953, Howard Bowen's *Social Responsibilities of the Businessman* defined the social responsibility of businessmen as "*the obligations of businessmen to pursue those policies, to make those decisions, or to follow those lines of action which are desirable in terms of the objectives and values of our society*" (p. 6). While Bowen's contribution represented a milestone in the debate on social responsibility, during the 1960s, definitions of Corporate Social Responsibility (CSR) began to spread: Davis (1960), for example, argued that CSR refers to "*businessmen's decisions and actions taken for reasons at least partially beyond the firm's direct economic or technical interest*" (p. 70). In so doing, he also suggested that some socially responsible business decisions could be justified by the long-run economic gains of the firm; Frederick (1960), instead, argued that "*social responsibility in the final analysis implies a public posture toward society's economic an human resources, as a willingness to see that those resources are used for broad social ends and not simply for the narrowly circumscribed interests of private persons and firms*" (p. 60). During the 1980s and 1990s, alternative approaches to CSR were elaborated, such as stakeholder theory (Freeman 1984), corporate citizenship (Andriof and McIntosh 2001) and business ethics (Kilcullen and Ohles Kooistra 1999).

From a UN perspective, after the 1997 Kyoto Conference on Climate change, a key milestone for addressing social concerns was represented by the *Millennium Development Goals* (MDGs) established in 2000 for the period 2000–2015. The MDGs focused on a set of rights and needs encompassing themes such as poverty, health and discrimination. Subsequently, according to Drexhage and Murphy (2010), the following 2002 Johannesburg World Summit on Sustainable Development (WSSD) "*demonstrated a major shift in the perception of sustainable development—away from environmental issues toward social and economic development*" (p. 8). By integrating MDGs with additional socio-economic aspects, WSSD "*did make a constructive change by focusing considerably more attention on development issues*" (Drexhage and Murphy 2010, p. 9).

Importantly, a 20-year follow-up to the 1992 Earth Summit took place in Rio de Janeiro in 2012 through the United Nations Conference on Sustainable Development (UNCSD). The Conference is also known as Rio+20 and was aimed at securing renewed political commitment for sustainable development, assessing the progress and implementation gaps in meeting previous commitments, and addressing new and emerging challenges. Within Rio +20 the UN agreed on the need for Sustainable Development Goals (SDGs) by emphasising the importance of both social and environmental concerns and the need for a more comprehensive definition of the role of business for sustainable development.

2.2.3   The Business Discourse

A third main discourse which has emerged within the debate on sustainability concerns the relationships between modern corporations and both social and environmental matters (we will label this discourse as the 'business discourse'). As argued by Gray (2010, p. 57), "*Capitalism and its destructive tendencies are manifest through its greatest creation—the corporation*". Given the depletion of natural resources that is caused through their activities, corporations are required to move towards a state in which they "*use only resources that are consumed at a rate below the natural reproduction, or at a rate below the development of substitutes. They do not cause emissions that accumulate in the environment at a rate beyond the capacity of the natural system to absorb and assimilate these emissions. Finally they do not engage in activity that degrades eco-system services*" (Dyllick and Hockerts 2002, p. 133). This situation encompasses not only *eco-efficiency* (WBCSD 2000) but also *eco-effectiveness* (Braungart and McDonough 1998) and *sufficiency* (Schumacher 1973).

Moreover, from a business perspective, sustainability has been referred to as the capability of a corporation to last in time, both in terms of profitability, productivity and financial performance, as well as in terms of managing environmental and social assets that compose its capitals. In one sentence, business sustainability is the *business of staying in business* (Doane and MacGillivray 2001). Dyllick and Hockerts (2002) define business sustainability as "*meeting the needs of a firm's direct and indirect stakeholders [...] without compromising its ability to meet the needs of future stakeholders as well*" (p. 131). In this respect, the business discourse on sustainability has also revealed an inherent paradox between corporations and sustainability (Gray 2010). On the one hand, given the power of corporations to exert control over society and to produce large scale innovations, they are increasingly regarded by governments as an unavoidable means through which (social and environmental) sustainability can be implemented (Hawken et al. 1999; Gray 2010). On the other hand, they are placed at the heart of concerns about the deterioration of natural resources and the production of social inequalities. This (apparent) paradox requires further understanding regarding the relationships between social, environmental and business discourses.

2.3 Conceptualising the Key Dimensions of Sustainability: Towards an Integrated Approach

The literature reviewed in the previous section, as well as the three evolving (environmental, social and business) discourses make it possible to identify and conceptualise the key dimensions of the concept of sustainability, as well as to emphasise the need for an integrated approach among the three dimensions. This need has also been acknowledged by Drexhage and Murphy (2010): we need to take *"sustainable development out of the environment "box" and considering wider social, economic, and geopolitical agendas"* (p. 20). In other words *"sustainable development embodies integration, and understanding and acting on the complex interconnections that exist between the environment, economy, and society"* (p. 6).

The multidimensionality of sustainability has also been reiterated by Rio+20. In fact, the Rio+20 outcome document, *The Future We Want*, refers to three dimensions of sustainable development: economic, social and environmental. It also refers to good governance as the basis for sustainable development. This idea is embraced by SDSN, which refers to four dimensions: economic development (including the end of extreme poverty), social inclusion, environmental sustainability, and good governance (including peace and security). Also SDSN stresses the need for an integrated approach to sustainability: this is clearly expressed by the document entitled *An Action Agenda for Sustainable Development* (SDSN 2013), according to which *"the challenges addressed by the proposed SDGs are inherently integrated"* (p. x).

The initiatives and documents mentioned above have highlighted the need for an integrated approach towards sustainability at a systems level. This need has also been emphasized at the level of the corporation. For instance, in providing guidelines to companies for sustainability reporting, the Global Reporting Initiative (GRI) has highlighted various dimensions of sustainability (i.e. economic, social and environmental dimensions) to be included and disclosed within reporting activities. In this respect, sustainability reporting should provide reliable information on the progress towards sustainability in all its different dimensions. The idea of sustainability as a multidimensional concept emerges clearly from GRI's *G4 Sustainability Reporting Guidelines—Reporting Principles and Standard Disclosure* (2013), which highlights that *"a sustainability report conveys disclosures on an organization's impacts—be they positive or negative—on the environment, society and the economy"* (p. 3). The multidimensional nature of sustainability reporting and the need for integration have also been emphasized by the International Integrated Reporting Council (IIRC). According to the *Consultation Draft of The International IR Framework* of 2013 (CD), integrated reporting *"is a process that results in communication by an organization, most visibly a periodic integrated report, about value creation over time"* (p. 8); furthermore, the integrated report is defined as "*a concise communication about how an organization's strategy, governance, performance and prospects, in the context of its external environment, lead to the creation of value over the short, medium and long term*" (p. 8). The CD points out that the integrated report aims to "*enhance accountability and stewardship with respect to the broad base of capitals (financial, manufactured, intellectual, human, social and relationship, and natural) and promote understanding of the interdependencies between them*" (p. 8). In this way, the CD stresses not only the need to preserve the various capitals, but also hints at the aim of integration. In fact, as emphasized within the CD, the integrated report supports "*integrated thinking, decision-making and actions that focus on the creation of value over the short, medium and long term*" (p. 8).

By relying upon the initiatives and documents mentioned above, as well as upon the analysis of the main discourses which have informed the debate on sustainability, next we will refer to the concept of integrated sustainability at the company level. This approach towards sustainability requires that organizations address all main dimensions of sustainability simultaneously. In simple terms, these dimensions include: the *Financial* dimension, in terms of ensuring long term economic and financial performance; the *Social* dimension, by creating value for the society; the *Environmental* dimension, through a responsible management and re-construction of natural resources. As we will see in the following section, integrated sustainability implies the effective management of the inherent tensions between these different dimensions.

2.4   The Challenges of Integrated Sustainability

Whereas the need for an integrated approach towards sustainability has been recently advocated by academics, institutions and cross country initiatives, the implications and challenges involved in implementing this integration have received little attention. As argued by Gray (2010, p. 53), "Sustainability is not only a complex and elusive notion, but one which is fraught with potential contradictions". Some of these 'potential contradictions' stem from the tensions between the different dimensions of sustainability, which may occur when attempting to implement all dimensions simultaneously, according to an integrated approach.

For example, if we consider the financial and social dimensions of sustainability from the company perspective, whereas some studies have demonstrated that addressing social performance is good for financial performance, other studies highlight that conflicts between the two dimensions do exist in numerous circumstances (see Boyd et al. 2009; Orlitzky et al. 2003). These mixed results offered by the literature can be explained in light of the tensions between the social and financial dimensions of company performance. Social performance requires freedom and flexibility from financial constraints and business logics, in order to find solutions to social problems. Whereas the pursuit of social performance should aim at creating value primarily for society as a whole rather than for the individual company, the search for financial performance works in the opposite way (Pache and Santos 2011). Tensions between social and financial performance are also related to various institutional pressures and stakeholders that converge within corporations, in which customers, employees, suppliers, beneficiaries, partners, and investors address multiple social or financial needs (Coda 1988). These tensions increase during scale-up processes, when social performance has to be considered while taking into account the financial needs of a larger number of stakeholders.

Similarly, if we consider the environmental and financial dimensions of sustainability from the company perspective, several studies have argued that effective environmental management may lead to increased production efficiency, cost reduction and improved market reputation with benefits for financial performance (see Molina-Azorín et al. 2009; Ambec and Lanoie 2008; Miles and Covin 2000). Simultaneously, the search for environmental performance may imply high costs of compliance (Jaffe et al. 1995), huge investments for re-constructing the consumed resources and may limit opportunities for growth and for competitive improvement, at the detriment of financial performance (see, for example, Hull and Rothenberg 2008). Also, on a large scale, financial performance and commercial needs may imply the use of technologies for increasing resource consumption, to the detriment of environmental performance.

Finally, the social and environmental dimensions of sustainability may also reveal inherent tensions. For instance, a new solution for a more effective management of environmental resources may conflict with social needs. In contrast, new solutions to social problems may conflict with the need to preserve natural resources. In this context, Gray (2010) draws on Dresner (2002) to suggest the existence of a 'sustainability continuum' between strong and weak sustainability. On one hand, weak sustainability relies upon the idea that human-made resources can compensate for the consumption of natural resources. On the other end of the continuum, very strong sustainability suggests that human life is incompatible with sustainability. Within this continuum, organizations are likely to play a role in contributing to weak sustainability to the extent in which they search for solutions to compensate for the consumption of natural resources.

Far from constituting paradoxes which need to be solved, the relationships between social, financial and environmental dimensions (highlighted above) represent tensions which need to be adequately managed when implementing integrated sustainability. The management of these tensions does not necessarily mean achieving a stable proportion between all dimensions, but rather addressing all (financial, environmental and social) dimensions simultaneously and through an integrated approach. In so doing, the management of tensions becomes crucial for avoiding the drift in favour of one single dimension to the detriment of the others and to fully realize the potentials of all dimensions at the same time. As we will argue next, in implementing integrated sustainability within organizations, a key role should be played by governance systems, business models, as well as management, measurement and reporting systems. All these systems need to be adequately designed and practiced within organizations according to an integrated approach.

Fig. 2.1 Implementing
integrated sustainability: key
levels

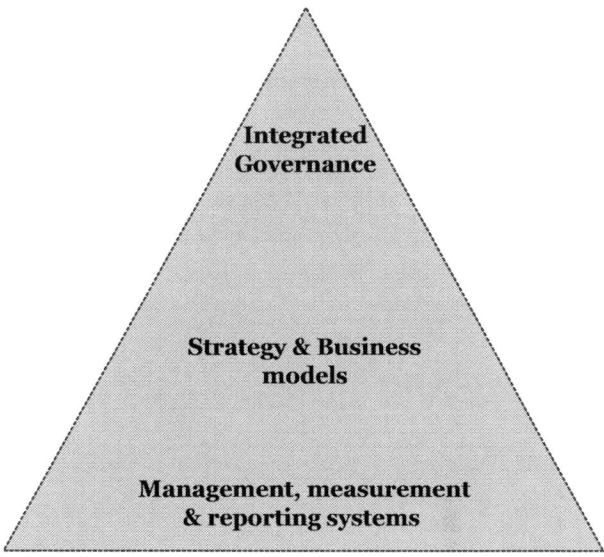

2.5   Implementing Integrated Sustainability Beyond Rhetoric: From Governance to Integrated Reporting Systems

In this section, we suggest that the actual implementation of integrated sustainability should take place at different organizational levels, ranging from the level of corporate governance to the strategic and business model level, while also including the level of management, measurement and reporting (see Fig. 2.1). At these various levels, structures, processes and systems should be designed and practiced according to an integrated approach. Far from providing an extensive analysis of the levels mentioned above, in this section we build on some recent, key studies which have addressed governance issues, business models, management and measurement systems according to an integrated and multidimensional approach. The aim is to suggest how these studies could be extended to include broader issues of sustainability from an integrated perspective.

2.5.1   Implementing Integrated Governance: Compliance, Integrated Sustainability, Risk and Knowledge Management

Within the debate on sustainability, governance issues have acquired increasing relevance. For example, the holistic framework on sustainability proposed by the Rio+20 outcome document considers good governance as a key element for sustainable development. This view is embraced by the SDSN, that includes good governance among the key dimensions of sustainability.

The need to align governance systems to sustainability is also acknowledged at the company level (Cartwright and Craig 2006). Following recent corporate scandals and episodes of managerial misconduct, the corporate governance debate has pointed to certain corporations whose ways of doing business have been too profit-oriented and overly focused on the financial aspects of organisational performance (see Abdel-khalik 2002; Benston and Hartgraves 2002). In particular, it has been broadly acknowledged that creating value only for shareholders is not enough (see, among others, Charreaux and Desbrières 2001; Catturi 2007; Coda 1988). Rather, value creation is an integrated process that is rooted around a broad perspective of governance, encompassing the interest of multiple stakeholders. In the attempt to ensure effective accountability towards different stakeholders, national and international regulations have largely proliferated. Simultaneously, following the increasing attention given to compliance issues within the corporate governance debate, some studies have emphasised that, in order to implement effective governance, compliance is not enough. In this context, a broader perspective on governance is suggested; one that combines compliance with the achievement of financial and non-financial objectives, ethical behaviour, environmental concerns, and risk awareness (see Seal 2006; Bhimani and Soonawalla 2005; Fahy et al. 2004). Such a broadened perspective also suggests going beyond formal structures of governance to consider the actual processes and mechanisms through which governance principles and practices are operationalised (Mouritsen and Thrane 2006).

Within this debate, recent studies have suggested an integrated approach to governance (labelled as 'integrated governance'); one which encompasses four main dimensions, namely, compliance, performance, risk and knowledge (see Busco et al. 2005). From this point of view, integrated governance includes: compliance to rules and regulations; the achievement of the company's performance; effective risk management; and knowledge management. These dimensions are strongly related to each other and, as such, should be sought out and managed simultaneously. For example, actual compliance to laws, rules and recommendations requires effective knowledge management, which implies the management of skills, competencies, cultural and ethical underpinnings of the individuals that comprise the organization. Furthermore, whereas the achievement of the company's performance should take place within the boundaries provided by compliance issues, within the integrated governance system these boundaries should enable rather than constrain value creation processes. Finally, risk management should be based on both compliance to recommendations (see, for instance, COSO 2004), as well as on effective knowledge management in order to actually support value creation and the strategic management of company performance. Although it is within the compliance-driven corporate governance debate that risk management has acquired growing relevance, regulatory power and legitimacy (Mikes 2008), risk management should also be considered as a system for strategizing and performance management (Collier and Berry 2002; Collier et al. 2004). Therefore, a key role is played not only by formal prescriptions and frameworks for risk management, but also by the relationships between risk management (compliance) and the effective knowledge management of the different groups of experts (accountants, risk managers, internal auditors, directors, top

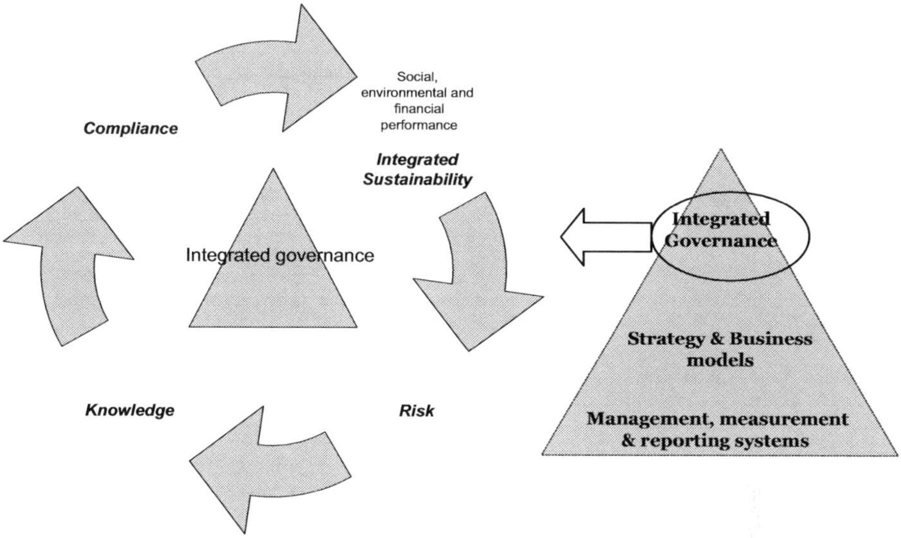

Compliance

Social,
environmental and
financial
performance

Integrated
Sustainability

Integrated governance

Integrated Governance

Knowledge   Risk

Strategy & Business
models

Management, measurement
& reporting systems

Fig. 2.2 Integrated governance [*source*: adapted from Busco et al. (2005)]

managers, etc.) that comprise the various parts of the organization and of its governance systems.

The integrated approach to governance described above (and proposed by Busco et al. 2005) is meant to assist the actual implementation of governance beyond simple issues of compliance and beyond the mere search for external legitimization and consensus, which have catalysed the recent debate on corporate governance. In the attempt to align this approach with the concept of integrated sustainability, the dimensions of integrated governance could be further developed to include social, environmental and financial dimensions of sustainability (see Fig. 2.2). In so doing, integrated governance would result from the simultaneous search for:

– compliance to national and international rules, regulations and recommendations;
– integrated sustainability, which combines social, environmental and financial performance dimensions;
– risk management, broadened through a holistic approach to include both quantifiable and non-quantifiable risks, providing managers with a more strategic perspective, and improving accountability towards all stakeholders within the strategic decision-making process;
– knowledge management, which should provide the subtle links for combining all of the previous dimensions by embracing the development of the skills, competencies, cultural and ethical underpinnings needed to ensure integration.

2.5.2 (Hybrid) Business Models for Integrated Sustainability

In addition to an integrated approach to the governance system, the implementation of integrated sustainability requires the definition of *ad hoc* strategies and business models that should capture social, environmental and financial dimensions, as well as their intertwining relationships.

Although new strategies have been recently emerging from the adoption of the founding principles of sustainable development from corporations, in the resulting business models charity and social programs have often been merely added to for-profit models. In this context, sustainability and business performance are managed separately and represent the objects of two distinct strategies carried out by an organization. The separation between sustainability and business strategies can undermine the actual implementation of sustainability, relegating it to ineffective solutions or to the mere 'sustainability rhetoric' in the search for legitimization. This situation calls for the definition and implementation of new, more effective business models, in which to ensure an integrated strategic move towards sustainability beyond its mere rhetoric.

In general, a business model should capture the internal and external patterns of interactions that shape a company's value chain, value proposition and value system. Given the tensions between the business needs of corporations and the social and environmental dimensions of sustainability highlighted in the previous sections, the definition and implementation of sustainable business models is a challenging process. Despite these challenges, new business models have emerged as forms of 'hybrid organizations' (or 'hybrid business models'), in which social (and/or environmental) and commercial performance are sought after simultaneously through a single, unified strategy (Battilana et al. 2012; see also Battilana and Dorado 2010—see Fig. 2.3)[5]. According to recent studies, hybrid business models are experiencing a rapid growth in a number of sectors (Porter and Kramer 2011; Battilana et al. 2012). Many hybrid organizations originated as forms of social entrepreneurship and, then they turned into hybrids by searching for autonomy from donations and subsidies, as well as by attempting to scale up in order to reach a larger market. More recently, hybrid business models are growing in new (and for-profit) sectors, such as consulting, retail, consumer products and IT (information technology). Hybrid organizations are also emerging among high tech R&D firms, as a result of the joint efforts and collaboration between industry and academia (Lamb and Davidson 2004).

As is similar to any hybrid species, hybrid business models face both the challenges and opportunities that come from the integration of diverse elements within the same strategy (Phills et al. 2008). On one hand, this diversity is interpreted as a unique source of innovation. With an approach that is different from pure social or pure commercial models, in hybrid organizations managers do

---

[5] In general, hybrids have been defined as new phenomena (practices, tools, organizations, etc.) produced out of two or more elements that are normally found separately (Miller et al. 2008).

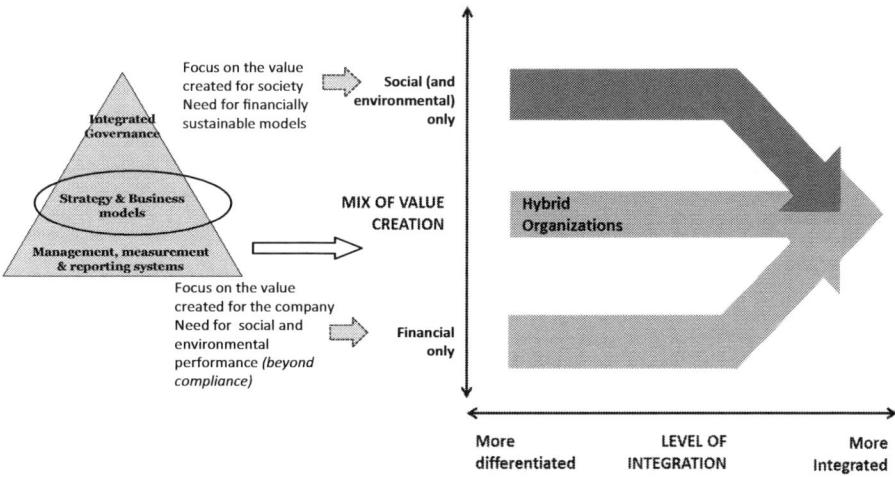

Fig. 2.3 Hybrid business models [*source*: adapted from Battilana et al. (2012)]

not have to choose between social (or environmental) and financial/commercial performance. The co-existence of different performance dimensions may allow a virtuous cycle of long term financial results and reinvestment in the social mission (Battilana et al. 2012). On the other hand, this co-existence can create tensions which may challenge the very nature of hybrids by causing a mission drift towards one dimension to the detriment of the other and of the hybrid nature itself. As argued by Battilana et al. (2012, p. 51), "Hybrid must also strike a delicate balance between social and economic objectives, to avoid 'mission drift'—in this case, a focus on profits to the detriment of social good". As a result, hybrid business models are said to be characterized by an ubiquitous and unstable nature (Miller et al. 2008), which does not allow one-off solutions to take place but rather requires the continuous search for the 'hybrid ideal'. According to Battilana et al. (2012, p. 51), "When organizations combine social mission with commercial activities, they create unfamiliar combinations of activities for which a supportive ecosystem may not yet exist".

Whereas hybrid business models may address some of the challenges of integrated sustainability, still the management of tensions between the different dimensions of sustainability, which co-exist within the hybrid, is a critical process. Similarly, as emphasized in the previous subsection, the relationships between the different dimensions of integrated governance requires *ad hoc* management systems. As we will see later, to support an integrated approach to sustainability, governance systems and business models need to be assisted by adequate management, measurement and reporting systems.

2.5.3 The Role of Integrated Management, Measurement and Reporting Systems

The role of management and measurement systems in addressing different (social, environmental and financial) performance dimensions have been the object of numerous studies that have, nevertheless, provided mixed results. Some studies have emphasised that traditional management control systems are limited in the pursuit of social or environmental performance because they focus managers' attention on financial concerns (Gond et al. 2012). Other studies have highlighted that, if designed to include social and environmental matters, management control systems can help to address social and environmental performance (Henri and Journeault 2010; Gond et al. 2012). The reasons for such mixed results can be related to the fact that these studies have mainly concentrated on isolated and fragmented elements or systems, without considering the broader spectrum of management controls, which can be involved in the management of different dimensions of sustainability.

The need for overcoming the fragmentation highlighted above has been advocated also in the recent debate on integrated reporting. The *CD* calls for an 'integrated thinking' to overcome the traditional 'silo thinking' within the performance measurement and reporting system, as well as in managing the overall value creation process. According to the *CD*, such integrated thinking should encompass all ranges of factors (from the firm's capitals, to governance structures, business models, as well as performance drivers and outcomes) which take part in the value creation process, as well as the interactions between them. From this point of view, integrated thinking should be a guiding logic of the (integrated) reporting system.

The logic of integrated thinking described in the *CD* displays potentials for providing integrated reporting with a key role in implementing integrated sustainability beyond compliance. In fact, integrated thinking does not imply the mere sum or systematization of financial, social and environmental reporting systems. Nor does it require adding an isolated measurement system for integrated reporting. Rather, the adoption of integrated reporting should provide an opportunity for a broader re-thinking of all pre-existing systems by suggesting how to overcome the isolation between them for the purpose of implementing and practicing integrated sustainability beyond compliance. Therefore, rather than representing an isolated element disconnected from the other management and measurement systems, and responding mainly to compliance and legitimizing needs, the integrated report should be aligned with other measurement systems (such as the business plan, the balanced scorecard, the budgeting system, the quality and production efficiency management systems, etc.) and should be conceived of as an active and constructive element within the process of planning, enacting, monitoring and communicating integrated sustainability on an ongoing basis and throughout all organizational levels (see Fig. 2.4).

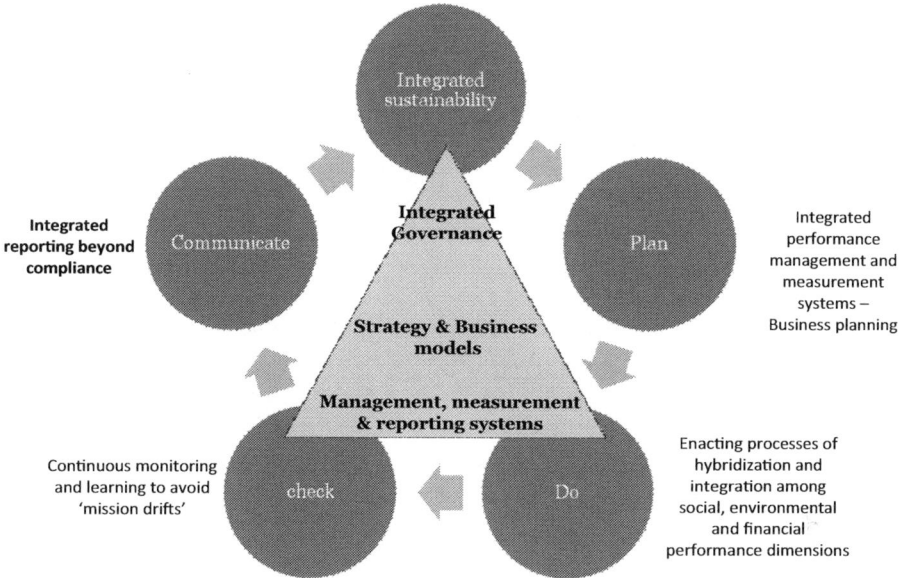

Fig. 2.4   Implementing integrated sustainability: which role for integrated reporting?

Summary and Conclusions

In this chapter we have highlighted the practical implications of exploring the key dimensions of sustainability, as well as their interconnections, going beyond the sustainability rhetoric. By relying upon the evolving debate regarding sustainability, and upon the different discourses which have informed this debate, we have emphasised the multidimensional and integrated nature of sustainability, as well as the tensions between its different dimensions. Rather than eliminating tensions, effective integration requires a full realisation of the potentials of all dimensions simultaneously. This process is challenging and, if we take the perspective of organizations, it should happen at various organizational levels. In this context, we have built on various studies that have explored governance, business models and performance management, measurement and reporting systems through integrated approaches, in order to highlight the opportunities that these approaches offer for incorporating the different dimensions of sustainability, and for understanding their management process. In so doing, rather than offering prescriptive solutions, we have outlined the following key elements and levels which we believe should be taken into account in the implementation of integrated sustainability:

- the integrated governance system, whose actual implementation requires the effective management of compliance; financial, social and environmental performance; risk management; and knowledge management;

- the definition of adequate (hybrid) business models, which are required to address social, financial and environmental performance dimensions simultaneously;
- integrated management, measurement and reporting systems, which may allow an integrated approach to sustainability through planning, execution, monitoring and communication.

Importantly, by drawing upon the elements mentioned above, our analysis highlights the potential role played by integrated reporting in the implementation of integrated sustainability. Given the driving principles and content elements for integrated reporting provided by the CD, we argue that, if adequately designed and implemented, integrated reporting can play an active and constructive role in managing sustainability beyond compliance. Therefore, integrated reporting should be conceived beyond mere issues of compliance and legitimization and should be framed within a broader approach. This approach requires that companies actually alter their existing practices beyond mere rhetoric and allow a concrete strategic move towards sustainable development.

References

Abdel-khalik A (2002) Reforming corporate governance post Enron: Shareholders Board of Trustees and the auditor. J Account Public Pol 21:97–103

Ambec S, Lanoie P (2008) Does it pay to be green? A systematic overview. Acad Manage Perspect 22(4):45–62

Andriof J, McIntosh M (eds) (2001) Perspectives on corporate citizenship. Greenleaf, Sheffield

Battilana J, Dorado S (2010) Building sustainable hybrid organizations: the case of commercial microfinance organizations. Acad Manage J 53(6):2010

Battilana J, Lee M, Walker J, Dorsey C (2012) In search of the hybrid ideal. Stanfor Soc Innov Rev Summer:51–55

Benston G, Hartgraves A (2002) Enron: what happened and what we can learn from it. J Account Public Pol 21:105–127

Berry MA, Rondinelli DA (1998) Proactive corporate environmental management: a new industrial revolution. Acad Manage Exec 12:38–50

Bhimani A, Soonawalla K (2005) From conformance to performance: the corporate responsibilities continuum. J Account Public Pol 24:165–174

Bowen HR (1953) Social responsibilities of the businessman. Harper & Row, New York, NY

Boyd B, Henning N, Reyna E, Wang DE, Welch MD (2009) Hybrid organizations: new business models for environmental leadership. Greenleaf, Sheffield

Braungart M, McDonough W (1998) The next industrial revolution. The Atlantic Monthly. October 282(2):82–92

Busco C, Frigo M, Giovannoni E, Riccaboni A, Scapens RW (2005) Beyond compliance: why integrated governance matters today, Strategic Finance, August, pp. 35–43

Cartwright W, Craig JL (2006) Sustainability: aligning corporate governance, strategy and operations with the planet. Bus Process Manag J 12(6):741–750

Catturi G (2007) La valorialità aziendale, vol 1. Cedam, Padova

Charreaux G, Desbrières P (2001) Corporate governance: stakeholder value versus shareholder value. J Manag Gov 5:107–128

Coda V (1988) L'orientamento strategico dell'impresa. UTET, Torino

Collier PM, Berry AJ (2002) Risk in the process of budgeting. Manag Account Res 13(3):273–297

Collier PM, Berry AJ, Burke G (2004) Risk and control: drivers, practices and consequences. Chartered Institute of Management Accountant

COSO (2004) Enterprise risk management—Integrated framework, Executive summary. Committee of Sponsoring Organisation of the Treadway Commission

Davis K (1960) Can business afford to ignore social responsibilities? Calif Manag Rev 2:70–76

Dempsey N, Bramley G, Power S, Brown C (2011) The social dimension of sustainable development: defining urban social sustainability. Sustain Dev 19:289–300

Dixon JA, Fallon LA (1989) The concept of sustainability: origins, extensions and usefulness for policy. Soc Natur Resour 2:73–84

Doane D, MacGillivray A (2001) Economic Sustainability-the business of staying in business, New Economics Foundation, London. http://www.projectsigma.co.uk/RnDStreams/RD_economic_sustain.pdf

Dresner S (2002) The principles of sustainability. Earthscan, London

Drexhage J, Murphy D (2010) Sustainable development: from Brundtland to Rio 2012, Background paper for the high level panel on global sustainability, United Nations, New York. http://www.un.org/wcm/webdav/site/climatechange/shared/gsp/docs/GSP1-6_Background%20on%20Sustainable%20Devt.pdf

Dyllick T, Hockerts K (2002) Beyond the case for corporate sustainability. Bus Strat Environ 11:130–141

Fahy M, Roche J, Weiner A (2004) Beyond corporate governance: creating corporate value through performance, conformance and responsibility. Wiley, Chichester

Frederick WC (1960) The growing concern over business responsibility. Calif Manag Rev 2:54–61

Freeman RE (1984) Strategic management: a stakeholder approach. Pitman, Boston, MA

Global Reporting Initiative (GRI) (2013) G4 sustainability reporting guidelines—reporting principles and standard disclosure. https://www.globalreporting.org/resourcelibrary/GRIG4-Part1-Reporting-Principles-and-Standard-Disclosures.pdf

Gond J, Grubnic S, Herzig C, Moon J (2012) Configuring management control systems. Theorizing the integration of strategy and sustainability. Manage Account Res 23:205–223

Gray R (2010) Is accounting for sustainability actually accounting for sustainability... and how would we know? An exploration of narratives of organisations and the planet. Account Org Soc 35(1):47–62

Hawken P, Lovins A, Lovins LH (1999) Natural capitalism: creating the next industrial revolution. Little, Brown, Boston, MA

Henri J, Journeault M (2010) Eco-control: the influence of management control systems on environmental and economic performance. Account Org Soc 35:63–80

Hopwood AG (2009) Accounting and the environment. Account Org Soc 34(3–4):433–439

Hull C, Rothenberg S (2008) Firm performance: the interactions of corporate social performance with innovation and industry differentiation. Strateg Manag J 29(7):781–789

International Integrated Reporting Council (IIRC) (2013) Consultation draft of the international IR framework. http://www.theiirc.org/wp-content/uploads/Consultation-Draft/Consultation-Draft-of-the-InternationalIRFramework.pdf

International Union for Conservation of Nature/United Nations Environment Programme/World Wildlife Fund (IUCN/UNEP/WWF) (1980) World conservation strategy: living resource conservation for sustainable development. http://data.iucn.org/dbtw-wpd/edocs/WCS-004.pdf

Jaffe A, Peterson S, Portney P, Stavins R (1995) Environmental regulation and the competitiveness of US manufacturing: what does the evidence tell us? J Econ Lit 33(1):132–163

Joseph G (2012) Ambiguous but tethered: an accounting basis for sustainability reporting. Crit Perspect Account 23:93–106

Kidd CV (1992) The evolution of sustainability. J Agr Environ Ethic 5(1):1–26

Kilcullen M, Ohles Kooistra J (1999) At least do no harm: sources on the changing role of business ethics and corporate social responsibility. Ref Serv Rev 27(2):158–178

KPMG (2011) KPMG international survey of corporate responsibility reporting 2011. http://www. kpmg.com/PT/pt/IssuesAndInsights/Documents/corporate-responsibility2011.pdf

Lamb R, Davidson E (2004) Hybrid organization in high-tech enterprise. Paper presented at the 17th Bled eCommerce Conference, Slovenia, 21–23 June 2004, pp. 1–14

Meadows DH, Meadows DL, Randers J, Behrens WW III (1972) The limits to growth. Universe Books, New York, NY

Melnyk SA, Sroufe RP, Calantone R (2003) Assessing the impact of environmental management systems on corporate and environmental performance. J Oper Manag 21:329–351

Mikes A (2008) Chief risk officers at crunch time: compliance champions or business partners? J Risk Manag Financ Inst 2(1):7–25

Miles M, Covin J (2000) Environmental marketing: a source of reputational, competitive and financial advantage. J Bus Ethic 23(3):299–311

Miller P, Kurunmäki L, O'Leary T (2008) Accounting hybrids and the management of risk. Account Org Soc 33:942–967

Molina-Azorín JF, Claver-Cortés E, López-Gamero MD, Tarí JJ (2009) Green management and financial performance: a literature review. Manag Decis 47(7):1080–1100

Mouritsen J, Thrane S (2006) Accounting network complementarities and the development of inter-organisational relations. Account Org Soc 31:241–275

Orlitzky M, Schmidt FL, Rynes SL (2003) Corporate social and financial performance: a meta-analysis. Organ Stud 24(3):403–441

Pache AC, Santos F (2011) Inside the hybrid organization-an organizational level view of responses to conflicting institutional. ESSEC Working Paper 11001. http://www.essec.edu/ faculty/showDeclFileRes.do?declId=9761&key=__workpaper__

Phills JA Jr, Deiglmeier K, Miller DT (2008) Rediscovering social innovation. Stanfor Soc Innov Rev Fall:35–43

Pierson J (2002) Tackling social exclusion. Routledge, London

Porter ME, Kramer MR (2011) Creating shared value. Harvard Bus Rev January–February:1–17

Ratcliffe P (2000) Is the assertion of minority identity compatible with the idea of a socially inclusive society? In: Askonas P, Stewart A (eds) Social inclusion: possibilities and tensions. Macmillan, Basingstoke, pp 169–185

Riddell R (1981) Ecodevelopment: economics, ecology, and development: an alternative to growth imperative models. Gower, London

Sachs I (1984) The strategies of ecodevelopment. FAO Ceres 17:17–21

Schumacher EF (1973) Small is beautiful: economics as if people mattered. Harper & Row, New York, NY

Seal W (2006) Management accounting and corporate governance: an institutional interpretation of the agency problem. Manag Account Res 17:389–408

Tivy J, O'Hare G (1982) Human impact on the eco-system. Oliver and Boyd, Edinburgh

United Nations (UN) (1972) Report of the United Nations Conference on the human environment. http://www.un-documents.net/aconf48-14r1.pdf

United Nations Sustainable Development Solutions Network (UNSDN) (2013) An action agenda for sustainable development. http://www.unsdsn.org/files/2013/06/130613-SDSN-An-Action-Agenda-for-Sustainable-Development-FINAL.pdf

Werbach A (2009) Strategy for sustainability: a business manifesto. Harvard Business, Boston, MA

World Business Council for Sustainable Development (WBCSD) (2000) Eco-efficiency: creating more value with less impact. World Business Council for Sustainable Development, Geneva

World Commission on Environment and Development (WCED) (1987) Our common future. Oxford University Press, Oxford

World Resources Institute/ International Institute for Environment and Development (WRI/IIED) (1986) World resources 1986. Basic Books, New York, NY

Annual Reports, Sustainability Reports and Integrated Reports: Trends in Corporate Disclosure

3

Marco Fasan

Abstract

This chapter aims at providing a comprehensive comparison between Annual Reports (ARs), Sustainability Reports (SRs) and Integrated Reports (IRs), focusing on their similarities and differences from an evolutionary perspective. In particular, it provides an argument for the main limitations AR has faced during recent years and of the main characteristics of SR, focusing in particular on the recent G4 guidelines from the Global Reporting Initiative. The IR, as framed in the Consultation Draft proposed by the International Integrated Reporting Council, can be considered the cutting-edge and probably the future of corporate disclosure. It is fundamental to compare it with previous forms of corporate disclosure in order to properly understand the current debate and to forecast its future development. IR presents some similarities with AR and SR, while at the same time introducing some relevant innovations, aimed at overcoming the limitations of the two traditional forms of reporting. Nevertheless, it still needs to undergo some scrutiny in order to become a widespread disclosure pattern.

3.1 Introduction

Corporate disclosure has been changing significantly in recent years. Integrated Reporting represents the cutting-edge and probably the future of corporate reporting worldwide. Scholars (among others, Arnold et al. 2012; Eccles and Krzus 2010; Frias-Aceituno et al. 2012), policymakers (European Commission 2009) and standard-setters (IIRC 2013; GRI 2013) are looking at this new way of reporting with great interest and, given the severe limitations and expectations of Annual Reports and Sustainability Reports, with great hope as well.

M. Fasan (✉)
Department of Management, Ca' Foscari University of Venice, Venice, Italy
e-mail: marco.fasan@unive.it

C. Busco et al. (eds.), *Integrated Reporting*, DOI 10.1007/978-3-319-02168-3_3,
© Springer International Publishing Switzerland 2013

This chapter aims to provide a comprehensive analysis and comparison between Annual Reports (AR), Sustainability Reports (SR) and Integrated Reports (IR), focusing on their similarities and differences from an evolutionary perspective. In order to properly understand the current debate about IR and to forecast its future developments, it is fundamental to link IR to the other forms of reporting, which are currently employed.

The second section analyses the current standards of financial disclosure, focusing in particular on AR's limitations: complexity, lack of non-financial information and short-termism. The third section discusses the main features of SR, devoting particular attention to the most important standard of disclosure [proposed by the Global Reporting Initiative (GRI)]. The fourth section briefly defines the main characteristics of IR according to the International Integrated Reporting Council (IIRC) framework.

Finally, the last section discusses similarities and differences between IR, AR and SR. In particular, it is argued that IR needs to be considered as an evolution of AR rather than SR, because, according to the IIRC framework, the intended users of the report are clearly identified as investors and providers of financial capital. Also the "capitals" (objective, thus referred to the final impact on the company) approach proposed by the IIRC is quite different from the "stakeholder" (subjective, thus referred to the single individuals or entities) approach typical of SR. IR presents some relevant differences as well, when compared to AR: the most important being the way of interpreting the value creation process and time horizon. IR is long-term oriented and focuses on the impact of a company's activities on the capitals and on the interrelations generated by such actions. This may create a problem for investors and companies that are short-term oriented, because they may see IR as a threat rather than as a way to disclose their performance more comprehensively.

Below are some challenges the IIRC will have to face in order for IR to become a widely employed pattern of disclosure.

3.2 Financial Disclosure and Limitations of Annual Reports

According to accounting standards (both IAS/IFRS and the national GAAPs of the various countries), the main purpose of ARs is to provide relevant information to investors in order to allow them to make informed economic decisions (see Revised IAS 1; Deloitte 2013). The topic is central to the field of accounting, where there is a vast body of literature analysing the value relevance (defined by Barth et al. 2001, p. 25, as "the association between accounting amounts and security market values") of accounting numbers, identifying the information which investors rely upon most heavily. Although AR is a tool used primarily by investors, it is also employed by managers in order to make decisions on resource allocation and, as such, is studied in the management field as well.

Although AR undoubtedly represents the main way investors gather information still today, during the last 10 years this form of reporting has proven to have some severe limitations. Such limitations arise from the inability of ARs to evolve coherently with change in the economic context without losing reliability and clarity (see Schroeder 2002; Cox 2007). In the last years, companies' values have been influenced to a greater extent by elements that are not properly represented in ARs, such as the way in which operations' safety is managed. A striking example is the 2006 Deepwater Horizon oil spill, which greatly damaged the reputation (and financial performance) of British Petroleum. In addition, companies have employed new financial instruments, such as derivatives and credit default swaps, which have had to be disclosed through ARs, increasing their complexity and decreasing, in turn, their reliability (see Plumee 2003; Li 2008; Miller 2010). The worlds of business and society are changing, and traditional reporting has not managed to successfully adapt to such evolution. As a consequence, AR's reliability and capability to provide a true and fair view of the companies' financial performance have decreased. Although mainly due to corporate governance failures, the cases of Enron, Parmalat and, more recently, Lehman Brothers, have decreased the confidence of investors in AR (see, among the others, Baker and Hayes 2004).

The challenges that AR is facing and that have caused its decrease in reliability and in its capability to provide a true and fair view can be grouped in three broad categories. ARs are too long and too complex; they do not disclose some information (mainly, non-financial information) that investors need; and they do not provide enough information to allow investors to predict the long-term financial performance of the company (see Plumee 2003; Li 2008; Miller 2010). Somehow, they disclose too much financial performance (ARs are often unable to disclose what is really relevant in explaining the ability of a company to create value in the long term) and too little non-financial performance (ARs do not disclose nor measure determinant aspects of company performance).

Already in the late 1990s, Holland (1998) pointed out that ARs were too large and cumbersome, generating an information overload for unsophisticated users, who need to process a very large amount of information. One of the most severe (and most widely debated) limitations of AR is complexity. As business evolves, new types of transactions emerge that cannot be readily captured by traditional accounting measures (see You and Zhang 2009). These new transactions (for instance, stock options awarded to employees) require firms to significantly expand their disclosure regarding the transaction. In this way, companies have been accumulating information in their ARs, decreasing their relevancy (see Loughran and McDonald 2010; Miller 2010). ARs become longer and longer but the disclosure system has been weakened overall. Plumee (2003) and Gu and Wang (2005) find that analysts assimilate more easily less complex information compared to more complex information. These empirical findings are rooted in the work by Hirst and Hopkins (1998), who argue: "research in psychology suggests that information will not be used unless it is both available and readily processable (i.e. clear)" (Hirst and Hopkins 1998, p. 48).

The second limitation of AR deals with the fact that it does not provide enough non-financial information on issues such as management quality, customer satisfaction, and environmental and social performance. It is commonly believed (see The Atlantic 2013) that information is relevant only if it can be translated into monetary terms (i.e. if it cannot be expressed through a monetary number, it is not relevant). This paradigm is based on the assumption that the market and exchanges on the market allow the measurement of everything. But in the last few years the fact that price is the only measure of value and that the market exchange is the only mechanism regulating values has been severely questioned. Non-financial information (which, by definition, is not expressed in monetary terms) is central even for investors interested only in the financial profitability of firms. In recent years, the belief that only financial information provides elements on which to predict future performance has changed. Many studies have analysed the relationship between the social performance of a company (mostly measurable through non-financial information) and its financial performance, finding that some association may exist (see Pava and Krausz 1996; Orlitzky et al. 2003; Margolis and Walsh 2003). Other studies—dealing with disclosure rather than with performance—have devoted increasing attention to the role of non-financial information (NFI) in informing investors and, more broadly, stakeholders, about a company's performance (see, among the others, Amir and Lev 1996; Healy and Palepu 2001; Fifka and Drabble 2012). A widely-cited study by Ocean Tomo (2011) provides evidence confirming that financial information is not enough for investors and stakeholders to have a complete understanding of a company's performance and value.

The third limitation is the limited usefulness of AR in predicting the long-term performance of a company. ARs are essentially backward-oriented, thus they report a company's past financial performance, and they disclose no information about the future outlook of performance. Many of the studies cited above investigating the impact of other-than-financial performance on corporate financial performance recognize that the positive impact of social performance would eventually occur in the long term. ARs, neglecting non-financial information, lack these important pieces of information. Not only that, they also lack other KPIs measuring other-than-financial performance that, though not directly connected to social or environmental issues, are fundamental in predicting the future long-term performance of a company. This limitation has some important consequences, even on the way the company is managed. A manager facing the decision whether to cut the company's R&D investments, for instance, is more likely to do so if the main benchmark on which he/she is evaluated is the AR. Investors would eventually recognize this, decreasing the company's stock price, but even this control mechanism (the market) can work only if information about R&D (like all other information about company performance captured by non-financial information) is more clearly disclosed by the company (see Hirst and Hopkins 1998).

In summary, business cases, empirical evidence and the recent financial crisis seriously put in question the ability of financial data to provide adequate information on a firm's capability to create value and to sustain it over time.

Policymakers have taken the issue into serious consideration, such that, in many countries, companies are now required to complement their ARs with non-financial information. In April 2013, the European Commission adopted a proposal for a directive enhancing the transparency of certain large companies on social and environmental matters (see European Commission 2013). Large companies will

Table 3.1 Annual reports main features

	Annual reports
Target	Specific stakeholders (shareholders and investors)
Mandatory/voluntary	Mandatory
Regulation or guidelines	National and international laws and GAAP (or IAS/IFRS)
Comparability	High
Industry customization	Low
Assurance level	High
Scope	Financial reporting entity (company or group of companies)

need to disclose information on policies, risks and results as regards environmental matters, social and employee-related aspects, respect for human rights, anti-corruption and bribery issues, and diversity on the boards of directors.

Table 3.1 summarizes the main features of Annual Reports. Besides the aspects discussed above, it is important to point out that comparability among ARs is high, even if some work still needs to be done (mainly in terms of convergence between US GAAP and IAS/IFRS). This high comparability is reached at the expense of low ARs industry customization, as accounting standards do not provide any additional guidelines for companies operating in specific industries, although companies have the possibility to include some additional relevant information in the notes. The assurance (audit) level is high, in the sense that auditing standards and procedures and the nature of the financial information makes ARs easier to be audited, compared to SRs or IRs and, finally, the report is limited to legal entities (a company or group of companies).

3.3   Sustainability Reports

SRs provide "information relating to a corporation's activities, aspirations and public image with regard to environmental, community, employee and consumer issues. Within these headings will be subsumed other, more detailed, matters such as energy usage, equal opportunities, fair trade, corporate governance and the like" (see Gray et al. 2001, p. 329). SRs are typically intended to inform a wide range of stakeholders, from activist groups operating in the community to shareholders and investors, which may be interested in the social performance of the company as a predictor of its financial performance (see Klok 2003; Daub 2007). This fundamental characteristic of SR is evident also in the framework proposed by the GRI, which organizes the various elements proposed by stakeholder groups. Given the broadness of the concept of stakeholder and, consequently, of the boundaries of the report, an increasing amount of attention has been placed lately on the definition of material issues, which are those that might have an impact on the company's ability to create value in the long-term. Companies need to carefully evaluate which are the relevant stakeholders and issues they wish to communicate and therefore which are the strategic and most important KPIs. This presents the difficult task of defining the real targets of SRs, which is fundamental in order to avoid SRs becoming too wide and too complex.

According to KPMG (2011), the vast majority of the 250 largest companies in the world (95 %) report on their corporate responsibility activities. Among the best performing countries, in terms of sustainability disclosure's strong communication and professionalism over time, there are many European countries and India, which takes a striking position, showing that the limited number of Indian companies that report on their sustainability performance take it rather seriously. The Americas seem to have focused so far on communication rather than corporate responsibility processes, and according to KPMG this may represent an issue in terms of reputational risk. In this region, the cases of Mexico and Brazil are striking: 66 % of Mexican companies included in the 250 largest global firms now report on their corporate responsibility activities, versus just 17 % in 2008; in Brazil, the percentage of companies reporting has now grown, bringing the country up to an impressive 88 %. Finally, Chinese and South Korean companies are demonstrating due regard to implementing processes and systems to measure and govern corporate responsibility issues (KPMG 2011). Among the reasons and motivations for companies to report, reputational consideration continues to drive sustainability reporting, with innovation and learning motivations rapidly gaining appreciation, compared to 2008.

ARs are usually viewed to be mandatory, while SRs voluntary. This is not entirely correct, since different countries' legislations have different positions on the issue, with some countries requiring the disclosure of social information by law while others do not, with the trend being, as the 2013 EU directive shows, to make non-financial information mandatory more often. The lack of a common worldwide policy on the compulsoriness of SR derives from the lack of consensus on the issue. Those that consider SR better suited for the voluntary reporting sphere argue that the gap between regulators and the industry is too wide, that mandatory SR would reduce the incentives to innovate, and that legal requirements would fail to recognize and take into account the differences among different industries. Conversely, others argue that it is necessary to make SR mandatory in order to change corporate culture, and that voluntary reports are not complete, not easily comparable and do not disclose negative performance.

To ensure comparability and to avoid "window dressing" solutions, SR needs a widely-accepted disclosure standard that would provide guidance and foster comparability among reports. This is true both in cases where SR is voluntary and where it is compulsory, because policymakers often refer to internationally accepted standards in order to guide companies towards the issuance of SRs. The Global Reporting Initiative (GRI) is a non-profit organization that contributes to the fulfilment of this need for standard guidelines. It was launched in 1997 and its standards are widely employed by global companies in order to frame their SRs. The GRI has recently published the G4 guidelines, the latest evolution of the GRI framework created in 1999, when the first exposure draft of the Sustainability Reporting Guidelines was released. The G4 guidelines are divided into two main documents: the "Reporting Principles and Standard Disclosure" and the

"Implementation Manual". Each company has the possibility to prepare its guidelines in accordance with the "Core" option or the "Comprehensive" option, with the Comprehensive option requiring additional disclosures compared to the Core option. This approach is an attempt to make the GRI G4 accessible also to companies implementing their SR for the first time (such as, for instance, Asian companies or SMEs) and is at the same time a reaction to the critique of being too challenging for small companies and first-time adopters to implement.

The two pillars of the GRI framework are the reporting principles and elements. The reporting principles defined by the G4 are the following: stakeholder inclusiveness, sustainability context, materiality, completeness, balance, comparability, accuracy, timeliness, clarity and reliability. GRI elements (both those required to be disclosed in accordance to the Core option and those to the Comprehensive option) are divided into the following categories: strategy and analysis, organizational profile, identified material aspects and boundaries, stakeholder engagement, report profile, governance and ethics and integrity. The G4 provides companies with the opportunity to disclose how they specifically manage some particular aspects of their environmental, social or governance performance through the Disclosures on Management Approach (DMA). The DMA provides narrative information on how an organization identifies, analyses and responds to its actual and potential material, economic, environmental and social impacts. DMA is ultimately the way GRI balances standardization and customization.

GRI is undoubtedly the most common standard for disclosure of comprehensive non-financial information in the context of SR. Among the specific reports, special mention should be made of the Carbon Disclosure Project (CDP), dealing with environmental disclosure and, in particular, carbon footprint disclosure. This is important given the increasing economic, social and environmental relevance of climate change. The CDP is an international, UK-based, not-for-profit organization providing a global system for companies (and cities) to measure, disclose, manage and share vital environmental information. In 2008, the CDP published the emissions data for 1,550 of the world's largest corporations, accounting for 26 % of global anthropogenic emissions. The CDP ultimately represents a form of market self-regulation, attempting to overcome the limitations of the Kyoto Protocol. In fact, the CDP focuses on companies rather than on countries (which have sometimes been reluctant to develop stringent national requirements on emissions) and leverages on institutional investors that focus their attention on carbon emission and energy usage. One of the most challenging topics in today's environment is to define which are the boundaries of the reporting entity. Given the central role of the supply chain, the CDP provides indication on how to collect, manage and disclose the climate change information of the entities included in the supply chain, which often accounts for most of the emissions and which can be indirectly managed by the company. The CDP also focuses its attention on cities and on the supply chain of governments, allowing them to efficiently manage suppliers' energy use.

Table 3.2 summarizes the main characteristics of SR, as compared to AR. The target of SRs is much wider, as it is intended to inform several different groups of stakeholders. As pointed out above, this challenges the usefulness of SR and

Table 3.2 Annual and sustainability reports main features

	Annual reports	Sustainability reports
Target	Specific stakeholders (shareholders and investors)	Several stakeholders (social and environmental perspective)
Mandatory/voluntary	Mandatory	Voluntary (with some exceptions: Denmark, Sweden, France)
Regulation or guidelines	National and international laws and GAAP (or IAS/IFRS)	Global reporting Initiative (GRI)
Comparability	High	Medium
Industry customization	Low	Medium (Sector supplements)
Assurance level	High	Low
Scope	Financial reporting entity (company or group of companies)	Broader than financial reporting entity (supply chain, LCA approach)

stresses the role of materiality. SR is voluntary, with the exception of some countries and in the context of a continuingly evolving situation. The guidelines employed by the GRI are the most widely employed standards for disclosure, which propose "sector supplements", additional guidelines for specific industries. Because of this, industry customization is medium. Assurance level is low, in the sense that non-financial information is more challenging to assure, compared to financial information. Finally, the scope of SR goes beyond the legal entity and includes also other entities that are not formally part of the group, for instance, including part of the supply chain.

3.4   Integrated Reporting

Recently, both the business and the academic world have been devoting increasing attention to the IR. In August 2010, through the initiative of the Prince's Accounting for Sustainability Project (A4S) and of the Global Reporting Initiative (GRI), the "International Integrated Reporting Committee" (IIRC) was launched. The 2013 IIRC Consultation Draft defines IR as follows: "<IR> is a process that results in communication by an organization, most visibly a periodic integrated report, about value creation over time. An integrated report is a concise communication about how an organization's strategy, governance, performance and prospects, in the context of its external environment, lead to the creation of value over the short, medium and long term" (IIRC 2013, p. 8). The aim of IR is to provide insights into the external environment that affects an organization, the resources and relationships used and affected by the organization (capitals) and the way in which the organization interacts with the external environment and capitals to create value.

The IIRC clearly states that the targets of IR are investors and providers of financial capital. Differently from SR, the framework is not based on stakeholders, but the focus is rather on the measurement and evaluation of capitals, if they have an impact on the long-term value creation process of the firm. In the context of the IIRC framework, the term "capitals" refers to any store of value that an organization can use in the production of goods and services. The six capitals the IIRC framework proposes are the following: financial; manufactured; intellectual; social and relationship; human; natural. All the capitals are fundamental for the company to operate, as the capitals are ultimately the input of an organization's business model. Through its activity, the company is increasing, decreasing or transforming the capitals. It is the company itself that identifies the relevant capitals modified by managerial action according to its perception and decision making process.

According to the IIRC objectives, the IR needs to provide a wide array of information, able to represent the reporting entity's long-term value creation process, which needs to be disclosed in an integrated way. The content elements that must be included in an IR are the following: organizational overview and external environment, governance, opportunities and risks, business model, strategy and resource allocation, performance and future outlook. Such elements need to be contextualized, coherently with the IIRC's principle-based approach. The guiding principles, and therefore the way such content elements must be disclosed, are the following: strategic focus and future orientation, connectivity of information, stakeholder responsiveness, materiality and conciseness, reliability and completeness, consistency and comparability.

Ultimately, IR aims to make it easier for the user to draw insightful connections between key pieces of information in the context of the investment decision-making process, to give a clear view of the firm's strategy and process and to allow long-term quantifiable risks or opportunities to be taken into account (UBS 2012).

IR aims to provide information mainly to providers of financial capital, even though the IIRC framework points out that other stakeholders may also find relevant information in the IR (see paragraph 3.24 of the IIRC Consultation Draft (IIRC 2013). Nowadays, IR is mostly voluntary, with the pilot program of the IIRC grouping those companies willing to implement—on a voluntary basis—their IR. Nevertheless, companies listed on the Johannesburg Securities Exchange (JSE) were required to adopt Integrated Reporting from years commencing on or after 1 March 2010. An interesting research stream could analyse the changes in corporate disclosure before and after the issuance of IR, the JSE being an interesting context to be analysed. IR has a principle-based approach, and this causes, on the one hand, a low comparability among IRs but, on the other, a high industry (and company) customization. The principle-based approach also confers more responsibilities to the top management, and it can potentially hide some opportunistic behaviours. The assurance level is low, because of the nature of non-financial information. Besides this, the IIRC framework encourages that information be disclosed also in narrative form, which is clearly much more challenging to assure, compared to financial information. Finally, the scope of the reporting, as for SR, goes beyond the legal entity (Table 3.3).

Terna S.p.a. (the largest independent grid operator for electricity transmission in Europe) is part of the IIRC pilot program, and it is currently working in the

Table 3.3 Annual, sustainability and integrated reports main features

	Annual reports	Sustainability reports	Integrated reports
Target	Specific stakeholders (shareholders and investors)	Several stakeholders (social and environmental perspective)	Primarily providers of financial capital
Mandatory/voluntary	Mandatory	Voluntary (with some exceptions: Denmark, Sweden, France)	Voluntary (with some exceptions: South Africa)
Regulation or guidelines	National and international laws and GAAP (or IAS/IFRS)	Global reporting initiative (GRI)	IIRC framework
Comparability	High	Medium	Low
Industry customization	Low	Medium (Sector supplements)	High
Assurance level	High	Low	Low
Scope	Financial reporting entity (company or group of companies)	Broader than financial reporting entity (supply chain, LCA approach)	Broader than financial reporting entity (supply chain, LCA approach)

implementation of its IR. The company started its "Integrated Report Project 2012" in order to progress towards "an innovative, concise, transparent and complete representation of its performance". In this initial phase of the process, Terna is working on the content elements proposed by the IIRC (organizational overview and external environment; governance; opportunities and risks; business model; strategy and resource allocation; performance; future outlook). Below, the disclosure by Terna of the main content elements will be discussed (Fig. 3.1).

About the business model, which, as recognized by the company as well, is one of the central elements of the IR framework, Terna argues that the Italian electricity system supply chain consists of four segments: the production, transmission, distribution and sale of electricity. Terna ensures the electricity transmission phase, an essential service to the community but one that does not involve a commercial relationship with end-users: it is a business to business activity. Specifically, Terna—through its subsidiary Terna Rete Italia—manages the dispatching of electricity and the development and maintenance of electricity transmission infrastructure. These operations are managed under the government-granted monopoly; the means of payment is determined by the Authority for Electricity and Gas. Increased operational efficiency—including procurement management—the timely realization of investments and financial management optimization all have a positive impact on value creation. Good performance in response to specific incentive schemes can further improve results.

About the performance content element, the company points out that Terna continually monitors and measures the implementation of its business model and the resulting impact on its capital. It then publishes the results in a report, for the benefit of all interested stakeholders. In this sense, the two most significant reports are the Annual Financial Report and the Sustainability Report. This element is

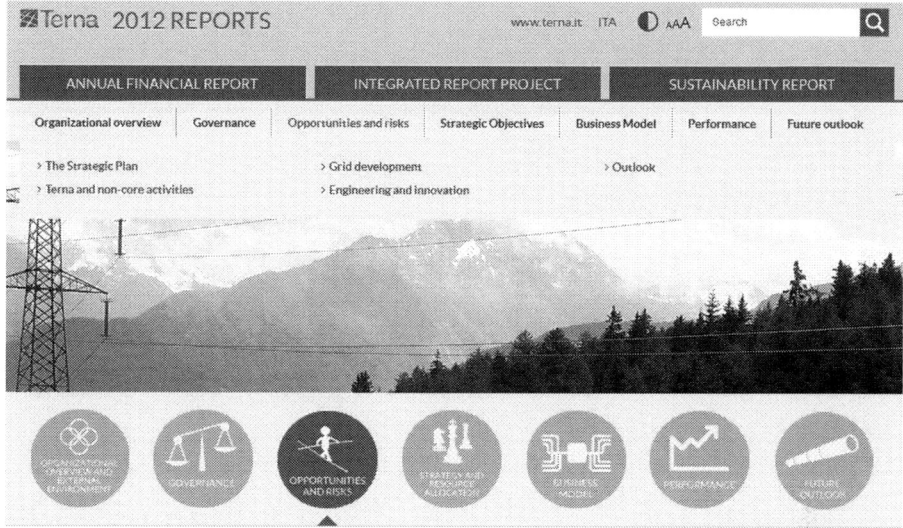

Fig 3.1 Terna integrated report project 2012

dedicated to Terna's financial and sustainability performance, including the impact on stakeholders—from human resources to local communities—as well as the impact on the environment and biodiversity. The current framework of reporting is going to be modified by the implementation of the IR, as Terna AR and SR will probably converge into the IR, despite being still existing.

Future outlooks aim at pointing out problems, uncertainties and potential implications for the business model and performance that Terna will have to face in order to implement its strategy. Terna's Strategic Plan, with its 5-year outlook, outlines the objectives, priorities and investments that guide the Group towards the right tools in order to continue to create value. To achieve this, the company needs to identify trends that could pose challenges in the medium and long term, and to find solutions. For example, the evolution of energy usage and the resulting need to adapt the electricity transmission grid, or even the increasing integration of grid management across Europe. In the long term, the increased importance of non-traditional business is expected, including in the creation of value. Focusing on stakeholders, and maintaining a relationship of trust with them, encourages sustainable policies that help to ensure the stability of the business model in the medium and long term.

3.5 Integrated Reporting: Evolution and Nature

AR, SR and IR ultimately represent different aspects of the evolution of corporate reporting over the years. The previous sections provided descriptions of the main characteristics of the three forms of reporting. This section, instead, aims at comparing the main characteristics of AR, SR and IR, pointing out similarities and differences, trying to make sense of this evolutionary process in corporate disclosure. IR represents the latest and most advanced stage of corporate reporting worldwide, but it derives from the evolution of already-existing forms of disclosure (AR and SR). The understanding of the connections between IR, AR and SR is fundamental in order to judge the effectiveness of the current IR framework and to predict its future development.

3.5.1 Integrated Reporting and Annual Reporting

The first issue it will be discussed deals with the origin of IR. Can IR be considered an evolution of SR? Or rather, does it derive from a broader approach to AR? Following the considerations made above, IR is a tool that has the potential to overcome the limitations of both AR (complexity, short-termism, shortage of non-financial information) and SR (low reliability and trust from investors, disconnection with financial performance). Nevertheless, there is an important element that ought to be taken into consideration in this reasoning. The IIRC framework clearly states that: "an integrated report should be prepared primarily for providers of financial capital in order to support their financial capital allocation assessments" (IIRC 2013, p. 8). Even if the subsequent paragraph states that "an integrated report and other communications resulting from the <IR> will be of benefit to all stakeholders interested in an organization's ability to create value over time, including employees, customers, suppliers, business partners, local communities, legislators, regulators and policymakers", the indication of the IIRC framework is clear in indicating investors and providers of financial capital as the intended users of IR. This has important consequences also in the way materiality and other fundamental IR aspects are defined. Because of this reason, IR may be viewed as an evolution of AR, rather than of SR, even if it captures some aspects of SR, aiming at providing information to the most "enlightened" markets.

While the intended users of the report is, to some extent, a common element between AR and IR, the time horizon represents one of the main differences and also poses some severe challenges to the successful implementation of IR. AR is focused on the past performance of the company and is short-term oriented, in the sense that it provides information mainly useful in predicting the short-term performance of a company. In contrast, one of the guiding principles of IR is "strategic focus and future orientation". According to this principle, "the report should provide insights into the organization's strategy and how that relates to its ability to create value in the short, medium and long term" (IIRC 2013, p. 18).

Even if the IIRC framework states that an IR allows providers of financial capital to assess the ability of the company also in the short term, it is clear that the main focus of an IR is on the long term. For instance, Unilever, a company joining the IIRC pilot program, has decided to abolish quarterly earnings guidance (Harvard Business 2012). IR took a clear position in its long-term orientation, and this also emerges clearly from the value creation paragraph.

The framework seems to be concerned with "reassuring" all typologies of investors and companies, both long-term and short-term oriented; both socially responsible and non socially responsible. In reality, there are some audiences that are likely not to be happy with IR but that would rather consider it a threat or, in the best-case scenario, useless. Short-term oriented investors need timely information on the last-year (last-quarter) performance of a company in order to forecast the future (short-term) performance of the company. How will these investors react to IR? Given the definition of value relevance provided above (see Barth et al. 2001), will these investors find the information disclosed in IR to be value relevant? Or will they simply ignore IR? Or will they disappear?

Short-term oriented companies may be creating short-term financial performance at the expense of some of the capitals. Paragraph 2.43 states that "value (. . .) is unlikely to be created through the maximization of one capital while disregarding the others". This is true only if reasoning with a long-term perspective, as recognized by the framework itself, which in the same paragraph states: "the maximization of financial capital (e.g., profit) at the expense of human capital (e.g., through inappropriate human resource policies and practices) is unlikely to maximize value in the long term". What is the approach of IR towards short-term oriented companies? Why should a short-term oriented company, which has ceased to invest in its human capital, disclose its performance according to the IIRC framework? If applied correctly, the IR would link the increase in financial capital to a decrease in human capital, and this would have some consequences on the long-term oriented investors' predictions of the company's ability to produce long-term financial performance. Besides this, the IIRC framework takes a clear position on those companies increasing their financial capital at the expense of other capitals, when discussing the value creation issue, basically arguing that such companies will not be able to sustain value over time.

Another relevant difference between AR and IR is the way in which materiality is interpreted, which is tackled in the chapter on materiality by Mio.

The IR explicitly recalls some concepts that may be considered similar to those expressed by Kramer and Porter in their work on value creation (see Kramer and Porter 2011). In that context, the concept of shared value can be defined as policies and operating practices that enhance the competitiveness of a company while simultaneously advancing the economic and social conditions in the communities where it operates. According to Paragraph 2.37 of the IIRC Framework, "an organization can create and maximize value by serving the interest of, and working with, all its key stakeholders, such as employees, customers, suppliers, business partners, local communities, legislators, regulators and policymakers". Paragraph 2.38 states: "providers of financial capital are focused on value in the form of financial returns. Those returns are, however, dependent on inter-relationships between various types of capital in which other stakeholders have an interest."

The IIRC takes a strong position on the issue of value creation, basically stating that it depends on other forms of capital and that it cannot be sustained in the long term at the expense of other individuals or groups of individuals. This approach also recalls the instrumental stakeholder theory (see Donaldson and Peterson 1995). In this sense, it takes a step further, compared to other traditional accounting standards regulating AR, which are silent about drivers of value creation.

3.5.2 Integrated Reporting and Sustainability Reporting

The IIRC is very clear in stating that IR should comply with the principles-based requirements identified through its framework. The aim is to balance flexibility and prescriptions, in order to recognize a wide variation in individual circumstances of different organizations and industries. This approach, which allows IR to have a high industry customization but a low comparability, is clear even in the description and discussion of capitals, which is one of the main elements of the whole framework. The IIRC states: "not all capitals are equally relevant or applicable to all organizations" (IIRC 2013, p. 13), thus allowing for a flexible application of the framework. Conversely, SRs, and in particular those following the GRI approach, rely on a fixed list of elements that need to be disclosed. The GRI has introduced two mechanisms in order to mitigate this rigidity: the sector supplements (which allows companies to have a medium level of industry customization) and the concept of materiality. The GRI G4 guidelines provide a description of the methodology to be employed in order to identify material aspects, allowing companies not to disclose some aspects, if not considered to be material. Even with this form of "mitigation", the approach of the GRI is fairly rigid, and may be defined as "customized", while the approach by the IIRC is really "principle-based".

Another relevant difference between IR and SR is that the approach proposed by the IIRC is based on the concept of "capital", while the GRI is based on the concept of "stakeholders". On the one hand, according to the IIRC framework, "capitals are stores of value that, in one form or another, become inputs to an organization's business model. They are increased, decreased or transformed through the activities and outputs of the organization in that they are enhanced, consumed, modified, destroyed or otherwise affected by those activities and outputs" (IIRC 2013, p. 11). On the other hand, the GRI framework is mostly focused on stakeholders. The elements proposed by the GRI are in fact divided by aspect, thus divided into categories that are clearly inspired by the different stakeholders' groups (economic, environmental, social, human rights, product responsibility, etc.). Not only that, the G4 framework stresses the stakeholder inclusiveness principle, pointing out that the organization should identify its stakeholders, and explain how it has responded to their expectations and interests. The capital approach proposed by the IIRC is "objective", rather than "subjective" and much more similar to financial accounting. The capitals do not refer to any specific category of stakeholder, and they recall a more relevant role of the company, which is the real focus of the IR.

The IR aims at reporting on the outcomes, rather than on outputs, further evolving the SR's model. According to the framework, the IR should answer the question: "to what extent has the organization achieved its strategic objectives and what are its outcomes in terms of effects on the capitals?". Outcomes are defined as the "internal and external consequences (positive and negative) on the capitals as a result of an organization's business activities and outputs" (IIRC 2013, p. 15). Even though the aim of the IIRC is to disclose outcomes, the KPIs proposed by the same framework do not measure outcomes, and, as it is today, IR is not able to measure the stocks for the six capitals and their variations (flows). For some capitals, IR only measures some specific aspects, employing such indicators as a proxy for the whole capital. Clearly outcomes are much more difficult to measure, and this may be a further evolution and one of the main challenges IR will have to face. While IRs takes into account the measurement (in terms of stock and flow) of capitals, which have clear similarities with balance sheets and income statements respectively, SRs report on the impacts of the company's activities.

Conclusions

The aim of this chapter was to provide a comprehensive comparison between Annual Reports (AR), Sustainability Reports (SR) and Integrated Reports (IR), focusing on their similarities and differences from an evolutionary perspective. While the first three sections discussed the main features and characteristics of AR, SR and IR respectively, the last section provided a comparison between them, pointing out similarities, differences and future challenges to be tackled.

IR is to be considered an evolution of AR rather than of SR, because the intended users of IR are clearly stated as the "providers of financial capital" (IIRC 2013). In addition, the way in which IR frames the capitals (much more "objective" and centred on the firm, compared to the "subjective" stakeholder approach of SR) leads to the conclusion that IR is really an evolution of AR rather than of SR.

Future research and attention by standard-setters ought to be spent on the definition of two issues of paramount importance for IR. The first is the way IR relates to short-term oriented investors and companies. The IIRC framework clearly states that financial performance cannot be sustained in the long term when obtained exclusively at the expense of the other capitals. On the one hand, short-term oriented companies may consider this approach to be a threat, because IR is likely to harm the market performance of the company. On the other hand, short-term investors may consider IR non-material. How is IR considered by these companies (investors)? Why should they implement (read) IR? What are the benefits (if any) would they get?

Second, IR aims at providing information on the outcomes produced by a company. Despite this, it fails to propose a set of KPIs on which a company may rely upon in disclosing the outcomes of their activity. Further guidance ought to be provided on this issue, as the communication of the company's performance is one of the main objectives of IR and therefore needs to be more carefully considered.

References

Amir E, Lev B (1996) Value-relevance of nonfinancial information: the wireless communications industry. J Account Econ 22(1–3):3–30

Arnold MC, Bassen A, Frank R (2012) Integrating sustainability reports into financial statements: an experimental study. http://ssrn.com/abstract=2030891. Accessed 10 Jul 2013

Baker CR, Hayes R (2004) Reflecting form over substance: the case of Enron Corp. Crit Perspect Account 15(6–7):767–785

Barth M, Beaver W, Landsman W (2001) The relevance of the value relevance literature for financial accounting standard setting: another view. J Account Econ 31:77–104

Cox C (2007) Closing remarks to the second annual corporate governance summit. Delivered at the USC Marshall School of Business, Los Angeles, CA. http://www.sec.gov/news/speech/2007/spch032307cc.htm. Accessed 23 Jul 2013

Daub C (2007) Assessing the quality of sustainability reporting: an alternative methodological approach. J Clean Prod 15(1):75–85

Deloitte (2013) IAS plus. http://www.iasplus.com/en/standards/framework. Accessed 10 Jul 2013

Donaldson T, Peterson LE (1995) The stakeholder theory of the corporation: concepts, evidence and implications. Acad Manage Rev 20(1):853–886

Eccles RG, Krzus MP (2010) One report: integrated reporting for a sustainable strategy. Wiley, Hoboken, NJ

European Commission (2009) European workshops on the disclosure of environmental, social and governance information. http://ec.europa.eu/enterprise/newsroom/cf/itemlongdetail.cfm?item_id=3723. Accessed 10 Jul 2013

European Commission (2013). http://ec.europa.eu/internal_market/accounting/docs/non-financial-reporting/com_2013_207-ia-full_en.pdf. Accessed 10 Jul 2013

Fifka MS, Drabble M (2012) Focus and standardization of sustainability reporting–A comparative study of the United Kingdom and Finland. Bus Strateg Environ 21(7):455–474

Frias-Aceituno J, Rodriguez-Ariza L, Garcia-Sanchez IM (2012) The role of the board in the dissemination of integrated corporate social reporting. Corp Soc Responsibility Environ Manage 20(4):219–233

Gray R, Javad M, Power DM, Sinclair CD (2001) Social and environmental disclosure and corporate characteristics: a research note and extension. J Bus Finance Account 28(3):327–356

GRI (2013) G4 sustainability reporting guidelines. https://www.globalreporting.org/reporting/g4/Pages/default.aspx. Accessed 10 Jul 2013

Gu F, Wang W (2005) Intangible assets, information complexity and analysts' earnings forecasts. J Bus Finance Account 32(9):1673–1702

Harvard Business Review (2012). http://blogs.hbr.org/ideacast/2012/05/unilevers-ceo-on-making-respon.html. Accessed 10 Jul 2013

Healy PM, Palepu KG (2001) Information asymmetry, corporate disclosure, and the capital markets: a review of the empirical disclosure literature. J Account Econ 31(1–3):405–440

Hirst D, Hopkins P (1998) Comprehensive income reporting and analysts' valuation judgments. J Account Res 36:47–74

Holland J (1998) Private disclosure and financial reporting. Account Bus Res 28(4):255–269

IIRC (2013) Consultation draft of the international < IR > framework. http://www.theiirc.org/consultationdraft2013. Accessed 10 Jul 2013

Klok A (2003) Trend in sustainability reporting by the Fortune Global 250. Bus Strateg Environ 12 (5):279–291

KPMG (2011) International integrated reporting survey. http://www.kpmg.com/global/en/issuesandinsights/articlespublications/corporate-responsibility/pages/2011-survey.aspx. Accessed 10 Jul 2013

Li F (2008) Annual report readability, current earnings, and earnings persistence. J Account Econ 45(2–3):221–247

Loughran T, McDonald B (2010) Measuring readability in financial text. Working paper, University of Notre Dame

Margolis JD, Walsh JP (2003) Misery loves companies: whither social initiatives by business? Adm Sci Q 48(2):268–305

Miller PB (2010) The effects of reporting complexity on small and large investor trading. Account Rev 85(6):2107–2143

Ocean Tomo (2011) Intangible asset market value. http://www.oceantomo.com/about/intellectualcapitalequity. Accessed 10 Jul 2013

Orlitzky M, Schmidt F, Rynes SL (2003) Corporate social and financial performance: a meta-analysis. Organ Stud 24:403–441

Pava ML, Krausz J (1996) The association between corporate social responsibility and financial performance: the paradox of social cost. J Bus Ethic 15(3):321–357

Plumee MA (2003) The effect of information complextity on analysts' use of that information. Accout Rev 78(1):275–296

Porter ME, Kramer MR (2011) Creating shared value. Harv Bus Rev 89(January–February):64–77

Schroeder M (2002) SEC proposes rules to improve disclosure by public companies. Wall St J May 1:C5

The Atlantic (2013). http://www.theatlantic.com/magazine/archive/2012/04/what-isnt-for-sale/308902. Accessed 10 Jul 2013

UBS (2012) What is integrated reporting? http://www.sasb.org/wp-content/uploads/2012/06/UBS-on-Integrated-Reporting.pdf. Accessed 10 Jul 2013

You H, Zhang X (2009) Financial reporting complexity and investor underreaction to 10-K information. Rev Account Stud 14:559–586

The Connectivity of Information for the Integrated Reporting

4

Sergio Paternostro

Abstract

The purpose of this chapter is to shed light on the guiding principle of connectivity of information which the Integrated Reporting Framework presents as a way of translating the integrated thinking into action. In doing so, the chapter moves from the analysis of the main reports that are a source of information for Integrated Reporting, defining them as "partial" reports because they represent only a part of the comprehensive value creation story. The ways in which these reports are aggregated and/or integrated during the process of construction of an Integrated Report have the potential to affect the level of connectivity of information. In addressing these issues, the chapter proposes three different approaches to the construction of an Integrated Report, also providing examples to illustrate the main features of each approach. Then, the chapter suggests the need to further explore the role of connectivity for a global and integrated reporting system.

4.1 Introduction

Connectivity of information is one of the guiding principles of the Integrated Reporting (IR) Framework. The Consultation Draft of the International IR Framework defines connectivity as:

"The combination, inter-relatedness and dependencies between the components that are material to the organization's ability to create value over time" (IIRC 2013a, p. 18).

Thus, in the IR Framework connectivity is seen as a way of translating the integrated thinking into action (IIRC 2013b). The connectivity concept had already been included in the Discussion Paper (IIRC 2011), but its relevance has been

S. Paternostro (✉)

Department of Economics, Business and Finance, University of Palermo, Palermo, Italy

e-mail: sergio.paternostro@unipa.it

C. Busco et al. (eds.), *Integrated Reporting*, DOI 10.1007/978-3-319-02168-3_4,

© Springer International Publishing Switzerland 2013

stressed after the public consultation process. This principle is considered essential in order to make the report more effective in giving a comprehensive vision of a firm's capacity for creating value over time.

Paragraphs 3.10 and 3.11 of the IR Framework (IIRC 2013a, pp. 18–19) list the following components of information between which connections are required:

- *content elements*: the organization's overview and external environment, governance, opportunities and risks, strategy and resource allocation, business model, performance, and future outlook;
- *time*: past, present and future;
- *capitals*: financial, manufactured, intellectual, social and relationship, human and natural;
- *financial information and other information*;
- *quantitative and qualitative information*;
- *management information, board information and information reported externally*;
- *information in the integrated report, information in the organization's other communications, and information from other sources.*

In recent decades, both the academic literature and standard setters have sought to pursue connectivity (more or less implicitly), proposing a number of frameworks in which various information and reports were integrated. In the academic debate, Hutton (2004) and Burgman and Ross (2007) have proposed to integrate financial information with other non-financial information in order to shed light on the main drivers involved in the value creation process. Pedrini (2007) suggests a *Global* or *Holistic Report* that integrates social and intellectual capital reports. Along the same line of thought, albeit with different nuances, are the proposals by Cordazzo (2005) and Branwijck (2012), while the integration between social and corporate governance reports is the idea proposed by Kolk and Pinske (2010). Instead, according to Yongvanich and Guthrie (2006), social and intellectual capital reports should be linked to wider performance measurement systems such as the Balanced Scorecard. The need to combine heterogeneous information is also claimed by Eccles and Krzus (2010), who propose to integrate the financial information included in the financial statement with non-financial information provided by other reports. In particular, the non-financial information includes (Eccles and Krzus 2010, p. 84): intangibles, key performance indicators, social and environmental information and corporate governance information. In line with the IR Framework, Eccles and Krzus state that the integration between information provided by different reports is needed in order to think in an integrated manner.

As for the standard setters, the Prince's Accountability for Sustainability Project (2007) published the *Accounting For Sustainability Report: The Connected Reporting Framework*, and then the guide *Connected Reporting: A practical guide with worked examples* (2009). This framework combined financial, sustainability and governance information stressing the concept of connectivity as it emerges from the name of the framework itself ("*Connected reporting*"). Moreover, in 2009 the *King Code of Governance for South Africa* required the preparation of an Integrated Report that included financial, economic and social information (Institute of Directors Southern Africa 2009).

This brief overview highlights the significant role played by the different types of reports and the several attempts to exploit their potential integration. In this chapter, these reports will be generally defined as "partial" reports because each of them is able to represent only a part of the comprehensive value creation process. According to the IR Framework, these reports contain the original source of different information that should be included in an Integrated Report within a holistic perspective in order to ensure the connectivity of information. As stated in paragraph 1.18 (IIRC 2013a, p. 9):

> "Organizations may provide additional reports and communications (e.g., financial statements and sustainability reports) for compliance purposes or to satisfy the particular information needs of a range of stakeholders. The integrated report may include links to these other reports and communications."

Therefore, the IR Framework identifies a different function for an Integrated Report and a partial report. The former aims at communicating to the stakeholders all factors influencing the firm's ability to create value. The latter has the purpose to tell a part of the so-called "value creation story" (IIRC 2013a, p. 9) and to provide specific information dealing with a particular kind of capital (i.e. financial, manufactured, intellectual, social and relationship, human and natural).

Starting from these assumptions, the aim of this chapter is to explore the potential role of the connectivity of information in IR. In particular, it will be investigated the relationship between an Integrated Report and the several partial reports which are at the basis of its construction. To this purpose, the following section describes the informative role of the main partial reports that can be drawn up by an organization. The analysis of each report properly focuses on the components of the connectivity of information identified in the IR Framework. Then, the third section proposes three different approaches that can be used to combine the information included in the partial reports. In particular, the cases of some Italian companies are discussed in order to illustrate each of these approaches. Finally, the fourth section discusses the final remarks.

4.2 The Informative Role of the Partial Reports

A shared and comprehensive taxonomy of all possible organizational reports does not exist. Thus, to the purpose of this chapter, the partial reports that have been considered are those specified by the International Integrated Reporting Council (IIRC) in the Discussion Paper in 2011 (IIRC 2011, p. 6), namely Financial Statement, Management Commentary, Social and Environmental Report, Corporate Governance Report, and Intellectual Capital Report. According to the IR Framework, these reports are able to assess all the various forms of capitals (IIRC 2013a, p. 10). Moreover, they are heterogeneous not only due to the information provided but also because some are mandatory and others are voluntary.

In the following sub-sections, each partial report will be firstly analysed in its main features and functions. Then, the focus will be on how these reports address the components of the connectivity of information identified in the IR Framework, with particular reference to the content elements, time, capitals, financial and other information, quantitative *vs* qualitative information.

4.2.1 The Financial Statement

The Financial Statement is a mandatory report with a content that depends on specific accounting regulation systems. However, in the attempt to describe the informative content of this report, here the International Accounting Standards Board (IASB) model has been considered as a reference since it aims at achieving international accounting harmonization and its adoption is mandatory in a large number of European countries. The IASB Conceptual Framework (IASB 2010a, p. 21) states that the aim of the Financial Statement is "*to provide financial information about the reporting entity that is useful to existing and potential investors, lenders and other creditors in making decisions about providing resources to the entity*". According to the IAS standard n.1 (IASB 2011), the Financial Statement should include the following documents: a statement of financial position; a statement of profit or loss and other comprehensive income for the period; a statement of change in equity in the period; a statement of cash flow in the period; notes; and comparative information in respect to the preceding period. In summary, the main information requested deals with: assets, liabilities, equity, income and expenses, contributions by and distributions to owners in their capacity as owners, and cash flows.

In terms of content elements required in the IR Framework, the Financial Statement only provides information on performance by the determination of profit and cash flows. Although Financial Statement contributes to giving an organization's overview as requested in the Framework, this overview is limited to the financial capital. As widely acknowledged (Kaplan and Norton 1996), quantitative financial information is oriented to the short term period and is not outward-looking. Thus, the Financial Statement is not able to provide a comprehensive picture of all the value creation drivers.

4.2.2 The Management Commentary

The Management Commentary is a document aimed at completing the information of the Financial Statement by using a more narrative approach. While its publication is mandatory, the structure it can assume is generally flexible. Because of this flexible nature, it is difficult to illustrate its content. In this sense, a possible reference may be found in the IFRS Practice Statement about Management Commentary published by IASB in 2010. Its adoption is not mandatory but it represents a framework for the presentation of the Management Commentary, which is related to financial statements that have been prepared in accordance with IFRS (IASB 2010b). In this framework, the Management Commentary is a narrative report that provides "*a context within which to interpret the financial position, financial performance and cash flows of an entity*" (IASB 2010b, p. 5). The main elements to be considered are: the nature of business; management's objectives and the strategies for meeting those objectives; the most significant resources, risks and opportunities; the results of operations and prospects; the critical performance measures and indicators that management uses to evaluate performance against stated objectives.

This report shows a greater informative potential than the Financial Statement due to its complementary function. The crucial elements indicated in the IFRS document (IASB 2010b) allow to provide information about several of the content elements specified in the IR Framework, namely the organization's overview, opportunities and risks, strategy and resource allocation, business model, performance, and future outlook. In particular, the provision of performance indicators and forward-looking information is able to bridge time horizons, allowing the analysis of "past to present" value creation, and also the connection with the future as required in the IR Framework (IIRC 2013b, p. 5). Therefore, in terms of capitals, the Management Commentary provides information both on financial capital and manufactured capital since it contains financial data, as well as operative data.

Notwithstanding, recent research has showed the limits of the Management Commentary (or the narrative part of the annual report). Firstly, it is often used as an "impression management" practice (Stanton et al. 2004). Secondly, some studies shed light on the gaps between the suggestions of the IFRS Practice Statement and the actual content of the reports realized by the organizations (Argento and Di Pietra 2010).

4.2.3 Social and Environmental Report

The Social and Environmental Report (also referred to as a Sustainability Report if the approach is more oriented towards sustainable development) can be described as a report through which an organization communicates the effects of its decisions and behaviours to the stakeholders in a well-defined social context. Many scholars (Medawar 1976; Ramanathan 1976; Guthrie and Parker 1989; Woodward et al. 1996; Ogden and Watson 1999; Toms 2002; Solomon 2007) have studied social accounting using heterogeneous approaches such as: legitimacy theory, political economic theory, agency theory, risk society theory, stakeholder theory, contractualism, and the democratic approach. The same variety is found in practice due to the voluntary nature of the report and its flexibility. In the attempt to standardize these reports and to avoid self-referentiality, in 2002 the Coalition for Environmental Responsible Economies (CERES) published the guidelines Global Report Initiative (GRI), which have achieved worldwide diffusion. In the online database of the GRI, there are 12,342 reports registered in compliance with the guidelines. In 2013, an updated version of the guidelines was published (GRI4). In this section of the chapter, this last version will be used as a reference for a brief overview on the content of the Social Report. According to GRI4 (GRI 2013), the content of a Social and Environmental Report should deal with: strategy and analysis, organizational profile, identified material aspect and boundaries, stakeholder engagement, report profile, governance, ethics and integrity, and indicators. The indicators regard both economic, environmental and social aspects.

The informative potential of the Social and Environmental Report according to GRI4 is huge, allowing the provision of information about each of the content elements of the IR Framework. Only the business model is not fully described according to what the IR Framework prescribes. The past is considered through the request for comparability of results over time, while the future is considered in the strategy and analysis section of the report. The information is mainly non-financial and is both quantitative and qualitative. In terms of capitals, the Social Report can describe the social and relationship capital and the human and natural capitals.

Notwithstanding, the guidelines do not contemplate the integration between the different categories of information. Consequently, they do not provide real connectivity. GRI4 considers the relation between an Integrated Report and other reports, in particular with the Sustainability Report, by stating: *"the integrated report interacts with other reports and communications by making reference to additional detailed information that is provided separately. Although the objectives of sustainability reporting and integrated reporting may be different, sustainability reporting is an intrinsic element of integrated reporting"* (GRI 2013, p. 85). The Sustainability Report is thus seen as a crucial foundation of the Integrated Report, but it has a specific and independent (although connected) function.

4.2.4 The Corporate Governance Report

In response to many financial scandals (Lehman Brothers, Xerox, Arthur Anderson, Enron, WorldCom, Tyco, Parmalat, etc.) that have occurred since the 1990s, in several countries and at a global level, many reforms of corporate governance have been realized: *Cadbury Committee* in the UK, *Sarbanes-Oxley act* in the USA, the OECD *Principles of Corporate Governance*, the *Vietti law* in Italy, etc. Within this context, disclosure on corporate governance has received a wide attention to the extent that it is more and more becoming a possible way of realizing techniques of "impression management" (Collett and Hrasky 2005).

In spite of this growing attention, at a global level initiatives aimed at standardizing corporate governance disclosure have not been developed yet. Indeed, the provision of corporate governance information is ruled by national laws with different solutions, such as, a specific report with a rigid format; a specific report with a flexible format; information included in other reports (for example, the Management Commentary); and full, voluntary disclosure. However, in the OECD Principles of Corporate Governance (OECD 2004), suggestions to national policy makers aimed at developing regulatory frameworks of corporate governance are provided. In these Principles, there is a specific section about disclosure and transparency where it is highlighted that: *"The corporate governance framework should ensure that timely and accurate disclosure is made on all material matters regarding the corporation, including the financial situation, performance, ownership, and governance of the company."* (OECD 2004, p. 22). In particular, the OECD principles enhance disclosure about the following topics: the financial and operating results of the company; company objectives; major share ownership and voting rights; remuneration policy for members of the board and key executives; information about board members including their qualifications, the selection process, other company directorships and whether they are regarded as independent by the board; related party transactions; foreseeable risk factors; issues regarding employees and other stakeholders and governance structures and policies; the content of any corporate governance code or policy and the process by which it is implemented.

Some information highlighted in the OECD Principles (*e.g.* financial and operating results, objectives, issues regarding employees and other stakeholders) is already included in other reports. As regarding the specific information on corporate governance, this is able to cover one of the content elements of the IR Framework, that is governance, and to improve the representation of the organization's overview. Moreover, this type of information aims at describing the current situation of the organization, even if the disclosure of corporate governance policies can also open up a view towards the future. In terms of capitals, disclosure on corporate governance mainly refers to the financial capital. Finally, the information is both financial and non financial, and both quantitative and qualitative.

4.2.5 The Intellectual Capital Report

Intellectual capital can be generically understood as the set of intangible assets available within an organization. The lack of information on intellectual capital in Financial Statements has long been considered one of the main causes of the loss of relevance of these reports (Johnson and Kaplan 1987). The most internationally shared classification of intellectual capital divides it into three sub-categories (Edvinsson and Malone 1997; Stewart 1997; Sveiby 1997): human capital, relational capital, and structural or organizational capital. However, the methodologies for representing intellectual capital are not agreed upon in academic literature and in practice. Andriessen (2004) found 30 different techniques for evaluating intellectual capital. Among the different methods, the frameworks provided by MERITUM (2002) and DMSTI (2003) are considered as the most influential (Guthrie et al. 2003; Lev et al. 2005).

The MERITUM framework is the result of a research project carried out by the European Commission. According to this set of guidelines, the structure of an Intellectual Capital Report should include: a vision of the firm, a summary of intangible resources and activities, and a system of indicators (MERITUM 2002, p. 22). On the other hand, the DMSTI framework was developed by the Danish

Ministry of Science, Technology and Innovation. In this framework the Intellectual Capital Report consists of the following sections: an annual report (with key information regarding objectives, challenges and results with respect to knowledge resources); a company description; a knowledge narrative; an intellectual statement model; management challenges including initiatives and indicators; and accounting policies (DMSTI 2003, p. 49).

Therefore, with reference to the content elements specified in the IR Framework, Intellectual Capital Report can provide information about the organization's overview and external environment, strategy and resource allocation, and business model. The Intellectual Capital Report represents the current organizational situation in terms of the stock of the available intangible resources, but it can also provide information about future trends since intellectual capital is considered one of the main drivers of long term financial performance (Abeysekera 2006).

As for the capitals, this report mainly refers to the intellectual, relationship, and human capitals. It mainly includes non-financial information, both quantitative and qualitative.

4.2.6 The Partial Reports as a Source of Information for the Integrated Report

A summary of how each partial report deals with the components of the connectivity of information (i.e. content elements, time, capitals, financial and other information, quantitative and qualitative information) is shown in Table 4.1. From a comparative analysis of the informative potential of the reports, it seems clear that a comprehensive vision of the five components is possible only by taking into account all the partial reports.

The partial reports represent a source of information for preparing an Integrated Report. Through the various kinds of information they provide, two guiding principles of the IR Framework are satisfied, namely stakeholder responsiveness and completeness. As for stakeholder responsiveness, the IR Framework states: "*An integrated report should provide insight into the quality of the organization's relationships with its key stakeholders and how and to what extent the organization understands, takes into account and responds to their legitimate needs, interests and expectations*" (IIRC 2013a, p. 19). Each report meets specific information needs derived from different stakeholder categories. For instance, the Financial Statement satisfies primarily the interest of providers of capital, while the Social and Environmental Report specifically meets the needs of a broader range of stakeholders including, for example, the mass media, non-profit organizations and the local community. Referring to completeness, the IR Framework claims that: "*A complete integrated report includes all material information, both positive and negative*" (IIRC 2013a, p. 22). In this sense, each report stresses a particular aspect of the organizational activity, and only by collecting all the information they provide it is possible to consider all the material dimensions. If each partial report is considered separately it is difficult for them to fully convey their potential in an

Table 4.1 The informative potential of partial reports according to the components of the connectivity

	Content elements	Time	Capitals	Financial and other information	Quantitative *vs* qualitative information
Financial statement	Performance and overview of the firm	Past and present	Financial	Financial	Quantitative
Management commentary	Potentially all content elements	Past, present and future	Financial and manufactured	Financial and other information	Quantitative and qualitative
Social and environmental report	Potentially all content elements	Past, present and future	Social and relationship, human and natural	Mainly other information	Quantitative and qualitative
Corporate governance report	Organization's overview and governance	Past and present	Financial and human	Financial and other information	Quantitative and qualitative
Intellectual capital report	Organization's overview and external environment, strategy and resource allocation and business model	Past, present and future	Intellectual, relationship and human	Mainly other information	Quantitative and qualitative

integrated logic due to the lack of connectivity between reports and between the information they present.

Connectivity is also linked to two other principles of the IR Framework, namely materiality and conciseness. The former is related to the possibility to "*influence the assessments of the primary intended report users with regard to the organization's ability to create value over the short, medium and long term*" (IIRC 2013a, p. 21). Materiality is ensured only if the information is interpreted through a complete and integrated vision of the value creation story which allows to explain the main drivers of performance. On the other hand, conciseness refers to the necessity of avoiding redundant information (IIIRC 2013a, p. 21). Indeed, the information included in a partial report can be significant in relation to the specific aims of that document, but it may not be useful for explaining a company's ability to create value in the long term, and so may not be interesting to include in an Integrated Report.

In particular, the ways in which partial reports can be combined to construct an Integrated Report will be discussed in the following section.

4.3   Three Possible Approaches to the Construction of an Integrated Report

The level of connectivity of information in the construction of an Integrated Report depends on the ways in which the partial reports are combined. In particular, in this chapter it is argued that three different approaches can be followed during this process: a "weak" aggregation (Fig. 4.1), a "strong" aggregation (Fig. 4.2), and an "integration" in a narrow sense (Fig. 4.3). To better explain the main differences between these approaches, in the following sub-sections examples from Italian companies will be used to highlight the main features of different reporting practices.[1] The choice to focus on the Italian context is due to the fact that Italy is one of the most active countries in the adoption of the IR Framework. This is witnessed by Italy's strong presence in the Pilot Program of the IIRC. Indeed, among the 88 organizations included in the list published online, eight are Italian. Only the United Kingdom, Netherlands and Brazil have more organizations than Italy involved in the Pilot Program.

4.3.1   A Weak Aggregation Between the Partial Reports

Within the weak aggregation approach, the Integrated Report is constructed starting from a main partial report which the organization 'enhances' simply adding other information perceived as secondary (Fig. 4.1). Typically, there are two possibilities. In a first case, the Integrated Report derives from the Financial Statement that is 'enhanced' including social and environmental information. In a second case, the Integrated Report is instead constructed on the basis of the Social and Environmental Report to which further financial information is aggregated.

Actually, the final report resulting from this aggregation cannot be considered as a real Integrated Report for various reasons. First of all, it does not respect the principle of completeness because the focus remains the same as the original main report (financial or social). Secondly, there is no connectivity between information that is only added without any process of integration. This weak approach to the construction of the Integrated Report could be followed by an organization that aims at implementing gradually the report or that is adopting a mere technique of communication strategy.

The examples provided for this approach are the cases of Sorgenia and Guna.

---

[1] The cases selected for this chapter have been conducted within a broader research project to which the author is currently taking part. Here, only some evidence has been presented in order to support the specific aim of the chapter. The research has been carried out through qualitative content analysis applied to the organizational reports of each company, available on their institutional websites.

Fig. 4.1 A "weak" aggregation between partial reports

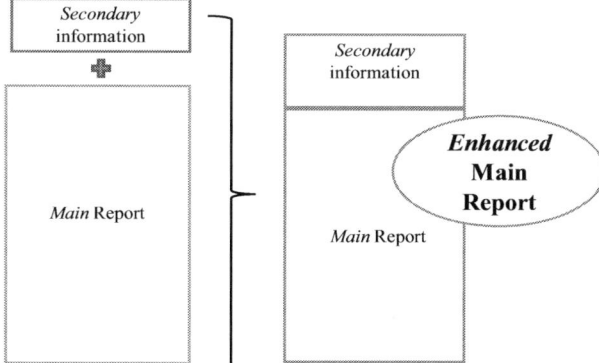

Fig. 4.2 A "strong" aggregation between partial reports

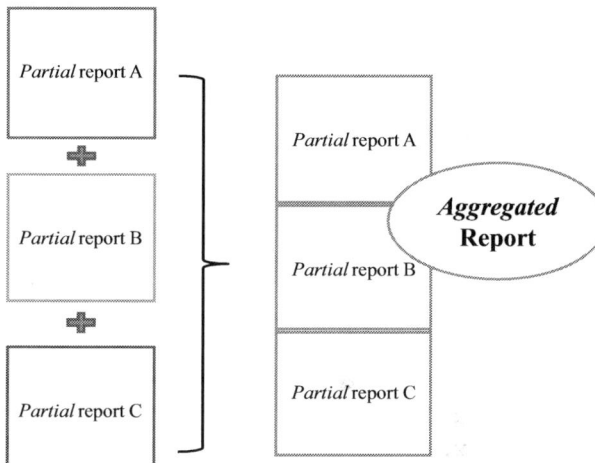

Fig. 4.3 Integration in a narrow sense

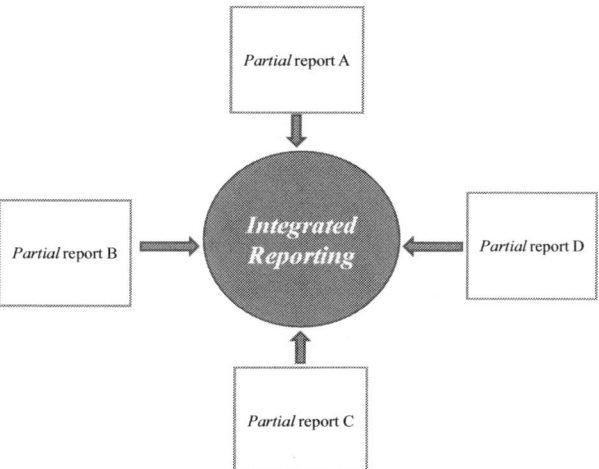

4.3.1.1 Sorgenia[2]

Sorgenia is an Italian group operating in each stage of the energy supply chain. The practice of IR began in 2010 with the first Annual Report which included a section dedicated to the "Company, Environment and Community". This Annual Report appears as a typical Italian Financial Statement (Accounts and Management Commentary) with the addition of some information about the external society and environment. The structure of the report is simple and it contains: some preliminary information about the group, the Report of the Board of Directors on the performance of the group and of the parent company, and the Accounts. The Report of the Board of Directors is a Management Commentary consisting in four sections: background information, results of main business activities, other relevant information (included some information about risk and governance), and the social and environmental section. The length of the social and environmental section is about the 23 % of the report. Between the financial and non-financial information there is no integration and the sustainability section represents only a supplement to the main report.

In 2011 the structure of the Annual Report underwent some changes. The sustainability section (called the "Report on the Value Generated") became an independent section from the Management Commentary and it was prepared according to GRI guidelines. The length of this section was still about the 23 % of the Annual Report. The structure of the 2012 Annual Report is the same as the previous version.

From the analysis of these reports it emerges that the connectivity of information is quite low, even though the provision of both financial and social-environmental information (*e.g.* distributed value, information about employees and CO_2 emissions) in the preliminary section stresses the multidimensionality of the company.

In the case of Sorgenia, the Financial Statement has been "enhanced" by adding social and environmental information that, however, does not allow to understand how social and environmental aspects affect the organizational capacity to create value in the long term.

4.3.1.2 Guna[3]

Guna is a company operating in the production and distribution of homeopathic medicines. The reporting strategy of Guna is quite different from that one of Sorgenia. In 2009 Guna started the practice of social accounting, publishing the first edition of its Social Report. In 2010, it realized an Integrated Report, derived from the practice of social reporting. The structure of the report is quite original and it includes the following sections: introduction; understanding the world of Guna; corporate social responsibility activities and stakeholder relationships; negative

---

[2] The Annual Reports of Sorgenia are available at: http://www.sorgenia.com/sorgenia-the-sensible-energy/investor-kit/annual-reports/

[3] Guna's Integrated Reports are available at: http://www.guna.it/mondoguna

results and future priorities; financial statement (with management commentary); and attached documents. The construction of the Integrated Report based on the approach of corporate social responsibility is clear in its introduction, in which the report is presented as a stage in implementing a social responsibility strategy. The structure is innovative, above all, because it includes a section about negative results, which confers reliability to the report that is tailored to the specific characteristics of the firm (no particular guideline is adopted). The financial statement and management commentary (taking up about 22 % of the report) provide the information that "enhances" the content of the Social Report. They are at the end of the Integrated Report without be linked to the other sections. The structure of the 2011 report maintains the same features but the financial section is larger (about 27 % of the report).

Therefore, Guna's Integrated Report is actually an "enhanced" Social and Environmental Report through which the company, that has a strong commitment to social responsibility, launched the message that its strategy does not consider the financial dimension as being separate from the social dimension. However, the connectivity of information is low because there is no real integration between social and financial information.

4.3.2 The Strong Aggregation Between the Partial Reports

Within the strong aggregation approach, the Integrated Report derives from the aggregation of a number of partial reports (Fig. 4.2). Unlike the first approach, in this case there is not a "main" report to which secondary information is added, but instead there is an equilibrium between the different reports. In this approach the partial reports do not lose their identity and they can be easily recognizable as part of the Integrated Report. Thus the partial reports do not coexist with the Integrated Report, but the latter contains them. The information that is derived from the different reports is not interconnected and the Integrated Report does not provide a comprehensive synthesis.

The resulting report is a document rich of information that however does not stress the interdependences affecting the value creation process. In this sense, this report remains at a level of "aggregation", within which the whole is equal to the sum of the parts.

The example provided for this second approach is Sabaf.

4.3.2.1 Sabaf[4]

Sabaf produces components for gas cooking equipment. The company has produced a sort of Integrated Report (called Annual Report) since 2005. From 2005 to 2010 the report included: an identity statement, a governance report, a sustainability report, a management commentary and a financial statement. From the 2011

---

[4] The annual reports of Sabaf are available at: http://www.sabaf.it

edition, the structure changed, showing an evolution towards a format that is more similar to the IR Framework. Indeed, the report contains sections on: business model and strategic approach; international dimension and markets of reference; corporate governance; risk management; compliance and remuneration; social and environmental sustainability; management commentary; financial statement; and remuneration report.

Until the 2010 edition, the Annual Report was a typical "aggregated" report made up of the different partial reports (each with a balanced length) with low connectivity between the various sources of information. The only synthesis between the different information was provided by some highlights regarding financial, intellectual capital, and social and environmental indicators presented in the introduction of the report. Instead, from 2011 the level of connectivity has increased due to the section regarding the business model of the organization. In this section, the interdependencies related to the drivers of performance are fully explained. The mission, vision and values of the company are linked to the productive activity by the four pillars of the Sabaf business model: sustainability, continuous learning, quality and internationalization.

Sabaf's reporting system shows an evolution towards stronger connectivity even though, apart from the section on business model, the rest of the Annual Report remains a sum of partial reports.

4.3.3 Integration in a Narrow Sense

The approach that best promotes connectivity between information is the one that relates to the so-called integration in a narrow sense. In this approach, the partial reports are only a means to provide information that is interpreted differently when it "enters" the Integrated Report (Fig. 4.3).

In this case, the sections of the Integrated Report are not identified by the partial reports and not all the information included in the partial reports is inserted in the Integrated Report. Indeed, the principle of materiality requires that only the information relevant to describing the value creation process is reported. Moreover, for the principle of conciseness it is necessary to avoid overload (IIRC 2013a). Between the partial reports there are some overlaps (for example, between the Social Report and the Intellectual Capital Report, or between the Management Commentary and the Governance Reports, etc.) which can create an excessive amount of information if the Integrated Report is a simple sum of the various parts. Therefore, to respect the principle of conciseness (IIRC 2013a, p. 21) the information contained in partial reports is assimilated within the Integrated Report without identifying the original source.

Only in this manner, the Integrated Report and the partial reports are fully autonomous and they have different functions as required by the IR Framework. Accordingly, the Integrated Report provides a holistic and global evaluation of the value creation ability of the company, while the partial reports respond to specific information needs relating to particular aspects of the organizational activity.

Despite a great deal of experimentation, the development of an actual "integrated" reporting system in organizational practice is still in an early stage (IIRC 2013a, p. 1). Therefore, it is difficult to find a clear example of an organization which approaches IR in this broader perspective. In the Italian context, two significant cases are Cassa Rurale Treviglio and Terna.

4.3.3.1 Cassa Rurale Treviglio[5]

Cassa Rurale Treviglio is a cooperative bank that in 2011 started to adopt the Integrated Report. Since the adoption of this report, the bank decided not to continue publishing its Social and Environmental Report as though the Integrated Report was a substitute for it. Actually, the structure of the latter is absolutely different than the previous edition of the Social Report; therefore, it fully represents a new kind of report for the bank.

The Integrated Report consists of 12 sections: mission and strategy; governance and human resources; presence in the territory; bank activity; members of the cooperative bank; support of local community; environmental policies and behaviours; relations with cooperative banking system; financial analysis; financial statement; board of statutory auditor report; board and composition of other bank bodies.

The Integrated Report is not a sum of reports but an original synthesis deriving from various sources and in which many sections are fully cross-dimensional. The choice to create this kind of report is explained in the introduction by the President of the bank as a decision that is consistent with the values of the organization and aimed at integrating the economic, social and environmental aspects within the spirit of a cooperative bank. The connectivity between heterogeneous information is pursued in almost every section combining different elements. For instance, in the section regarding the analysis of the results, the added value that was generated and distributed among the stakeholders is calculated. Again, in the section about the bank activity, the description of anti-crises policies for the families' benefit is included. Finally, in the section regarding the bank's presence in the territory there is a mix of financial strategy information and information about social support for the local community.

4.3.3.2 Terna[6]

Terna is a company operating in the energy sector and it participates in the Pilot Program of IIRC. Terna does not publish an Integrated Report but it uses its website for the so-called Integrated Reporting Project. The use of technology to improve the connectivity of information is a solution suggested both in the literature (Eccles and Krzus 2010) and by the IIRC (2013b).

---

[5] The Integrated Reports of Cassa Rurale Treviglio are available at: http://www.cassarurale-treviglio.it/template/default.asp?i_menuID=39625

[6] The Integrated Report Project is available at: http://www.ternaintegratedreport2011.message-asp.com/it

Terna separately publishes two main documents in its reporting system: a financial statement (with a management commentary) and a sustainability report. In 2011 (the 2012 version is still a work-in-progress), Terna created an online platform within a specific website, which was based on the content elements of the IIRC Discussion Paper (IIRC 2011): the organizational overview and business model; strategic objectives; operating context; governance and remuneration; performance; future outlook. Clicking on each of these sections, it is possible to select links to specific parts of the Financial Statement, Management Commentary or Sustainability Report containing information on each topic. The user can then build a "virtual" Integrated Report and connect the information according to his/her information needs. The choice of information is left to the user without being driven by the company.

The solution is innovative and flexible and it could be further improved by allowing for the creation of a sort of "customized" report that the user could also download. In this way, the Integrated Report and the partial reports can coexist in a reporting system in which both global and specific information needs are satisfied.

4.4   Final Remarks

This chapter has offered some reflections on the centrality of the guiding principle of connectivity in the IR Framework, focusing on the relationships between the Integrated Report and the several partial reports which are at the basis of its construction. Partial reports have been here defined as all the possible reports drawn up by an organization to represent a specific part of its value creation process. In particular, this chapter referred to Financial Statement, Management Commentary, Social and Environmental Report, Corporate Governance Report and Intellectual Capital Report. These reports have been analysed according to the key-components of the connectivity of information identified in the IR Framework (i.e. content elements, time, capitals, financial and other information, quantitative *vs* qualitative information). Connectivity can be ensured only if these components are represented within the Integrated Report. Thus, partial reports play the important role of providing all the needed information.

Notwithstanding, the ways in which the different partial reports are combined can affect the actual level of connectivity of information in the Integrated Report. In this chapter, it has been argued that three different approaches can be identified in the process of aggregation and/or integration of the partial reports to construct the Integrated Report, namely a "weak" aggregation, a "strong" aggregation, and an "integration" in a narrow sense. Only the third approach allows for a real integration of the partial reports since all the interdependencies between different information are considered to explain the value creation process. In this case, the Integrated Report and the partial reports can coexist in a global and integrated reporting system. Only through the interpretation of information contained in partial reports is it possible to have a complete vision of the multi-dimensionality of the organization. Connectivity, through the interpretation of this multi-dimensionality, makes the concept of integrated thinking evident, as proposed in the IR Framework.

The path towards achieving an integration, in a narrow sense, is difficult and complex due to the fact that it entails changes in many aspects of organizational life, from the implementation of new information systems and organizational structures to the development of new cultural basis. For this reason, a gradual adoption of the Integrated Report can facilitate this organizational change. In this sense, the three approaches proposed in this chapter could be considered as three gradual stages towards the Integrated Report.

Moreover, from the analysis of the two companies that seem to follow an integrated approach in a narrow sense, some interesting points emerge. Firstly, the role of technology could be very relevant as in the case of Terna. In particular, the use of the Web could increase the level of connectivity of information giving also the opportunity to build up "customized" Integrated Reports. Secondly, the use of Integrated Report should not be limited only to large and complex organizations as shown in the case of Cassa Rurale Treviglio. Indeed, the Integrated Report is not a rigid tool but it can be adapted to the contextual features of each organization.

Although in the IR Framework the concept of connectivity is fully developed with reference to the information needed to explain the value creation process, more efforts could be taken to apply the concept of connectivity also to the notion of performance. In particular, the challenges ahead for corporate reporting should lead to the redefinition of the notion of performance in an "integrated" perspective.

References

Abeysekera I (2006) The project of intellectual capital disclosure: researching the research. J Intellect Cap 7(1):61–77

Andriessen D (2004) IC valuation and measurement: classifying the state of the art. J Intellect Cap 5(2):230–242

Argento D, Di Pietra R (2010) IASB ED management commentary versus European regulation: the impact on management reports of companies listed on the Italian stock exchange. Paper presented at 5th international workshop on accounting and regulation, Siena

Branwijck D (2012) Corporate social responsibility + intellectual capital = integrated reporting? In: Proceedings of the 4th European conference on intellectual capital held at Arcada University of Applied Sciences, Helsinki, 75–85

Burgman R, Roos G (2007) The importance of intellectual capital reporting: evidence and implications. J Intellect Cap 8(1):7–51

Collett P, Hrasky S (2005) Voluntary disclosure of corporate governance practices by listed Australian companies. J Corp Govern Int Rev 13(2):188–196

Cordazzo M (2005) IC Statement versus Environmental and Social Reports. An Empirical Analysis of their convergencies in Italian Context. Int J Intellect Capital 6(3):441–464

DMSTI (Danish Ministry of Science, Technology and Innovation) (2003) Intellectual capital statements - the new guidelines. http://www.vtu.dk. Accessed 15 Jun 2013

Eccles R, Krzus M (2010) One report. Integrated reporting for a sustainable strategy. Wiley, New Jersey, NJ

Edvinsson L, Malone MS (1997) Intellectual capital—realizing your company's true value by finding its hidden brainpower. Harper Business, New York, NY

Guthrie J, Parker LD (1989) Corporate social reporting: a rebuttal of legitimacy theory. Account Bus Res 19(76):343–352

Guthrie J, Johanson U, Bukh PN, Sanchez P (2003) Intangibles and trasparent enterprise: new strands of knowledge. J Intellect Cap 4(4):429–440

Hutton A (2004) Beyond financial reporting—an integrated approach to disclosure. J Appl Corp Finance 16(4):8–16

IASB (2010a) The conceptual framework for financial reporting. http://www.eifrs.ifrs.org/eifrs/bnstandards/en/2013/conceptualframework.pdf. Accessed 10 Jul 2013

IASB (2010b) Ifrs practice statement—management commentary. A framework to presentation. http://www.ifrs.org/Current-Projects/IASB-Projects/Management-Commentary/IFRS-Practice-Statement/Pages/IFRS Practice-Statement.aspx. Accessed 10 Jun 2013

IASB (2011) IAS n.1. Presentation of financial statement. http://www.eifrs.ifrs.org/eifrs/bnstandards/en/2013/ias1.pdf. Accessed 10 Jul 2013

IIRC (2011) Towards integrated reporting. Communicating value in the 21st century, IIRC, New York. http://www.theiirc.org/wp-content/uploads/2011/09/IR-Discussion-Paper-2011_spreads.pdf. Accessed 14 April 2013

IIRC (2013a) Consultation draft of the international <IR> framework, IIRC, New York. http://www.theiirc.org/wp-content/uploads/Consultation-Draft/Consultation-Draft-of-the InternationalIRFramework.pdf. Accessed 14 April 2013

IIRC (2013b) Connectivity. background paper for IR, IIRC, New York. http://www.theiirc.org/wp-content/uploads/2013/07/IR-Background-Paper-Connectivity.pdf. Accessed 15 Jul 2013

Institute of Directors Southern Africa (2009) King code of governance for South Africa. http://www.african.ipapercms.dk/IOD/KINGIII/kingiiireport/. Accessed 10 Oct 2012

Johnson TH, Kaplan RS (1987) Relevance lost: the rise and the fall of management accounting. Harvard Business School, Boston, MA

Kaplan RS, Norton DP (1996) Translating strategy into action: the balanced scorecard. Harvard Business School, Boston, MA

Kolk A, Pinkse J (2010) The integration of corporate governance in corporate social responsibility disclosures. Corp Soc Responsib Environ Manag 17(1):15–26

Lev B, Cañibao L, Marr B (2005) An accounting perspective of intellectual capital. In: Marr B (ed) Pespectives of intellectual capital. Elsevier, Amsterdam, pp 42–55

Medawar C (1976) The social audit: a political view. Account Organ Soc 1(4):389–394

MERITUM (2002) Guidelines for managing and reporting on intangibles (intellectual capital report). European Commission, Brussels

OECD (2004) OECD principles of corporate governance. http://www.oecd.org/daf/ca/corporategovernanceprinciples/31557724.pdf. Accessed 16 Jun 2013

Ogden S, Watson R (1999) Corporate performance and stakeholder management: balancing shareholder and customer interest in the U.K. privatized water industry. Acad Manage J 42 (5):526–538

Pedrini M (2007) Human capital convergences in intellectual capital and sustainability reports. J Intellect Cap 8(2):346–366

Ramanathan KV (1976) Toward a theory of corporate social accounting. Account Rev 21 (3):516–528

GRI (Global Reporting Initiative) (2013) G4 sustainability reporting guidelines. http://www.globalreporting.org/resourcelibrary/GRIG4-Part1-Reporting-Principles-and-Standard-Disclosures.pdf. Accessed 1 Jul 2013

Solomon J (2007) Corporate governance and accountability. Wiley, Chicester

Stanton P, Stanton J, Pires G (2004) Impressions of an annual report: an experimental study. Corp Comm Int J 9(1):57–69

Stewart TA (1997) Intellectual capital: the new wealth of organizations. Nicholas Brealey, London

Sveiby K-E (1997) The new organizational wealth. Managing and measuring knowledge-based assets. Berret-Koehler, San Francisco

The Prince's Accountability for Sustainability Project (2007) Accounting for sustainability report: the connected reporting framework. http://www.accountingforsustainability.org. Accessed 1 Jun 2013

The Prince's Accountability for Sustainability Project (2009) Connected reporting. A practical guide with worked examples. http://www.accountingforsustainability.org. Accessed 1 Jun 2013

Toms JS (2002) Firm resources, quality signal and determinants of corporate environmental reputation: UK. Br Account Rev 34(3):257–282

Woodward DG, Edwards P, Birkin F (1996) Organizational legitimacy and stakeholder information provision. Br J Manag 7:329–347

Yongvanich K, Guthrie J (2006) An extended performance reporting framework for social and environmental accounting. Bus Strateg Environ 15:309–321

Materiality and Assurance: Building the Link

5

Chiara Mio

Abstract

This chapter provides a comprehensive discussion of materiality and assurance in the context of Integrated Reporting (IR). On the one hand, materiality has gained much importance following the introduction of IR, since one of the main objectives of this innovative form of reporting is to reach conciseness. On the other hand, assurance may play a crucial role in conferring reliability to the materiality determination process proposed by the International Integrated Reporting Council (IIRC) and to the whole process of IR. This chapter provides a discussion of the state of the art of materiality and assurance in the context of non-financial information and, more specifically, IR. It also points out some of the main challenges the IIRC materiality determination process will have to face in order for companies to implement it correctly. Finally, drawing on the peculiarities of IR, the chapter points out some issues that will have to be discussed regarding assurance and its effectiveness. Some insights for future development of the debate are also proposed.

5.1 Introduction

The recent debate about Integrated Reporting (IR) has pushed the academic and practitioner discussion to focus on the issue of materiality, given that one of the guiding principles proposed by the International Integrated Reporting Council (IIRC) in its framework is "materiality and conciseness." The Consultation Draft (CD) by the Council proposes the IIRC's materiality determination process in order to allow companies to effectively identify material issues. Because such a process requires a company to exercise a high degree of judgment, assurance may play a central role in order to confer reliability to the information disclosed in the IR.

C. Mio (✉)
Department of Management, Ca' Foscari University of Venice, Venice, Italy
e-mail: mio@unive.it

C. Busco et al. (eds.), *Integrated Reporting*, DOI 10.1007/978-3-319-02168-3_5,
© Springer International Publishing Switzerland 2013

This chapter provides a discussion of the state of the art in materiality and assurance, focusing in particular on the peculiarities of these concepts in the context of IR, as compared to Annual Reports (AR) and Sustainability Reports (SR). It also points out some issues arising in the definition of materiality by the IIRC and in the methodology assurance providers ought to follow for IR. Finally, it proposes some insights for future development of the debate on materiality and assurance in IR.

In more detail, the second section provides an overview of the academic literature and professional standards on materiality in the context of non-financial information, focusing on the differences with that of financial information and on the main standards employed (the Global Reporting Initiative (GRI) G4 and the AccountAbility AA1000). The third section focuses on IR, discussing the materiality determination process proposed by the IIRC and also providing some examples drawn from IR included in the IIRC examples database. The fourth section points out some of the main crucial issues of the IIRC materiality determination process, mainly deriving from the predominant/exclusive focus on providers of financial capital, which confer to companies a high degree of judgment in identifying material issues. Assurance may potentially represent a mechanism that may partially provide a solution to such issues, thus increasing the reliability of IR. The fifth section provides an overview of assurance in the field of non-financial information. In particular, it discusses the main standards employed for the assurance process (i.e. ISAE3000 and AA1000AS) and analyses the role the GRI and the IIRC assign to assurance in the context of Sustainability and Integrated Reporting respectively. Some examples of assurance from the IIRC examples database are also provided.

Finally, the sixth section points out some of the challenges in materiality and assurance implementation that will need to be tackled in the future and which, to a large extent, derive from the peculiarities of IR. In the context of IR, in fact, it is not possible to rely on quantitative thresholds to determine materiality, the materiality determination process is to a large extent subjective, IR provides future-oriented information, performance targets play a relevant role and the boundaries of the report are difficult to determine. Given these peculiarities and the related challenges, some insights for future development of the debate are also presented.

5.2   Materiality: The State of the Art

The first definitions of materiality were proposed in the context of financial reporting, since the first reports disclosed mainly financial information (for a review, see Messier et al. 2005). In accordance with the user utility theory (see Faux 2012), a piece of information is considered to be "material" if its omission or misstatement would influence the economic decision made by the report's user (i.e. the investor). If the comparison is kept at a broad enough level of analysis, it is possible to identify some similarities between definitions in the financial and non-financial reporting contexts (see Dhaliwal et al. 2011). According to AccountAbility (2006), non-financial information materiality requires that the Assurance Provider states whether the Reporting Organization has included in the report the information about its sustainability performance required by its stakeholders for them to be able to make informed judgments, decisions and actions. This definition relies on the concept of the "decision usefulness of the information for the intended report's user". *Mutatis mutandis*, the definition is fairly similar to those found for the financial context. AccountAbility (2006) focuses on "stakeholders" rather than "investors" and "judgments, decisions and actions" rather than "investment decisions". Nevertheless, the underlying criterion is the same both for the financial and the NFI contexts: the decision usefulness of the information.

Despite this apparent homogeneity, digging deeper into the definitions and into the actual implementation of the materiality concept, some crucial differences and consequences arise. The International Standard on Accounting (ISA) 320 mentions, among the main characteristics of materiality definitions in financial reporting frameworks (ISA 2009), that "judgments about materiality are affected by the size or nature of a misstatement or a combination of both". In the context of financial information, the quantitative threshold is very important, as it allows the assessment of materiality by making a comparison between specific financial performance items, such as assets or revenues. This approach is particularly useful to investors, who are interested in understanding the impact of material issues on the financial capital of a company.

Some authors (Tuttle et al. 2002; Lydenberg 2012) and standards (AASB 2010) attribute a predominant importance to thresholds in determining materiality. This methodology is particularly effective (because it simplifies the materiality assessment process) for audit firms, which do not have a deep knowledge of the company and of its operations and that must rely on quantitative methods to proxy for materiality as they can only rely on accounting numbers. Such quantitative thresholds employed for defining financial materiality cannot be employed for non-financial information (see Guthrie and Parker 1990) for various reasons. First, non-financial information captures a wider concept of firm value as compared to financial information. Therefore, when materiality is assessed, the relationship between the issue to be assessed and firm value as represented by non-financial information is more difficult to determine, as non-financial pieces of information present many intersection levels in their definition. Second, even if the impact of a certain issue on the firm value can be determined, in the field of non-financial information it is not possible to employ a unique threshold, because the issues considered may have an impact on different capitals. Non-financial information is often relevant for many stakeholders, which have different and non-aligned interests (see Berthelot et al. 2003; Brammer and Pavelin 2004; Patten 2002). To rely only on financial capital would be a satisfactory approach only for one specific category of stakeholder (investors). Third, non-financial information cannot always be expressed in monetary terms. Fourth, non-financial information is often long-term oriented, meaning there may be some issues that are material despite not having an immediate impact on the item employed as a threshold. The long-term impact may be evaluated, but necessarily relying on models, which would need to make strong assumptions. Fifth, non-financial information is often derived from a life-cycle approach, therefore in order to properly assess it, information about events and phenomena that are external to the company would be needed.

While non-financial information refers to objects that are often not traded on a market, financial information refers to a market in which goods and services are being exchanged and often have a well-defined price. Conversely, objects represented by non-financial information cannot be "priced" in a market, simply because an efficient market does not exist. Is it possible to set a quantitative threshold to determine how many deaths in the workplace are tolerable? How much is a death in the workplace worth? How much is damaging the reputation of the firm worth? This is impossible to define, at least by relying on an active market. More precisely, quantitative thresholds may be determined even for non-financial information, but their calculation would have to rely on such heavy assumptions that would make the threshold too discretionary, and these assumptions would affect both values and methodology. Since a quantitative value does not exist, it is not possible to apply the thresholds as in the context of financial information, making it more difficult to separate material from non-material information. As will be discussed in depth below, these difficulties in defining thresholds for non-financial information have led assurance providers to mainly focus on the assurance of the stakeholder engagement and of the materiality determination process, rather than on the definition of a threshold.

The lack of a clear definition of materiality in the context of non-financial information, also due to the issues described above, has not represented a major problem for sustainability reports, since the most widely employed standards do not focus on the conciseness of the reports, but rather on their completeness (see GRI 2013a, b). With the introduction of IR into the debate, the issue of how to define materiality gained more relevance. The IIRC argues that "a matter is material if it is of such relevance and significance that it could substantively influence the assessments and decisions of the organization's highest governing body, or change the assessments and decisions of intended users with regard to the organization's ability to create value over time" (IIRC 2013a, b, c, p. 21). The IIRC introduces the concept of usefulness not only for the external users of the report but also for the "organization's highest governing body". This is coherent with the attention the IIRC devotes to the process of integrated reporting, which ought to provide relevant information for the company decision makers and, in some cases, also shape the corporate governance of the company.

Besides the one proposed by the IIRC, which will be discussed in more detail in the following section, the other two main standards that provide some guidance on the issue of materiality are the GRI Guidelines and the AccountAbility AA1000. The latest version of the GRI guidelines (G4) defines information as "material" when it reflects the organization's significant economic, environmental, and social impact or when it would substantively influence the assessments and decisions of stakeholders ("relevant topics are those that may reasonably be considered important for reflecting the organization's economic, environmental and social impacts, or influencing the decisions of stakeholders, and, therefore, potentially merit inclusion in the report. Materiality is the threshold at which Aspects become sufficiently important that they should be reported" GRI 2013a, b, p. 17).

By considering both internal (i.e. the organization's mission) and external (i.e. influence of the organization on other entities) factors, companies ought to define whether information is material or not, following two parameters: influence on disclosed assessments and disclosures, and significance on economic, environmental and social impacts. In the final part of its principles, the GRI also proposes some tests in order to determine the significance to stakeholders and the significance to the organization, thus making it clear that both perspectives ought to be considered ("in defining material Aspects, the organization takes into account the following factors: Reasonably estimable sustainability impacts, risks, or opportunities (...); Main sustainability interests and topics, and Indicators raised by stakeholders (such as vulnerable groups within local communities, civil society); The main topics and future challenges for the sector reported by peers and competitors; Relevant laws, regulations, international agreements, or voluntary agreements with strategic significance to the organization and its stakeholders (...)" GRI 2013b, p. 12). The GRI—which has also proposed the Sector Supplement—has the merit of framing the issue of materiality in a sector-specific way. According to Eccles et al (2012), this is an aspect that ought to be improved in the current reporting framework: "developing sector-specific guidelines on what sustainability issues are material to that sector and the Key Performance Indicators (KPIs) for reporting on them would significantly improve the ability of companies to report on their ESG performance" (Eccles et al. 2012, p. 13).

AccountAbility established a standard for sustainability disclosure under its AA1000 framework, updated in 2008. AA1000 (2008) determines some criteria that ought to be met when tackling the issue of materiality. In particular, it proposes a five-step test in order to determine materiality (AccountAbility 2008). This is aimed at providing companies with some more information, compared to the definitions already discussed above. The first test is "direct short-term financial impacts". Some non-financial performance indicators (such as carbon emission) may have a financial impact in the short term and, for this reason, need to be disclosed. The second test is "policy-related performance", requiring the disclosure of those issues that do not have any impact on short-term financial performance but that are related to policies the company has agreed upon. The third test is "business peer-based norms". According to this test, information that the company's competitors deem to be material ought to be considered material by the company as well. The fourth test is "stakeholder behaviour and concerns", which considers issues that will impact stakeholders' behaviour as material. This test is fairly similar to the definitions proposed following the user utility theory, and is probably the least insightful of the five tests proposed by AccountAbility (2008), because it does not add much to the indications provided by the materiality definitions discussed above. Finally, the fifth test ("societal norms") requires companies to disclose issues or matters that are embedded in regulations or that will likely become regulated in the future. While the GRI Guidelines framework is mostly "principles-based", the AccountAbility (2008) framework is "process-based".

Thus, it focuses on the relationship of the company with its stakeholders. On the one hand, this "process-based" approach is positive because it focuses on the company's peculiarities to the highest extent. On the other hand, it lacks "standardization" of the process outcome.

5.3   Materiality in Integrated Reporting

Before the introduction of IR, the debate on materiality in the context of non-financial information was certainly less fierce (see Deloitte 2012; IFAC 2011). The issue was taken into consideration by AccountAbility (2008) and GRI, but it did not have the relevance it has gathered today. The GRI proposed a list of indicators and issues the company ought to report on. The more of these indicators a company manages to cover, the higher the (perceived) report's robustness and completeness will be. The problem with this approach is that the indicators may be considered a fixed list to be complied with, with only few adjustments done according to the materiality principle. This is particularly evident in the comprehensive version of the G4 GRI guidelines, which requires all the proposed elements to be disclosed. Inevitably, in following this approach the issue of materiality loses some relevance, despite being listed among the "Reporting Principles for defining Content" by the GRI. Conversely, IR, especially in the IIRC framework, confers a central role to materiality. The IR "conciseness" is one of the key features stressed by the framework, and to gather a clear and accepted definition of materiality is, in the IR context, fundamental and much more important than it was for previous standards.

The latest (and probably the most complete) framework for the identification of material issues is provided by the IIRC (2013c) in the "Background paper for <IR>" about materiality. The IIRC (2013c) stresses the importance of materiality since it is one of the main principles that ought to guide the creation of an IR. According to IIRC (2013c), the process leading to the definition of materiality "requires a high degree of judgment and involves numerous strategic considerations. This requires senior management and those charged with governance collectively to exercise judgment to determine which matters are material for the purposes of <IR> and to ensure that they are appropriately disclosed, given the specific circumstances of the organization, including the application of generally accepted measurement and disclosure methods as appropriate" (IIRC 2013a, b, c, paragraph 1.13).

The IIRC takes a step further towards the identification of who the intended users of IR are and, as a consequence, to whom a certain matter or information ought to be considered material in order to be disclosed in the report. According to IIRC (IIRC 2013a, b, c), "while the communications that result from <IR> will be of benefit to a range of stakeholders, they are principally aimed at providers of financial capital, in order to support their financial capital allocation assessment" (IIRC 2013a, b, c, p. 8). This clarification is embedded into the definition of materiality, which is the following: "a matter is material if it is of such relevance and importance that it could substantively influence the assessments of providers of financial capital with regard to the organization's ability to create value over the short, medium and long term" (IIRC 2013a, b, c, p. 21). As argued by the detractors of the user utility theory (see Faux 2012), there may be issues relevant to certain stakeholders but, at the same time, not relevant to other stakeholders. This creates a problem for the organization. The decision made by the IIRC to choose the "providers of financial capital" as the main intended users of the IR helps in reaching a clearer framework that can be useful for companies and represents a necessary and "unavoidable" first step towards the identification of material information. As argued in the chapter by Fasan, IR may be considered an evolution of AR, therefore focused on the providers of financial capital (investors) rather than on the wider category of stakeholders. This makes it easier for companies to reach a definition of materiality in IR and AR as compared to in SR.

The framework proposes three steps in the "<IR> materiality determination process". The first is to identify relevant matters for inclusion in the integrated report, defined by the IIRC as "those matters that have a past, present or future effect on the organization's ability to create value over time". In order to identify such issues, the management would need to consider: the organization value drivers, matters identified during stakeholder analysis and engagement and other factors internal/external to the organization. It seems clear that this activity depends on a full understanding of the business model of the firm, which is defined by the IIRC (2013b) as "the chosen system of inputs, business activities, outputs and outcomes that aims to create value over the short, medium and long term" (IIRC 2013b, p. 6). The IIRC (2013b) also specifies that: "features that can enhance the effectiveness and readability of the description of the business model include (...) identification of critical stakeholders and other dependencies, key value drivers and important external factors" (IIRC 2013b, p. 13). The process of identifying such "relevant matters" touches upon many aspects of the company business model and strategy and therefore needs to be tackled by the top managers of the organization. Also particularly important is the long-term/short-term orientation of the company, because short-term oriented companies are not likely to disclose much ESG information. This approach is tightly linked to the belief (which is in some ways too optimistic) that the market will reward long-term oriented companies. Unfortunately, actual business cases show how often short-term oriented companies survive and make profit, since the market and consumers do not punish their short-termism.

The second step is the determination of the importance of relevant matters, in order to prioritize issues. The IIRC (2013c) proposes two dimensions in order to assess importance: magnitude of the effect (for matters that have occurred, currently exist or will occur with certainty); magnitude of the effect and likelihood of its occurrence (for matters where there is uncertainty about whether or not the matter will occur). Since the most important phase is the determination of the potential magnitude of the effect on the organization's ability to create value over time, the IIRC proposes some factors which companies ought to consider: quantitative and qualitative factors; the financial, operational, strategic, reputational and regulatory perspective of the effect; the area of the effect; and the time frame of the effect.

Finally, the third and final step requires the prioritization of material matters, based on their importance. Therefore IR, as compared to AR, includes other capitals and stakeholders in the framework, but at the end it is the company that needs to prioritize the issues derived from this inclusion. Following this approach, there are material issues generally speaking and material issues according to the company. The risk is that the company (maybe because of low stakeholder engagement activity) does not recognize the materiality of some issues, and thus does not disclose them. Following a more sustainability-oriented approach, the IIRC would need to require the disclosure of some elements regardless of the materiality assessment by the company, which is subject to great subjective judgment and to possibility of mistake or misconduct.

Among the pilot companies now adopting the IIRC framework, some good examples can be found; the IIRC website provides an "examples database" which includes some IR examples, intended to provide companies with a range of emerging reporting practices, with the selection being reviewed by the IIRC's Secretariat and Technical Task Force. Among the reports flagged for the "Conciseness, reliability and materiality", there is the Absa IR. According to the IR, the five material issues that have been identified stemmed from the consideration of: what stakeholders consider important; core issues and future challenges; relevant laws and regulations; key organizational values, policies, strategies, goals and targets; significant risks; critical factors for enabling organizational success; and core competences of the organization. Some performance indicators have been assured on a limited assurance basis by two audit firms. The material issues identified are the following: sustainable financial viability; process and systems effectiveness; customer experience; our people; and economic equity. Another interesting report included in the examples database is the IR by Hyundai, which classifies the issues according to two dimensions: external relevance and internal relevance. The issues have been divided into three categories: key reporting issues (high external and internal relevance); main reporting issues (medium external and internal relevance); issues to be monitored (low external and internal relevance). Each issue is listed below the Hyundai matrix, with reference to the page of the IR where that topic is discussed.

5.4   Materiality and Assurance in Integrated Reporting

According to the IIRC framework, an issue is material if it could substantively influence the assessment of providers of financial capital with regard to the organization's ability to create value (IIRC 2013a, paragraph 3.23). As recognized by the IIRC itself, the materiality determination process requires a high degree of judgment by senior management and by those charged with governance. These characteristics lead to the possibility for the report's preparers to leverage on such judgments in order to exclude some issues, which may damage the company in terms of investors' expectations about its ability to generate future cash flows.

Suppose three different cases. In the first, a company is deciding whether to disclose an issue that is relevant for both investors and stakeholders. In this case, according to the IIRC framework, the company would have to disclose the issue. In the second case, a company is considering an issue that is relevant for investors but not relevant for stakeholders. Also in this situation, the issue would have to be disclosed, even if the representation of the issue, as in the first case, would be significantly influenced by the perspective of the investors. Finally, in the third case, a company is deciding whether to disclose an issue that is relevant for stakeholders but not relevant to investors. In this case, according to the framework, the issue would not have to be disclosed, given the definition of materiality.

Because of the high degree of judgment involved in this process, there is the possibility that some issues that are material but could damage the reputation or performance of the company if disclosed, could be considered not relevant for the providers of financial capital by the management to be and could be, therefore, excluded from the IR. Therefore, companies may employ the materiality definition as a "shield" in order to avoid the disclosure of information that is actually relevant. This is a serious shortcoming of IR, which may generate a significant gap between the expectations that IR is creating and the actual completeness of information, even if the IIRC clearly specifies that the ESG information is not to be abandoned but rather included in the Sustainability Report. Some concerns need to be raised about this IIRC methodology, which relies only on the investors' perspective, because it is based only on the good faith of the company and on its willingness to provide an adequate disclosure of the process. In this way, the judgment on the adequate application of the materiality principle is ultimately left to the report's user. And it is relevant to assess whether users are really able to assess each company's application of materiality, using only limited and periodic external information.

In this context of a high degree of judgment, assurance may play a crucial role in increasing report readers' confidence that the materiality determination process was properly implemented and that material issues were not excluded from the report because of some misjudgement such as the one exemplified above. Clearly, the assurance providers would face major challenges in determining whether an issue is really material or not, because they lack detailed knowledge of the firm. In the context of financial information, this problem has, to a great extent, been overcome through the employment of thresholds, which are not applicable to IRs assurance.

5.5   Assurance: The State of the Art

This section provides a brief discussion of the characteristics of the two most important assurance standards for non-financial information disclosure, one more accounting-oriented than the other, which are respectively ISAE3000 and

AA1000AS. Besides this, the role GRI and IIRC assign to assurance in the context of Sustainability and Integrated Reporting respectively will be analysed.

The International Standard on Assurance Engagement (ISAE) 3000 is a widely recognized international standard that ensures the quality of assurance work, including report verification as well as assurance on environmental performance, corporate governance, internal compliance, stakeholder engagement and other areas central to corporate responsibility. The standard was developed by the International Federation of Accountants and is designed to guide accountants, auditors and assurance professionals as they undertake non-financial audits. One of the key characteristics of the standard is the distinction it introduces between limited and reasonable assurance. A limited assurance engagement is one in which the practitioner reduces the engagement risk to a level that is acceptable in the circumstances of the engagement but where that risk is greater than for a reasonable assurance engagement. Usually, limited assurance is in the form of negative statements (i.e. "nothing suggesting that the content of the report is not reliable has come to our knowledge") while the reasonable assurance is in the form of positive statement ("we found the content of the report to be reliable"). The standard focuses on the following areas: ethical requirements, quality control, engagement acceptance, terms of engagement, planning and performance of engagement, the use of experts, obtaining evidence, the consideration of subsequent events, documentation and the preparation of the assurance report.

ISAE 3000 defines materiality, coherently with previous literature and audit standards, as the ability of the information to influence relevant decisions of intended users (see ISAE3000 2011, paragraph A86). According to the standard, both quantitative and qualitative factors ought to be considered in the materiality assessment. Among the qualitative factors, the assurance providers ought to consider the previous communication to users and, if applicable, the nature of observed deviations from a control (see ISAE3000 2011, paragraph A88).

The AA1000 is a standard introduced by the Institute of Social and Ethical AccountAbility (ISEA), which aims to provide guidelines for the assurance of social reports and for stakeholder engagement. Such standards have been issued with the aim to help organizations understand their responsibilities and the consequences of their actions. There are two main standards: the AA1000APS (Accountability Principles Standard), which focuses on the main principles that should be followed in the reporting process, and the AA1000AS (Assurance Standard), which deals with the assurance of sustainability reports. The AA1000AS was introduced in 2003 as the first assurance standard for sustainability reporting with the aim of reinforcing the credibility and quality of performance in the sustainability field. This standard is mostly principle-based and, according to AA1000 (2008), "it provides a means for assurance providers to go beyond mere verification of data, to evaluate the way reporting organizations manage sustainability, and to reflect that management and resulting performance in its assurance statements" (AA1000 2008, p. 6).

The assurance provided according to the AA1000AS has two types: it can be focused only on the adherence of the organization to the AA1000 AccountAbility principles, or it can also be focused on the reliability of some specific sustainability performance information. Similar to those for ISAE3000, assurance statements according to AA1000AS may also have a high or low level of assurance.

The GRI G4 recommends the assurance of the report, but does not pose this as a necessary requirement (GRI 2013a, b, paragraph 3.3). The G4 also requires the company to report on the relationship between the organization and the assurance provider and, in particular, it requires disclosing whether or not the highest governance body or senior executives are involved in seeking the assurance for the report. Therefore, it poses management independence and engagement as two of the main conditions to be met in order to reach a credible assurance. Assurance process should be conducted by competent groups of individuals external to the organization who follow professional standards for assurance or who apply systematic, documented and evidence-based processes (GRI 2013a, b). Beside this, assurance providers should be independent from the organization and therefore be able to reach and publish an objective and impartial opinion on the report, apply quality control procedures to the assurance engagement, conduct the engagement in a manner that is systematic, documented, evidence-based, and characterized by defined procedures.

Similar to the GRI G4, the IIRC framework does not require an external assurance to be performed on the IR and the external assurance is seen as a mechanism to increase the reliability of the report (see paragraph 3.31 of the Consultation Draft (IIRC 2013a, b, c). Even if external assurance has been provided, the IIRC framework makes it clear that the responsibility still is on "those charged with governance", who are the ones that need to exercise the judgment. According to IIRC (2013a, b, c) "Independent, external assurance may also provide comfort, in addition to the internal mechanisms, to those charged with governance" (paragraph 5.20 of the Consultation Draft (IIRC 2013a, b, c). Finally, the IIRC makes it clear that, while it does provide the reporting criteria against which organizations and assurance providers assess a report's adherence, it does not provide the protocols for performing assurance engagements. It is interesting to note that the topic of assurance is among the consultation questions proposed by the IIRC in the consultation Draft, meaning that the issue is considered to be relevant by the standard-setter. In particular, the questions/comments are: "If assurance is to be obtained, should it cover the integrated report as a whole or specific aspects of the report?" and "assurance providers are particularly asked to comment on whether they consider the Framework to provide suitable criteria for an assurance engagement".

Among the reports included in the IIRC examples database, the assurance statement of most companies refers to ISAE 3000, some companies refer to AA1000AS, and others have decided to omit an external assurance at this stage. The Hyundai 2012 IR has been performed according to AA1000AS, at a moderate level of assurance. The scope of the assurance includes, among other things, the verification of the sustainability policy, goals, initiatives, practices and performance; the processes for defining the boundaries, focus and content of the report; and the extent to which the principles of materiality, inclusivity and responsiveness are adopted. The assurance statement of the Absa 2012 IR was performed by Ernst & Young and Pricewaterhousecoopers following the ISAE3000 principles. The assurance activity included interviews with the management, inspection of documentation and verification of the processes Absa has in place for determining material information. Truworths, another South-African based company, does not include any assurance information in its 2012 IR, and it states: "at this early stage of integrated reporting the Group has not sought external verification of the content of the Integrated Annual Report. We are however committed to adopting an assurance process and will initially seek assurance from the Group's Internal Audit department. Thereafter the intention is to move towards the independent verification of specific elements of the Integrated Annual Report before progressing to external assurance of the entire Report."

5.6 Materiality, Assurance and the Value of Information

This section analyses the role of assurance for IR and, more specifically, for materiality in the IR context. There are a number of issues both concerning reporting companies and assurance providers that still need to be discussed and on which academic literature may offer a significant contribution.

First of all, it is necessary to assess whether companies really need to assure their IRs. Is the market able to distinguish reliable from non-reliable information disclosed through IRs, even without an assurance statement? According to the liberal perspective, the company issuing the IR takes responsibility for the fairness and reliability of the information disclosed. If the IR was proven not to provide adequate disclosure, the firm's reputation would be damaged. Besides, the final users of the information may be able to understand whether or not to trust the company by relying on previous experience and other "observable" company characteristics, such as the effectiveness of its governance system.

On the one hand, this approach considers assurance as not necessary, but on the other, it oversees the protection of the interests of minority shareholders or of other stakeholders who have less access to information and who may give credence to companies not really worthy of trust. This is the reason both academics and practitioners give value to assurance. According to legitimacy theory (among the others, see Guthrie and Parker 1989; Wilmshurst and Frost 2000), since the worst performers on ESG would provide an IR (or SR) before a good performer, the potential expectation gap would be also greater.

The competing view, which seems to be supported by the IIRC, argues that the assurance statement does provide IRs with some additional reliability, conferring to the IR a higher level of credibility that allows users to make their decisions according to the IR. An interesting research topic would be to examine whether the assurance provides any additional value to the company and which are the determinants of such an eventual increase. The incremental value of a company with assurance, compared to the company without assurance, will probably depend on the level of its intangible assets and on the quantity of ESG information disclosed in the report.

An assurance provider would have to face some important challenges in assuring an IR, as indirectly recognized by the same IIRC [see the consultation questions proposed in the Consultation Draft IIRC (2013a, b, c)]. Such challenges may be better identified by looking at the five main differences existing between IRs and ARs, in terms of assurance. Given that IR may be considered an evolution of AR (see the Chap. 3), IR assurance should also look at the AR auditing process in order to reach a successful evolutionary pattern.

First, differently from AR, IR assurance providers cannot rely on quantitative thresholds in order to assess materiality, as has already been discussed above.

Second, the IR materiality determination process is much more subjective if compared to that of AR. Given a certain company, two different management teams may identify different materiality aspects, depending on their strategy, and different understandings of the business model, the future orientation and the relationships with stakeholders. Despite being totally different, the two approaches may both be correct because they are both consistent with the strategic approach.

Third, while AR is almost exclusively backward-oriented, one of the guiding principles of IR is the "strategic focus and future orientation", and indeed the IIRC framework requires companies to disclose future-oriented information. The same framework (see paragraph 3.6) admits that "future-oriented information is by nature more uncertain and, therefore, less precise than historical information". This is particularly true and relevant for the IR assurer, and to assure future-oriented information is unrealistic.

The fourth difference between AR and IR deals with the fact that in the IR (and SR) context, the performance targets play a much more important role. By nature, non-financial information is difficult to evaluate, if provided as "stand alone". In order to assess whether the performance of a company has been satisfactory with reference to a certain KPI, it is fundamental for the IR readers to have a target against which to compare the actual performance. In this case, the assurance should be focused on the process leading to the benchmark.

Finally, different from ARs, which rely on a "legalistic" view of the firm, IRs also need to report on the performance of companies not included in the group because of lack of legal control. According to the IIRC framework, the company should take into account, in determining the boundaries of an integrated report, "opportunities, risks and outcomes attributable to or associated with other entities/ stakeholders beyond the financial reporting entity that have a material effect on the ability of the financial reporting entity to create value over time" (IIRC 2013a, b, c, p. 33). The entities to be included in the broader boundaries are not related to the financial reporting entity by virtue of control or significant influence, but rather by the nature and proximity of the opportunities, risks and outcomes. Therefore, virtually all the entities that have some relationship with the company may be relevant and may be included into the IR. This may create some problems for the assurer, who would need to virtually examine a huge amount of information—all the information relative to the entities that have relationships with the reporting company. How can the assurer test whether the supply chain or other entities have been considered to be included in the reporting entity? This process would be costly and would need to access some information that, referring to other legal entities, may be impossible to obtain.

Two issues that should be tackled in order to obtain reliable assurance in the field of IR, with particular reference to materiality, are hereby proposed.

First, the assurance provider may implement a check of "internal consistency" between the declared materiality of specific items/issues and the relevance the management itself gives to them in its current decisions. Clearly this is not an easy task, as companies may just pretend to give importance to issues such as the environment, sustainability etc.; or they may organize the company efficiently, having excellent procedures for evaluating capitals, but not employing them to make decisions. Following this approach, the assurer may look at some observable elements that may proxy for the importance and relevance given by the management itself to the same issue. For instance, the assurer may look at the time the board of directors spent discussing a certain issue (or at the number of words related to that issue in the memorandum of the board of directors meeting). If the board of directors has devoted a proper amount of time discussing a certain issue it probably means that the issue is material. If that issue, in turn, is not disclosed in the IR, some further analysis may be required.

Second, the assurance provider may focus on the process leading to materiality assessment rather than on the outcome, which, as argued above, is to a large extent subjective. Thus, the assurer would need to check the process leading to a certain materiality assessment rather than the materiality assessment itself. For instance, according to the <IR> materiality determination process, the management needs to assess the likelihood of the occurrence of a certain event. The assurance provider may check how the management assessed the probability of the event, in terms of subjects involved in the process and methodology employed. If no process has been carried out or the process is demonstrated not to be a due process, then probably the outcome of the materiality determination process cannot be considered a reliable one.

Conclusions

This chapter aimed at providing a discussion of materiality and assurance in the context of IR. The first part of the chapter described materiality in the context of non-financial information, focusing in particular on the differences existing with financial information and on the main standards of Sustainability Report (G4 and AA1000) for its assessment. It then moves on to the IIRC and, in particular, to the discussion of the IIRC materiality determination process, which presents some challenges that will need to be tackled in the near future. One of the possible mechanisms for overcoming (at least partially) such issues is assurance, in particular where the high degree of judgement that is left to the company in identifying its material issues is concerned.

After discussing the main assurance standards (ISAE3000 and AA1000AS) now applied to SR and the position of the IIRC and GRI on assurance, some issues about materiality and assurance are discussed.

The first issue deals with the necessity for companies to actually provide an assurance to their IR. Is the market able to recognize non-reliable information? Is the possibility of damaging the company's reputation sufficient for avoiding opportunistic behaviour by managers?

The other issue deals with the difficulties an assurance provider will need to face when assuring an IR, which is a more difficult task as compared to the auditing of an AR because of some characteristics intrinsic to IR. In the context of IR, in fact, it is not possible to rely on quantitative thresholds to determine materiality; the materiality determination process is to a large extent subjective; IR also provides future-oriented information; targets of performance play a much more relevant role and it is difficult to determine the boundaries of the report.

These peculiarities require assurance providers to employ innovative procedures in order to assure IRs. There are two themes (which are at the same time possible solutions for an effective assurance) that will have to be tackled and discussed in future literature.

The first one is the "internal consistency" control, which requires analysis of the consistency between the relevance actually given by the management to a certain issue and the coverage (materiality) of that issue in the IR. The actual relevance may be measured through the observation of some elements that proxy for the importance and relevance given by the management itself to a certain issue, such as the time the board of directors spent discussing it or the inclusion of this issue in the KPIs used as performance measurement linked to compensation.

Secondly, it should be decided if the assurance provider may focus on the process leading to the materiality assessment rather than on its outcome, which is highly subjective. To this extent, some specific IR standards for assuring the process would be needed.

References

AASB (2010) Standard AASB 1031, Prepared on 23 February 2010 by the staff of the Australian Accounting Standards Board. http://www.cpaaustralia.com.au/cps/rde/xbcr/cpa-site/aasb_1031_materiality.pdf. Accessed 20 Jul 2013

AccountAbility (2006) Guidance note on the principles of materiality, completeness and responsiveness as they relate to the AA1000 assurance standard. http://www.accountability.org/images/content/1/8/189/AA1000%20Guidance%20Note%20-%20Low%20Res.pdf. Accessed 20 Jul 2013

AccountAbility (2008) AA1000 accountability principles standard 2008. http://www.accountability.org/about-us/publications/aa1000.html. Accessed 20 Jul 2013

Berthelot S, Cormier D, Magnam M (2003) Environmental disclosure research: review and synthesis. J Account Lit 22:1–44

Brammer S, Pavelin S (2004) Voluntary social disclosures by large UK companies. Bus Ethics Eur Rev 13(2/3):86–99

Deloitte (2012) Does materiality matter? Should the principle of materiality be applied more consistently to non-financial reporting? http://www.deloitte.com/assets/Dcom-UnitedStates/Local%20Assets/Documents/us_scc_materialitydebate_032712.pdf. Accessed 20 Jul 2013

Dhaliwal DS, Li OZ, Tsang A, Yang GY (2011) Voluntary nonfinancial disclosure and the cost of equity capital: the initiation of corporate social reporting. Account Rev 86(1):59–100

Eccles RG, Krzus MP, Rogers J, Serafeim G (2012) The need for sector-specific materiality and sustainability reporting standards. J Appl Corp Finance 24(2):8–14

Faux J (2012) Environmental event materiality and decision making. Manag Audit J 27(3):284–298

GRI (2013a) G4 sustainability reporting guidelines—reporting principles and standard disclosures. https://www.globalreporting.org/resourcelibrary/GRIG4-Part1-Reporting-Principles-and-Standard-Disclosures.pdf. Accessed 20 Jul 2013

GRI (2013b) G4 sustainability reporting guidelines—implementation manual. https://www.globalreporting.org/resourcelibrary/GRIG4-Part2-Implementation-Manual.pdf. Accessed 20 Jul 2013

Guthrie J, Parker LD (1989) Corporate social reporting: a rebuttal of legitimacy theory. Account Bus Res 19(76):343–352

Guthrie J, Parker LD (1990) Corporate social disclosure practice: a comparative international analysis. Adv Publ Interest Account 3:159–176

IFAC (2011) Sustainability framework 2.0. http://www.ifac.org/publications-resources/ifac-sustainability-framework-20. Accessed 20 Jul 2013

IIRC (2013a) Consultation draft of the international <IR> framework. IIRC, New York. http://www.theiirc.org/consultationdraft2013. Accessed 20 Jul 2013

IIRC (2013b) Business model–background paper for < IR>. IIRC, New York. http://www.theiirc.org/wp-content/uploads/2013/03/Business_Model.pdf. Accessed 20 Jul 2013

IIRC (2013c) Materiality - background paper for <IR>. IIRC, New York. http://www.theiirc.org/wp-content/uploads/2013/03/IR-Background-Paper-Materiality.pdf. Accessed 20 Jul 2013

ISA (2009) Materiality in planning and performing audit. http://www.aicpa.org/research/standards/auditattest/downloadabledocuments/au-c-00320.pdf. Accessed 20 Jul 2013

ISAE3000 (2011) ISAE3000 (Revised), assurance engagements other than audits or reviews of historical financial information. http://www.ifac.org/sites/default/files/publications/exposure-drafts/IAASB_ISAE_3000_ED.pdf. Accessed 20 Jul 2013

Lydenberg (2012) On materiality and sustainability: the value of disclosure in the capital markets. Initiative for responsible investment hauser center for nonprofit organizations at harvard university. http://hausercenter.org/iri/wpcontent/uploads/2010/05/OnMateriality_Final.pdf. Accessed 20 Jul 2013

Messier WF, Martinov-Bennie N, Eilifsen A (2005) A review and integration of empirical research on materiality: two decades later. Audit J Pract Theory 24(2):153–187

Patten DM (2002) The relation between environmental performance and environmental disclosure: a research note. Account Organ Soc 27(8):763–773

Tuttle B, Coller M, Plumlee R (2002) The effect of misstatements on decisions of financial statement users: an experimental investigation of auditor materiality thresholds. Audit J Pract Theory. 11–27

Wilmshurst TD, Frost GR (2000) Corporate environmental reporting: a test of legitimacy theory. Account Audit Account J 13(1):10–26

Stakeholder Engagement

6

Leonardo Rinaldi

Abstract

One of the main purposes claimed for reporting is the provision of an account to a range of stakeholders regarding how managers have acted in relation to the social, environmental, economic and ethical responsibilities these managers and their corporation feel they have towards stakeholders. Engagement and dialogue initiatives, therefore, are increasingly recognised as crucial elements of this accountability process. Only through stakeholder engagement companies can develop knowledge of what stakeholders believe should be their economic, environmental, ethical and social responsibilities to discharge. This chapter addresses this important aspect of corporate life investigating the role of stakeholder engagement within the reporting process in general, and the Integrated Reporting in particular. After describing the main traits of stakeholder engagement as of the most recent development in the academic literature, this process is placed within the context of Integrated Reporting and various theoretical perspectives that have the potential to prove useful in the interpretation of stakeholder engagement and dialogue practices are introduced.

6.1 Introduction

The Integrated Reporting (IR) framework aims at stimulating innovation in disclosure mechanisms by bringing "together material information about an organization's strategy, governance, performance and prospects in a way that reflects the commercial, social and environmental context within which it operates" (IIRC 2011, p. 3). Although it does not explicitly link with existing initiatives, it is acknowledged as developing from earlier progresses and initiatives in the field of

L. Rinaldi (✉)

School of Management, Centre for Research Into Sustainability (CRIS), Royal Holloway University of London, Egham Hill, UK

e-mail: leonardo.rinaldi@rhul.ac.uk

C. Busco et al. (eds.), *Integrated Reporting*, DOI 10.1007/978-3-319-02168-3_6,   95

© Springer International Publishing Switzerland 2013

social and environmental accounting, sustainability reporting (KPMG 2012; Deloitte & Touche 2012; Ernst & Young 2012). In this regard, this new initiative has been criticised by some commentator pointing out at the focus on investor information needs and the de-emphasis of sustainability and accountability in the IIRC's recent Integrated Reporting discussion paper (IIRC 2011). For this reason, it was argued that the Integrated Reporting could be unable to achieve significant change thus preventing a real transition towards a sustainable economy with stakeholder oversight enabled by a full recognition of corporate responsibilities and accountabilities. A possible way forward to overcome this risk could be the implementation of effective stakeholder engagement schemes. As the Consultation Draft of the International IR framework maintains.

> *"An integrated report should provide insight into the quality of the organization's relationships with its key stakeholders and how and to what extent the organization understands, takes into account and responds to their legitimate needs, interests and expectations"* (IIR 2013, p. 19)

The above quotation indicates that engagement and dialogue with stakeholders are increasingly recognised as crucial elements of IR. In addressing this point the aims of the chapter are to explain:
- the important function of stakeholder engagement within the reporting process;
- the main traits of stakeholder engagement;
- various theoretical perspectives regarding the interpretation of stakeholder engagement.

But before addressing these issues, it may be helpful to outline what is meant by the term. Thomson and Bebbington (2005, p. 517) provide a helpful definition when they argue that:

> *"Stakeholder engagement describes a range of practices where organisations take a structured approach to consulting with potential stakeholders. There are a number of possible practices which achieve this aim including: Internet bulletin boards, questionnaire surveys mailed to stakeholders, phone surveys, and community based and/or open meetings designed to bring stakeholders and organisational representatives together"*.

Another outlook on the meaning and role of stakeholder engagement is given by Accountability[1] within the final exposure draft standard on stakeholder engagement in 2011 (AccountAbility 2011, p. 6):

> *"Stakeholder engagement [. . .] is the process used by an organisation to engage relevant stakeholders for a clear purpose to achieve accepted outcomes. It is now also recognised as a fundamental accountability mechanism, since it obliges an organisation to involve stakeholders in identifying, understanding and responding to sustainability issues and concerns, and to report, explain and be answerable to stakeholders for decisions, actions and performance."*

---

[1] AccountAbility is a global organisation that works with companies to help them facing the most critical challenges in corporate responsibility and sustainable development. One critical component of this practice consists in building effective approaches to stakeholder engagement (for more details regarding the AA1000 Stakeholder Engagement Standard framework, see http://www.accountability.org).

The importance of stakeholder engagement was further emphasised by the United Nation Environment Programme (UNEP) that has highlighted the need to understand engagement from multiple perspectives and reflect practitioners' views (including NGOs, labour associations and trade and industry associations). They stated that:

> *"[e]ngagement can help organisations meet tactical and strategic needs ranging from gathering information and spotting trends that may impact their activities, to improving transparency and building the trust of the individuals or groups whose support is critical to an organisation's long- term success, to sparking the innovation and organisational change needed to meet new challenges and opportunities"* (UNEP 2005, p. 13).

Their finding also seems to suggest that there is "a growing recognition of the intrinsic value of engagement and, in some cases, the practice of stakeholder engagement as an element of an organisation's routine business processes" (UNEP 2005, p. 8).

After this broad overview of the meaning stakeholder engagement, the next section will now explore the extent to which these practices are central to the reporting process.

6.2   The Function of Stakeholder Engagement

Stakeholder engagement is regarded a key element in the earlier development of IR, that of sustainability reporting (Unerman 2007; Accounting for Sustainability 2008; Hopwood et al. 2010; AccountAbility 2011). One of the main purposes claimed for sustainability reporting (SR) is the provision of an account to a range of stakeholders regarding how managers have acted in relation to the social, environmental, economic and ethical responsibilities these managers and their corporation feel they have towards stakeholders (Unerman et al. 2007). In addressing this role, sustainability reporting is a channel of communication from a corporation's managers to some of their stakeholders. However, stakeholder engagement in sustainability reporting is not limited to stakeholders being recipients of unidirectional communication from managers. To develop knowledge and understanding of what stakeholders believe should be the company's economic, environmental, ethical and social responsibilities that the sustainability reporting seeks to address managers need to engage in dialogue with stakeholders to ascertain their views and expectations regarding acceptable corporate behaviour and responsibility (Thomson and Bebbington 2005; Bebbington and Thomson 2007).

The mechanisms behind dialogue and communication are not purely linguistic in nature. In several cases the semantic content of the statement represents only the starting point for its interpretation. Question of power, legitimacy and urgency are also relevant in that symbolic statements may be appropriate to manage stakeholders (Mitchell et al. 1997). The full understanding of the matter conveyed through a specific argument requires the interlocutors to reflect upon the aims and the intents behind a specific assertion and the analysis of the process through which aims and intents takes shape.

For these reasons, stakeholder engagement has increasingly been regarded as an important part of corporate social, environmental, economic and ethical governance and accountability mechanisms (Archel et al. 2011; Deegan and Unerman 2011; O'Dwyer et al. 2011; Brown and Dillard 2013; Barone et al., forthcoming). The stated prominence of stakeholder interaction is that only consulting with potential stakeholders organizations can develop knowledge and understanding of their needs and expectations while addressing these expectations should be the aim of 'good' corporate governance and accountability (Unerman and Bennett 2004; Thomson and Bebbington 2005; Bebbington et al. 2007).

Some commentators argue that if companies are serious about engaging in effective stakeholder dialogue, they should offer their stakeholders a variety of channels both to request and obtain information about the companies' economic, environmental, ethical and social behaviour, and to provide criticism in a timely fashion (Owen et al. 2001). The role of criticism is important because not only does it allow stakeholders to express their views and expectations to the company, but it can also contribute to problematise companies' performance and challenge their practice through an evidence-based strategy (Miller and Rose 1990; Sikka 2006; Brown 2009).

Achieving these outcomes requires organisations to shift from a business centred stakeholder engagement perspective based on internally generated content towards a more independent stakeholder driven approach. In this approach interested parties can ascertain organisational performance and also contribute to a wider debate by submitting their own perspectives that can be quickly and conveniently confronted and contrasted both by the organisation and by other stakeholders.

As such, stakeholder engagement comprises a vast and heterogeneous set of activities ranging from conversations, to written exchange of ideas, and general availability to confrontation (Burchell and Cook 2008). Many accounts of stakeholder engagement focus on principles and mechanisms directed towards designing, implementing and evaluating frameworks to engage with the various constituency groups (Bebbington et al. 2007; Brown 2009; Belal and Roberts 2010) and assessing the quality of such engagement (Freedman and Jaggi 2006; Manetti 2011). Nevertheless, stakeholder engagement remains an under-theorised area (Greenwood 2007).

The next section of this chapter examines the main traits of stakeholder engagement so see how they comply with the functions discussed above.

6.3 Main Traits of Stakeholder Engagement and Dialogue

Numerous scholars have variously conceptualised and analysed the practices of stakeholder engagement. Such research has resulted in a broad range of engagement attributes being developed stretching from 'formal' (Gray et al. 1995) versus 'informal' dissemination (Agyemang et al. 2009) to the 'explicit' versus the 'silent' character of accounts (Gray 1997) and their 'shadowed' or 'unshaded' nature (Dey 2007). Other authors have also stressed the written and oral type of dialogue, either conducted 'directly' (Spence and Rinaldi, forthcoming) or 'mediated' by an online system (Sikka 2006; Rowbottom and Lymer 2009; Scott and Orlikowski 2012). Accounting practitioners have also emphasised the role of stakeholder engagement practices in effective corporate accountability and transparency (ACCA 2004; AccountAbility 2007; KPMG 2008; 2011).

Despite this, there is still no widespread agreement on how to envisage stakeholder engagement and dialogue. Dillard and Yuthas (2013) notice that the growing emphasis upon the role of dialogue comes from the recent management strategies' focus upon the identification and management of relationships with stakeholders in order to minimise reputational risks related to unsustainable practices. This need was firstly fulfilled through the provision of information about the social and environmental impact of corporate activities and progressed through forms of mutual responsibility, information-sharing, and open and interactive two-way process of stakeholder engagement.

Arenas et al. (2009) reveal the emotional aspects, perception and assumption among organisations, NGOs and other stakeholders looking at the entire network of stakeholder relationships. Since most approaches to stakeholder dialogue do not explore the broad set of these relationships, it is maintained that the role of opinions, beliefs and worldviews of stakeholders are essential to understanding the problems in the advancing of sustainability reporting because stakeholders and organisations make sense of each other, of themselves and of what constitutes an appropriate relationship through such mutual perceptions (Kwok and Sharp 2005).

Tsoi (2010) found that local and regional stakeholders in Hong Kong and China perceive corporate responsibility as fairly significant to the export orientated businesses and rank stakeholder engagement among the mechanisms able to bring about improvement in the social and environmental conditions of the firm. In a similar vein Boesso and Kumar (2009) observe that organisations possess a broader social obligation that spreads beyond the sole financial interests. A wider set of responsibilities for which they should report on and held accountable to various stakeholders. In this regard, stakeholder dialogue initiatives seem to be associated with the importance of stakeholders for the organisations and the guidelines for such dialogue aim at building, governing the relations with them. Grenwood (2007), indeed, transcends the assumption that stakeholder engagement and dialogue is always a responsible practice. He maintains that despite engagement and dialogue processes may be seen as mechanisms for consent, control cooperation, can involve employee participation and have the potential to enhance trust and fairness, the assumption that dialogue is directly linked to the responsible treatment of stakeholders is simplistic.

Having established the main traits of stakeholder engagement, we can now address its importance within sustainability management and reporting.

6.3.1 Importance of Stakeholder Engagement Within Sustainability Management and Reporting

Organisations' concerns with sustainable development have led to an interest in how companies engage and deploy stakeholder engagement initiatives. Elijido-Ten et al. (2010) analyse a consultation process initiated by a company in order to be able to construct an account of the corporate social and environmental impact. The process is aimed at obtaining a better understanding about which stakeholder seems to be most affected by the distribution, sale and consumption of the company's products and at how responsibility within the company could be allocated to alleviate those impacts. In a similar fashion Habisch et al. (2011) have empirically investigated engagement practices undertaken by firms in Germany, Italy and the U.S. Results suggest that despite the increasing attention on sustainable development favours stakeholder engagement, these initiatives seem to disregard the level of involvement and diversity of stakeholder participation. The lack of consensus around a specific definition of stakeholder dialogue, however, has led to a confusion as to the appropriate method for understanding and meeting the needs of stakeholders who are no longer confined to shareholders and employees but include a wide variety of societal groups (Kelsall 2011).

Another example is that provided by Boesso and Kumar (2009) who emphasise the role of stakeholder engagement in both "identifying and soliciting the views of all stakeholders affected by an organization's activities" (Boesso and Kumar 2009, p. 163). Given the diverse range of existing and prospective stakeholder's demands, it is emphasised that in practice when conflicts among interests of various stakeholder groups occur priorities among these could be established through an arbitrary managerial process rather than through a democratic effort upon a shared set of social, environmental, economic and ethical responsibilities (O'Dwyer 2003; Baker 2010).

Against this unilateral manager—stakeholder relation, Burchell and Cook (2006) argue that a kind of reciprocal engagement could pave the way towards forms of collective cognition. By focusing upon interaction organizations can react to the issues and demands rose by stakeholders rather than define for themselves stakeholders' needs and expectations. Dialogue, and with it the commitment of listening and learning from each other, may therefore have the potential to extricate intertwined economic, social and environmental concerns.

A cooperative effort aimed at empowering individuals to challenge their perspectives has the potential to move stakeholders and organizations away from the protection of subjective positions, thus leading to a greater mutual understanding of the complexity of sustainability (Moore 2005; Mitchell et al. 2012). As a result, the achievement of holistic sustainability requires the recognition and the integration of a wide range of perspectives and entails an inclusive engagement framework to facilitate change.

6.4 Theoretical Perspectives for Interpreting Stakeholder Engagement

To appreciate the centrality of stakeholder engagement it seems important to place this process within the context of IR. Several scholars have argued that the reporting process is characterised by a hierarchical staged structure where decisions taken at each stages are likely to have an effect upon the subsequent stages (Deegan and Unerman 2011). One of the key stages is represented by the identification (and prioritization) of the social, economic, environmental, ethical and social expectations of those stakeholders to whom organizations feel they have a duty of accountability to discharge.

While there might be a variety of different reasons driving organizations to engage with stakeholders to ascertain their needs and expectations, the academic literature examining these motives can be broadly divided into two perspectives which may be regarded as two opposite ends of a continuum. The first broad perspective regards engagement as the move to broaden corporate accountability to include stakeholders. Proponents of this holistic nature of engagement argue that organizations should be considered responsible for their integrated impact. The main consequence of such approach is that all stakeholders (not just those who hold more power) should be considered as equally important and their views ascertained through a long term, open and mutually respectful relationship.

The other perspective regards stakeholder engagement as a strategic tool aimed at winning or maintaining the support of those stakeholders who have the power (usually economic power) to influence organizations' goal. In this context the views and expectations of powerful stakeholders are prioritised over the others whereas the engagement is inspired almost from a purpose of reputation branding process.

Against this background, various theoretical standpoints highlights how stakeholder engagement can be interpreted as either a holistic or strategic tool. The former perspective (holistic) will be discussed using the dialogic learning framework advocated by Paulo Freire (1996) as a guide to examine the extent to which stakeholder engagement provides the possibility for dialogue and mutual learning between organizations and stakeholders. The latter perspective (strategic) will adopt Michel Foucault governmentality framework (Foucault 1991) as extended by Mitchell Dean's (2009). The analysis of stakeholder engagement initiatives through Dean's analytics of governmentality framework, it is argued, has the potential to provide useful insights into how engagement can be regarded as a strategic tool to control/govern stakeholders' perceptions of organizational actions.

The following section will adopt Paulo Freire's dialogic learning framework as further extended by Thomson and Bebbington (2005), to interpret the practical application to stakeholder engagement and dialogue.

6.4.1 Understanding Stakeholder Dialogue Through Dialogic Theoretical Framework

According to Freire (1996) dialogue is a form of learning whereby human subjects can achieve a truer sense of reality my means of communication. Only through respectful and cooperative dialogue, he argues, human subjects can be set free from oppressive subordination.

Freire considered oppressive the process that presupposes two distinct sides within the learning relationship, an active and a passive side, each of which holding specific powers and characters. The active side is thought as entirely responsible of the process, and takes the role of filling-up their counterpart with "correct" and "truthful" knowledge. As a result, the other side of the process becomes almost a listening receptacle. For Freire this kind of practice is oppressive and changes the act of knowing into an act by which subjects are transformed into objects that uncritically and obediently accept the content others impart to them (Irwin 2012).

Thomson and Bebbington (2005) maintain that while oppression often possesses a physical nature, it "may also be created and sustained via cultural factors" (p. 513). Individuals need to be liberated from the predetermined understanding of reality, in order to act free. This happens through reflection upon their conditions in order to bring about change (Freire 1996). Consequently, a true commitment to freedom that enable particular aspirations of reform—such as sustainability—to be constituted is the rejection of the mechanical concepts of knowledge as an empty vessel to be filled by virtue of a problem-posing concept of learning. Freire argues, in fact, that problem-posing concept embodies the essence of knowledge and consists in acts of reasoning rather than transfer of information.

If the process of dialogic learning has the power to create a more enlightened and sustainable society, then the development of stakeholders as human subjects requires at the same time the recognition that our understandings is socially constructed and the challenging of these understandings (Thomson and Bebbington 2005). Interpreting stakeholder engagement using the dialogic learning framework as analytical lens has the potential to offer a range of useful explanations of the ways in which organizations engage with stakeholders for their economic, environmental, ethical and social practices and provide an integrated report about these performance. Organizations that promote a holistic nature of engagement, should first allow a less objective and verifiable representations of problems raised and discussed within the process. This has the potential help stakeholders change their perspectives, expand meanings and understanding, or even identify common purposes and intersecting interests. In other words, multiplicity of interpretations though dialogue allow confrontation and problematization of organizations and stakeholder views, thus creating the premises for a consensus among potentially mutually exclusive needs and expectations. For example, the acknowledgment that sustainability is a complex issue and the presence of independent discussant that introduce of a range of different perspectives at meetings with stakeholders can create the conditions for stakeholders to take up critical consciousness.

Second, a stakeholder engagement aimed at expanding corporate accountability towards stakeholders should provide (potentially) unlimited possibilities for discussions with organizations and the provision of feedback from stakeholders in light of an increased inclusion and openness to confrontation. For example the adoption of on-line technology such as video and audio streaming, social network and other form of bidirectional communication media for the process, would move in this direction (Gallhofer et al. 2006).

Third, in a holistic engagement process companies should promote an active and reflective participation in the direction of stakeholders to the organisation. If companies are serious about promoting mutual learning—that is learning from stakeholders while at the same time allowing stakeholders to learn from them—they should move away from a limited the scope or content of engagement. For example, removing any limitation to the set of stakeholders that are considered legitimated to take part to the process.

Fourth, and related, a more participative process where potentially everyone is entitled to engage diminishes the power differential between organizations and stakeholders (see also, Unerman and Bennett 2004).

As a result, Freire's conceptualization of a dialogic process is the determination that it involves respect and cooperation (or partnership), in the sense that dialogue should not implicate one subject acting on others, but rather "subjects working with each other" (Freire 1996, p. 56).

6.4.2 Understanding Stakeholder Dialogue Through Governmentality Theoretical Framework

The other theoretical perspective that can be useful to interpret stakeholder engagement practices is that of governmentality, introduced by Michel Foucault in his lectures at Collège de France in 1977 and 1978 (2007) and further developed by various scholars in areas such as sociology and accounting (Miller and O'Leary 1987; Miller and Rose 1990, 2008; Dean 2009). Mitchell Dean (2009) adopted some of the notions proposed by Foucault and developed a theoretical framework known as the "analytics of government". In the following, Dean's framework will be explored as a conceptual perspective for understanding the engagement exercises between stakeholders and organisations as a form of governance, also providing empirical examples from the academic literature.

The analytics of government investigates the distinct conditions whereby a program of stakeholder engagement originates, is maintained and changes through a set of "regimes of practices" put in place by organizations. A regime of practice could be described as the assemblage of mechanisms that contribute to make ideas and beliefs applicable in particular times and places. As such, organisations tend to possess many regimes of practices. They comprise and often connect collegiate (e.g. committees, representatives, groups, categories) individual (e.g. customers, employees, managers, suppliers, shareholders) and institutional agents, so that we often attribute to them the traits of a system (e.g. reporting system, control system, information system, etc.). Regimes of practices are triggered and shaped by a variety of forms of knowledge (e.g. chemistry, medicine, geography, psychology, sociology, auditing, accounting etc.) and contribute to describe the object of such regime. Dean's framework allows the investigation of these practices along four entwined but still reasonably independent dimensions: *field of visibility*, *techne of government*, *episteme of government* and *identity formation analytic*.

The first dimension of the analytics of government is known as *field of visibility*. It consists of the peculiar characteristics and means by which a specific system of governance seeks to illuminate some object and obscure others. Management flow chart, tables, and KPIs are examples of items that are meant to define object and subject of governance. They show how individuals are connected relate to one another within the organizational space (Dean 2009). For example, performance indicators concerning stakeholder engagement initiatives can be used as a means to render visible what companies see as important for the achievement of their ends and therefore as a technology of governance influencing stakeholders' perceptions (Boesso and Kumar 2009). Another example of this conduct is also embodied into the "CSR identity" organisations build and follow. Bolton et al. (2011) argue that an instrumental approach to understanding stakeholders, that define who might be classified as such, has the potential to neglect of some agents as stakeholders. As consequence, the concealed stakeholders cannot have their voice heard in the engagement process and, consequently, cannot be accounted for within the integrated reporting process. Overall, this dimension of the framework seeks to expose the means by which some aspects are made visible and other are concealed, thus unveiling how organisations' power allows control and prioritisation of the aspects that significant to them within the engagement process.

The second dimension, the *techne* of government, is interpreted as specific ways of acting adopted by the organization that rely on specific mechanisms such as accounting, systems of training and professional specialisms. The technologies of government practiced by companies can be related to various ends, including education, regulation, control and normalization (Russell and Thomson 2009).

The educational rationale of government, for instance, is aimed at spreading the corporate views and leading stakeholders to echo them uncritically. In this regard, Tsoi (2010) demonstrated that organizations link the effectiveness of dialogue to a kind of educational practice and occurs when it is time to specify what 'sustainability' entails. According to Tsoi, organizations seeks to establish a common language between them and stakeholder during the engagement process (arguably that of corporations'). This educational role attributed to stakeholder engagement is likely to have a big influence upon stakeholders' perceptions of social and environmental impacts, up to the point of transforming their overall identity as stakeholders of the firm. Other governing technologies employed by organisations consist of forms of internal auditing against self-imposed specifications. A notable example of this dimension of government is represented by the Self-Diagnostic checklist that Adams and McNicholas (2007) have found in their research. The completion of the checklist represented the first step of the organization towards sustainability reporting and played the role of establishing an order between compliant and non compliant stakeholder thus creating the premises for their prioritization. Additionally, it also rendered some areas within the engagement initiatives visible (allegedly arbitrarily selected) thus governable. Overall this dimension explores how the companies connect the constituted visibilities to the practices of engagement.

The third dimension of the framework, the *episteme* of government, is understood as a specific form of thinking that relies on specific expertise, vocabularies and procedures. For instance, some commentator (Baker 2010; O'Dwyer 2003) have observed forms of engagement relying on economic cost-benefit analyses aimed at winning or retaining support of those stakeholders who have power to influence the achievement of an organisations' goal. In a similar vein, the development and reporting of KPIs to measure the effectiveness of stakeholder engagement practices (Boesso and Kumar 2009) may portray engagement as a measurable activity, thus suggesting that particular goals could be established and, subsequently, its advancements against a certain level of performance could be measured.

The *identity* is the final dimension of the framework. It examines how stakeholders assume their role during the engagement and the characters associated with it within the integrated reporting process. For instance, the process itself of engaging with stakeholders, requires identifying them, assign them a label and an implicit or sometimes explicit role to play within the process (not necessarily that stakeholders may see themselves with).

In this regard, Arenas et al. (2009) while examining the new forms of business-NGOs noticed the use of 'breadth of focus' and 'coordination' as criteria to formulate the identity of NGOS and divide them into populations on the basis of those possessing certain characteristics and those without. By marking the dissimilarities between the two groups, an ideal-type identity for NGOs is crated and contrasted against an arguably less appealing type. Similarly, the process of identity formation can also be seen in combination with the commercial perspective of organisations. Bui (2010), for example, maintained that notwithstanding the looseness of the concept of Corporate Social Responsibility to consumers they are often organised as 'ethical', although tags such as 'green', and 'responsible' are also quite common association to stakeholders and business practices (Russell and Thomson 2009).

The examination of the field of visibility, techne, episteme and identity formation analytics of governance within stakeholder engagement has the potential to reveal the transformation of the role of such regime of practice. The combination of the four dimensions of the analytics of government, therefore, may contribute to increase knowledge and understanding of the governing role of stakeholder engagement within the integrated reporting process.

Summary and Conclusions

This chapter has investigated a range of matters related to stakeholder engagement and its importance for the integrated reporting process. It has outlined the notion of engagement by clarifying its function, the underlying mechanisms and key characters. It further discussed of the nature of engagement within sustainability management and reporting processes and provided a review of some of the latest research by examining the main traits of stakeholder engagement practices to see how they comply with the functions discussed above. It discussed the problem of interpreting stakeholder engagement by looking at the motives for engaging with stakeholders. In this regard, the chapter has explored two perspectives, which may be regarded as two opposite ends of a continuum: holistic motivation and strategic motivation for engaging with stakeholders.

If "corporate reporting needs to evolve to provide a concise communication about how an organization's strategy, governance, performance and prospects n the context of its external environment, lead to the creation of value over the short, medium and long term" (IIRC 2013) then engagement initiatives that remove the obstacles to open and cooperative dialogue between organizations and stakeholders needs to be conceived and implemented. Else, corporate reporting may continue to be criticised for concealing economically driven goals.

References

ACCA (2004) UK awards for sustainability reporting 2004. The Association of Chartered Certified Accountants, London

AccountAbility (2007) Development as accountability. Accountability innovators in action. London. http://www.accountability.org. Accessed 23 Jun 2013

AccountAbility (2011) Stakeholder engagement standard–exposure draft. London. http://www. accountability.org. Accessed 10 Jan 2013

Accounting for Sustainability (2008) Connected reporting in practice. A consolidated case study. http://www.suatainabilityatwork.org.uk

Adams CA, McNicholas P (2007) Making a difference: sustainability reporting, accountability and organisational change. Account Audit Account J 20:382–402

Agyemang G, Awumbila M, O'Dwyer B (2009) A critical reflection on the use of focus groups as a research method: lessons from trying to hear the voices of NGO beneficiaries in Ghana. Soc Environ Account J 29:4–16

Archel P, Husillos J, Spence C (2011) The institutionalisation of unaccountability: loading the dice of corporate social responsibility discourse. Account Organ Soc 36:327–343

Arenas D, Lozano JM, Albareda L (2009) The role of NGOs in CSR: mutual perceptions among stakeholders. J Bus Ethics 88:175–197

Baker M (2010) Re-conceiving managerial capture. Account Audit Account J 23:847–867

Barone E, Ranamagar N, Solomon JF (2013) A Habermasian model of stakeholder (non)engagement and corporate (ir)responsibility reporting. Accounting Forum 37(3):163–181

Bebbington J, Thomson I (2007) Social and environmental accounting, auditing, and reporting: a potential source of organisational risk governance? Environ Plann C Govern Pol 25:38–55

Bebbington J, Brown J, Frame B, Thomson I (2007) Theorizing engagement: the potential of a critical dialogic approach. Account Audit Account J 20:356–381

Belal AR, Roberts RW (2010) Stakeholders' perceptions of corporate social reporting in Bangladesh. J Bus Ethics 97:311–324

Bolton SC, Kim RC, O'Gorman KD (2011) Corporate social responsibility as a dynamic internal organizational process: a case study. J Bus Ethics 101(1):64–74

Boesso G, Kumar K (2009) Stakeholder prioritization and reporting: evidence from Italy and the US. Account Forum 33:162–175

Brown J (2009) Democracy, sustainability and dialogic accounting technologies: taking pluralism seriously. Crit Perspect Account 20:313–342

Brown J, Dillard J (2013) Critical accounting and communicative action: on the limits of consensual deliberation. Crit Perspect Account 24:176–190

Bui TLH (2010) The Vietnamese consumer perception on corporate social responsibility. J Int Bus Res 9:75–87

Burchell J, Cook J (2006) It's good to talk? Examining attitudes towards corporate social responsibility dialogue and engagement processes. Bus Ethics Eur Rev 15:154–170

Burchell J, Cook J (2008) Stakeholder dialogue and organisational learning: changing relationships between companies and NGOs. Bus Ethics Eur Rev 17:35–46

Dean M (2009) Governmentality: power and rule in modern society. Sage, London

Deegan C, Unerman J (2011) Financial accounting theory. Second European edition. McGraw-Hill, Maidenhead

Dey C (2007) Social accounting at Traidcraft plc: a struggle for the meaning of fair trade. Account Audit Account J 20:423–445

Dillard J, Yuthas K (2013) Critical dialogics, agonistic pluralism, and accounting information systems. Int J Account Inf Syst 14:113–119

Elijido-Ten E, Kloot L, Clarkson P (2010) Extending the application of stakeholder influence strategies to environmental disclosures: an exploratory study from a developing country. Account Audit Account J 23:1032–1059

Foucault M (1991) Governmentality. In: Foucault M, Burchell G, Gordon C, Miller P (eds) The foucault effect: studies in governmentality with two lectures by and an interview with Michel Foucault. University of Chicago Press, Chicago, IL

Foucault M, Senellart M, Ewald F, Fontana A (2007) Security, territory, population: lectures at the College de France, 1977–78. Palgrave Macmillan, Basingstoke

Freedman M, Jaggi B (eds) (2006) Environmental accounting: commitment or propaganda. JAI Press, Oxford

Freire P (1996) Pedagogy of the oppressed. Continuum, New York, NY

Gallhofer S, Haslam J, Monk E, Roberts C (2006) The emancipatory potential of online reporting: the case of counter accounting. Account Audit Account J 19:681–718

Gray R (1997) The practice of silent accounting. In: Zadek S, Pruzan PM, Evans R (eds) Building corporate accountability: emerging practices in social and ethical accounting, auditing, and reporting. Earthscan, London

Gray R, Kouhy R, Lavers S (1995) Corporate social and environmental reporting a review of the literature and a longitudinal study of UK disclosure. Account Audit Account J 8:47–77

Greenwood M (2007) Stakeholder engagement: beyond the myth of corporate responsibility. J Bus Ethics 74:315–327

Habisch A, Patelli L, Pedrini M, Schwartz C (2011) Different talks with different folks: a comparative survey of stakeholder dialog in Germany, Italy, and the U.S. J Bus Ethics 100:381–404

Hopwood AG, Unerman J, Fries J (eds) (2010) Accounting for sustainability. Practical insights. Earthscan, London

IIRC (2011) Towards integrated reporting. Communicating value in the 21st century. IIRC, New York. http://www.theiirc.org/wp-content/uploads/2011/09/IR-Discussion-Paper-2011_spreads.pdf. Accessed 14 Apr 2013

IIRC (2013) Consultation draft of the international < IR > framework. IIRC, New York. http://www.theiirc.org/wp-content/uploads/Consultation-Draft/Consultation-Draft-of-the-InternationalIRFramework.pdf. Accessed 14 Apr 2013

Irwin J (2012) Paulo Freire's philosophy of education origins, developments, impacts and legacies. Continuum, London

Kelsall C (2011) Analysing the sustainability discourse within the accounting community. British Accounting and Finance Association Annual Conference. Aston University, Birmingham

KPMG (2008) KPMG international survey of corporate responsibility reporting 2008. Amsterdam. http://www.kpmg.com/EU/en/Documents/KPMG_International_survey_Corporate_responsi bility_Survey_Reporting_2008.pdf. Accessed 26 Jun 2013

KPMG (2011) KPMG international survey of corporate responsibility reporting 2011. Amsterdam. http://www.kpmg.com/Global/en/IssuesAndInsights/ArticlesPublications/corporate-responsi bility/Documents/2011-survey.pdf. Accessed 23 Feb 2013

KPMG (2012) Integrated reporting. performance insight through better business reporting. http://www.kpmg.com/integratedreporting. Accessed 10 Jul 2013

Kwok WCC, Sharp D (2005) Power and international accounting standard setting: evidence from segment reporting and intangible assets projects. Account Audit Account J 18:74–99

Manetti G (2011) The quality of stakeholder engagement in sustainability reporting: empirical evidence and critical points. Corp Soc Responsib Environ Manag 18:110–122

Miller P, O'Leary T (1987) Accounting and the construction of the governable person. Account Organ Soc 12:235–265

Miller P, Rose N (1990) Governing economic life. Econ Soc 19:1–31

Miller P, Rose NS (2008) Governing the present: administering economic, social and personal life. Polity, Cambridge

Mitchell RK, Agle BR, Wood DJ (1997) Toward a theory of stakeholder identification and salience: defining the principle of who and what really counts. Acad Manage Rev 22:853–886

Mitchell M, Curtis A, Davidson P (2012) Can triple bottom line reporting become a cycle for "double loop" learning and radical change? Account Audit Account J 25:1048–1068

Moore J (2005) Is higher education ready for transformative learning? A question explored in the study of sustainability. J Transform Educ 3:76–91

Neu D, Warsame H, Pedwell K (1998) Managing public impressions: environmental disclosures in annual reports. Account Organ Soc 23:265–282

O'Dwyer B (2003) Conceptions of corporate social responsibility: the nature of managerial capture. Account Audit Account J 16:523–557

O'Dwyer B, Owen D, Unerman J (2011) Seeking legitimacy for new assurance forms: the case of assurance on sustainability reporting. Account Organ Soc 36:31–52

Owen DL, Swift T, Hunt K (2001) Questioning the role of stakeholder engagement in social and ethical accounting, auditing and reporting. Account Forum 25:264–282

Rowbottom N, Lymer A (2009) Exploring the use of online corporate sustainability information. Account Forum 33:176–186

Russell SL, Thomson I (2009) Analysing the role of sustainable development indicators in accounting for and constructing a Sustainable Scotland. Account Forum 33:225–244

Scott SV, Orlikowski WJ (2012) Reconfiguring relations of accountability: materialization of social media in the travel sector. Account Organ Soc 37:26–40

Sikka P (2006) The internet and possibilities for counter accounts: some reflections. Account Audit Account J 19:759–769

Spence LJ, Rinaldi L. Governmentality in accounting and accountability: a case study of embedding sustainability in a supply chain. Accounting, Organizations and Society. (forthcoming)

Thomson I, Bebbington J (2005) Social and environmental reporting in the UK: a pedagogic evaluation. Crit Perspect Account 16:507–533

Deloitte & Touche (2012) Integrated reporting. navigating your way to a truly integrated report. TOUCHE, D, Johannesburg. http://www.deloitte.com. Accessed 10 Jul 2013

Tsoi J (2010) Stakeholders' perceptions and future scenarios to improve corporate social responsibility in Hong Kong and Mainland China. J Bus Ethics 91:391–404

UNEP (2005) The stakeholder engagement manual. Volume 1: the guide to practitioners' perspectives on stakeholder engagement. http://www.uneptie.org. Accessed 5 Nov 2007

Unerman J (2007) Stakeholder engagement and dialogue. In: Unerman J, Bebbington J, O'Dwyer B (eds) Sustainability accounting and accountability. Routledge, London

Unerman J, Bennett M (2004) Increased stakeholder dialogue and the internet: towards greater corporate accountability or reinforcing capitalist hegemony? Account Organ Soc 29:685–707

Unerman J, Bebbington J, O'Dwyer B (eds) (2007) Sustainability accounting and accountability. Routledge, London

Ernst & Young (2012) Driving value by combining financial and non-financial information into a single, investor-grade document. http://www.ey.com. Accessed 10 Jul 2013

"Integrating" Business Model and Strategy

7

Federico Barnabè and Maria Cleofe Giorgino

Abstract

This chapter explores the potential role of Integrated Reporting in supporting the relationships between a company's strategy and the development (i.e. design and implementation) of its business model. To this aim, we draw on the relevant literature on strategy and on business models, as well as on the recent guidelines provided by the International Integrated Reporting Council framework, to suggest a three step process for linking the company's strategy to the development of the related business model. An example of such process is presented in the context of low-cost airline companies.

7.1 Introduction[1]

During the last twenty years, many academics and practitioners have focused their attention on the concept of "business model", hardly agreeing on what it really indicates (Zott et al. 2011). Despite the growing use of this concept, a clear definition has rarely been provided. Some scholars considered the concept of business model coinciding with that of strategy or the first as being a component

---

[1] Although this chapter is the result of a joint collaboration, Federico Barnabè should be considered the author of the Sects. 7.4, 7.5, and 7.6, while Maria Cleofe Giorgino should be considered the author of the Sects. 7.1, 7.2, and 7.3.

F. Barnabè (✉)
Department of Business Studies and Law, University of Siena, Siena, Italy
e-mail: barnabe@unisi.it

M.C. Giorgino
Department of Business Administration, Finance, Management and Law, University of Milano-Bicocca, Milan, Italy
e-mail: maria.giorgino@unimib.it

C. Busco et al. (eds.), *Integrated Reporting*, DOI 10.1007/978-3-319-02168-3_7,
© Springer International Publishing Switzerland 2013

of the second. Other scholars considered business model and strategy as separate although interconnected concepts.

Recently, the International Integrated Reporting Council (IIRC) defined the business model as "The organization's chosen system of inputs, business activities, outputs and outcomes that aims to create value over the short, medium and long term" (IIRC 2013a, p. 6). In so doing the IIRC suggested guidelines on how to disclose information about the company's business model into the Integrated Report (IR). By drawing on the definition of business model provided by IIRC, this chapter aims to explore the potential role of Integrated Reporting in supporting the relationships between an organization's strategy and the development (i.e. design and implementation) of its business model. To this aim, we draw on the relevant literature on strategy and on business models (analysed in Sect. 7.2), as well as on the recent guidelines provided by the International Integrated Reporting Council framework (Sect. 7.3), to suggest a three step process for linking the organization's strategy to the development of the related business model (Sect. 7.4). An exemplification of such process is presented in the context of low-cost airline companies (Sect. 7.5).

7.2   The Concept of Business Model

Several scholars have attempted to define the notion of business model, identifying different components of this notion. For instance, according to Timmers (1998, p. 2), the business model is an "architecture of the product, service and information flow, including a description of the various business actors and their roles; a description of the potential benefits for the various business actors; a description of the sources of revenues", while Tucker (2001) has defined the concept as "a description of how your company creates value for customers that in turn generated revenue and profits for your company". According to other scholars, the business model is "the heuristic logic that connects technical potential with the realisations of economic value" (Chesbrough and Rosenbloom 2002, p. 529), "the content, structure, and governance of transactions designed so as to create value through the exploitation of business opportunities" (Amit and Zott 2001, p. 511), or "an abstract representation of some aspects of an organisation's strategy; it outlines the essential details one needs to know to understand how an organisation can successfully deliver value to its customers" (Seddon and Lewis 2003, p. 246). By reading these definitions, the lack of convergence is evident, especially if we consider the different terms used for referring to the concept of business model (i.e. representation, architecture, statement, conceptual tool, description, framework, and so on).

In a similar way, several scholars have attempted to identify which the components or elements of a business model are, reaching different conclusions. In particular, taking into consideration strategy theory and Porter's framework (1985), Hedman and Kalling (2002) have identified five groups of components, i.e., (a) industry, customers and competitors, (b) product offering, (c) activities and organisation, (d) resources and competencies, (e) factor markets and suppliers. In a more comprehensive way, Chesbrough and Rosenbloom (2002) have identified six elements constituting a business model (i.e. value proposition, market segment, value chain, cost structure with profit potential, value network, and competitive strategy). Six fundamental components are also included in the scheme proposed by Morris et al. (2005) and each concerns questions underlying a business model: (1) *How does the organisation create value?*—factors related to the offering; (2) *Who does the organisation create value for?*—market factors; (3) *What is its source of competence?*—internal capability factors; (4) *How does the organisation position itself competitively?*—competitive strategy factors; (5) *How does the organisation make money?*—economic factors; (6) *What are its time, scope, and size ambitions?*—personal/investor factors. In this context, the competitive strategy is considered a component of the business model; however, other scholars disagree with this assumption, considering strategy, instead, as an external driver for business model creation and evaluation[2].

The variety of components that has been theorised for the business model can make the meaning of the concept even more confusing. To resolve the potential confusion surrounding this concept, it would be more useful to define "what a business model does" and what needs it addresses, rather than searching for "what a business model is" (Doganova and Eyquem-Renault 2009), but also on this topic there is not agreement: according to some scholars, the business model primarily provides a transparent representation of the organization's features for its relevant stakeholders (Seddon and Lewis 2003); instead, according to other scholars, the business model is mainly useful to evaluate the organization's capacity to create value through its activities (Magretta 2002; Chesbrough 2006).

Moreover, the disagreement and confusion about the concept of business model have resulted in a considerable variety of modalities adopted for its representation and disclosure, making the homogenization of these modalities necessary in order to facilitate comparisons between organisations. Furthermore, since some organisations have various business divisions or operate in multiple market segments, the disclosure of all business models may be useful in order to support the decision-making process of the various stakeholders.

Moving forward from the conceptual analysis abovementioned, this chapter explores the links between an organisation's business model and its strategy. In this regard, the concepts of "business model" and "strategy" should be considered as separate yet related concepts (Zott and Amit 2008; Teece 2010; IIRC 2013a), with some areas of overlapping[3]. In this context, we argue that the IIRC framework could provide guidelines for addressing their intertwined relationships.

---

[2] For instance, Osterwalder and Pigneur (2010) have proposed a scheme based on a set of nine components (i.e. customer segments, value propositions, distribution channels, customer relationships, revenue streams, key resources, key activities, key partners, and cost structure), arguing the necessity of "re-interpreting strategy through the lens of the Business Model Canvas". According to this other perspective, strategy is so not included in the business model, rather the former supports the assessment and management of the latter.

[3] On these topics see Ansoff (1965); Andrews (1971); Wernerfelt (1984); Porter (1985, 1996); Barney (1991); Warren (2002, 2008) and Morecroft (2007).

7.3   The Business Model in Integrated Reporting

In the search for disclosure harmonisation, IIRC provided a relevant contribution to business model reporting. In fact, the reference framework proposed by IIRC (2013a) included a clear definition of the business model and its key elements. In particular, according to this framework, "at the heart of the organisation is its business model", i.e. its "chosen system of inputs, business activities, outputs, and outcomes that aims to create value over the short, medium and long term" (IIRC 2013a, p. 6). The definition identifies four key elements for a business model, i.e. inputs, activities, outputs, and outcomes. They are strictly interconnected since, at the beginning, the organisation acquires its capitals or inputs and then converts them into outputs through business activities. The final phase of the process, related to the output placement in the market, determines outcomes that affect the initial situation, causing the regular review of the entire model. The system is then dynamic and it inevitably connects to other aspects of the organisation, such as governance, opportunities and risks, external environment, etc.

Figure 7.1 provides a graphical representation of the business model proposed by the IIRC framework, highlighting its positioning with respect to the other relevant factors.

Each key element of the business model requires a specific disclosure in order to communicate its characteristics, relationships and changes over time. Therefore, the following sections will provide a broader description of the components of the business model and a disclosure map for their representation in IR.

7.3.1   Business Model Components Within the IIRC Framework

According to IIRC, the first component of a business model coincides with inputs, i.e. the organisation's capitals that are suitable to support the achievement of its mission. Each capital is indeed a holder of value and can contribute to create other value through the activities realised by the organisation. According to the IIRC framework, an organisation has six categories of capitals, having specific interconnections among them (Fig. 7.2).

Specifically, financial and manufactured capitals lay at the core of the diagram represented above. These capitals are often seen as the organisation's only real capitals, since they are the traditional factors of production. The first category includes all funds available to the organisation. They are usually distinguished in debt and equity finance, referring to their source. The second category represents the set of equipment and tools used in the production process. These capitals are typically distinguished according to their lifetime, which usually impacts also on their accounting treatment (e.g. inventories are generally divided by plants, following different rules of valuation, taxation, etc.).

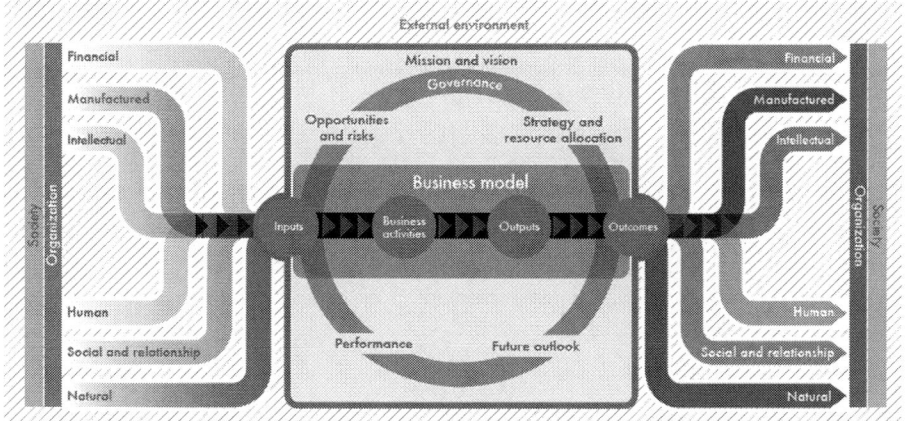

Fig. 7.1 Business model functioning and positioning (reproduced from IIRC (2013a), p. 8)

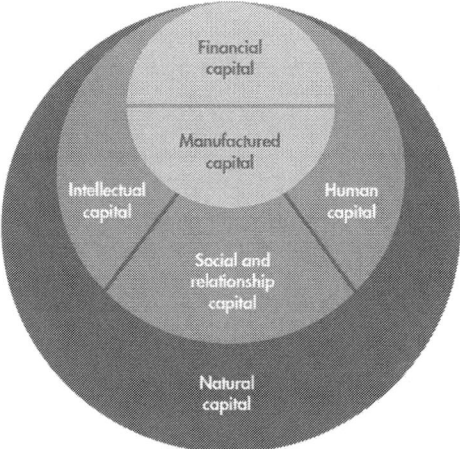

Fig. 7.2 Capitals in organisations (reproduced from IIRC (2013b), p. 3)

The intangible assets of the organisation lay "around" these first two types of capitals, being strictly interconnected with them. Intangibles are usually divided into three categories: human, intellectual, and social and relationship capitals.

The first category includes the stock of knowledge, skills, and abilities embodied in the organisation's people, including both employees and managers (Coff 2002). Human capital refers to both explicit and implicit embodied competencies, acquired through formal education and on-the-job training. Although it is often difficult to be defined, human capital certainly plays an important role in any organisation, having potentially important performance implications (Crook et al. 2011).

Intellectual capital, instead, includes other types of intangible assets that provide a competitive advantage to the organisation. Specifically, this capital usually refers to, on one hand, the value of brand and reputation developed by the organisation, and, on the other hand, its intellectual property, such as licences, patents, copyrights, and organisational systems or procedures, but this definition is not shared among scholars (Petty and Guthrie 2000).

The third category of intangible capitals refers to the organisation's ability to establish effective relationships with other economic actors (first of all, its actual and potential clients) in order to mediate economic transactions, enhancing individual and collective well-being (Granovetter 1985; Pennings et al. 1998). In this sense, social and relationship capital can be formed in different ways and includes values shared with the community, and loyalty and trust built with the various categories of stakeholders.

The last input of the business model coincides with natural capital, i.e. the stock of natural resources or environmental assets (such as air, soil, water, etc.) that contribute to the development of the organisation's activities, coming out affected, positively or negatively (Brand 2009).

Not all abovementioned capitals are owned by the organisation, but each capital is considered as an "input" since they constitute or affect the business process. Specifically, there is a continuous flow of capitals between the external environment and the organisation where such capitals are modified (i.e. increased, decreased or transformed) due to the business activities (e.g. planning, design and manufacture of products). In this way, the value of each capital is directly (such as for labour and raw materials) or indirectly (such as for infrastructure or legislation) cumulated in order to create new value for all the parties involved. In this sense, in a business model activities "can be viewed as the engagement of human, physical and/or capital resources (. . .) to serve a specific purpose toward the fulfilment of the overall objective" (Zott and Amit 2010, p. 217).

Through business activities, inputs are converted into outputs, i.e. the organisation's products or services and potentially by-products and wastes. In other words, outputs coincide with the organisation's offering defined in order to optimise and maximise the value creation (Anderson and Narus 1999). It depends on many factors such as the customer segments chosen, the available set of inputs and the process architecture designed. Generally, outputs vary over time in relation to changes in customer's needs and according to the organisation's ability to innovate and adapt its inputs and business activities.

However, outputs do not represent the final objective of the production process, since their realisation really aims at generating valuable outcomes, i.e. internal or external effects on the organisation's capitals. In principle, outcomes can be divided into two categories, i.e. techno-economic outcomes, such as product and process innovation and customer relationship profitability, and psychosocial outcomes, such as feelings of success and trust (Tikkanen and Alajoutsijärvi 2001). The first outcomes are more objective than the second ones, but both have an impact on the organisation's inputs and on the subsequent new implementation of the business model.

7.3.2 Reporting on the Business Model

In order to better understand the business model structure according to the IIRC framework, we will rely upon a general example, taking into consideration a car manufacturer. The inputs of its business model may be all the raw materials used to produce the finished goods. Example of activities would include the single operations through which the raw materials are transformed, aggregated or assembled into the manufactured goods. The outputs are represented by the cars sold on the market. The outcomes lagging behind the outputs may be divided into those that are internal within the organisation and those that are external and related to a wide range of stakeholders. In this example, the outcomes to a consumer may be the mobility, safety and comfort provided and associated with the product, whilst outcomes that have an impact reaching beyond a single consumer may include environmental impacts arising from car emissions or traffic congestion.

Each component of the business model structure requires a specific information disclosure in the integrated report in order to support the decision-making process of the organisation and provide useful elements for business development. For instance, IR might aid the understanding of how the organisation creates value for its stakeholders, what its positioning is in the market segments in which it operates and what impact its activities produce on the capitals in the short, medium and long term (IIRC 2013a).

With specific reference to the inputs, IR might provide some quantitative or qualitative/narrative indicators aimed at measuring the capitals' availability and their changes at the end of the business process. These indicators should vary according to the particular nature of the capital considered and the aspects that are useful to IR purposes. For instance, whether financial capitals require an analysis of their entity and the funding model adopted, social capitals need a description of the relationship structure adopted by the organisation and the actions programmed in order to develop connections with its stakeholders.

In reference to business activities, IR should, instead, describe all the actions implemented by the organisation, providing a comparison with the competitors' activities and valuating their effectiveness and efficiency in relation to the innovations being implemented as well.

Finally, IR should describe all the products or services provided by the organisation, constituting its outputs together with contingent by-products and waste, as well as the outcomes that arise from the process, especially in terms of the impact on the organisation's capitals.

7.4   IR for Integrating Business Model and Strategy

The business model is the core element of the organisation's strategy and it is at the basis of the decisions, plans and activities that are carried out in order to create value in the short, medium and long term. Moreover, the business model is not only the starting point for any investor's analysis, but it is also to be regarded as the key element linking an organisation's strategy, governance and performance.

Starting from these considerations, we will combine the literature on business model analysed in the previous sections with the key contents and principles of IR as addressed by IIRC. Afterwards, we will propose a three-step process which could be followed to develop, implement and use IR to support the links between an organisation's business model and its strategy.

As shown in Fig. 7.1, the business model draws from the 6 capitals (included in the IR framework) as its main inputs. These inputs are then transformed into outputs through business activities. Both business activities and outputs will generate a range of outcomes that, in turn, will eventually affect the various capitals. From what we have previously stated, it is clear that a proper and complete analysis of outputs and outcomes is particularly relevant for a correct understanding of the effectiveness of the organisation's strategy *and* business model. In this regard, IR plays a role in providing not only actual values of outputs and outcomes, but also past values and historical trends. Furthermore, such data should be assessed in comparison to market expectations, strategic objectives and/or other benchmarks (e.g. competitors' actual and past performance). This process may eventually lead to modifying (or on the contrary confirming) the organisation's business model in order to better achieve the current strategy and strategic goals, or at a higher level may even "oblige" the managers to introduce changes in reference to the strategic objectives that affect the current business model (IIRC 2013a, p. 6).

In summary, the IR framework clearly depicts an overall *integrated management* and *integrated thinking* system where the business model is to be considered as the core. However, the system extends well beyond the business model and even extends outside the organisation's borders, also embedding the organisation's mission and vision, its strategy, and the external environment, as previously shown in Fig. 7.1.

Within this system, *strategy* should define how to maximise opportunities and mitigate or manage risks, and set out long term goals and efficient plans that should be able to achieve such objectives. Shorter term allocation plans are developed and carried out in order to effectively implement the current strategy and the business model, which can be viewed as the operational toolkit system meant for pursuing this goal.

It is relevant to stress that this system is highly dynamic and not static. It is based on a continuous cycle of planning, execution, performance monitoring and assessing, review and revision of strategic goals, as well as business model and decision-making issues. Furthermore, as clearly described by IIRC (2013a, p. 9), the overall value creation process is to be considered as a cyclical and feedback-based system "in which the stock of capitals at the end of a period become the capitals available for use by the business model in the following period", as portrayed in Fig. 7.3.

All these elements have a direct or indirect influence on the organisation's strategy and on its short, medium and long-term policies and strategies since actual performance is periodically assessed against target strategic goals. Obviously, this

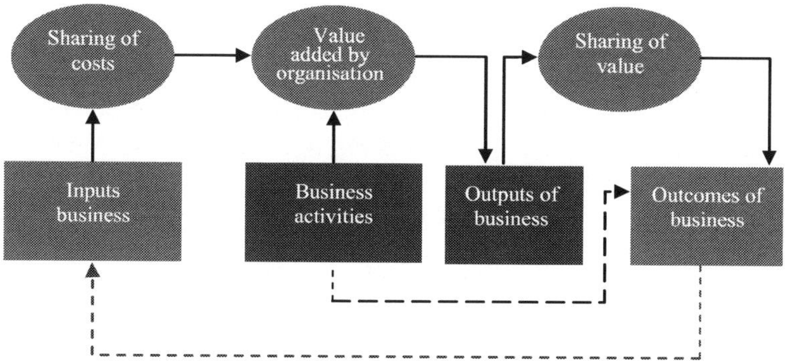

Fig. 7.3 Interaction of the business model with internal and external capitals (adapted from IIRC (2013a), p. 9)

may lead to changes in the business model (or any part of it) and/or potentially in the organisation's strategy. Moreover, gaps between actual performance and desired targets should be analysed in connection to the whole value chain rather than in exclusive reference to the organisation. This could in turn generate changes to the overall business model and the modalities in which the value chain is designed, organised and managed.

In brief, the IR framework entails to consider the various linkages between an organisation's business model and its strategy, clearly suggesting their mutual influence and the need for an integrated thinking approach to decision-making. In principle, when dealing with specific organisations, business sectors or industries, it may be consequently useful to design a multi-stage approach to IR that encompasses the following steps: (a) focus on the concepts of strategy and the business model in use; (b) identify their main components and relationships, and understand how they are linked with the external environment; (c) combine all these elements within the integrated report, receiving an information feedback in terms of performance metrics and recommendation for future changes.

These three steps entail a sequential approach to strategy development, business design, and—at a later stage—business (integrated) reporting which is in line with the suggestions given by the relevant literature on business model. In more detail, the three phase approach under analysis is suitable to support managers to develop their decisions and subsequently carry out actions, whereas the IIRC framework would provide not only the underlying logical infrastructure, but also several examples about the business model components.

7.5 IR in Action: The Example of Low Cost Carriers

Based on the considerations and information provided above and in order to clarify how IR may be operationalised, this section focuses on the airline sector; in particular, attention is placed on "low cost carriers" (LCCs). With this in mind, it is relevant to first provide a broad classification of business models within the airline sector.

The literature highlights the presence of several business models that can be adopted when operating an airline company (see Hunter 2006; Wensveen and Leick 2009; Diaconu 2012; Lohman and Koo 2013), with the following being the most common: Low Cost Carriers (LCCs—based on cost leadership and cost minimisation) and Full Service Carrier (FSC—the more traditional approach). Other business models that can be adopted include Holiday Carriers, Regional Carriers, Traditional Freight Carriers, Integrators, Hybrid Carriers, and Airlines within Airlines.

As mentioned, this section focuses on the LCC model which has recently emerged as a profitable method for operating airline companies. In particular, LCCs have emerged from the mid-1990s as powerful competitors on several different markets due to both a far-reaching process of deregulation that first affected the USA and then Europe, and also due to the overall financial crisis that has had a strong impact on customers' spending power.

In general terms, the LCC strategy is based on their capacity to focus on cost minimisation and on reaching a price leadership position within the specific markets in which they operate. To accomplish this, they usually operate a young and homogeneous fleet, fly to and from secondary airports with short and frequent flights, eliminate most of the traditional services and simplify many operational procedures (e.g. on-line booking is required and no seating reservation is provided).

Following, we will take into consideration the "typical" LCC business model in order to provide an example of how IR may be used in this specific business sector according to three steps as abovementioned.

a) *Defining the organisation's strategy and drawing its connections with the business model.*

To pursue this aim, IIRC (2013a) may provide a core set of guidelines to develop the organisation's strategy and define its connections to the business model and its various components.

Thus, the first step of the analysis requires the identification of the main elements defining the specific LCC strategy and the generation of the business model in use.

In principle, LCCs pursue the strategic goal of gaining market share through strategies of cost minimisation and price leadership (Alamdari and Fagan 2005; Hunter 2006). The LCC business model can be consequently seen as the direct consequence of this strategy; therefore, although there are some differences, LCC strategies and business models usually have common elements regarding the reduction of costs and low-priced fares.

As to the reduction in revenues, the pricing policy of LCCs is usually a very dynamic one. Very often LCCs sell discounted tickets or tickets at very low prices, thus acquiring a competitive advantage in comparison to traditional FSCs. However, the prices tend to rise to a point where they are comparable or even more expensive than a FSC ticket. To makeup for the lower revenues resulting from lower ticket prices, LCCs usually charge fees for a series of other services and place specific emphasis on ancillary revenues coming from a variety of goods and services sold to customers (e.g. food and beverages on board, priority boarding, seating reservation, extra-baggage, etc.).

As regards the minimisation of costs, LCCs are usually able to reduce expenses basing their operational policies on the following elements (Alamdari and Fagan 2005; Hunter 2006):

- standardised fleet, made of relatively new airplanes that are fuel-efficient, need lower maintenance and provide a higher seat density; relying on a homogeneous fleet also reduces staff training time and personnel costs;
- elimination of all non-essential features (e.g. reclining seats) which further allows the reduction of operating costs/activities, including cleaning the aircraft;
- use of secondary airports, which are usually smaller and less-crowded (with a consequent reduction in traffic delays, offload service and re-loading the aircraft), and which charge lower landing fees;
- simplified or reduced services, such as on-line ticket sale and on-line check-in, no seating reservations; in other words, "no frills—no additional costs";
- rapid turnaround, with frequent short flights and less time on the ground;
- employment of a multi-role staff;
- "fly point to point" scheme, i.e. no services for flight connections for passengers or baggage transfer are provided.

Even though LCCs may have different services and operational solutions, most of the elements mentioned above usually characterize their strategy and business model. However, as the number of LCCs has grown during the last 15 years, thus also increasing their competition, many companies have responded by introducing variations to their business model.

Therefore, it is relevant to understand how the external environment, the organisation's strategy and the specific business model are mutually related and influence each other in this sector.

With this in mind, it is essential to highlight at least three elements:

1) the overall air travel industry is characterized by strong competition, in which LCCs have gradually emerged as strong players alongside the FSCs;
2) the emergence of LCCs was made possible due to relevant deregulation, in different time periods and in different geographical areas. In particular, in the USA this process started in 1978 with the Airline Deregulation Act, while in Europe such deregulation began only in 1987 and was completed by the end of 1993 with the so-called "third deregulation package" (see Diaconu 2012);
3) the opportunity to serve new markets and expand on other geographical areas (e.g. Morocco destinations) is creating an additional incentive to further introduce new strategies and diversify from the original LCC business model. In particular, LCCs are increasingly expanding their services to medium-haul markets. The result of this change is the so-called "hybrid business model" (e.g. see Vidović et al. 2013), which

combines the traditional LCC cost-reduction solutions with the services and route structure of a FSC.

b) *Identifying the key components of the business model.*

As also specified by IIRC (2013a), the main components of an organisation's business model are inputs, business activities, outputs, and outcomes. Therefore, the second step of the analysis requires exploring and providing in depth examples of the single elements included in the value creation chain of the specific business model that was adopted. Focusing on LCCs, some examples are as follows.

- *Inputs*: the *capitals* (financial, manufactured, intellectual, human, social and relationship, natural) identified by the IIRC (2013a) are to be considered the key inputs to any organisation's business model. Whereas, some capitals are quite common to a variety of organisations across various industries and business sectors, more specific capitals can be identified in reference to LCCs, such as (Warren 2008):
  - Fleet. LCCs usually have a young and homogeneous fleet, based on newer and fuel-efficient medium-sized planes (e.g. Airbus 319 and 320 or Boeing 737-700/800). Moreover, these planes are usually cost efficient also in terms of maintenance and personnel costs, and are more affordable in terms of capital costs as compared to long-haul aircrafts.
  - Routes. The routes are a key element for any airline company. LCCs usually operate short flights, to and from secondary regional airports. Moreover, no interlining is accommodated, since the business model is based on a point to point scheme in order to save time, increase the number of daily flights and reduce costs.
  - Staff. LCCs very often hire employees which are assigned multiple tasks, in order to reduce costs. Employees are consequently assigned not only cabin duties, but are also required to provide assistance at gate or clean the aircraft.
  - Customers. LCCs usually aim to attract customers which are highly sensitive to pricing. Customers are also attracted by the number of routes operated by the company and, to a smaller degree, by other variables (such as brand strength). Among these customers, a substantial number will be frequent travellers with the airline.
- *Business activities* are used to transform inputs into outputs. In doing so, they are aimed at generating valuable outcomes and eventually creating short, medium and long term value. The list of business activities related to a LCC is substantially broad and includes, for instance, all the activities needed to operate flights, hire and train personnel, open new routes or introduce new services. In broad terms, other activities which could be listed in this category include quality controls, relationship management, and service provision.
- *Outputs* are mainly the key products or services that an organisation produces, but are also other by-products which create (or erode) value, and waste. When considering a LCC, examples of outputs include: routes and flights, services and by-products (usually sold as add-on products and

generating ancillary revenues), as well as wastes that result from the different stages of the production process.

- *Outcomes* can be defined as the internal and external consequences for the capitals as a result of an organisation's business activities and outputs. In principle, outcomes may be both internal (e.g. reputation and staff morale) and external (e.g. customer value and environmental impacts).

With reference to a LCC, typical outcomes may be analysed in light of financial performance results, such as operating revenues, operating margin, net income, and net income per share. Further indicators are related to the number of passengers carried during the year, such as the Passenger Load factor, Revenue Passenger Miles (RPMs), and Revenue Passengers carried.

Moreover, some outcomes are related to the organisation's staff and its management, for example, by highlighting the degree of job creation (e.g. the number of Full-time Equivalent Employees at year-end, compared to previous years). Further data aim to clarify how the organisation is creating value that is reinvested, increasing its fleet or modernising the existing aircrafts.

Considering more intangible outcomes, a LCC may be interested in understanding if (and how) its reputation, brand strength and customer satisfaction has improved during the previous year. For instance, a typical way of analysing changes in reputation and brand strength suggests reporting on accolades and awards received by the company, while customer satisfaction may be assessed by counting the number of complaints made to the organisation.

Finally, some outcomes that should be analysed include the environmental impacts generated by LCC flights and economic implications.

With reference to the first issue, it should be noted that the airline industry is among the most controlled business sectors due to its potentially high environmental impacts. Moreover, LCCs are numerically the major contributor to the significant growth in flights in the airline sector. However, at least in general terms, LCCs are characterised by relatively low CO_2 emissions per passenger kilometer index (RPK) and by fewer overall GHG emissions, by relying on young and fuel-efficient fleets (and carrying more passengers than their FSC competitors). In addition, many LCCs are actively trying to reduce their environmental impacts by developing "green procurement" policies, recycling materials, and periodically reporting on their environmental efforts and achievements.

Regarding economic impacts, the presence of LCCs in secondary regional airports is often seen as having a positive effect in those areas, by contributing to the development of the regional economy (for some examples see Vidović et al. 2013, p. 73).

Lastly, some LCCs are very active in the field of human rights, not only by complying with state laws regarding child or forced labour, but also by promoting programs aimed at increasing the awareness of suppliers and customers regarding this problematic issue.

c) *Drafting the integrated report*

In this last stage, the integrated report is drawn up and used for disclosing how the organisation has performed, and the actual performance is assessed in comparison to desired outcomes and strategic goals. Therefore, we can see that strategy and business model should be considered as "distinct disclosure elements" (IIRC 2013a, p. 5), even though they are clearly related to each other.

Consequently, eventual gaps between goals and actual values may lead to changes in the business model and/or in the organisation's strategy and strategic objectives. For instance, a specific LCC may decide to increase the number of routes, modernize its fleet, enter into new markets, introduce a new pricing policy, etc.

Finally, it is also important to note that any change decided by the organisation should take into careful consideration the relationship with the external environment and should be made with a long term, value creating perspective.

Summary and Conclusions

This chapter has explored the concept of business model as a fundamental element at the heart of any organisation. In so doing, the chapter began with a literature review highlighting some possible definitions of the business model concept, specifying that it may be influenced by the presence of regional legislation, corporate governance codes and listing requirements; moreover, we have discussed the link between an organisation's business model and its strategy.

On this basis, the chapter has adopted the definition of business model as provided by IIRC (2013a), presenting its fundamental components (inputs, business activities, outputs and outcomes) and discussing its linkages with the company's strategy and the external environment.

Consequently, the chapter has described a three-step process which could be followed to develop, implement and use IR to support the links between an organisation's strategy and its business model.

In brief, the chapter has explored the dynamic process through which IR may assist managers in the development of an *integrated decision-making system*.

References

Alamdari F, Fagan S (2005) Impact of the adherence to the original low-cost model on the profitability of low-cost airlines. Transp Rev 25(3):377–392

Amit R, Zott C (2001) Value creation in e-business. Strateg Manag J 22(6–7):493–520

Anderson JC, Narus J (1999) Business market management. Understanding, creating, and delivering value. Prentice-Hall, Englewood Cliffs, NJ

Andrews KR (1971) The concept of corporate strategy. Dow Jones Irwin, Homewood, IL

Ansoff HI (1965) Corporate strategy. McGraw-Hill, New York, NY

Barney J (1991) Firm resources and sustained competitive advantage. J Manag 17(1):99–120

Brand F (2009) Critical natural capital revisited: ecological resilience and sustainable development. Ecol Econ 68(3):605–612

Chesbrough HW (2006) Open business models how to thrive in the new innovation landscape. Harvard Business School Press, Boston, MA

Chesbrough HW, Rosenbloom RS (2002) The role of the business model in capturing value from innovation: evidence from xerox corporation's technology spin-off companies. Ind Corp Chang 11(3):529–555

Coff RW (2002) Human capital, shared expertise, and the likelihood of impasse on corporate acquisitions. J Manag 28:107–128

Crook TR, Todd SY, Combs JG, Woehr DJ, Ketchen DJ (2011) Does human capital matter? A meta-analysis of the relationship between human capital and firm performance. J Appl Psychol 96(3):443–456

Diaconu L (2012) The evolution of the European low-cost airlines' business model. Ryanair case study. Procedia Soc Behav Sci 62:342–346

Doganova L, Eyquem-Renault M (2009) What do business models do? Innovation devices in technology entrepreneurship. Res Policy 38(10):1559–1570

Granovetter MS (1985) Economic action and social structure: the problem of social embeddedness. Am J Sociol 31:481–510

Hedman J, Kalling T (2002) IT and business models: concepts and theories. Copenhagen Business School Press, Copenhagen

Hunter L (2006) Low cost airlines: business model and employment relations. Eur Manag J 24(5): 315–321

International Integrated Reporting Council (2013a) Business model. Background paper for. IIRC, New York. http://www.theiirc.org/wp-content/uploads/2013/03/Business_Model.pdf. Accessed 20 May 2013

International Integrated Reporting Council (2013b) Capitals. Background paper for < IR>. IIRC, New York. http://www.theiirc.org/wp-content/uploads/2013/03/IR-Background-Paper-Capitals.pdf. Accessed 20 May 2013

Lohman G, Koo TTR (2013) The airline business model spectrum. J Air Transp Manag 31:7–9

Magretta J (2002) Why business models matter. Harv Bus Rev 80(5):86–92

Morecroft JDW (2007) Strategic modelling and business dynamics. Wiley, Chichester

Morris M, Schindehutte M, Allen J (2005) The entrepreneur's business model: toward a unified perspective. J Bus Res 58(6):726–735

Osterwalder A, Pigneur Y (2010) Business model generation: a handbook for visionaries, game changers, and challengers. Wiley, Hoboken, NJ

Pennings JM, Lee K, van Witteloostuijn A (1998) Human capital, social capital, and firm dissolution. Acad Manag J 41(4):425–440

Petty R, Guthrie J (2000) Intellectual capital literature review. Measurement, reporting and management. J Intellect Cap 1(2):155–176

Porter M (1985) Competitive advantage. Free, New York, NY

Porter ME (1996) What is strategy? Harv Bus Rev Nov–Dec:61–78

Seddon P, Lewis G (2003) Strategy and business models: what is the difference? In: Hanisch J et al (eds) Proceedings of 7th Pacific Asia Conference on Information Systems, Adelaide, South Australia, pp. 236–248

Teece DJ (2010) Business models, business strategy and innovation. Long Range Plann 43(2–3): 172–194

Tikkanen H, Alajoutsijärvi K (2001) Competence strategies of growth firms. MET Publishing, Helsinki

Timmers P (1998) Business models for electronic markets. Electron Mark 8(2):3–8

Tucker R (2001) Strategy innovation takes imagination. J Bus Strateg 22(3):23–27

Vidović A, Stimac I, Vince D (2013) Development of business models of low-cost airlines. Int J Traffic Transport Eng 3(1):69–81

Warren K (2002) Competitive strategy dynamics. Wiley, Chichester

Warren K (2008) Strategic management dynamics. Wiley, Chichester

Wensveen JG, Leick R (2009) The long-haul low-cost carrier: a unique business model. J Air Transp Manag 15:127–133

Wernerfelt B (1984) A resource-based view of the firm. Strateg Manag J 5(2):171–180

Zott C, Amit R (2008) The fit between product market strategy and business model: implications for firm performance. Strateg Manag J 29(1):1–26

Zott C, Amit R (2010) Business model design: an activity system perspective. Long Range Plann 43:216–226

Zott C, Amit R, Massa L (2011) The business model: recent developments and future research. J Manag 37(4):1019–1042

Performance Measurement and Capitals

8

Monica Bartolini, Fabio Santini, and Riccardo Silvi

Abstract

This chapter focuses on the most important characteristics that Key Performance Indicators (KPIs) should have in order to reinforce their informative effectiveness in stakeholders' decision processes. To this aim, we discuss the role that KPIs can potentially play within Integrated Reporting (IR)—i.e. measuring the ability of the company to create value, by increasing or transforming its tangible and intangible capital. Moreover, given the lack of a generally accepted model for measuring and communicating the integrated performance of a company, this chapter introduces a theoretical framework in accordance with IR guidelines and principles. It provides an innovative perspective that contributes to integrate internal- and external-oriented performance measurement systems.

8.1 Introduction

Integrated Reporting (IR) provides an effective and concise description of the ability of a company to create sustainable value and combines information about governance, strategy, risk, operations, financial and non-financial performance. Environmental, social, and governance issues are increasingly recognized as being responsible for filling the gap between the accounting and market value of firms. It is widely recognized that the firm's value creation depends on the ability to manage a diversified set of capitals (financial, manufactured, human, intellectual, natural, social). Non-financial data disclosed in annual reporting on a voluntary

M. Bartolini (✉) • R. Silvi
Department of Management Sciences, University of Bologna, Bologna, Italy
e-mail: monica.bartolini4@unibo.it; riccardo.silvi@unibo.it

F. Santini
Department of Accounting, Business and Law, University of Perugia, Perugia, Italy
e-mail: fabio.santini@unipg.it

C. Busco et al. (eds.), *Integrated Reporting*, DOI 10.1007/978-3-319-02168-3_8,
© Springer International Publishing Switzerland 2013

basis is usually perceived as being not reliable, not comparable and, therefore, unable to affect investors decisions.

Despite some companies are developing innovative approaches to strengthen accountability for these different capital configurations, stakeholders are demanding more objective and unambiguous data. Therefore, the use of non-financial performance measures can establish trust in the communication towards stakeholders, making the non-financial information more robust. While managers are already using Key Performance Indicators (KPIs) in their decision-making processes, analysts and investors could also make greater use of them in the future.

This chapter describes the role in performance management and measurement systems of a variety of capitals, as defined in the Consultation Draft of the International <IR> Framework (CD, IIRC 2013a, pp. 12–13) and exhibited in the Capitals Background Paper for <IR> (IIRC 2013b). After discussing the role that KPIs can potentially play in IR—measuring the ability of the company to create sustainable value, by increasing or transforming its tangible and intangible capital -, this chapter focuses on the most important characteristics that KPIs should have to be useful for stakeholders' decision making.

Afterwards, given the lack of generally accepted models for performance measurement within IR, the chapter provides a framework for an Integrated Performance Measurement System coherent with IR purposes. The framework is structured on four different value creation dimensions (competitors and best practice, the entire value chain, innovation and knowledge, internal processes), that should be measured through the adoption of specific KPIs and disclosed in IR to offer a complete overview of the company's ability to create value. Each dimension is observed through a triple perspective: economic, environmental, and social. Examples of KPIs are provided, taking into account the GRI's framework in the Sustainability Reporting Guidelines G4 (2012).

8.2   The Role of Capitals in Performance Reporting

The CD of the IIRC is based on the understanding that "value is not created by or within an organization alone, but is: (i) influenced by the external environment (including economic conditions, technological change, societal issues and environmental challenges), which creates the context within which the organization operates; (ii) created through relationships with others (including employees, customers, suppliers, business partners, and local communities); (iii) dependent on the availability, affordability, quality and management of various resources" (CD, section 2.1).

In accordance with traditional models of business strategy, the innovative scope of this notion involves the review of the concepts of "resources" and "value".

The reference to resources is not limited to those that can currently be employed, but extends to potential factors that may affect the company's ability to generate future income. Current and potential resources are expressed in the concept of "capitals", which may take the following forms:

- *financial* (the funds available to an organization);
- *manufactured* (manufactured physical objects—as distinct from natural physical objects—that are available to an organization for use in the production of goods or the provision of services);
- *intellectual* (organizational, knowledge-based intangibles);
- *human* (competencies, capabilities and experience, and the motivation to innovate);
- *social and relationship*s (institutions and relationships within and between communities, groups of stakeholders and other networks, and the ability to share information to enhance individual and collective well-being);
- *natural* (all renewable and non-renewable environmental resources and processes that provide goods or services that support the past, current or future prosperity of an organization).

Organizations employ the capitals "in one form or another as inputs and, through its business activities, converts them to outputs (products, services, by-products and waste). The organization's activities and its outputs lead to outcomes in terms of effects on the capitals" (CD, Section 2.9). In this fashion, they are "increased, decreased or transformed through the activities and outputs of the organization in that they are enhanced, consumed, modified, destroyed or otherwise affected by those activities and outputs".

The concept of "Capitals" is also related to the idea of "Value", which is interpreted by the CD not only with regard to the functions of financial variables (variations in financial capital), but also as a "measure of the positive and negative effects generated across all of these capitals". This implies a relevant change in business performance measurement, and shifts the perspective of analysis from the short to medium-long term.

It should be noted that the consideration of fluctuations in the value of capitals does not alter the primary firm's purpose of maximizing the present value of future income (or market value), to which all firms should aim (Jensen 2002), but rather represents a logical precondition to ensure the continued focus of management on the creation of sustainable development conditions for the business. The company's ability to achieve this aim can be verified by demonstrating the relationship that exists between financial and non-financial results, the role of different capitals in the company's value creation process, and the manner in which the business intends to generate and exploit emerging opportunities.

The decision to shift the focus to the role played by the different capitals that benefit the company has significant consequences.

Although one might assume that each form of capital corresponds with one or more stakeholders, with a consequent lack of distinction between the two categories, it should be made clear that there are significant differences between them.

To illustrate this assertion, one can take the example of the difference that exists between employees (stakeholder) and human capital (capital). On the one hand, employees represent the current workers, with associated characteristics and company expectations; on the other hand, human capital can be conceived as composed not only of employees. The latter regards all people who gravitate towards the company's field of activity, and who may eventually enter into working relations in the future. In this sense, initiatives such as training the current workforce, and the provision of funding to local high schools, with the aim of developing certain vocational skills, may have similar effects in terms of their impact on human capital value. Both are capable of affecting the ability to generate future income, but only training activities concern current employees. If the ultimate goal of IR is to illustrate the extent to which the organization achieves its strategic objectives, and outlines business performance, any detail which affects human capital value is relevant.

In brief, the two categories of stakeholders and capitals must be treated separately even though they are interlinked as "some of the capitals belong to the organization, while others belong to stakeholders or to society more broadly [. . .] the organization and society therefore share both the cost of the capitals used as inputs and the value created by the organization" (CD, section 2.9).

The conceptual distinction between stakeholders and capitals also makes it difficult to ignore the effects that business activity has on the local community and environment, which is often overlooked when the attention is focused on the relationship between the organization and social partners. Because of the lack of trade-off between business success and benefits created for society, which in turn "create economic costs in the firm's value chain" (Porter and Kramer 2011, p. 68), the performance measurement based on changes in the value of financial and non financial capitals leads management towards the path of social responsibility.

Porter and Kramer (2011, p. 66), also affirmed that "a business needs a success-ful community, not only to create demand for its products but also to provide critical public assets and a supportive environment". In their paper titled "Creating shared value", the two authors completely overturn the traditional idea that running a business in itself creates sufficient social benefits due to the fact that companies generate employment, investment and taxes (Friedman 1970).

As a means towards achieving a long-term competitive advantage, a firm should be committed to creating shared value through "policies and operating practices that enhance the competitiveness [. . .] while simultaneously advancing the economic and social conditions in the communities in which it operates". In this sense, "Profits involving a social purpose represent a higher form of capitalism—one that will enable society to advance more rapidly while allowing companies to grow even more. The result is a positive cycle of company and community prosperity, which leads to profits that endure" (Porter and Kramer 2011, p. 75).

One example presented by the authors is that of Nespresso (a business division of Nestle), which between 2000 and 2011 recorded an annual increase in turnover of 30 %. This success, while also the result of improved reliability and quality in the supply of coffee, has been achieved by working closely with suppliers—mostly small business owners in extremely poor rural areas of Africa and Latin America—giving them advice on cultivation practices, guaranteeing bank loans, helping to ensure the necessary production factors, and encouraging supply of the highest quality. This has led to an increase in producers' income and an improvement in the lifestyle of rural communities.

This policy, as well as affecting the current expectations of stakeholders (suppliers), has produced many other effects: it has guaranteed optimal supply conditions for the future, stimulated non-agricultural players to engage in similar activities, strengthened awareness of the Nespresso brand among a population which has seen an increase in their purchasing power, and improved business expertise through the development of new initiatives and interaction with local communities. The effects generated do not only apply to direct stakeholders, but also offer significant benefits for manufactured, intellectual, social and relationship capitals. It is for this reason that the authors state that this managerial philosophy "is not philanthropy but self-interested behaviour to create economic value by creating societal value" (Porter and Kramer 2011, p. 77).

While the CD proposes a range of reporting options, it can be envisioned that two possible approaches to the role of capitals may be favoured in practice:

• *a focus on internal stakeholders*. In this case the capitals would be exclusively directed to represent the qualitative characteristics of current company stakeholders (in the case of Nespresso the emphasis would be on the increased professionalism of suppliers and compliance with related income expectations);
• *a distinction between stakeholders and capital*. The value created would be considered in terms of increased current and potential resources that might be employed in the short and medium-long term in order to maximize future income.

The latter is evidently more appropriate, and corresponds with the IIRC's framework guidelines, although it also tends to amplify the already significant issues of representation and measurement of created value. The following section explores the role of performance measurement in IR.

8.3 The Role of Performance Measurement in Integrated Reporting

Investors and other stakeholders need to understand how an organization creates and sustains value over time. The description of a company business model explains how resources (capitals) are used and which activities add value, increasing and transforming those capitals. It also provides insight into risks and opportunities arising from external capitals and factors, such as economic conditions, social and environmental issues, competitive forces and technological factors.

IR has the stated objective of providing an effective and concise description of the company's ability to create current and future sustainable value, by presenting information normally reported in several separated documents as a coherent whole. Separate and disconnected strands increase the complexity of information and fail to highlighting critical interdependencies between strategic issues—for example, governance, strategy, risk, operations, financial and non-financial performance, value creation along the value chain, etc.

It is widely recognized that a diversified set of tangible and intangible resources creates value in the short as well as in the medium and long term. For this reason, IR should report both financial results and accounting for the social and environmental effects of a company's business model, including information on reputation, market positioning, innovation, employees' skills and talents, etc. (IIRC 2012). Briefly, IR should highlight the importance of different capitals for the past and future performance of the company.

Capital market players increasingly ask for clarification of the difference between the accounting and market value of firms, emphasising the role of additional non-financial data (Anderson et al. 2005; IFAC 2008; Pozen Committee 2008). A survey by the Radley Yeldar commissioned by GRI (2012) on a sample of investors and analysts reveals that 80 % of the interviewees believe that non-financial information is very relevant or at least relevant to their investment decision-making, showing a clear preference for more comprehensive sources of financial and non-financial information. 84 % stated that it is either very important or important to make explicit links between different dimensions of performance. This empirical evidence strongly supports an integrated approach to annual reporting and, in particular, the connection of financial and non-financial results.

In addition, while Environmental, Social, and Governance (ESG) information is increasingly used by investors to develop financial valuation associated with a company, many investors perceive ESG information as being complex, not integrated, difficult to access and hard to compare. According to a survey by Radley Yeldar (2012), 61 % of a sample of analysts and investors stated that social information is difficult to compare; moreover, 41 % believe the same as regard to environmental information. Devinney (2009) argues that the link between corporate social performance and corporate financial performance is complex, affected by many contingencies. Nonetheless, from a strategic point of view, companies neglecting these dimensions underestimate risks and, at the same time, miss opportunities. As a consequence, measuring ESG factors becomes a key emerging issue. The perceived accountants' inability to measure the effect of ESG factors on financial performance is the most common barrier to enlarge their role in annual reporting. Accounting rigor in the collection, analysis, and reporting of ESG data should then encourage the incorporation of ESG factors into a company's information system, both for management and external disclosure purposes. If ESG data and analysis met the same international standards as financial data, investors would be encouraged to take these factors into bigger consideration in their decision-making. Moreover, standards on reporting environmental and social performance information would aid comparability as well. Therefore, the use of non-financial performance measures can establish trust in the communication to stakeholders of company's results, making non-financial information more robust, rather than looking like subjective and non-quantifiable assertions (PricewaterhouseCoopers 2007a). Stakeholders are demanding objective and unambiguous data about company business models, governance, risk management, etc.

In this context, KPIs can play a crucial role. Thanks to KPIs, ESG factors can be measured and monitored. While managers are already using KPIs to assess their business, analysts and investors could make greater use of them in the future. KPIs can translate ESG factors into figure and even attempt to describe their impact on financial performance. As an example, the UK framework introduces some

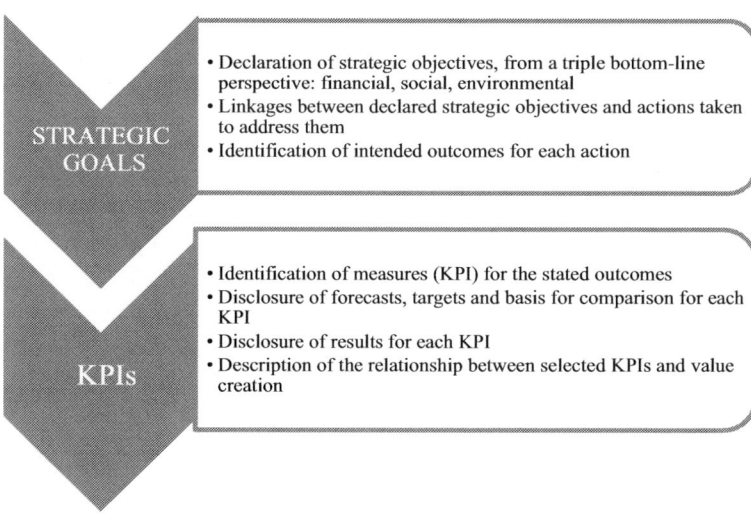

Fig. 8.1 From strategic objectives to KPIs

elements on the possible role of KPIs within Enhanced Business Reporting. Reporting standard 1 (ASB, May 2005)—concerning the Operating and Financial Reviews—states that that document should include an analysis using financial KPIs and, where appropriate, analysis using KPIs on other dimensions, with a particular focus on environmental and employee information. Trend data should also be reported to allow an assessing of the management strategic success. As stated in this document, if used correctly, KPIs can offer concise and solid data as a key complement to the narrative discussion in company annual reporting. The way KPIs are used and explained is a critical issue and greatly affects their effectiveness. In fact, if not properly *explained, contextualized* and if not *consistently* used, KPIs can even result in misleading information.

Furthermore, KPIs could enhance the comparability of the company results within the industry, if they reflected widely accepted metrics. A survey by PricewaterhouseCoopers (2007b, p. 21) reports a high demand by investors and analysts for industry-specific performance data. In particular, they call for international standards to be developed to address the comparability issue of data, in terms of calculation and presentation.

Figure 8.1 shows the process for identifying KPIs for annual reporting. The flow starts with the identification of the company's strategic objectives, taking into account both tangible and intangible aspects, financial and non-financial dimensions. Strategic objectives should be linked to the expectations of each category of stakeholders. According to the indications given by the CD's principle of stakeholder responsiveness, "an integrated report should provide insight into the quality of the organization's relationships with its key stakeholders and how and to what extent the organization understands, takes into account and responds to their legitimate needs, interests and expectations" (CD, section 3.13). Indeed, an understanding of the needs of stakeholders is crucial, not only to ensure their effective contribution, but also to correctly measure the overall business performance. Stakeholders' satisfaction (or lack of satisfaction) is reflected in the variation of capitals. The absence of understanding may lead management to believe that they have created value, when in reality it is the opposite. To avoid this, it is necessary to establish a direct dialogue with stakeholders, in order to ensure trust and engagement (Wheeler and Elkington 2001).

After their specification, strategic objectives should be linked to the actions taken to address them. The identification of intended outcome for each action allows managers to translate objectives into concrete intended results.

IR should explain how each stated outcome has been translated into measures, i.e. KPIs able to quantify the ability of the management to achieve strategic objectives. While KPIs presented in isolation from strategies and value creation processes can increase the complexity of business-reporting, a comprehensive set of values linked to the strategy and supported by a context-giving narration would constitute a useful way to enhance business model's disclosures (Buck 2002; Mouritsen and Larsen 2005).

KPIs should cover short, medium and long-term periods, including differentiated forecasts and targets. The comparison between estimated data and real data -with evidence of the degree of accuracy of management forecasts- is of great importance to stockholders. This comparison allows the transformation of the IR performance section into an extension and qualification of management earnings forecasts, which are generally considered to be essential for investment decisions in financial markets (Anilowsky et al. 2007; Ball and Shivakumar 2008), and responsible for the largest variation in quarterly stock returns (Beyer et al. 2010).

It is interesting to underline the manner in which forecasts effectively condition investment choices, due to their estimated reliability and the perceived predictive abilities of managers (Kennedy 1999). In other words, "investors respond more strongly to forecasts issued by managers with the highest prior forecasting accuracy", especially in the case of information uncertainty (Yang 2012). Indeed, correct predictions, as well as being an effective element in business success (Singh 2013), are testament to the presence of managers that are aware of business realities and future prospects, which represents a guarantee for investors. Given the difficulties investors find themselves, and non-professionals in particular, in verifying the predictive capabilities of managers, the presence of the deviation between forecasts and final results in the IR analysis (which may be limited to the principal KPIs) should cause a notable decrease in information asymmetries in the financial market. This would affect the quality and completeness of data reported, until now not considered sufficient to describe the company's value creation process (Houston et al. 2010).

In order to be useful, KPIs should have some important characteristics. Firstly, they should be included in the performance measurement systems set up for internal purposes. According to recent national and international regulations, the reporting package should clearly align information reported externally with information reported to senior management for decision purposes. This implies that large part of the information used/reported by managers to run the business and to evaluate the achievement of the company's strategy coincides with the capital providers and other stakeholders' requirements for efficient decision making.

Secondly, KPIs should be clear and understandable (CD, section 4.31). Thus, IR should provide any information that enables stakeholders to clearly understand each KPI disclosed. In particular, the following should be included for each KPI: its definition and calculation method; its purpose and the reason why it is "key"; and the source of underlying data and any assumptions.

Thirdly, KPIs should be comparable (CD, section 4.31), over time and between organizations (at least, within the same industry). So comparability should be provided at two different levels: (1) inter-firm comparability (PricewaterhouseCoopers 2007a, p. 21), (2) inter-period consistency.

As for the first level of comparability, generally-accepted indicators provided by international institutions (like GRI, for instance) could strongly support this need. Taking into consideration that KPIs tend to be industry and process-specific, the EBRC (2007, p. 4) suggested the involvement of industry-specific and market-based committees. As an example, a Gartner/EBRC AICPA's document (2010) summarizes the results of a KPIs initiative to identify and develop industry-wide standard measures that forecast corporate performance. Also standardized taxonomy—such as XBRL—if available for relevant industry KPIs, would make it easier for investors and stakeholders to compare and, thereafter, make use of KPIs in decision-making (Doni and Inghirami 2011). XBRL could also enhance accessibility of data via Internet.

Considering the second level of comparability (inter-period consistency), IR should reveal any changes and comparisons between different calculation methods over different periods, as well as the impact of changes in accounting policies. Moreover, trend and past data should also be reported (for three or more past periods) as they provide the reader with a way of assessing the success of management strategies.

After discussing results, including the reasons for successes and failures, IR should adopt a forward-looking perspective, introducing challenges to progress and plans for the delivery of strategic future objectives, in relation to targets and projections for each KPI for two or more future periods.

IR should finally offer a description of the relationship between selected KPIs and financial results, in a narrative form and preferably, when possible, in quantitative terms. As an example, this would require a quantification of the relationship between KPIs and revenues, expenditures, investments, cash flow, profitability ratios, etc. This last step would anchor results of single areas of management to the global business financial performance achieved over the period, especially if mathematical cause-effect relationships are defined. The focus on capitals of the CD suggests that IR also discloses a quantitative description, when possible, of cause-effect relationships between KPIs and the variations of the non-financial forms of capitals.

8.4   An Integrated Performance Measurement System's Framework

The ability of a company to create financial value can be measured using existing and generally-accepted standards; but few approaches have been developed to measure and report business value creation through intangible factors, like creating knowledge and increasing employees' skills, supporting public policy, respecting natural environment, reducing waste and environmental pollution, etc.

Perrini et al. (2009) aims at showing the multiple levels of analysis at which corporate social responsibility's performance consequences can be appreciated and evaluated. The analysis provides a value creation framework based on the following value drivers: organizational, customer, society, natural environment, innovation, and corporate governance. According to this model, those value drivers turn into (1) revenue-related outcomes (such as growth opportunities, competitiveness positioning, brand equity), and (2) cost-related outcomes (i.e. cost of labor, operational efficiency, cost of capital, risk management).

Ferguson (2009) explores methods for making more explicit the issues surrounding corporate responsibility and financial value and provides approaches for selecting, measuring and evaluating performance. However, they are only developed for internal purposes, to support strategies, policies and processes.

Epstein and Wisner (2001) suggest a framework based on the Balanced Scorecard to implement sustainability and to measure its effects from a multidimensional perspective.

Given the lack of a generally accepted model to coherently measure the integrated performance of a company, this section introduces a theoretical framework, that provides an innovative perspective for both scholars and practitioners. It is characterized by a comprehensive and complete view of a number of factors affecting companies' performance and leads to an integration between internal- and external-oriented Performance Measurement Systems. While companies can adopt this framework for management purposes—to assess and orient strategy and their own behaviour—investors and other stakeholders can use it to clearly read and appreciate the real quality of management and the ability of the company to create value.

Figure 8.2 highlights four different value creation dimensions (competitors and best practice, the entire value chain, innovation and knowledge, internal processes) that companies should include in their Integrated Performance Management System (IPMS) to assess their ability to create value. Each dimension can be observed and managed through a triple perspective: economic, environmental, and social (i.e. the *triple bottom-line*). Moreover, each dimension involves all the various forms of capital (human, social and relationship, natural, intellectual, manufactured, and financial) on which the organization depends.

What follows is a brief description of the benefits of measuring and reporting to stakeholders each value dimension. In general, business benefits consist of maximizing opportunities and minimizing risks.

Fig. 8.2 An integrated performance measurement system (IPMS) framework

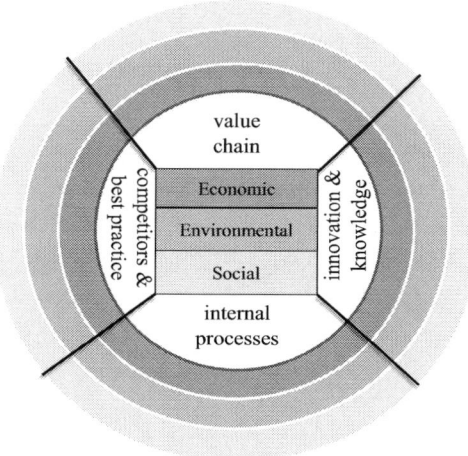

8.4.1 The Value Chain dimension

The analysis of the value chain dimension includes three sub-dimensions:
- The value chain as a whole;
- Customers;
- Suppliers.

8.4.1.1 The Value Chain as a Whole
The focus of this sub-dimension is on the value chain's economic, social and environmental performances. It helps to understand the impact on capitals of:
- How the business model works, its dynamics and key relationships;
- The distribution of the value generated among the various value chain actors, reflecting both their different level of bargaining power, and the customers' perception about the different content of value inside each activity;
- The reasons explaining companies' profitability in different stages of the value chain, characterized by specific competitive factors and levels of competition;
- Opportunities to increase collaboration between businesses within the value chain and to protect and reinforce relationships with customers and suppliers;
- Opportunities to reduce the environmental impact along the value chain (pollution due to transportations, packaging, waste of materials, energy and other resources due to inefficient processes and transaction costs, etc.);
- Opportunities to contribute to the development of organizations in specific geographical areas (districts, poor areas, developing countries, etc.) or with particular social relevance.

8.4.1.2 The Customers
In competitive markets it is essential to offer products and services that meet customer requirements from a multidimensional perspective. Therefore, the

identification of the most relevant value attributes in the eyes of the customer becomes essential. Subsequently, these can be translated, into parameters and KPIs, as leading indicators of the company's ability to create value by increasing its capitals through:

- Engaging customers;
- Providing products and services aligned with customers expectations and able to generate value for them;
- Achieving acceptable levels of customer profitability;
- Controlling the financial risk based on the possibility that customers (or segments of customers) will not fulfill their financial obligations;
- Building and protecting the corporate brand;
- Mitigating the environmental impacts of products and services and, as a consequence, providing savings and waste reduction for customers (e.g. thanks to packaging affecting transportations cost, more regulation compliant features, etc.);
- Establishing more valuable and synergistic relationships and partnerships with customers (e.g. through training activities and/or delivery of safer materials/products/services).

8.4.1.3 The Suppliers

The supply chain is a relevant driver of competitive advantage and sustainable performance. By measuring this dimension management can control and report:

- Suppliers' performance (or of groups of suppliers) in terms of defect rate and quality;
- The quality of service, in terms of timeliness of delivery, on-time delivery, etc.;
- The cost of the procurement process in terms of total cost of ownership (Ittner and Carr 1999), which, in addition to the purchase cost of inputs, also considers purchasing activities' costs (issuing of orders, receiving of goods, incoming inspections, etc.), of stocks maintenance (physical space, cost of capital, inspection, etc.) and other qualitative aspects (like waste, rework, returned goods);
- Suppliers' sustainability, in terms of their ability to produce recycled input materials, of environmental impacts of transporting goods and materials, etc.;
- The opportunities deriving from more valuable and synergistic relationships and partnerships with suppliers;
- Human rights' performance of significant suppliers and their role in the local community.

8.4.2   The Internal Processes Dimension

This IPMS's dimension pursues two main objectives. The first relates to the appraisal of the operational performance of internal processes in terms of efficiency, which affects all the various forms of capital available to the organization. As a consequence, processes' efficiency is relevant to the creation of economic value and, at the same time, strongly affects the environmental and social impacts. Thorough this section some key information can be investigated:

- Productivity of internal processes;
- Cost of operations;
- Environmental impacts of technology used, in terms of pollution, emissions, energy consumption, recycling, etc.;
- Labour practice and working conditions, absenteeism and sickness, gender balance, child labour;
- Ability to create employment, directly and indirectly;
- Compliance with regulations and voluntary codes concerning the health and safety impact of internal processes' activities, products and services during their entire life cycle.

A second aim is to appreciate the content of value of each company's activity performed along its processes. According to this goal, process activities can be classified in value adding, non-value adding or waste (McNair et al. 2013). In particular, a better understanding of waste has implications for both management and stakeholders interested in environmental issues (see Chap. 9). For example, KPIs related to this aspect could reflect:

- The cost of value, non-value and waste activities and their impact on lead time. This kind of analysis is strategic in monitoring and controlling the ability of the company to devote lacking resources to the most valuable activities;
- The cost of different typologies of waste;
- Opportunities of waste reduction;
- Opportunities of reduction of fines and litigation exposure.

8.4.3   The Innovation and Knowledge Dimension

Innovation and knowledge are fundamental values. As a consequence, IPMS should pay attention to this dimension, in order to detect useful elements for evaluating current and future competitive advantages and sustainability of the business model.

KPIs can measure the innovative potential of the company in terms of:

- New products/services developed over the reporting period and their economic, social and environmental effects;
- New technologies/processes/materials introduced in the reporting period;
- The ability of the company to protect innovation through patents and trademarks;
- Product life-cycle efficiency;
- The efficiency of the innovation process;
- The efforts towards innovation (investments, expenditures, etc.).

However this dimension also concerns knowledge management and human resource management and their impact on:

- Employees' satisfaction, productivity, and loyalty, maintaining employee motivation, retaining expertise and the best people, attracting the best skilled people, and providing staff development opportunities;
- Organizational learning;
- Organizational climate, freedom of association, redundancy support;
- Safety in the workplace, respect of human rights and equal opportunities;

- Impact on the local community (school/educational programs, employee volunteer programs, etc.).

Given the creative and non-repetitive contents of innovation and knowledge management processes, the measurement of this dimension is a real challenge, but it is also extremely important, given its strong impact on every form of firms' capitals.

8.4.4 The Competitors and Best Practice Dimension

The Competitors & Best practice dimension is intended to monitor competitors and their performance and enables comparison and benchmarking processes. Thanks to this dimension IPMS achieves inter-firm comparability as a key issue in IR. The company's performance can be better appreciated comparing to the economic, environmental and social results of specific competitors or to the entire industry-sector. This section of the IPMS highlights strengths and weaknesses investigating:
- Profitability and growth of comparable groups of competitors;
- Different cost structures, reflecting alternative process configurations, technology, customer targets, etc.;
- Alternative strategies and their social and environmental outcomes.

Furthermore, analysis about best practices within and outwith the industry highlights opportunities to emulate them and catalyzes radical and continuous improvements.

Basically, the consideration of this dimension involves the provision of comparative data for the other IPMS dimensions presented above, when data is available and, by nature, industry-driven.

8.4.5 Some Examples of KPIs Grouped for Capitals

Table 8.1 reports some examples of suggested KPIs for each dimension of the IPMS discussed in the previous section. They follow a triple bottom-line perspective (economic, environmental, social) and are mainly derived from the framework provided by the Sustainability Reporting Guidelines G4 (GRI 2012).

Single KPIs can address more than one dimension at the same time, for instance when industry or competitors' values are disclosed, filling in the Competitors & Best practice section of the IPMS.

Table 8.1 also shows how each KPI can be connected to a specific form of capital; in other words, KPIs can measure the outcome of the organization's activities in terms of effects on each capital. As stated in the Capitals background paper for IR (IIRC 2013b, section 3.5), "Quantitative indicators, such as [. . .] KPI and in some cases monetized metrics, can be very important in explaining an organization's uses of and effects on various capitals". Nonetheless, the same document points out that it would not be practicable to expect organizations to attempt to quantify all capitals, because many uses of and effects on the capitals are best -and in some cases can only be- reported on in narrative form.

Table 8.1 Examples of KPIs for each dimensions of the integrated performance measurement system (IPMS), from a triple bottom-line perspective

KPIs	Value Chain	Internal processes	Innovation & knowledge	Competitors & best practice
ECONOMIC PERSPECTIVE				
FINANCIAL CAPITAL				
Revenues by customers, market, etc.	■			
% of revenues by new products/services			■	
Market share				■
Profitability ratios	■			■
Liquidity and financial position ratios	■			■
Value adding operating costs	■	■		■
Payments to providers of capital (return on equity, EPS, etc.)	■			■
Timely payments to suppliers	■			■
New markets penetration rate	■			■
MANUFACTURED CAPITAL				
Investment in new technologies			■	
INTELLECTUAL CAPITAL				
Investment in new brands development			■	■
No. and value of new patents/copyrights			■	■
Etc.				
ENVIRONMENTAL PERSPECTIVE				
NATURAL CAPITAL				
Hazardous waste treated	■	■	■	■
No. of suppliers identified as having significant actual and potential negative environmental impacts	■			
% of new suppliers/customers that were screened using environmental criteria	■			
Total weight of waste disposed by reuse, recycling, composting, incineration, …	■	■	■	■
Waste reduction over the period	■	■	■	■
Volume of sills by categories (oil, fuel, chemicals, etc.)		■		■
Total weight of waste disposed by reuse, recycling, composting, incineration, …	■	■	■	■
Amount of significant air emissions		■	■	
FINANCIAL CAPITAL				
Total monetary value of fines for non-compliance with environmental laws and regulations	■	■		
Prevention and environmental management costs		■	■	
Etc.				

SOCIAL PERSPECTIVE

FINANCIAL CAPITAL

Cost of actions taken to manage risks or opportunities				

HUMAN CAPITAL

No. or % of new employee hires during the reporting period, by age group, gender, region, etc.				
Employee turnover rate during the reporting period				
Injury rate				
Occupational diseases rate				
No. of incidents for non-compliance with regulations				

INTELLECTUAL CAPITAL

Average hours of training by categories				

SOCIAL AND RELATIONSHIP CAPITAL

No. of ethical/legal violations				
No. of suppliers/customers subject to impact assessments for labour practices				
% of suppliers covered by ethical procurement				
Negative impacts for labour practices identified in the supply chain				
% of new suppliers/customers that were screened using human rights criteria				
No. of community complaints				
Customer satisfaction				
Etc.				

Conclusions

This chapter focuses on the role of KPIs in IR and introduces a framework for developing an IPMS giving an innovative perspective to both scholars and practitioners. The framework is characterized by a comprehensive and complete view of the different performance dimensions and, most of all, it integrates internal- and external-oriented performance measurement systems. Integration among different information systems is a major issue in management accounting studies. «Increasingly, accounting standards are requiring disclosure on the financial statements of information consistent with that internally reported to management. This is facilitating an organization's ability to align certain financial statement disclosures with internal reporting and Management Commentary provided to investors» (KPMG 2010, p. 4).

The cost of acquiring/collecting/gathering/integrating information is also a relevant aspect; this could be reduced using common accounting systems and technology. Thus, the overlap between KPIs information for annual reporting and for management accounting is an opportunity to reduce information cost, as well as to increase its effectiveness (see Chap. 9).

The opportunity to convey measures provided by management accounting systems towards annual reporting for external purposes has consequences also in terms of reliability of the data reported, which reflects the faithfulness level and the degree to which information is verifiable. This requirement is obviously considerable for external reporting; in fact, from prior research users turned out to be very concerned about the reliability of data in annual reporting, in particular with regard to information with a forward-looking orientation. The CD (section 3.31) states that "reliability is enhanced by mechanisms such as robust internal reporting systems, appropriate stakeholder engagement, and independent external assurance".

The increased attention to KPIs in annual reporting could also have positive effects on management control systems for internal purposes. In fact, in order to comply with national and international regulations, management could be forced to reinforce and improve the company's management control tools, to formalize and communicate their strategic priorities, and to produce the necessary measurement data.

Neutrality is also essential, because stakeholders need to believe that the information provided is not aimed at determining or influencing their decisions. Guidelines from external independent entities can help to address this issue.

References

Anderson A, Herring P, Pawlicki A (2005) EBR: the next step. J Account June:71–73
Anilowsky C, Feng M, Skinner DJ (2007) Does earning guidance affect market returns? The nature and information content of aggregate earnings guidance. J Account Econ 44:36–63
Ball R, Shivakumar L (2008) How much new information is there in earnings? J Account Res 46:975–1016

Beyer A, Cohen DA, Lys TZ, Walther BR (2010) The financial reporting environment: review of the literature. J Account Econ 50:296–343

Buck PN (2002) Disclosure of intellectual capital–Indicator or models? A matter of accounting or strategy, Working Paper, Aarhus School of Business

EBRC (Enhanced Business Reporting Consortium) (2007) Discussion paper for consideration by the SEC Advisory Committee on Improvements to Financial Reporting, 24 Oct 2007

Devinney TM (2009) Is the socially responsible corporation a myth? The good, the bad, and the ugly of corporate social responsibility. Acad Manag Perspect 23(2):44–56

Doni F, Inghirami IE (2011) Performance measurement models: the role of IAS / IFRS standards and XBRL language. Paper presented at the 6th Conference on performance measurement and management control, nice

Epstein MJ, Wisner P (2001) Using a balanced scorecard to implement sustainability. Environ Qual Manag 11(2):1–10

Ferguson DL (2009) Measuring business value and sustainability performance. http://www.scribd.com/doc/40230333/Measuring-Business-Value-and-Sustainability-Performance-2009. Accessed 25 Jul 2013

Friedman M (1970) The social responsibility of business is to increase its profits. The New York Time Magazine, 13 Sept 1970

Gartner–EBRC (2010) Standard key performance indicators. http://www.aicpa.org/InterestAreas/AccountingAndAuditing/Resources/EBR/Pages/GartnerEBRCKPIInitiative.aspx. Accessed 1 Jul 2011

GRI (Global Reporting Initiative) (2012) Sustainability reporting guidelines G4. http://www.globalreporting.org. Accessed 19 Jul 2013

Houston J, Lev B, Tucker JW (2010) To guide or not to guide? Causes and consequences of stopping quarterly earnings guidance. Contemp Account Res 27:143–185

IFAC (2008) Financial reporting supply chain: current perspectives and directions. International Federation of Accountants, New York, NY

IIRC (The International Integrated Reporting Council) (2012) The pilot programme 2012 yearbook, capturing the experiences of global business and investors. http://www.theiirc.org. Accessed 15 Jul 2013

IIRC (The International Integrated Reporting Council) (2013a) Consultation draft of the international <IR> framework. http://www.theiirc.org. Accessed 26 Jul 2013

IIRC (The International Integrated Reporting Council) (2013b). Capitals background paper for IR, March

Ittner CD, Carr LP (1999) Measuring the cost of ownership. J Cost Manage Fall:42–51

Jensen CJ (2002) Value maximization, stakeholder theory, and the corporate objective function. Bus Ethics Q 12:235–256

Kennedy J (1999) Discussion of the joint effect of management's prior forecasting accuracy and the form of its financial forecasts on investor judgment. J Account Res 37:125–134

KPMG (2010) Better business reporting: enhancing financial reporting, Australia

McNair-Connolly CJ, Polutnik L, Silvi R, Watts T (2013) Value creation in management accounting: using information to capture customer value. Business Experts, New York, NY

Mouritsen J, Larsen HT (2005) The 2nd wave of knowledge management: the management control of knowledge resources through intellectual capital information. Manag Account Res 16(4):371–394

Perrini F, Russo A, Tencati A, Vurro C (2009) Going beyond a long-lasting debate: what is behind the relationship between corporate social and financial performance? http://www.som.cranfield.ac.uk/som/search.aspx?s=perrini+2009. Accessed 25 Jul 2013

Porter ME, Kramer MR (2011) Creating shared value. Harv Bus Rev January–February:62–77

Pozen Committee (2008), Final report of the advisory committee on improvements to financial reporting to the United States Securities and Exchange Commission, US Securities and Exchange Commission. Washington, DC

PricewaterhouseCoopers (2007a) Guide to forward-looking information. http://www.pwc.com/gx/en/corporate-reporting/integrated-reporting/index.jhtml. Accessed 6 Sep 2011

PricewaterhouseCoopers (2007b) Corporate reporting. Is it what investment professionals expect? http://www.pwc.com/gx/en/corporate-reporting/integrated-reporting/index.jhtml. Accessed 6 Sep 2011

Radley Yeldar (2012) The value of extra financial disclosure. What investors and analysts said. http://www.globalreporting.org. Accessed 1 Oct 2012

Singh S (2013) What is the cost of your forecast error? J Bus Forecast Spring:26–28

Wheeler D, Elkington J (2001) The end of the corporate environmental report? Or the adbent of cybernetic sustainability reporting and communication. Bus Strateg Environ 10:1–14

Yang HI (2012) Capital market consequences of manager's voluntary disclosure styles. J Account Econ 53:167–184

Integrated Reporting and Value-Based Cost Management: A Natural Union

9

Carol J. McNair-Connolly, Riccardo Silvi, and Monica Bartolini

Abstract

Integrated reporting systems are the wave of the future from two points of view: for their support to management decision making processes, and as strategic information source for annual Integrated Reporting (IR). This chapter describes Value-based Cost Management (VCMS) as one tool available to the financial and marketing communities that can be used in the integration effort because it naturally joins data streams from across the organization to provide a unified picture of the firm's performance. Furthermore this chapter shows the twofold potential contribution of VCMS to IR. First, it supports the management and monitoring of the company performance with specific regard to customers and internal processes as fundamental dimensions of an integrated performance measurement system. Second, the role played by waste in VCMS is argued to support the sustainability movement and reporting.

9.1 Value-Based Cost Management

Value-based Cost Management (VCMS) is a relatively new tool that has been added to the financial toolbox for a company. Focused on looking at both revenues and costs through the lens of customer preferences, VCMS provides new insights into the way that companies spend their money meeting customer demands. It starts with a focus on final consumer preferences and works its way through the

C.J. McNair-Connolly (✉)
Honorary Principal Fellow, University of Wollongong, Wollongong, Australia
e-mail: cjconnolly126@gmail.com

R. Silvi • M. Bartolini
Department of Management Studies, School of Economics, Management and Statistics, University of Bologna, Bologna, Italy
e-mail: riccardo.silvi@unibo.it; monica.bartolini4@unibo.it

C. Busco et al. (eds.), *Integrated Reporting*, DOI 10.1007/978-3-319-02168-3_9,
© Springer International Publishing Switzerland 2013

traditional financial model to more closely align financial metrics with those used in strategy, marketing, and operations.

9.1.1 Value from the Consumer's Perspective

There are countless articles in the marketing literature about the concept of value from a customer's perspective. Moller (2006, p. 914) notes that there have been four recurring characteristics of value in recent marketing studies: (1) customer value is a subjective concept, (2) it is conceptualized as a tradeoff between benefits and sacrifices, (3) benefits and sacrifices can be multi-faceted, and (4) value perceptions are relative to competition. The author notes that these findings are based on a comprehensive review done by Ulaga and Eggert (2005, pp. 75–76).

Priem (2007, p. 219) brings the lens of value creation more tightly into the realm of consumers, noting that "consumers must be an important consideration in strategy formation, because consumers experiencing benefits are essential to company success [. . .] value creation, by offering benefits that induce payments from willing consumers, is a precondition for value capture". Value creation, then, starts with the final customer of the value chain—the consumer. In a competitive marketplace each company in the value chain is constrained by the final value placed on the chain's products and services by a willing consumer. These firms compete for the rewards of value creation by attempting to capture the most value within their chains.

The VCMS at the heart of this chapter ties to literature that emphasizes the demand side of the value creation puzzle. This is because willing consumers validate the value of products and services (Priem 2007, p. 219), not the chain of companies that supply portions of these products and services to the consumer. Starting from the recognition that the only place true revenues are earned in the marketplace is when consumers part with their own resources to obtain a good or service, the VCMS joins the league of strategic and marketing tools that put customers first in the quest for profit and as preferential stakeholder.

9.1.2 Tying Value to Revenues

How does the VCMS take the consumer-defined concept of value creation and bring it into the financial domain? It does so by redefining the revenues earned by a firm in terms of the value attributes, or key points of value creation, that the consumer identifies with and uses in their selection process. Specifically, the VCMS creates what are called revenue equivalents, which proportion revenues earned to value attributes based on how important they are to the consumer's choice decision.

An example of revenue equivalents can be seen in Table 9.1. Here we have a window manufacturer who is trying to understand exactly what aspects of a window purchase matter the most to consumers. As we see from Table 9.1, the concept of a competitive price weights very heavily in the consumers' decisions. This is not

Table 9.1 Revenue equivalents

Total sales revenue for window products: $1.5 billion		
Value attribute	Value weighting	Revenue equivalent
Competitive price	40 %	600,000,000
Weather tight	15 %	225,000,000
Color	5 %	75,000,000
Style	8 %	120,000,000
Sizes available	10 %	150,000,000
Warranty	15 %	225,000,000
Service	7 %	105,000,000
Totals	100 %	1,500,000,000

market price, per se, but rather the "table stakes" component of price—the amount of money that the consumer assigns to the basic features of the product or service (Nagle and Holden 1999).

The other six features of a window that consumers care about are differentiators—they lead to the ability of a firm to charge more for its product than the basic commodity window replacement would earn. Here we see that weather tightness and warranty both make up a large portion of the revenues earned by the firm—15 % or $225 million each. This amount directs attention in the firm to how much money it has available to spend to provide these features for its products. Revenue equivalents lay the baseline for the costing exercise.

9.1.3 Looking at Costs Through a Value Lens

Having tied the VCMS to the top line of the firm (revenues), attention now turns to the costing side of the economic puzzle. Revenue equivalents tell a firm how much it can afford to spend to deliver on a specific value attribute if it intends to make any money on the product. Clearly, costs cannot be equal to revenue or there will be no profit left in the firm. Let's say a company wants to earn a 20 % profit on its window sales. Then all of the costs for producing these windows, marketing them, and supporting them with internal activities has to be less than or equal to $1.2 billion for our window company.

This sounds reasonable, but very few companies make this magic 20 %. The why behind this problem is excess cost. Cost takes on many forms in a company, making it hard to make a clear linkage between a value attribute and a specific cost element. It is here that the VCMS makes its second major contribution to the existing cost management literature (McNair-Connolly et al. 2013). Specifically, the VCMS model splits the spending of the firm into five categories of cost (value-add; business value-add indirect, such as invoicing; business value-add future, such as R&D; business value-add administrative, such as personnel; and waste) and then ties the value-add dollars of this total to the specific value attributes.

In total terms, a company can see whether it is spending most of its money on the things consumers directly value or whether more of the funds are going to support the business itself. In study after study, only 20 % at most of the total spending of the participating firms in the McNair-Connolly et al. (2013) report was tied directly to value-added from the consumer's perspective. The rest of the spending was spread across the other four dimensions of cost in a wide range of ways. More successful firms tended to concentrate on business value-add indirect (activities that impact consumers indirectly) and business value-add future (activities that build future competencies).

This brief overview of the VCMS approach will hopefully provide the baseline understanding to now look at how this model integrates with the rest of the firm's information datasets to form an integrated reporting system. For a much more detailed discussion of the model, the reader is referred to McNair-Connolly et al. (2013). It is to these integration issues that we now turn our attention.

9.2   Integrating VCMS with Other Information Systems

PriceWaterhouseCoopers (2010, p. 3) suggests that the goal of Integrated Reporting (IR) is to provide a "cohesive and persuasive picture of a business, including the way it is managed and governed". The five key elements of this new reporting approach are an enhanced marketing set of insights, the delivery of the long-term strategy, the revealing of the behavioral triangle (governance, risk, and remuneration), the dynamics and key relationships underlying the firm's business model, and rethinking measurement and presentation in the light of a highly resource-constrained world (PriceWaterhouseCoopers 2010, p. 3). IR should be useful to both internal and external stakeholders in assessing the value of the organization or in making decisions about how to best leverage the firm's assets to generate positive, sustainable value (see the Chap. 8).

The value of a free-standing information source, such as the VCMS, is enhanced if it can be integrated with other sources of information in the firm. To achieve this objective, though, the information in all affected systems needs to reflect the same basic beliefs, assumptions, and approaches to measurement. This set of expectations is actually a strength of the VCMS, which uses activity-based language defined in terms of consumer-driven concepts that underlie strategy, marketing, product development and process management fields. Let's now turn to specifics about this integration.

9.2.1   VCMS and Marketing Databases

The major focus of marketing databases is the firm's customers. Looking at both what the customer expects from the company (the value profile) and how well these expectations are met (satisfaction and loyalty metrics) the marketing database provides a vital link with the revenue-generating aspects of the firm's competitive positioning. Brand loyalty is one of the key value attributes for a consumer product firm. Finding out how important brand is in the decision process of the purchasing

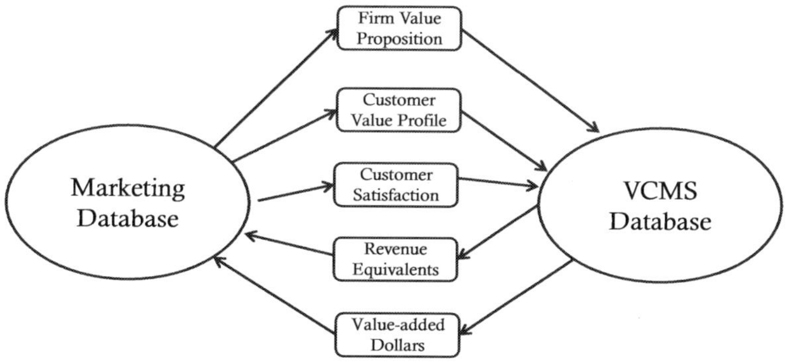

Fig. 9.1 The interplay of marketing and VCMS data

consumer helps a company understand what funding should be made available to build brand image and gain a competitive advantage from this branding.

The VCMS focus on separating out the revenue portion of the firm to match the consumer's value preferences tightly links these two systems together. In fact, the VCMS helps translate financial language into marketing language, providing a common baseline for the various managers to use when trying to describe, shape, and act on marketing opportunities. By tying marketing language tightly to the financial reporting process, the VCMS makes it easier to make decisions regarding where additional marketing dollars should be spent to yield the greatest benefits.

There are many linkages, therefore, between the marketing and VCMS databases, as suggested by Fig. 9.1. The VCMS pulls three key pieces of information from the marketing database to launch its analysis. Once this data is input into the VCMS database, two vital pieces of strategic marketing data emerge—the revenue equivalents, and the value-add cost distribution.

As the figure suggests, then, there are tight ties between the VCMS data and the marketing insights used to drive company decisions and actions. Moreover, as it has been noted earlier, the VCMS provides a natural point of linkage between marketing and finance, one that can significantly improve communication and reporting practices. Placing the entire organization into a framework that is driven by the consumer ties everyone in the organization to the firm's ultimate goal—to meet or exceed customer expectations.

9.2.2   VCMS and Operational Databases

An important part of any organization's dataset is its operational metrics. Reflecting how efficiently and effectively firm resources are being transformed into value-added products and services, the operational database of metrics is one of the key sources of information used to guide internal decision-making and process improvement. Consisting of metrics of the quality, timely and accurate delivery, cost, and productivity of the firm's productive assets, the operational database lies at the heart of any integrated information system.

The VCMS has a natural tie to the operational database in several ways. First and foremost, it relies upon activity and capacity analysis (McNair and Vangermeersch 1998) to generate the list of activities that cost is matched to. These activities and the related capacity data originate in the operational world and have been proven to be a very valuable source for reformatting internal financial reporting systems to better align them with operational reality. Since the VCMS relies upon activity and capacity data, then, it is immediately linked to the facts as they exist in the operational pipeline where the firm earns the money that the consumer is willing to pay for products and services that are valued.

A second tie of the VCMS to the operational database, though, lies in the ease with which process coding is added to the VCMS dataset (Hines et al. 2002; Silvi et al. 2008). Process management is now considered best practice in the operational disciplines. With its list of activities and a fully fleshed out process chart such as that developed by the APQC Benchmarking Clearinghouse (1992), the basics of a process structure can be detailed for any organization.

9.2.3 VCMS and the Resource Level of Reporting

One of the primary levels of the organization that affects all decisions is the resource level. Keeping an eye on whether the firm has the right mix of human skills (i.e. human capital, according to the Capitals background paper for IR by IIRC 2013a) in the right proportions to meet customer expectations is one such critical piece of information. This is data that exists in the human resources database. It is data that is brought to life within the VCMS by its mapping of the workforce to activities and the value-add cost distribution framework.

Other resources are also picked up by the VCMS analysis. When the operating budget for a department or process is pulled together, the first question that needs to be asked is whether the rest of the resources of the group are used up proportionately to the human activity level or whether certain activities consume greater amounts of non-people resources. This question leads to a simple alteration in the data collection process, with the responding managers to the VCMS survey simply breaking out the non-people costs against specific activities.

In this way, then, the VCMS also allows a firm to integrate the data on both its human and physical resources (i.e. human and manufactured capitals, according to the IIRC Consultation Draft of the international <IR> framework, IIRC 2013b) into one unified picture of the types of activities and outcomes these resources consume. Once again, the VCMS sits in an integrative role, sharing data with resource-focused departments. In the case of a machine-intensive workplace, the VCMS relies upon capacity reporting databases to generate its value-add cost framework. This gives the VCMS two potential resource-focused points of integration—the activity grid of the organization and the utilization analysis of its capacity—in the form of manufactured capital (IIRC, Capitals background paper for IR, 2013a). As such, the VCMS can be an integral part of any IR system.

9.3   VCMS and Taking the Waste Out: Towards Sustainability

Sustainability requires organizations to provide goods and services in a way that is profitable and, at the same time, ethical and respecting the environment, individuals and the communities. This approach to the organization was expanded in the 2009 EABIS report on sustainable value by noting (EABIS 2009, p. 2): "Corporate sustainability [. . .] is a business approach that creates long-term shareholder value by embracing the opportunities and managing the risks associated with economic, environmental, and social development".

One of the primary drivers of the value creation framework suggested by the EABIS sustainability project (2009, p. 2) is the role played by wasted resources as an internal driver of performance. To sustain growth a company has to manage its total portfolio of capital in such a way that it uses clean technology, prevents pollution, develops a sustainable vision, and undertakes product stewardship. Critical to this set of goals is the need to actively manage the waste of resources, thereby reducing costs and enhancing profits within a sustainability framework.

In every measurement taken to build the VCMS database, an eye is kept on identifying the various places waste can creep into the company's structure. Waste, or *muda* in the Japanese language, is the focus of all of the continuous improvement tools currently in use. For instance, Total Quality Management (Ishikawa 1985; Simpson and Muthler 1990; Morse and Poston 1990; Shank and Govindarajan 1993) targets the waste from defects and seeks ways to drive this form of waste as near to zero as humanly possible (Six Sigma, Dahlgaard and Dahlgaard-Park 2006). On the lean management (Womack et al. 1990; Womack and Jones 1996a, b) side of modern management approaches, the waste that is focused upon is move and queue. One by one the new management techniques seek to ferret out waste. The various kinds of waste that are targeted are shown in Fig. 9.2.

9.3.1   Waste: The Hidden Gold for Future Sustainable Growth

As noted in Fig. 9.2, there are many places waste can be created in an organization. One of the most common places waste occurs is in the handoffs between different functions in a company. Fumbles occur, causing rework and scrap, making an entire process more costly to operate (Brache 2012).

Integrating the information systems of the organization into one unified set of measurements helps identify, manage, monitor, and report these areas where fumbles occur and sets a cost on these errors. Any time excess resources are consumed within the organization, the waste that results pollutes some aspect of the environment—it consumes scarce resources.

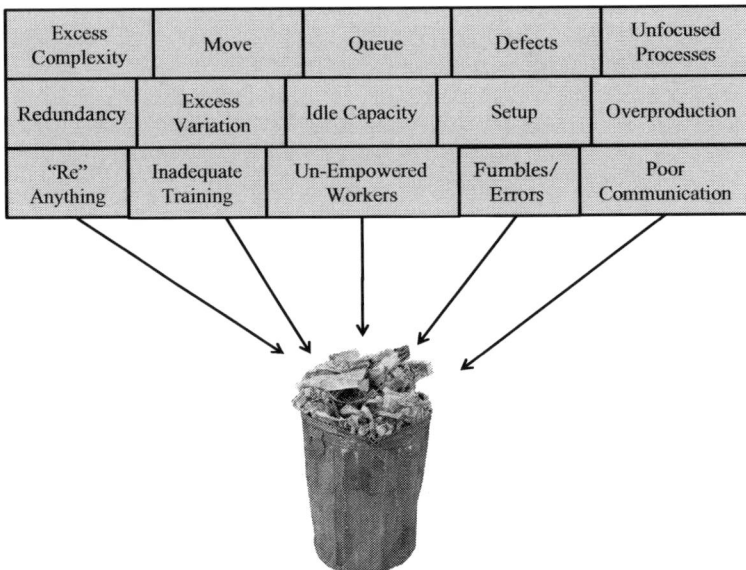

Excess Complexity	Move	Queue	Defects	Unfocused Processes
Redundancy	Excess Variation	Idle Capacity	Setup	Overproduction
"Re" Anything	Inadequate Training	Un-Empowered Workers	Fumbles/ Errors	Poor Communication

Fig. 9.2 The many faces of waste

To gain a sustainable growth pattern, then, an organization has to be actively managing all the sources of its waste. This waste can be structural in nature or embedded in the process flow where action takes place (McNair 1994). In terms of sustainability, then, waste metrics help identify where an organization is at risk when faced with changing environmental conditions. Waste is a unifying measure that helps an organization improve profits while at the same time supporting sustainable growth. Waste is the hidden gold of sustainability.

9.3.2   The Dominant Role of Removing Waste in a VCMS

Waste is one of the five categories of cost collected in the VCMS data collection exercise. Every activity has some portion of waste in it. Once again setting the VCMS apart from other forms of activity analysis, each activity can be represented as having portions of value-add, business value-add, and waste in it. It is not an all or nothing proposition, nor is it one that is based on internal perspectives on value. The VCMS, then, links to the sustainability movement because it details the costs of the organization in terms of how important each portion of spending is to the total value profile of the firm as defined by consumers and society.

Waste in the VCMS is the source for creating the growth cycle. Instead of simply dropping the savings from removing waste to the bottom line, the VCMS encourages firms to reinvest these savings into value-added work, thereby enhancing the growth potential of the firm. One time cost savings do little to enhance sustainability. A reinvestment strategy for savings that come from trimming waste in the firm's activities provides a baseline for gaining sustainable growth.

The area of waste is also one that can prove the most difficult to get responding managers to agree to disclose. While clearly every activity has some portion of waste that continuous improvement methods can help eliminate, managers are reluctant to confess to these levels of waste, thinking that doing so will result in reduced budgets. Under a sustainability approach, this fear is diminished as the savings from reducing waste become the basis for adding investments in value-add and business value-add future (R&D). Both of these results benefit the environment and the firm's stakeholders.

Taking a new approach to measuring waste once again serves to integrate the VCMS into the other organizational initiatives, such as lean management. Since lean initiatives to process management seek to understand waste at the task level, the implicit task-based data in the VCMS can help to identify the areas where potential savings are the greatest. Reaping sustainable value and growth is the ultimate goal of waste reporting in the VCMS.

9.4   VCMS and Performance Measurement for IR

The VCMS data collection exercise offers valuable information about the performance of the company, which can be reported to stakeholders to make them appreciate its ability to create sustainable value. In particular, it contributes to the appraisal of the operational performance of internal processes in terms of efficiency (see the Chap. 8), paying attention—at the same time—to the content of value of each activity. VCMS can gather data and metrics and key performance inditors—articulated by business, process, department, etc.—organized by the following categories:

- *Activity costs and value*, i.e. their distinction in value-adding, business value-adding indirect, business value-adding future, business value-adding administrative, and waste;
- *Cost and value alignment*, emphasizing gaps between the activities' cost and their importance to the total value profile of the firm as defined by consumers and society;
- *Customer satisfaction* and its impact on sales and growth;
- *Sustainability*, measuring, for instance, waste reduction and the connected effects on different forms of capital, such as financial (cost reduction, fines and litigation exposure containment), natural (pollution, emissions, energy consumption, recycling), and manufactured (unused capacity, productivity);
- *Processes configuration* and its impact on lead time, overproduction, poor communication, redundancy, excess complexity and the other forms of waste reported in Fig. 9.2, which affects all the capitals available to the firm, according to the Consultation Draft of the International <IR> Framework (IIRC 2013b, section 2.17).

9.5   Concluding Remarks

This chapter has briefly introduced the VCMS model and detailed how it fits into an integrated reporting system. Taking its primary input from consumer preferences, the model serves to identify strategic strengths and weaknesses. Because it relies on activity and capacity data sources, it also links to the tactical and operational levels of decision-making within the firm.

This chapter has also highlighted how the contribution of VCMS to IR is twofold. First, it supports the management and monitoring of the company performance with specific regard to customers and internal processes as fundamental dimensions of an integrated performance measurement system. Second, it focuses on waste reduction. In trying to create a sustainable future, the role of waste needs to be taken into account. The VCMS recognizes that, while few activities are made up totally of waste, there is waste embedded to some extent in every activity. Suggesting that these wasted resources can be recouped and reinvested in the organization to support future growth ties the VCMS approach not only to the IR movement but also reflects the growing concerns with creating sustainable value for the global community and the organization's primary stakeholders.

Moving forward in the future in cost management, then, will require a new set of perspectives. While financial accounting will still play a role in communicating results of operations to the market, new forms of information need to be developed that more closely and accurately represent organizational actions and outcomes. The result will be a more robust information database where external reporting more accurately and fully details the risks and returns resulting from management decisions and action. VCMS plays a vital role in this natural unions of resources (capitals) to outcomes, value creation to sustainable growth.

> *More people should learn to tell their dollars where to go instead of asking them where they went.*
>
>   *Roger Babson*

References

APQC International Benchmarking Clearinghouse (1992) Process classification framework. APQC International, Houston, TX

Brache A (2012) What is a process? Why should you care?. http://www.rummler-brache.com/case-studies-and-white-papers. Accessed 1 Dec 2012

Dahlgaard JJ, Dahlgaard-Park SM (2006) Lean production, six sigma quality, TQM and company culture. TQM Mag 18(3):263–281

EABIS (2009) Sustainable value. Corporate responsibility, market valuation and measuring the financial and non-financial performance of the firm. http://www.investorvalue.org/docs/EabisProjectFinal.pdf. Accessed 24 Sept 2013

Hines P, Silvi R, Bartolini M (2002) Demand chain management: an integrative approach in automotive retailing. J Oper Manag 3(6):707–728

IIRC (The International Integrated Reporting Council) (March 2013a) Capitals background paper for IR

IIRC (The International Integrated Reporting Council) (2013b) Consultation draft of the international <IR> framework. http://www.theiirc.org. Accessed 26 Jul 2013

Ishikawa K (1985) What is total quality control? The Japanese way. Prentice-Hall, Englewood Cliffs, NJ

McNair C (1994) The profit potential: taking high performance to the bottom line. Omneo, Essex Junction, VT

McNair CJ, Vangermeersch R (1998) Total capacity management. Optimizing at the operational, tactical and strategic level. St. Lucie, Boca Raton, FL

McNair-Connolly C, Polutnik L, Silvi R, Watts T (2013) Value creation in management accounting: using information to capture customer value. Business Experts, New York, NY

Moller K (2006) Role of competences in creating customer value: a value-creation logic approach. Ind Mark Manag 35:913–924

Morse WJ, Poston KM (1990) Accounting for quality cost in CIM. In: Brinker BJ (1990, a cura di) Emerging practices in cost management. Warren Gorham & Lamont, Boston, MA

Nagle TT, Holden RK (1999) Strategy and the tactics of pricing, 2nd edn. Prentice Hall, Englewood Cliffs, NJ

PriceWaterhouseCoopers (2010) What does your reporting say about you? International: PriceWaterhouseCoopers, Hong Kong

Priem RL (2007) A consumer perspective on value creation. Acad Manag Rev 32(1):219–235

Shank JK, Govindarajan V (1993) Strategic cost management. The Free, New York, NY

Silvi R, Hines P, Bartolini M (2008) SCM and lean thinking: a framework for management accounting. In: Cost management (USA, NY), January–February 2008

Simpson J, Muthler DL (1990) Quality cost: facilitating the quality initiative. In: Brinker BJ (ed) Emerging practices in cost management. Warren Gorham & Lamont, Boston, MA

Ulaga W, Eggert A (2005) Relationship value in business markets: the construct and its dimensions. J Bus Bus Market 12(1):73–99

Womack J, Jones D (1996a) Beyond Toyota: how to root out waste and pursue perfection. Harv Bus Rev September–October:140–144

Womack J, Jones D (1996b) Lean thinking: banish waste and create wealth in your corporation. Simon & Schuster, New York. trad. it. (1997) Come creare valore e bandire gli sprechi, Guerini e Associati, Milano

Womack J, Jones D, Roos D (1990) The machine that changed the world. Rawson Associates, New York, NY

Approaching Risk Management from a New Integrated Perspective

10

Sonia Quarchioni and Francesca Trovarelli

Abstract

In recent years, risk management has acquired increasing relevance within the organizational realm. Although the Integrated Reporting Framework includes 'risk' as one of the content elements of the Integrated Report, its main purpose does not specifically relate to risk management. Drawing on the evolving academic debate, this chapter aims to provide an overview of the different approaches to risk management and to highlight the need for a broader and integrated perspective. The chapter ends by highlighting the potential contribution of this perspective to the Integrated Reporting Framework.

10.1 Introduction[1]

The increasing uncertainty which characterizes the modern 'risk society' (Beck 1992) has led to growing interest about risk management (Power 2007). In this context, organizations are considered as 'critical agents' (Hutter and Power 2005) from a twofold perspective. Firstly, they represent the major *providers* of risk to the external community. Secondly, they are large *containers* of uncertainty, which needs to be managed appropriately in order to ensure long term value creation.

---

[1] This chapter is based on the results of a broader research project entitled "*From governance and risk management rules to performance: roles, tools and enabling conditions in Italian firms*". The authors would like to gratefully acknowledge the financial support for the research provided by national funding within PRIN 2009. Although this chapter is the result of shared research, Sonia Quarchioni authored the introduction and Sects. 10.2 and 10.3, while Francesca Trovarelli authored Sect. 10.4. The concluding remarks are the joint work of both authors.

S. Quarchioni (✉) • F. Trovarelli
Department of Business and Law, University of Siena, Siena, Italy
e-mail: quarchioni@unisi.it; trovarelli@unisi.it

C. Busco et al. (eds.), *Integrated Reporting*, DOI 10.1007/978-3-319-02168-3_10,
© Springer International Publishing Switzerland 2013

As argued by Power (2004a), this broad social movement of 'risk management of everything' has been translated into a growing formalized body of international frameworks that have prescribed how an organization should cope strategically with rising uncertainty, as well as create and communicate *sustainable* value to its external environment. Generally, these frameworks have enhanced both the importance of risk management as a mechanism of accountability (Spira and Page 2003) and the need to consider risk and performance as 'two sides of the same coin' (Van der Stede 2009).

The relevance of the relationships between risk and performance are also acknowledged by the International Integrated Reporting Council (IIRC), a global coalition of regulators, companies and professional institutions, which is currently developing the International Integrated Reporting (IR) Framework. Although this framework includes *risk* as one of the content elements of an Integrated Report, its main purpose does not specifically relate to risk management. Given the increasing relevance of sharing risk information with all stakeholders, this chapter draws on the evolving debate on risk management to provide an overview of the different approaches (Sects. 10.2 and 10.3) and to highlight the need for a broader and integrated perspective (Sect. 10.4), together with the potential contribution of this perspective to the IR Framework (Sect. 10.5).

10.2 The Traditional Concept of Risk

Risk has always been of considerable interest in various streams of research. In the economic literature, Knight (1921) made a basic distinction between the notion of *risk* and the notion of *uncertainty*. In his view, risk refers to those events which are in some way predictable and statistically calculable, while uncertainty represents the indeterminate and inestimable halo surrounding the human condition. Also, the notion of *hazard* has often been compared to risk and uncertainty. In this context, hazard usually refers to those adverse phenomena which could harm human society (Jones and Hood 1996).

The absence of a widely accepted definition of risk possibly explains the lack of a well-defined approach for assessing and managing risks within organizations. As argued by Bhimani (2009, p. 3), "this is because ambiguities render viable a multitude of plausibilities and interpretations and confer legitimacy on redefined boundaries which delimit organisational actions and objectives in novel ways".

However, in the attempt to identify the pattern through which the concept of risk has entered the organizational realm, it is important to highlight that according to several scholars (see, for instance, DeLoach 2000) modern risk *management* in organizations has started with risk *analysis*. Insurance, indeed, has been the most popular field in which the *traditional* risk calculation emerged. The development of statistical analysis of data and probability theory applied to practical issues enhanced the use of mathematical models to predict and quantify risk. Particularly, a milestone in the development of risk analysis is provided by Starr's (1969) seminal article on risk and voluntariness (see, Renn 1998). Power (2007) claimed that this was the starting point for a subsequent institutionalization of risk analysis with the growing establishment of new academic and professional associations and the evolution of techniques for modelling risk, above all in high-reliability organizations. Within this field, risk was mainly seen as the quantifiable level of probability for an accident or adverse event to occur. Moreover, as discussed by Power (2007), the need for *quantification* itself reflected an overall cultural approach which highlighted the role of *numbers* in creating acknowledgment and trust in given "forms of belief and action" (Porter 1992, p. 640). Indeed, in the history of organizations, measures have always been an important means of management, providing individuals with a sense of objectivity and neutrality (Power 2004b).

Pressures for change in the practice of risk analysis within organizations started to develop in the neo-liberal era (O'Malley 2000). These pressures derived from changes in the conception of risk in the wider institutional context where "new managerial and enterprise culture discourses have, in significant ways, challenged the 'mathematical' models of economics" (O'Malley 2000, p. 463). The idea of the *rational* individual, whose choices are based upon functional models, could no longer be acceptable in a competitive environment, within which increasing levels of complexity and turbulence had undoubtedly amplified the intensity of risk that each organization had to face. Globalization, digitalization of the markets, political and financial instability represent only some of the elements which have characterized the entrance into the new era. Also, the *quantitative* approach to risk has been challenged by new emerging conceptions of risk in social theories that flourished in the early 1990s with the well-known idea of Beck (1992) about the *Risk Society* (for a review, see Zinn 2004). Particularly, the idea that risk is essentially *man-made*, and thus represents an intrinsic feature of modern society itself, undermined the utility of the calculative technologies of risk. In this context, numbers and calculations came to be considered as not able to provide reasonable elements for decision-making processes any longer. Rather, it is the wider managerial belief system that affects the ways in which managers perceive risk according to both their individual taste and social norms and expectations (March and Shapira 1987). Thus, risk preferences are essential for understanding the organizational responses to risk.

The limited and inadequate role of risk analysis for organizational decision-making processes became particularly evident at the beginning of the 1990s, when several incidents of corporate failure, financial scandals, and world-wide disasters affected the whole global market. The shift from risk *analysis* to risk *management* is, therefore, evident. According to Jones and Hood (1996, p. 6), "the term 'risk management' means different things to different people, depending partly on which of the islands in the archipelago they inhabit". However, they claim that, like any other form of management, risk management can be generally described as a process involving the three fundamental elements of any control system: goal-setting; information gathering and interpretation; action to influence or modify human behaviour or physical structures. Specifically, in the business context this has implied that "risk analysis, the traditional technical home territory of risk management, has been subsumed within a larger accountability and control framework" (Power 2004a, p. 11). The main factors that can be detected behind this shift and what it actually implies for organizational activity are explained in the following section.

10.3 Criticism of Enterprise-Risk Management

Along with neo-liberal principles and new social conceptions of risk, the great emphasis on control for the integrity of corporate governance systems in the late 1990s had a central role in the changing discourses about risk for organizations. As outlined in the previous section, financial scandals and episodes of managerial misconduct provided the reasons for new regulations, to both prescribe stricter internal control requirements and ensure more transparency of financial information for stakeholders. The Cadbury Code (1992), the Hampel Report (1998), and the Turnbull report (1999) are just some examples of these new regulations that, at least initially, involved primarily the Anglo-Saxon world.

In particular, these codes and regulations allowed risk management to acquire more and more prominence in the regulatory area (Scheytt et al. 2006). Indeed, societal demands for more trustworthiness and transparency of organizational behaviour created new *objects* for risk regulation 'regimes' (Hood and Rothstein 2001) which dealt with financial controls, good governance systems, and reliable reporting processes. In Power's (2007, p. 3) terms, the shift from the "logic of calculation to that of organization and accountability" gave rise to a new managerial concept of risk management that overlapped mechanisms of internal control systems.

This shift was also visible in academic management research literature which abandoned a 'particularistic view' of risk (Hagigi and Sivakumar 2009) to focus towards a comprehensive notion of risk management within control, audit, and reporting discourses, giving rise to a strand of research which Van der Stede (2011) refers to with the label 'accounting risk'. These studies shed light on how organizations respond to new risk and corporate governance requirements in terms of struggles between changing internal roles (Fraser and Henry 2007) and explicit alignment between internal control and risk management (Spira and Page 2003).

Pressures for change towards a wide approach to risk management did not only come from regulatory forces. Since the mid-1990s professional associations and consultancy firms started to provide organizations with several blueprints for managing risks, highlighting the strategic significance of risk management and its link with performance and value creation processes. Thus, the new wide approach to risk management was both an attempt to spread a 'legalistic culture' in organizations (Hood 1996) and an effect of the growing provision of general blueprints (Power 2007).

Typically, these blueprints became a point of reference in the risk management agenda of every organization. In particular, the Enterprise Risk Management

(ERM) Framework (COSO 2004) is considered the foremost template for managing risk implemented within organizations. According to this framework, ERM is defined as:

> *"a process, effected by an entity's board of directors, management and other personnel, applied in strategy setting and across the enterprise, designed to identify potential events that may affect the entity, and manage risks to be within its risk appetite, to provide reasonable assurance regarding the achievement of entity objectives".*

Within this view, risk is not only to be managed to mitigate harm in the context of a risk society in Becks' terms and neither to strengthen internal controls in a world of financial scandals. It should also be managed in a logic of *opportunity* as neo-liberal conceptions of entrepreneurship suggest (O'Malley 2000). From this point of view, Power (2007, p. 68) considered ERM as a wider body of knowledge under which several standards and frameworks developed, like a sort of "semi-popular managerial discourse which exists at the interface between regulators, finance specialists, insurers, and accountants". From this point of view, ERM became a new way of considering control and organizational strategy, under which very different sets of risk practices and techniques flourished.

Specifically, with the ERM a new focus on outcomes, performance and value creation has invested risk management. The main vehicle has been the professional world in which the idea of ERM became increasingly prominent. In this sense, planning and budgeting processes started to be considered the natural settings in which risk management practices should be embedded in order to improve business results (Ow 2009), and grant long-term success (Beasley and Frigo 2007). Additionally, a broad practical body of literature on performance measurement systems began to focus on the determination of key-risk indicators for business strategy (Beasley et al. 2010), and to be integrated with pre-existing performance tools within the organization such as the Balanced Scorecard (Kaplan 2009). Several normative frameworks encompassing ideas of *integrated* and *holistic* risk management were also proposed. For instance, Van der Stede (2009) presented the conceptual framework for 'Enterprise governance' that addressed firms to be aware of the need for considering risk and performance under the same umbrella, both in the short and long term. Frigo and Ramaswamy (2009) proposed a framework to be used by executive teams in their strategic planning processes for evaluating the impact of events and different scenarios on performance. Along these lines, Frigo (2008) suggested the 'Strategic Risk Management' framework, while Simons (1999) even proposed a 'risk exposure calculator' in order to determine how much internal risk exists within a company. Finally, after the publication of ERM in 2004, updated versions of the framework were published in the following years by the COSO, and well-known consultant bodies continually published reports, studies, and practical models on risk management. All these models were centred around a *holistic* vision of risk, linking its management with planning, control and value creation processes.

Academic literature also started to consider an integrated view of risk and performance within the organizational governance system. For instance, Drew et al. (2006) presented an integrated corporate governance model in which five elements (i.e. Culture, Leadership, Alignment, System, and Structure) are identified as being fundamental in supporting a strong approach to corporate risks, helping organizational executives in meeting their strategic objectives. Busco et al. (2006) proposed an integrated governance framework which shows how risk management is functional for both a good governance system and a sustainable performance. Other studies specifically focused on ERM, exploring its main features (Levinsohn and Williams 2004), and analysing the factors associated with its implementation (Paape and Spakklé 2012).

Another strand of research has sought to analyze the actual meanings and effects of the introduction of risk management practices within an organization (Mikes 2009; Arena et al. 2010). These studies have questioned the real reasons behind the adoption of blueprints regarding how to manage risk, wondering whether it is just a compliance exercise for facing legislative and social pressures,or if its principles are embedded in organizational culture. Moreover, these studies highlighted the significant interconnections that exist between risk management practices (which are socially constructed) and the overall organizational processes. Indeed, as stated by Hutter and Power (2005, p. 9), "risk is not independent of management processes in organizations, but rather, representations of risk, its management and the organizations that do the managing are co-produced".

Actually, this strand of research criticizes the definition of standards and normative schemes, providing organizations with guidelines and *ready-made* solutions for implementation problems. Behind this criticism lays a profound reconsideration of the ERM principles. At the end of the first decade of the twenty-first century, what for Power (2004a) was the 'risk management of everything' became the 'risk management of nothing' (Power 2009). As stated by this scholar, the financial crisis in 2008 emphasized the limits of ERM. In this context, the RIMS Executive Report (2009) claimed the need for a wake-up call for ERM, which has not failed as a business discipline, but rather in its implementation within organizations.

Interestingly, Power (2009) identified three main reasons behind the ERM failure. Firstly, the notion of a singular risk appetite, intrinsic to ERM principles, has been too simplistic in organizational reality. Even though ERM appears to enhance a qualitative approach to risk, the processes of risk management that it depicts actually depends on an identifiable amount of risk appetite. Instead, the concept of risk appetite cannot be merely relegated to measurement issues because it is derived from a complex entanglement between internal processes and role interactions.

Secondly, despite the fact that ERM has been depicted as a strategic control system where notions of risk and performance are strictly related, its development was mainly derived from the broad logic of accounting and auditing during the mid-1990s. For Power (2009), this entailed a strong 'legitimacy-driven style' in implementing ERM frameworks within organizations. In other words, the perceived need to be compliant with external blueprints and models of organizing could have led organizations to implement 'ready-packages' which are actually *empty* inside (Power 2009). As shown by Hood and Rothstein (2001), risk management often enhances a 'culture of blame avoidance' in organizations, feeling more confident to defend themselves by demonstrating that they have followed the rules or fulfilled all social expectations.

Finally, the ERM framework is underpinned by an 'entity-based embeddedness' of risks which does not capture the relationships of the firm within its broader social network. Specifically, Power (2009) argues that the failure of ERM in facing financial crisis is due to its lack of understanding of the 'entity interconnectedness', which entails the consideration of wider *systemic* risks. This last criticism opens the way to a fruitful debate which provides a new knowledge base for rethinking risk management in the wake of more recent worldwide events. The background for this debate and the new approach to risk management which emerges will be explained in more depth in the following section.

10.4   Towards a New Approach to Risk Management

Beck's (1992) thesis of *self-produced* risks is still compelling today in a context of growing uncertainty and increasing scientific and technical knowledge. However, changes in the nature of threats in the new global scenario require further reflection on risk as a 'borderless phenomenon' (Fischbacher-Smith and Fischbacher-Smith 2009). This notion of risk underpins the idea of a risk society, but it still has not received much attention in the academic debate. Global crisis, worldwide scandals, and large-scale disasters have shown that risks are often *man-made* and that their level of predictability is increasingly low. However, there is further more relevant evidence on the fact that risk, both in its roots and in its effects, transcends the borders of every knowledge discipline and institution. Indeed, structural and cognitive boundaries cannot exist when dealing with risk management.

This has a great impact on 'organizational encounters with risk' (Hutter and Power 2005). The multi-disciplinary nature of risk and the higher level of *permeability* of organizations which operate in a *networked* society have affected the scale of disruptive events. The impact of these events depends on the level of integration between the *extended* organization and its environment. Starr et al. (2003, p. 5) identify these events under the umbrella of 'interdependence risk', which is defined as the "unanticipated risk exposure across the extended enterprise that is beyond an individual organization's direct control". This notion corresponds to what Power (2009) referred to as 'interconnectedness', referring to those risks which are derived from the level of embeddedness of the organization in wider social networks.

Thus, risk management models developed up to now under ERM principles reveal their current inadequacies. Despite calls for being open-minded, ERM did not actually challenge organizations to internally manage risks emerging from extended and interconnected systems (Power 2009). Moreover, these models did not fully consider the potential consequences of those risks for the external environment.

As stated by Power (2009), an increasingly relevant part of the changing risk management agenda nowadays is Business Continuity Management (BCM). Although BCM has recently developed in different fields such as IT and emergency management, its strategic significance for organizations is becoming broader (Herbane et al. 2004). The Business Continuity Institute defines BCM as (*italics added*) "a process that identifies potential impacts that threaten an organization and provides a framework for building *resilience* and the capability for an effective response that safeguards the interests of its stakeholders, reputation, brand and value creating activities". Although BCM has often been associated with crisis management and recovery strategies from major disruptions, the abovementioned definition highlights that it can provide a new way of interpreting risk management in everyday life. The underpinning principle of BCM is that a single organization never acts in isolation from the others and that its activity is strictly interdependent within the system which it inhabits. In this context, each organization needs to represent and manage the 'interconnectivity risks', recognizing that "security is only possible as a collective way" (Power 2009, p. 853). Moreover, organizations experience a growing need to manage resilience issues in the attempt to react, adapt and gain from new risk environments. The ways in which *resilience* is conceived and operationalized within organizations, and its influence on risk management strategies, deserve more attention.

Defining the concept of resilience is a complex task, as it is difficult to give a complete description and understanding of all its features. The term resilience is derived from the ancient Latin word *resilio* (*re* and *salio*) that literally means *to jump back*, but it also means, in a figurative sense, not to be touched by something negative. The available literature on resilience is characterized by a strong multi-disciplinary approach, fragmentation and a lack of a dominant paradigm.

The notion of resilience is also present within many branches of social sciences where it takes on various meanings and nuances depending on the context in which it is inserted and on the *moment* it is considered. Typically, researchers have analysed resilience as a concept *situated* before or after a shock, stressing in this way the tension between *speedy recovery* and *timely adaptation* (Westrum 2006). A broad definition of resilience is provided by Comfort et al. (2010, p. 9) who claim that "resilience is the capacity of a social system (e.g., an organization, city, or society) to proactively adapt to and recover from disturbances that are perceived within the system to fall outside the range of normal and expected disturbances".

In this context, the concept of resilience has become widely known also in organization and management literature. Particularly, the anticipation *vs.* resilience divide has been one of the major key areas of debate with specific reference to risk management (Hood et al. 1992). Recalling the link between risk, resilience and uncertainty, Wildavsky (1988) suggests resilience as the best strategy and the more successful management approach to be used from decision makers that have to deal with great uncertainty, while anticipation is a strategy effective only when threats and problems are known (Dalziell and McManus 2004). Wildavsky proposes to create a balance of *anticipation* and *resilience* for reducing risk in uncertain conditions (Comfort et al. 2001). He stresses the virtues of flexibility and adaptability of decision makers and suggests the use of elastic, malleable resources, such as knowledge, communication, wealth and organizational capacity, in order "to enable us to craft what we need, when we need it, even though we previously had no idea we would need it" (Wildavsky 1988, quoted in Comfort et al. 2010, p. 23). Hence, this also enhances the organizational capacity of adaptability to future change through continuous processes of learning (Comfort et al. 2010).

Although resilience has been under debate in previous years, especially within crisis and disaster literature, a new focus should be given to this notion in light of the current economic and security environment. Since an organization's competitive context has become progressively more uncertain and volatile, resilience gains importance in practice under two dimensions: operational and strategic. 'Operational resilience' is the ability to bounce back and is a *recovery-based resilience* persisting after experiencing a crisis. 'Strategic resilience', instead, is the ability to change without crisis and is a *renewal-based resilience*, turning threats into opportunities (Välikangas et al. 2012).

Within this perspective, resilience means being prepared for both the potential harms and benefits that accompany change, aligning all risk management activities accordingly. More interestingly, resilience provides a broader view on risk interdependencies across the 'extended enterprise' (Starr et al. 2003) and increases organizational flexibility. This can have a twofold effect. Firstly, organizations enhance their ongoing ability to create value through a more *integrated* approach to risk management that actually considers organizational life within an interconnected system. Secondly, the external environment can benefit from this new way to approach risk, that is necessarily outward-looking and very closed to notions of sustainability. Here, sustainability assumes the meaning of a framework for assessing how decisions in the present may impact individuals in the future within the core concept of 'futurity' (Krysiak 2009).

The importance of this new approach will be further discussed in the following final section. After a brief summary of the development process of risk management, we will argue that recent calls for new risk management approaches (following for instance BCM principles and the concept of resilience) converge with the suggestions provided by the IR Framework and its underlying principles.

10.5 Summary and Concluding Remarks

The aim of this chapter has been to provide an overview of the different approaches to risk management and to highlight the need for a broader and integrated perspective, together with the potential contribution of this perspective to the IR Framework.

Whereas risk management in organizations was traditionally linked to risk analysis and quantification, pressures from governments and new competitive environments intensified the need to manage uncertainty beyond numbers and calculations. In this context, several frameworks on how to manage risk properly for achieving organizational objectives have been widely diffused, reinforcing the inextricable link between risk, performance and value creation. Nevertheless, the recent financial crisis has shown the limits of some of these frameworks. Currently, organizations are being called on to assess and manage risks that are derived from a *networked* society, in which there are no longer boundaries between organizational activity and external environment. Thus, risk itself is becoming *borderless*.

The need for a wide perspective on risk is acknowledged also in the IR Framework, which considers *risk* as one of the content elements of the Integrated Report. Particularly, in the IR Framework it is argued that an Integrated Report should identify the risks that are specific to the organization, "including those that relate to the organization's effects on, and the continued availability, quality and affordability of, relevant capitals" (IIRC 2013, p. 26). The analysis of these risks allows for a comprehensive vision of the organizational capacity to create value over time. According to the IR Framework, value is derived from a number of interactions, activities, and relationships which could affect the increase, decrease or transformation of the various kinds of capitals (i.e. financial, manufactured, intellectual, human, social and relationship, and natural) of an organization. The value creation process develops within a broad picture in which primary attention is given to the value stored in the different forms of capital embedded in the external environment and then consumed, modified or destroyed by the organization through its own business model. This internal activity generates *outcomes* (internal *vs.* external and positive *vs.* negative) for the capitals affecting, in turn, the external society. These points highlight a high level of *permeability* of organizations, which are an integral part of a more *interconnected* environment.

From this perspective, the new approaches to risk management emerging from recent literature may provide useful insights to support the implementation of IR. Indeed, BCM principles and the concept of *resilience* are able to address the complexity of the *interconnected* systems in which an organization operates. BCM enhances the need for an organization to manage *systemic* risks, both identifying potential impacts and planning appropriate recovery strategies. Moreover, through *resilience* the organization develops capacity to react, adapt and gain from changes in new risk environments.

Therefore, recent calls for new risk management approaches appear to converge with the underlying principles of the IR Framework. In addition, the implementation of BCM practices within organizations may actually enhance the *integrated thinking*, which is at the basis of IR. *Integrated thinking* takes into account the interdependencies between the range of factors (and thus risks) that have significant effects on an organizations' ability to create value over time (IIRC 2013). Thus, BCM has a twofold effect (internal and external) for organizations. On the one hand, organizations can manage risk properly within a broader picture and plan their activity accordingly. On the other hand, they can demonstrate and communicate to all stakeholders that they take a *very* integrated approach to risk management.

Although these fundamental concepts emerge from the IR Framework, more efforts should be taken to provide further well-framed insights on how an organization should manage risks in this new perspective and then disclose its strategy to its stakeholders. In particular, reinforcing recent academic calls for new approaches to risk management, this chapter has offered some insights for encouraging a new agenda for debate.

References

Arena M, Arnaboldi M, Azzone G (2010) The organizational dynamics of enterprise risk management. Account Organ Soc 35(7):659–675

Beasley M, Branson B, Hancock B (2010) Developing key risk indicators to strengthen enterprise risk management. Committee of Sponsoring Organizations of the Treadway Commission, New York

Beasley M, Frigo M (2007) Strategic risk management: creating and protecting value. Strateg Financ May:25–53

Beck U (1992) Risk society. Towards a new modernity. London, Sage

Bhimani A (2009) Risk management, corporate governance and management accounting: emerging interdependencies. Manag Account Res 20:2–5

Busco C, Frigo M, Giovannoni E, Riccaboni A, Scapens R (2006) Beyond compliance: an integrated governance framework. The Institute of Chartered Accountants, London

Cadbury A (1992) Report of the committee on the financial aspects of corporate governance. Gee, London

Comfort LK, Boin A, Demchak CC (2010) Designing resilience: preparing for extreme events. University of Pittsburgh Press, Pittsburgh, PA

Comfort LK, Sungu Y, Johnson D, Dunn M (2001) Complex systems in crisis: anticipation and resilience in dynamic environments. J Contingencies Crisis Manage 9(3):144–158

Committee on Corporate Governance (1998) Final report. Gee, London

COSO (2004) Enterprise risk management—integrated framework. The Committee of Sponsoring Organizations of the Treadway Commission, New York

Dalziell EP, McManus ST (2004) Resilience, vulnerability, and adaptive capacity: implications for system performance. In: 1st International Forum for Engineering Decision Making (IFED), Stoos, Switzerland, 5–8 Dec 2004

DeLoach J (2000) Enterprise-wide risk management: strategies for linking risk and opportunity. Prentice Hall, Upper Saddle River

Drew SA, Kelley PC, Kendrick T (2006) CLASS: five elements of corporate governance to manage strategic risk. Bus Horiz 49:127–138

Fischbacher-Smith D, Fischbacher-Smith M (2009) The changing nature of risk and risk management: the challenge of borders, uncertainty and resilience. Risk Manage 11(1):1–12

Fraser I, Henry W (2007) Embedding risk management: structures and approaches. Manag Audit J 22(4):392–409

Frigo M (2008) Return driven. Lessons from high performance companies. Strateg Financ July:25–30

Frigo M, Ramaswamy V (2009) Co-creating strategic risk-return management. Strateg Financ May:3–10

Hagigi M, Sivakumar K (2009) Managing diverse risks: an integrative framework. J Int Manag 15:286–295

Herbane B, Elliott D, Swartz EM (2004) Business continuity management: time for a strategic role? Long Range Plann 37:435–457

Hood C (1996) Where extremes meet: "SPRAT" versus "SHARK" in public risk management. In: Hood C, Jones D (eds) Accident and design. London, UCL Press, pp 208–227

Hood CC, Jones DKC, Pidgeon NF, Turner BA, Gibson R (1992) Risk management. In: Royal Society Group (ed) Risk: analysis, perception and management. The Royal Society, London, pp 135–192

Hood C, Rothstein H (2001) Risk regulation under pressure: problem solving or blame shifting? Admin Soc 33(1):21–53

Hutter B, Power M (2005) Organizational encounters with risk: an introduction. In: Hutter B, Power
    M (eds) Organizational encounters with risk. Cambridge University Press, Cambridge, pp 1–32
IIRC (2013) Consultation draft of the international <IR> framework. IIRC, New York.
    http://www.theiirc.org/wp-content/uploads/Consultation-Draft/Consultation-Draft-of-the-
    InternationalIRFramework.pdf. Accessed 28 Jul 2013
Jones D, Hood C (1996) Introduction. In: Hood C, Jones D (eds) Accident and design. Contempo-
    rary debate on risk management. UCL Press, London, pp 1–9
Kaplan RS (2009) Risk management and the strategy execution system. Balanced Scorecard Rep
    November/December:3–8
Knight F (1921) Risk, uncertainty, and profit. Hart, Schaffner& Marx; Houghton Mifflin Co.,
    Boston, MA
Krysiak FC (2009) Risk management as a tool for sustainability. J Bus Eth 85:483–492
Levinsohn A, Williams K (2004) How to manage risk enterprise-wide. Strateg Financ 86(5):55–57
March JG, Shapira Z (1987) Managerial perspectives on risk and risk taking. Manag Sci 33
    (11):1404–1418
Mikes A (2009) Risk management and calculative cultures. Manag Account Res 20:18–40
O'Malley P (2000) Uncertain subjects: risks, liberalism and contract. Econ Soc 29(4):460–484
Ow P (2009) Embedding risk management practices for improved organisational performance.
    Accountants Today April:26–30
Paape L, Spakklé RF (2012) The adoption and design of enterprise risk management practices: an
    empirical study. Eur Account Rev 21(3):533–564
Porter TM (1992) Quantification and the accounting ideal in science. Soc Stud Sci 22(4):633–651
Power M (2004a) The risk management of everything. Demos, London
Power M (2004b) Counting, control and calculation: reflections on measuring and management.
    Hum Relat 57(6):765–783
Power M (2007) Organized uncertainty: designing a world of risk management. Oxford University
    Press, Oxford
Power M (2009) The risk management of nothing. Account Organ Soc 34:849–855
Renn O (1998) Three decades of risk research: accomplishments and new challenges. J Risk Res
    1:49–71
RIMS (2009) The 2008 financial crisis. A Wake-up Call for Enterprise Risk Management,
    Risk and Insurance Management Society. https://higherlogicdownload.s3.amazonaws.com/
    RIMS/2008%20Financial%20Crisis%20A%20Wake%20up%20Call%20for%20ERM.pdf?
    AWSAccessKeyId=AKIAJH5D4I4FWRALBOUA&Expires=1374767656&Signature=
    w44vxgt6Jdex%2BpK00JCMOauZRW8%3D. Accessed 28 Jul 2013
Scheytt T, Soin K, Sahlin-Andersson K, Power M (2006) Special research symposium:
    organizations and the management of risk. introduction: organizations, risk and regulation.
    J Manag Stud 43(6):1331–1337
Simons R (1999) How risky is your company? Harv Bus Rev May/June:85–94
Spira LF, Page M (2003) Risk management: the reinvention of internal control and the changing
    role of internal audit. Account Audit Account J 16(4):640–661
Starr C (1969) Social bene. ts vs. technological risks. Science 165:1232–1238
Starr R, Newfrock J, Delurey M (2003) Enterprise resilience: managing risk in the networked
    economy. Strategy Bus 30:1–13
Välikangas L, Georges A, Romme L (2012) Building resilience capabilities at "Big Brown Box,
    Inc. Strategy Leadersh 40(4):43–45
Van der Stede W (2009) Enterprise governance. Financial Manage February:38–40
Van der Stede W (2011) Management accounting research in the wake of the crisis: some
    reflections. Eur Account Rev 20(4):605–623
Westrum R (2006) A typology of resilience situations. In: Hollnagel E, Woods DD, Leveson NG
    (eds) Resilience engineering: concepts and precepts. Ashgate, Aldershot
Wildavsky A (1988) Searching for safety. Transaction, New Brunswick, NJ
Zinn JO (2004) Literature review: sociology and risk. Working paper for Social Contexts and
    Responses to Risk Network (SCARR). http://www.kent.ac.uk/scarr/papers/Sociology%20Lit
    erature%20Review%20WP1.04%20Zinn.pdf. Accessed 28 Jul 2013

The Relationship Between Multinational Enterprises and Territory in the Integrated Reporting

11

Christian Cavazzoni and Francesco Orlandi

Abstract

Multinational enterprises (MNEs) have long used both financial and sustainability reports to inform stakeholders of the different aspects of their business. Integrated Reporting, which has been developed as a result of shareholders' increasing demands for information, is an innovative tool that communicates the social and financial aspects of business operations as well as reporting companies' value creation processes over time. Integrated reporting is affected by the nature of a MNE's stakeholders and influenced by their territorial origin, which raises aspects of business analysis that must be investigated in an Integrated Report. This chapter, which begins with a review of the existing literature on the aforementioned topics, explores the relationships that exist between business activities and the territory in which it operates, proposing that MNEs consider analysing specific points when formulating their Integrated Reports. The link between MNEs and the territory is analysed with a dual perspective: the local value added, and the MNEs' relationships with the economic systems and governments of the country in which they operate. The authors believe that these two strongly interconnected factors underlie the social role that MNEs play also to the benefit of the territories in which they operate. In doing so, they qualify the contents and the use of the Integrated Report.

Although the present work is the result of joint work of both authors, paragraphs 1 and 3 are attributable to Christian Cavazzoni, paragraph 2 to Francesco Orlandi and paragraph 4 is written by both authors.

C. Cavazzoni (✉) • F. Orlandi
University of Perugia, Perugia, Italy
e-mail: christian.cavazzoni@unipg.it; francesco.orlandi1@studenti.perugia.it

C. Busco et al. (eds.), *Integrated Reporting*, DOI 10.1007/978-3-319-02168-3_11,   171
© Springer International Publishing Switzerland 2013

11.1   Introduction

Firms are institutes that operate in the social system, the purpose of which is to produce and deliver the goods and services required to satisfy the requirements of a number of individuals. As it attempts to achieve its objectives through a series of operations, the firm constantly plays a dynamic, interactive role in the social system. During this process the firm conditions and is conditioned by a bi-unique relationship of interdependency with the external environment, and by continually searching for a new equilibrium. It is able to adapt to external changes and stimuli, which will guarantee its long term survival (Ferrero 1968).

The firm interacts with a group of interest bearers from whom it continually encourages mechanisms of feedback. These are known as the company stakeholders, who can be considered to be "any group or individual who can affect or is affected by the achievement of a corporation's purpose. Stakeholders include employees, customers, suppliers, stockholders, banks, environmentalists, government and other groups who can help or hurt the corporation" (Freeman 1984, p. 46).

Studies of the stakeholder theory have established some commonly recognised principles, stating that firms should proactively pay attention to their stakeholders (Freeman 1984; Harrison and Wicks 2013), that the stakeholder theory has an equal status to that of the shareholder theory (Friedman 1970), that the stakeholder theory provides a vehicle for connecting ethics and strategy (Phillips 2003), and that firms that seek to serve the interests of a broad group of stakeholders have the opportunities to create more value over time (Freeman 1984; Freeman et al. 2007).

The academic approach behind the stakeholder theory has led to the growing role of corporate social responsibility (CSR) which has, over time, become widely recognised in corporate reports (Carroll 1991; Kiernan 2005; Wood 1991). In fact, the most open-minded organisations have switched from drawing up a financial report merely to show capital and income to provide a more detailed report to satisfy their stakeholders' demands for information. In this context the sustainability report plays a fundamental role in recognising the function of the firm within the economic system. Its purpose is to describe the ethical behaviour of the firm and to highlight how its operations interacts with the external environment, by contributing to economic development and improving the stakeholders' quality of life (Holme and Watts 2006). There is an overlap between social responsibility and corporate governance (Jamali et al. 2008), because firms are held responsible not only to internal stakeholders, but also to external stakeholders and society in general (see Huseynov and Klamm 2012). For these reasons, from the beginning of the new millennium, social and environmental reports have acquired prominence and reached a level of importance similar to financial reports.

From a theoretical viewpoint, Integrated Reporting (IR) represents a sort of synthesis of the two types of documents and also aims to combine the "*individualism*" of the financial report with the implied "*altruism*" of the sustainability report. If the CSR distinguishes, or at least places on separate levels, the achievement of profit levels and the social function of the enterprise, IR combines these two aspects as elements which simultaneously contribute to set out the competitive strategies for the firm.

The objective of IR remains that of highlighting the organisation's ability to create value in the medium-long term (Deloitte and Touche 2012; KPMG 2012; IIRC 2013). Only outwardly does it maintain a predominantly individualistic concept, as the design of this document requires the firm to widen its analytical perspective to inform stakeholders of the role played by the firm within the economic context in which it has been operating. Employment and production are at the foundation of the wealth of a community and only if both of these are present in an economic system at the same time, can a firm find a favourable environment in which to develop. If an enterprise contribute to enhance the social context in which it operates in terms of per capita income, individual skills, technological development and infrastructural services, it is likely to receive a return from its environment both in terms of demand and of employment quality and productivity.

Over the last few decades, the social and economic context has been characterised by the following: (i) increasing market globalisation, brought about mainly by the reduced number of barriers to production mobility and by the development of Information and Communication Technology tools; (ii) the growth of social expectations on the firm, which is required to implement a new management philosophy which knows how to adapt economic responsibility, understood as the capacity to produce wealth, and social responsibility (Ceccherelli 1961); (iii) the growing importance of intangibles as non-physical sources of value and generators of future profits, which currently are not adequately accounted for in corporate reports (Baruch 2001).

In a globalised economic system, where social differences tend to weaken, competition is on a global level and developing countries represent the markets of the future, it is impossible to develop a theory of the enterprise as standalone entity, but rather as an open, interconnected system which can only expand under favourable conditions. Physics reminds us that apparently static matter is actually a form of energy. Similarly, the enterprise which we imagine as a combination of productive factors is really the result of a network of relationships between individuals both inside and out.

Thus, the model of business reporting becomes the tool to display this relationships by informing the stakeholders about which activities are generating wealth and which levers the organisation is using to exploit it. In this process, the firm must try internalise the external environment, i.e. identify those social and general interests that influence its own processes to create value. Therefore, the firm uses IR to clarify its strategies, with the sole restriction of protecting its competitive advantages from competitors (IIRC 2013). The purpose is twofold: (i) providing financial investors with information concerning the firm's ability to generate medium-long term wealth, thus enabling them to evaluate not only the firm's accounting results but also the strategies it intends to implement to maintain or expand its position in the market; (ii) informing the other stakeholders of the role that the firms plays to improve the environment in which it operates in order to grow its reputation, generate recognition by the social context, and motivate workers, clients and suppliers interacting with it.

This contributes, amongst other things, to reducing the strong pressure on managers to maximise short term profit, often at the expense of a reduction in the medium-long term growth rate (Fuller and Jensen 2002; Michenaud 2008). This frequently occurs where corporate evaluation is calculated on the base of the firm's financial statement rather than on its corporate strategies. As a result, the ability of IR to effectively convey information to the stakeholders can become an essential prerequisite for a stable company in the market. This allows positive feedback to be given which, in turn, may enable the firm to increase its ability to generate value. In this sense, the process of developing the IR becomes a regular opportunity through which the firm must:

- identify the internal and external values in which it intends to invest and which it believes to be closely connected with its ability to create value;
- define its own stakeholders;
- identify the relationships between corporate values and the creation of value over time;
- build a strategic vision which bonds these elements and guarantees the definition of a common thought which will identify the behaviour of the organisation;
- formalise these internal processes in a document which is able to explain the information to the different stakeholders, bearing in mind their different interests and different learning skills, so as to maximise its usefulness;
- set up a continual feedback process in order to monitor and eventually amend the fundamental contents of IR according to changes in the social and economic context.

This process takes on a more linear connotation for firms operating in localised areas. However, for multinational enterprises (MNEs) with economic activities in various locations, it becomes extremely complex and relevant. MNES need to differentiate the information according to the stakeholders' geographical origin and, above all, describe and give the reasons for the different behaviour of the enterprise towards similar stakeholders living in different countries.

Although we are aware that "these large MNEs have been much more active in sustainability reporting than other firms, which means that evolving patterns noticeable amongst this panel can help shed light on the diversity of options, as well as aspects and/or dilemmas that play a role more generally in the way MNEs address organizational accountability on sustainability" (Perego and Kolk 2012, p. 174), we have approached some of the problems in the reporting of multinational enterprises operating in distant, disparate, geographical areas, in order to identify the main variables which may influence the relationship between the enterprise and area, and to propose some models to report this issue.

The principal parameter used in the analysis is represented by value added. Part 2 of this chapter describes the latter in detail, and introduces the concept of "local value added". Then, part 3 is dedicated to illustrating some of the elements qualifying the relationship between the MNEs and territory.

11.2   The Determination of Local Value Added in Multinational Enterprises

A manufacturing firm, which begins with a certain quantum of raw materials, and then engages itself in a conversion process to yield a product with a new utility and market value which differs from the original cost of materials (Chakraborty 1979), cannot consider to have concluded its activity until the profit already achieved is also distributed wisely among those who have collaborated towards its production (Zappa 1956).

Value added (VA) is possibly the most used indicator to summarise the overall evaluation of the company system, because it is capable of measuring the global value generated and distributed among the various parties that have contributed to its creation (Morley 1978; Mei 1992; Riahi-Belkaoui 1999). While, on the one hand, VA can offer significant information that will enable corporate performance to be assessed, on the other hand, it allows quantifying the share of corporate results among different stakeholder categories. VA is a tool which enables corporate activity to be appreciated, and consolidates the process of alignment between company stakeholders (Coda 1995).[1]

The value added concept can be expressed through the following equation:

$$VBS = W + T + I + D + R + DP. \qquad (11.1)$$

where:
V = value of production (sales revenue plus change in inventory)
BS = bought-in materials and services
W = salaries and wages
T = taxation
I = interest
D = dividend
R = retained earnings
DP = depreciation

Therefore, VA can be quantified on the one hand as the difference between the value of production and the cost of purchase of materials and services and, on the other, it represents the total return of the firm earned by all providers of capital, employees, government and the amount used to maintain and expand assets (retained earnings plus depreciation—Sarkar and Nandi 2011).

In line with the concepts and the equation illustrated above, value added can be shown in the Value Added Statement (VAS), consisting of two consequential and equally balanced tables showing the wealth created by the firm (see Table 11.1).

---

[1] Burchell et al. (1985) also state that value added has the property of revealing (or representing) something about the social character of production, something which is occluded by traditional profit and loss accounting. Value added reveals that the wealth created in production is the consequence of the combined effort of a number of agents who together form the co-operating team.

Table 11.1 Value added statement of shoprite

	June 2012 R'000	%	June 2011 R'000	%
Sale of merchandise (V)	82,730,587		72,297,777	
Investment income (V)	224,425		122,277	
Cost of goods and services (BS)	(70,135,100)		(61,341,791)	
Value added	**12,819,912**	**100.0**	**11,078,263**	**100.0**
Employed as follows:				
Employees				
Salaries, wages and service benefits (W)	6,930,791	54.1	6,089,252	55.0
Providers of capital				
Finance costs to providers of funds (I)	223,563	1.7	125,964	1.1
Dividends to providers of share capital (D)	1,421,598	11.1	1,189,411	10.7
Income tax				
Income tax on profits made (T)	1,438,889	11.2	1,346,826	12.2
Reinvested				
Depreciation and amortisation (DP)	1,200,106	9.4	1,006,442	9.1
Retained earnings (R)	1,604,965	12.5	1,320,369	11.9
Employment of value added	**12,819,912**	**100.0**	**11,078,263**	**100.0**

Source: Shoprite holdings integrated report, 2012

These will show the difference between the operational revenue of management and the costs sustained to buy in new external resources and the allocation them between the productive factors and the various stakeholders who, by taking part in the firm's operations, have contributed to its creation (Pendril 1977).

The value added statement has a fundamental role in the communication process developed by IR. It provides not only economic, but also social information, by identifying the portion of wealth to be distributed among the participants in the company's operations for their contribution (Prasad et al. 2012). For this reason, VA is a much broader performance measure than net income, since the latter is only able to capture the wealth produced for the shareholders.

MNEs are characterised by various, legally autonomous, operational units scattered in different regions or nations, yet connected by a bond of participation which draws them into a single economic entity that coordinates and control them. Value added is capable of providing far-reaching information on corporate operations, and this makes it particularly useful in reporting information within an MNE context (Ferrarese 2000; Narula and Dunning 2010; McCann and Zoltan 2011).

The fact that a firm characterised by a specific social and cultural context operates in territories that are different from its country of origin, inevitably leads to an alteration of the social and economic environment of the host country, which may potentially become a source of conflict. Furthermore, the divergence between the interest of MNEs in maximising their "global" corporate profit, and the interest that the host countries have in maximising the collective benefits of the operations in the territory, tends to create contrasts and misunderstandings between the various stakeholders (Mason 1974; Vernon 1977; Campbell et al. 2011).

The information provided in the report about the value added for the country in which an MNE operates is of fundamental importance in evaluating the policies that MNE uses to handle its relationships with different territories, and with parties belonging to the same category of stakeholders but residing in different countries.

Clearly, this information reveals the operational choices of MNEs, resulting in the firm being able to boast about its development policy in the countries in which it operates or, on the contrary, having to "justify" its behaviour towards certain stakeholders.

Therefore, this means that the MNE must provide a "customised" report for each country in which it operates, its aim being to measure the economic impact of the MNE on the territory. This can be shown by calculating the local value added (LVA) created by the enterprise, which can be compared to a sort of "balance of payments" of multinational business operations.[2]

LVA "adjusts" the calculation of the total value added (see the Eq. 11.1) of wages the multinational pays to overseas stakeholders. Therefore, LVA deducts from the multinational's total outputs (local sales plus change in inventory plus exports) the remuneration for its overseas productive factors and overseas stakeholders who have contributed to the creation of the value of production (cost of imported goods and services, sum of wages of foreign capital, amortisation of immobilisation purchased overseas). It makes it possible to estimate the wealth that the multinational has "distributed" in the specific area of operation (Rahman 1990).

LVA can be expressed by the following equation:

$$V - BS_F - W_F - I_F - D_F - DP_F = BS_L + W_L + T + I_L + D_L + R + DP_L. \quad (11.2)$$

where:

V = value of production (local sales plus change in inventory plus exports)
BS_F = imports of goods and services
W_F = wages and salaries to foreign workers
I_F = interest on foreign loans
D_F = dividend to foreign shareholder
DP_F = depreciation on imported fixed assets
BS_L = local bought-in materials and services
W_L = wages and salaries to local employees

---

[2] If, at most, corporate operations use only the productive factors from overseas countries compared to that in which the multinational operates, then any "local" sale by the multinational would represent a "subtraction of resources from the host country", because it would be paying stakeholders in another nation. On the other hand, we could conclude that if the production value was obtained entirely by using "local" productive factors, then any export of the commercialised product by the multinational would represent an "addition of foreign resources" into the country, which would pay local stakeholders.

Table 11.2 Local value added statement

	State A	State B	State C
Sales revenue (local sales plus exports) (V)	xxx	xxx	xxx
Variation in the inventories (V)	xxx	xxx	xxx
Import of goods (BS$_F$)	(xxx)	(xxx)	(xxx)
Import of services (BS$_F$)	(xxx)	(xxx)	(xxx)
Wages and salaries to foreign workers (W$_F$)	(xxx)	(xxx)	(xxx)
Interest on foreign loans (I$_F$)	(xxx)	(xxx)	(xxx)
Dividends to foreign shareholders (D$_F$)	(xxx)	(xxx)	(xxx)
Depreciation on imported fixed assets (DP$_F$)	(xxx)	(xxx)	(xxx)
Local value added	*XXX*	*XXX*	*XXX*
Local goods (BS$_L$)	xxx	xxx	xxx
Local services (BS$_L$)	xxx	xxx	xxx
Wages and salaries to local employees (W$_L$)	xxx	xxx	xxx
Tax payments (T)	xxx	xxx	xxx
Interest on local loans (I$_L$)	xxx	xxx	xxx
Dividends to local shareholders (D$_L$)	xxx	xxx	xxx
Retained earnings (R)	xxx	xxx	xxx
Local capital consumption (DP$_L$)	xxx	xxx	xxx
Distribution of local value added	*XXX*	*XXX*	*XXX*

T = taxation
I_L = interest on local loans
D_L = dividend to local shareholder
R = retained earnings
DP_L = depreciation on local fixed assets

The distribution of local value added can be represented and analysed qualitatively in the information provided by MNEs in order to allow them to demonstrate how the various components of the economy of the host country have been paid by the comprehensive operations carried out there by the multinational.

This distribution process can be shown in Table 11.2.

The proposed tables are an example of the quantitative information which can be extracted from LVA to provide an indication of the social role played by MNEs as they create and distribute wealth in the territory, pay staff, local shareholders and the State. However, IR adds to corporate reports by making qualitative information available to the user making it easier to understand the existing relationships between so many variables which determine corporate results. Therefore, the role of social responsibility of MNEs can be enriched to include a better understanding of the relationship between the enterprise and the territory. These elements will be discussed in the following section.

11.3 The Relationship Between Multinational Enterprises and Government. The Tax Component

A discussion of taxation in relation to corporate social responsibility (CSR) is a delicate proposition. Although the firm has a strong bond with territory in the countries in which it produces and sells under the maximum authority of its government, the contribution it makes by paying the taxes of individual countries reduces the resources available for it to make investments or distribute dividends. The company limits development, unless compensated by the indirect benefits the organisation enjoys in the context in which it operates. This potential conflict is polarised into two totally opposite points of view.

On the one hand, there are those who consider the enterprise to be one of many individuals in a wider community, of which it is an indistinguishable member to the extent that the interest of the individual is required for the common good. The most orthodox versions of this theory recall Aristotle's philosophical principles and presuppose an "Aristotelian approach to business ethics" (Solomon 1992a), according to which the ultimate purpose of productive organisations naturally tends to coincide with that of the surrounding social context.

On the other hand, there are those following an amoral, utilitarian approach placing taxes on the same level as other costs sustained by the firm. They conclude that taxation must be minimised in the same way as any other factor which decreases income (Hanlon and Heitzman 2010; Hanlon and Slemrod 2009; Robinson et al. 2010). This assumption gives rise to the axiom that any behaviour within the boundaries of the law which reduces taxation increases corporate value and responds to the shareholders' interests.

The comparison which has developed in the scientific world has found no synthesis in empirical evidence. In fact, the most recent studies of the relationship between CSR and aggressive tax have not identified a positive relationship between the two indicators. On the one hand, some authors have found that more socially responsible firms try to follow correct tax policies (Watson 2011; Lanis and Richardson 2012). On the other hand, other researchers have verified that some firms claiming to be socially responsible adopt forms of fiscal arbitrage (Carroll and Joulfaian 2005; Preuss 2010; Sikka 2010; Preuss 2012).

However, without having to theorise "humanised" enterprise strategies, (Andrews et al. 1989) which envisage a careful management of the "social nature of the persons and their capacity for acquiring virtues that perfect them and, as a consequence, for growing as human beings" (Melè 2003, p. 82), there are many reasons for an enterprise to show politically correct behaviour towards social questions, of which governments should be the bearers.

• Many external stakeholders judge enterprises which implement tax avoidance very negatively and consider them socially irresponsible (Erle 2008; Schön 2008) as it is in the public interest for the firm to fulfil its tax obligations correctly. Tax aggressiveness, tax shelters, and tax evasion could, therefore, seriously compromise corporate image and cause "isolation of the business".

- "There is no business world apart from the people who work in business, and the integrity of those people determines the integrity of the organization as well as vice versa" (Solomon 1992b, p. 338), and a management that "cheats the government" is a management that may also "cheat" its shareholders (Huseynov and Klamm 2012, p. 804).
- On the other hand, those same shareholders may find tax evasion or tax avoidance inopportune, believing that this exposes the firm to a potentially greater risk in the long term compared with the actual benefits produced.
- Whereas the firm's interest in profit may be considered separate from its surrounding economic context in the short term, this is unthinkable in the long term, as the growth of the economic system depends on that of the social context (Coda 1995; Catturi 1989) as the different dimensions of finalism of the enterprise, concerning the achievement of economic, competitive and social results, respectively, are constructed and connected with each other, so as to trigger a virtual circle which exalts and strengthens correct behaviour (Montrone 2000). Thus, an enterprise which does not invest in the territory is an enterprise which does not invest in its own future.
- It is increasingly difficult for enterprises to compete globally without the support of national governments which place them in the best position to produce efficiently by implementing infrastructural investments, contra-cyclical economic policies, income support for the population, and by maintaining adequate services for the enterprises (such as an efficient legal system), which guarantee stable social order.
- Equally, corruption, often very common in developing countries, diminishes transparency and correctness in competitive processes and can distort the economic system, and reward less efficient firms which are more inclined to unlawful practices or moral hazards.

Therefore, a correct relationship with government authorities appears preferable not merely for moral reasons, however relevant and commendable,[3] but above all from an economic point of view, as the enterprise contributes via direct or indirect taxation to the growth of the country system in which it operates. This behaviour creates economic and social development which, in the long term, can generate positive feedback, both directly via the support of public services and infrastructures which benefit production, and indirectly via the creation or development of new outlet markets for its products.

In other words, a tax aggressive behaviour constitutes a short term tactic aiming to temporarily maximise the profits and benefits of current shareholders and managers, whereas a correct fiscal policy guarantees the future growth of the enterprise within the economic system.

---

[3] "The philosophical myths that have grown almost cancerous in many business circles, the neo-Hobbesian view that business is *every man for himself* and the Darwinian view that *it's a jungle out there*, are direct denials of the Aristotelian view that we are, first of all, members of a community and our self-interest is for the most part identical to the larger interests of the group" (Solomon 1992a p. 326).

It is, therefore, evident how the relationships between enterprise and government and between enterprise and taxation, often considered as an expression of social responsibility, can constitute elements on which to base the information of IR, in that they demonstrate a link with the medium-long term strategies of the enterprise.

The relationship between enterprise and state can be expressed by numerous factors involving economic activity. The state provides social capital on behalf of society in the shape of education, healthcare, transport, social order, legal system and, as every form of capital expects to receive the requisite return on its investment, so the state expects to obtain payment by taxing its citizens (Sikka 2010).

On the other hand, the enterprise has specific interests in the activity of public administration in terms of services, support for internal consumption, implementation of infrastructures which assist production and the transport of goods and, last but not least, the upkeep of an adequate level of legality which guarantees economic activity can run correctly.

However, it must be said that, especially in the short term, the relationship between state and enterprise can be represented by the communicating channels in which fiscal planning can reduce or avoid taxation, thus generating immediate, direct benefits to the shareholders. Subsequently, it imposes a corresponding obligation on the community, which will see a decrease in the resources available to governments to put their economic and social policies into practice.

It is clear, therefore, that above and beyond the affirmation of the principle and a desirable, far-sighted long-term vision, taxation and the relationships of firms with governments constitute a grey area, in which there is a clash between shareholders' interests to receive profit, directors' interests to maximise the firm's income, and the indirect interests of internal and external stakeholders in the development of the territory. Furthermore, the analysis of this phenomenon cannot be separated from the consideration that "directors have no obligation, legal or even moral, to select the event (out of a choice of more than one) under which their company will pay a maximum amount of tax and, importantly, that democratic societies do not insist that they do make such a choice" (Hasseldine and Morris 2013, p. 11) and "stock markets rarely ask any questions about the social quality of profits" (Sikka 2013, p. 16). Neither can it exclude the expression of tax-related behaviour as forms of a different kind of fiscal arbitrage, with profoundly different economic contents and associated moral judgements: corruption, tax evasion, tax avoidance, abuse of rights, transfer pricing, and the adoption of economic choices conditioned by fiscal variables.

However, all these pieces, which together form a complex, conflictual picture, only make the role of IR more important. Its description of tax-related behaviour will take into account the choices made, how the managers have handled these opposing interests, and the existing relationships between tax policies and the strategy of the enterprise.

The information requested fulfils a double purpose: (i) it demonstrates the economic contribution the firm provides the country in which it operates, by paying taxes and guarantees transparent fiscal planning policies to highlight the absence of any tax evasion or avoidance, the movement of income between countries and the use of tax havens; (ii) it explains how the choices made not only respond to a moral commitment, but are also part of the strategic vision of the enterprise.

Fig. 11.1 Rio Tinto provides
an indication of its total tax
payments by type of tax.
Source: Rio Tinto—Tax Paid
in 2012

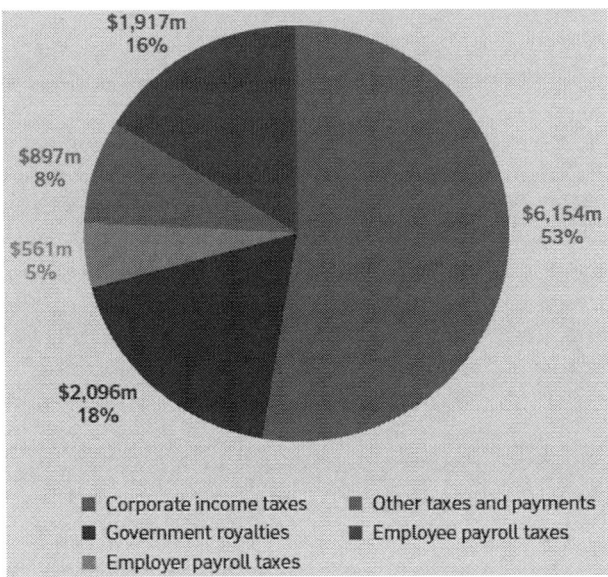

IR must, therefore, try to provide an answer to the following questions:

* how does the firm contribute to the development of the country in which it operates?
* how does the development implemented within the territory link with the ability of the enterprise to produce medium-long term wealth?
* what strategies does the enterprise put in place to create or strengthen the bi-unique relationship with the state?

In answer to the first question, enterprises usually show the final data concerning the taxes paid in each country (Fig. 11.1). However, taxation constitutes only one of the forms of contribution received either directly or indirectly from the enterprise. In fact, resources transferred by the enterprise to the state may include:

* income tax, i.e. taxes calculated on the profit produced by its economic activity in the country;
* income tax paid by workers, in direct proportion to the number and qualifications of the work force used by the enterprise;
* indirect taxes, mainly VAT and customs duties;
* fees for services, concessions, authorisations granted by the State to the enterprise;
* direct donations or donations to state-controlled organisations to achieve worthy aims.

This initial information, often provided by MNEs in absolute terms (Fig. 11.2), does not, however, express a value judgement on the behaviour and choices of the enterprise.

Thus, to provide the stakeholders with a better perspective of analysis sustained by measuring the quantitative terms of the phenomenon, it is possible to highlight

Fig. 11.2 Gold Fields sets out its contributions to government by region (US$/m). *Source*: Gold Fields Integrated Annual Review, 2012

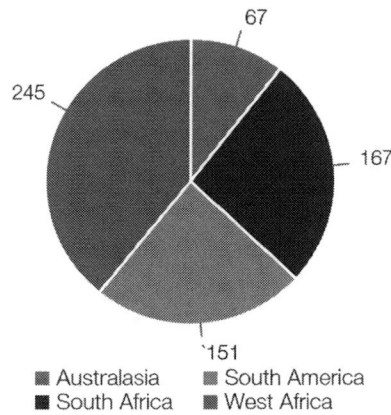

Australasia   South America
South Africa   West Africa

the relationships between valued added produced in the country and the direct and indirect contribution by the firm to state taxation. IR can, therefore be structured to record:

- the value added created in the country, highlighting the relationships with the activities of the value chain implemented in each establishment in the territory;
- the share of value added produced in the state which is destined to support the government under various forms of contribution;
- the interventions the enterprise carries out in the social system, replacing state intervention (Table 11.3).

This perspective not only provides proof of the taxes paid, but also correlates them with two fundamental economic processes: the activities of the value chain implemented within the state and the value added produced by each activity.

However, payment of taxes does not exhaust the information concerning the relationships between the enterprise and the territory in which it operates. This can be supplemented with some particularly significant aspects which qualify the firm's behaviour. In fact, when we speak of the state as a stakeholder, we must remember how this organisation is, in turn, the expression of a multitude of underlying interests which do not conclude simply by collecting taxes, but stem from the role played by the state in the social and economic system.

In this sense, an additional qualifying aspect of the enterprise-state relationship is the adoption of models of behaviour which contrast the use of forms of corruption by the managers. The firm will use IR to provide information on these subjects concerning the contents of its code of ethics, its support of initiatives aiming to contrast these practices and the actions undertaken to discourage such behaviour.

There are several initiatives of this kind. The World Economic Forum has promoted a Partnering Against Corruption Initiative that is a global, multi-industry, multi-stakeholder anti-corruption initiative set up to raise business standards and to contribute to a competitive, transparent, accountable and ethical business society.[4]

---

[4] http://www.weforum.org/issues/partnering-against-corruption-initiative

Table 11.3 Distribution of local value added by value chain

	State A	State B	GROUP
Contribution of activities to value added			
Primary activities			
Inbound logistics	xxx	xxx	xxx
Operations	xxx	xxx	xxx
Outbound logistics	xxx	xxx	xxx
Marketing & sales	xxx	xxx	xxx
Service	xxx	xxx	xxx
Support activities			
Firm infrastructure	xxx	xxx	xxx
Human resource management	xxx	xxx	xxx
Technology	xxx	xxx	xxx
Procurement	xxx	xxx	xxx
Value added	**XXX**	**XXX**	**XXX**
Payments to government			
Income taxes	(xxx)	(xxx)	(xxx)
Indirect taxes and duties	(xxx)	(xxx)	(xxx)
Property tax	(xxx)	(xxx)	(xxx)
Royalties	(xxx)	(xxx)	(xxx)
Employee taxes	(xxx)	(xxx)	(xxx)
Other contributions	(xxx)	(xxx)	(xxx)
Interventions replacing the government (construction of hospitals, schools, kindergartens)	(xxx)	(xxx)	(xxx)

Then again, the European Union has recently come to an agreement on the wording of the new Accounting Directive, introducing a principle of transparency for payments by the extractive industry to the Governments of countries holding mineral resources. The obligations envisaged by the Directive are very similar to those in the Dodd-Frank Act in the United States and include all types of firms, compared to the American model which referred to companies quoted on the stock market. This will enable citizens to know "how much money their governments receive for their natural resources and how this money is used" (Kaufmann D., president of Revenue Watch 2012[5]).

IR can use this information to explain how the company diffuses the principles and models of behaviour within its organisational structure, how it informs its managers of existing legislation in the various countries, and of the procedures to monitor compliance with internal directives by its directors and, more generally speaking, the results it obtains in its fight against unlawful practices.

Numerous firms have adopted IR to provide information regarding the risks of corruption, especially those enterprises operating as concession holders for the extraction of natural resources which are most open to these phenomena (Fig. 11.3).

---

[5] http://www.revenuewatch.org

Fig. 11.3 Bam Group proposes to share turnover according to Corruption Perception Index Country. *Source*: Royal Bam Group, Sustainability report, 2012. The Corruption Perception Index (CPI) is calculated annually by Transparency International

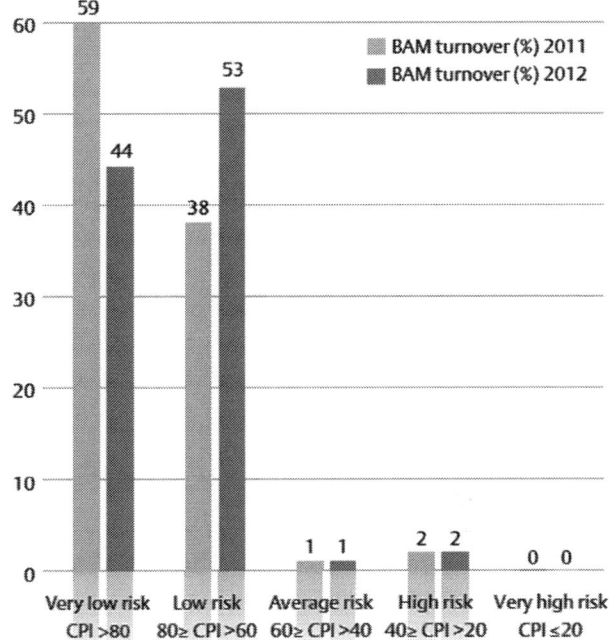

The analysis of country risk factors (Fig. 11.4) should be accompanied by a description of the behaviour adopted to oppose the various forms of corruption.

To fulfil this role, IR must highlight the functions given to the systems of internal audit, the operations of the control department, the warning situations recorded by the alert systems, any breach discovered and the reactions of the organisation to this type of behaviour (Table 11.4).

The additional element which clearly qualifies the relationships between enterprise and state is the existing economic and financial relationship between the associated entities present in the various countries. This phenomenon, which for the sake of convenience we will define as "transfer pricing", stems from the policies adopted by the firm regarding the exchange of goods, the payment of royalties and dividends, the payment for infra-group services and funding, and for the placement of relevant activities in terms of value added in Countries with low taxation.

These internal transactions in MNEs are continually on the increase and currently exceed 30 % of the entire international trade (United Nations, October 2012). They generate true flows of wealth which move "mysteriously" across transnational borders without a trace, since they disappear mainly within a single economic or legal individual.

Furthermore, the policies concerning transfer pricing not only determine the level of taxation of the enterprise in a particular country, but also demonstrate the wealth created and distributed in a territory as opposed to that transferred to other associated entities of the organisation. As regards IR, this information could lead to

	Transparency International Corruption Perceptions Index 2012	Maplecroft Governance Framework Risk Index 2012	Maplecroft Democratic Governance Index 2012	Maplecroft Rule of Law Index 2012	World Bank GDP Growth data 2011	Extractive Industries Transparency Initiative status
Australia	7th out of 176 countries	8.87 (Low risk)	10.00 (Low risk)	9.34 (Low risk)	1.8%	Not a signatory
Ghana	64th out of 176 countries	5.22 (Medium risk)	8.00 (Low risk)	6.24 (Medium risk)	14.4%	Compliant country
Peru	83rd out of 176 countries	5.43 (Medium risk)	10.00 (Low risk)	5.52 (Medium risk)	6.9%	Compliant country
South Africa	69th out of 176 countries	7.22 (Medium risk)	9.00 (Low risk)	7.56 (Low risk)	3.1%	Not a signatory

Fig. 11.4 Gold Field provides the following classification of the host country governance and growth indicators. *Source*: Gold Fields Integrated Annual Review, 2012

Table 11.4 Activities fulfilled by Snam internal audit

	2010	2011	2012
Total number of audits fulfilled	51	48	55
Reports received	26	22	17
... of which related to the Internal Control System	10	8	10
... of which related to the accounting system, auditors, fraud	–	–	–
... of which related to corporate responsibility ex D.Lgs. 231/2001	–	–	–
... of which related to violations of anti-corruption law	–	1	–
... of which related to other subjects (Code of Ethics, mobbing, theft, security)	16	13	7
Archived reports due to the absence of evidence or untrue evidence	16	11	13
Reports resulting in disciplinary or administrative action and/or submission to the Court	–	5	2
Reports under examination	6	6	2

Source: Snam Sustainability report, 2012

MNEs constructing an internal Balance of Payments in which the wealth produced and distributed in each country replaces imports and exports. The data acquired from the model concerning the Local Value Added Statement proposed in paragraph 2, together with a summary of these movements using a specific report, make it possible to identify the Local Added Value created and distributed for each associated entity compared to the value added transferred to other countries (Table 11.5).

The results of these dynamics within MNEs can be summarised to highlight the flows of wealth moving between associated entities (Fig. 11.5).

We should point out that many States adopt regulations which oppose forms of fiscal arbitrage and require transactions between countries to be assumed "on an arm's length basis". Nevertheless, even though it operates in full compliance with tax regulations, the company often shows significant margins which enable it to place or transfer valued added amongst its branches. In addition, these regulations, inspired by the OECD model (OECD 2010), do not radically influence the behaviour of the enterprise. However they normally protect only the government authorities, forcing the enterprise to tax an income which has been recalculated

Table 11.5 Balance of local value added

	State A
Local value added created in State A	*XXX*
Workers	xxx
Suppliers of goods and services	xxx
Local minority shareholders	xxx
Lenders	xxx
Government	xxx
Depreciations and amortisations	xxx
Others	xxx
A distribution of value added in State A	*XXX*
Parent MNEs	(xxx)
Indirect taxes and duties	(xxx)
Foreign minority shareholders	(xxx)
Foreign lenders	(xxx)
Foreign governments	(xxx)
Others	(xxx)
B value added transferred to foreign States	*(XXX)*
(A–B) Balance of local value added	**XXX**

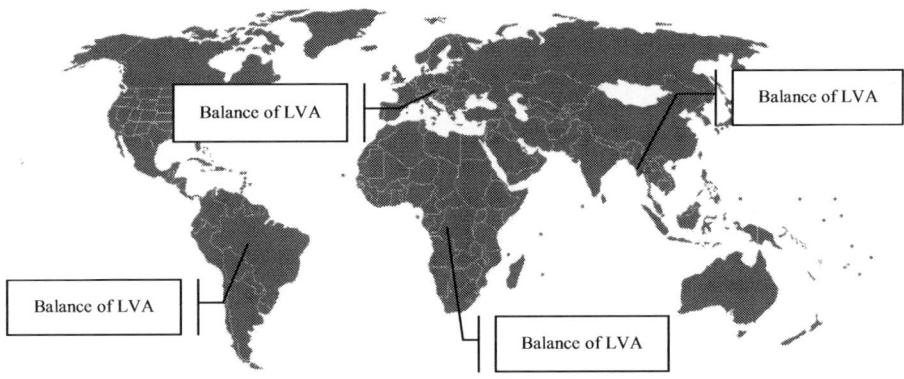

Fig. 11.5 Local value added flow

according to different transfer prices, whereas no influence is exerted on the effective transfer of wealth between branches of the MNEs.

On the contrary, IR, which includes a further breakdown of LVA, must take into account the policies of transfer pricing not merely from a physical viewpoint, but also in terms of social commitment to the growth of the countries in which production takes place. It should highlight how internal management choices influence the distribution of local value added.

The different levels of analysis of the enterprise–state relationship, which we have attempted to highlight, must in the long run find their synthesis in the definition of the strategies adopted by the enterprise to increase its value over time. This final descriptive stage is the definitive qualification of IR, as it outlines the relationships between the behaviour of the firm, its choices of fiscal planning and its value creation processes, by taking on the role to disclose corporate competitive strategies.

Thus, once the various forms of relationships have been identified between its behaviour towards the country system and the processes to create value this may encourage, IR will have to place corporate choices within a much wider strategic vision. The latter will have to highlight how and why the firm intends to invest a good reputation from a culture of legality into the social and economic growth of the territories in which it operates and in its relationship with local governments.

Conclusions

In this chapter, we have attempted to examine some of the problems regarding Integrated Reporting for enterprises with branches in different companies (MNEs). Commencing from an analysis of the literature on the subject of corporate social responsibility which has partially dealt with these topics, we have tried to identify the relationships between MNEs and territory which may influence IR.

For this purpose, we considered local value added to constitute the economic aggregate, which best summarises the overall activity and the existing relationships between the various components of the corporate system, representing a fundamental tool to measure the effects of the management choices made by firms on territory.

However, the relationship between MNEs and local interests presents numerous facets which, on the one hand, influence the interpretation of the LVA and, on the other, introduce further factors for the analysis of these dynamics. In this sense, the chapter focuses its attention on three particular areas of interest: the fiscal component, transfer pricing and the absence of unlawful practices.

We actually believe that these are the characteristic features which determine the relationship between MNEs and the state, and the contribution played by the firm to the economic development of the context in which it settles. Thus, the disclosure proposed on these topics within IR, goes beyond the "*numbers*" contained in financial statements or the "*good intentions*" of sustainability reports. It is able to report the strategic choices of MNEs concerning these dynamics by evaluating the role of the value creation process, and providing its stakeholders adequate information in order to strengthen the company's image in the global market.

References

Andrews K et al (1989) Ethics in practice: managing the moral corporation. Harvard Business School Press, Boston, MA

Baruch L (2001) Intangibles: management, measurement, and reporting. Brookings Institution Press, Washington, DC

Burchell S, Clubb C, Hopwood AG (1985) Accounting in its social context: towards a history of value added in the United Kingdom. Account Organ Soc 10(4):381–413

Campbell JT, Eden L, Miller SR (2011) Multinationals and corporate social responsibility in host countries: does distance matter? J Int Bus Stud 43(1):84–106

Carroll A (1991) The pyramid of corporate social responsibility: toward the moral management of organizational stakeholders. Bus Horiz 34(4):39–48

Carroll R, Joulfaian D (2005) Taxes and corporate giving to charity. Public Finan Rev 33 (3):300–317

Catturi G (1989) Teorie contabili e scenari economico—aziendali. Cedam, Padova

Ceccherelli A (1961) Economia aziendale e amministrazione delle imprese. Editrice universitaria, Firenze

Chakraborty SK (1979) New Perspective in Management Accounting. The McMillan Company of India, Delhi

Coda V (1995) L'orientamento strategico dell'impresa. Utet, Torino

Deloitte & Touche (2012) Integrated reporting. navigating your way to a truly integrated report. Accessed 10 Jul 2013

Erle B (2008) Tax risk management and board responsibility. In: Schön W (ed) Tax and corporate governance. Springer, Berlin, pp 205–220

Ferrarese MR (2000) Le istituzioni della globalizzazione. Il mulino, Bologna

Ferrero G (1968) Istituzioni di economia d'azienda. Giuffrè, Milano

Freeman RE (1984) Strategic management—a stakeholder approach. Pitman, Boston, MA

Freeman RE, Harrison JS, Wicks AC (2007) Managing for stakeholders: survival, reputation, and success. Yale University Press, New Haven, CT

Harrison JS, Wicks AC (2013) Stakeholder theory, value and firm performance. Bus Ethics Q 23:97–124

Friedman M (1970) The social responsibility of business is to increase its profits. *New York Time Magazine* (September 13), pp 32–33, 122–124

Fuller J, Jensen M (2002) Just say no to wall street: putting a stop to the earnings game. J Appl Corp Finance 14(4):41–46

Hanlon M, Heitzman S (2010) Review of tax research. J Account Econ 50(2–3):127–178

Hanlon M, Slemrod J (2009) What does tax aggressiveness signal? Evidence from stock price reactions to news about tax shelter involvement. J Public Econ 93(1):126–141

Hasseldine J, Morris G (2013) Corporate social responsibility and tax avoidance: a comment and reflection. Account Forum 37(1):1–14

Holme L, Watts P (2006) Human rights and corporate social responsibility. World Business Council for Sustainable Development, Geneva

Huseynov F, Klamm BK (2012) Tax avoidance, tax management and corporate social responsibility. J Corp Finance 18(4):804–827

IIRC (2013) Consultation draft of the international IR framework. IIRC, New York. Accessed 14 Apr 2013

Jamali D, Safieddine AM, Rabbath M (2008) Corporate governance and corporate social responsibility synergies and interrelationships. Corp Gov Int Rev 16(5):443–459

Kiernan MJ (2005) Corporate social responsibility—the investor's perspective. In: Hancock J (ed) Investing in corporate social responsibility: a guide to best practice, business planning & the UK's leading companies. Kogan Page, London, pp 67–79

KPMG (2012) Integrated reporting. Performance insight through better business reporting. Accessed 10 Jul 2013

Lanis R, Richardson G (2012) Corporate social responsibility and tax aggressiveness: an empirical analysis. J Account Public Pol 31(1):86–108

Mason RH (1974) Conflicts between host countries and the multinational enterprise. Calif Manag Rev 17(1):5–14

McCann P, Zoltan J (2011) Globalization: countries, cities and multinationals. Reg Stud 45 (1):17–32

Mei G (1992) Sistemi contabili e strutture del conto del risultato economico. Cedam, Padova
Melè D (2003) The challenge of humanistic management. J Bus Ethics 44(1):77–88
Michenaud S (2008) Corporate investment and analyst pressure (Working paper). Rice University, Houston, TX
Montrone A (2000) Il valore aggiunto nella misurazione della performance economica e sociale dell'impresa. FrancoAngeli, Milano
Morley FM (1978) The value added statement: a review of its use in corporate reports. for the institute of chartered accountants of Scotland. Gee & Co, London
Narula R, Dunning JH (2010) Multinational enterprises, development and globalization: some clarifications and research agenda. Oxf Dev Stud 38(3):263–287
OECD (2010) Transfer pricing guidelines for multinational enterprises and tax administrations. http://www.oecd.org
Pendril D (1977) Introducing a new comer—the value added statement. Accountancy 88 (1012):92–94
Perego P, Kolk A (2012) Multinationals' accountability on sustainability: the evolution of third-party assurance of sustainability reports. J Bus Ethics 110(2):173–190
Phillips RA (2003) Stakeholder theory and organizational ethics. Berrett-Koehler, San Francisco, CA
Prasad MSV, Sheela P, Prasada Rao SS (2012) Value-added accounting: an empirical illustration with reference to the port of Visakhapatnam. IUP J Account Res Audit Pract 11(2):33–57
Preuss L (2010) Tax avoidance and corporate social responsibility: you can't do both, or can you? Corp Gov 10(4):365–374
Preuss L (2012) Responsibility in paradise? The adoption of CSR tools by companies domiciled in tax havens. J Bus Ethics 110:1–14
Rahman MZ (1990) The local value added statement: a reporting requirement for multinationals in developing host countries. Int J Account 25(2):87–98
Riahi-Belkaoui A (1999) Value added reporting and research: state of the art. Quorum Books, New York, NY
Robinson JR, Kises SA, Weaver CD (2010) Performance measurement of corporate tax departments. Account Rev 85(3):1035–1064
Sarkar CR, Nandi KC (2011) Corporate social performance through value added reporting—a case study of hindustan petroleum corporation ltd. Int J Res Comm Econ Manage 1(6):89–95
Sikka P (2010) Smoke and mirrors: corporate social responsibility and tax avoidance. Account Forum 34(3):153–168
Sikka P (2013) Smoke and mirrors: corporate social responsibility and tax avoidance—A reply to Hasseldine and Morris. Account Forum 37(1):15–28
Schön W (2008) Tax and corporate governance. A legal approach. In: Schön W (ed) Tax and corporate governance. Springer, Berlin
Solomon RC (1992a) Corporate roles, personal virtues: an aristotelean approach to business ethics. Bus Ethics Q 2(3):317–339
Solomon RC (1992b) Ethics and excellence. Cooperation and integrity in business. Oxford University Press, New York, NY
United Nation (2012) Pratical tranfer pricing manual for developing countries. http://www.un.org/esa/ffd/tax/documents/bgrd_tp.htm
Vernon R (1977) The power of multinational enterprises in developing countries. In: Madden CH (ed) The case for multinational corporations. Praeger, New York, NY
Watson L (2011) Social influences on aggressive accounting: the impact of corporate social responsibility on tax aggressiveness. Paper presented at the American Accounting Association Annual Meeting, Denver, 6–10 August 2011
Wood DJ (1991) Corporate social performance revisited. Acad Manag Rev 16(4):691–718
Zappa G (1956) Le produzioni nell'economia delle imprese. Giuffrè, Milano

Towards Integrated Reporting in the Public Sector

12

Luca Bartocci and Francesca Picciaia

Abstract

During the last 20 years, social, political and economic changes have impacted on the accountability concept in the public sector. In this context, public organizations are requested to improve their reporting processes, and disclose more accurate and complete information about their activities and results. In April 2013 the International Integrated Reporting Council issued the Consultation Draft of the International Integrated Reporting Framework, with the aim of contributing—among other things—to the initial integration of information regarding different forms of "capital" involved in the value creation processes of an organization. While primarily designed for private companies, the Consultation Draft can also be extended to the public sector. For this reason, in order to discuss the possibility to improve the level of accountability of public sector, this chapter intends to provide an introductory analysis on the applicability of the International Integrated Reporting Framework to public institutions.

12.1 Introduction

The changes that have affected the public sector over recent decades have deeply impacted the relationship between public administrations and citizens. Due to the spread of New Public Management (NPM), public organizations have seen the role of citizens change through the years, from "a vague, textureless component of the environment of public administration" to a service user to be treated as a customer (Radin and Cooper 1989, p. 167). For this reason the evaluation of the performance of the administration and individual representatives should be based on the results achieved. More recently, following the Public Governance (PG) approach, citizens are conceived as partners of the public administration, participating in the decision

L. Bartocci (✉) • F. Picciaia
Faculty of Economics, University of Perugia, Perugia, Italy
e-mail: luca.bartocci@unipg.it; francesca.picciaia@unipg.it

C. Busco et al. (eds.), *Integrated Reporting*, DOI 10.1007/978-3-319-02168-3_12,   191
© Springer International Publishing Switzerland 2013

making, production, monitoring and evaluation processes of the public services supplied (Vigoda 2002).

These cultural changes have also affected the idea of accountability (Behn 1998). This has changed and continues to change the way in which public institutions become accountable, and also the expectations and demands for transparency made by citizens. New reporting instruments, as evidenced by the spread of environmental sustainability and social responsibility reporting systems, offer the opportunity to facilitate public administration in meeting citizen's needs. Citizens now have the possibility to be informed about aspects of public activities that cannot be described by traditional financial reporting alone.

In this scenario, the Consultation Draft (CD) of the International Integrated Reporting Framework, issued in April 2013 by the International Integrated Reporting Council (IIRC), represents a potential point of reference for the public sphere. The need to develop forms of integration between different types (social, environmental, sustainability based, etc.) of reporting systems has emerged in both government-owned companies and, with some specific attributes, in non-market-oriented public institutions.

The objective of this chapter is to provide a preliminary analysis of the opportunities to apply the CD guiding principles and content elements to public administrations. To achieve this purpose, the chapter is structured as follows. In order to highlight the limitations of traditional reporting, the second section briefly outlines the evolution of the concept of accountability in the public sector. The third section deals with the principal forms of non-financial reporting that public organizations have implemented in recent years. Then, the fourth section offers a reflection on the way in which the content of the CD may be reinterpreted within the context of the public sphere. The paper ends with some suggestions concerning the implementation of Integrated Reporting (IR) in the public sector.

12.2 Reporting as an Accountability Medium in the Public Sector

Even if widely discussed in the literature, the concept of accountability still presents considerable problems of interpretation. In general, accountability indicates the aptitude of subjects (*accountee* or *steward*) to account for their actions, and for their actions in relation to another person or group of people (*accountor* or *principal*). Therefore, the basis of the idea is inspired by agency theory: there is a relationship between a subject, who acts in the interest of another, and towards whom he has some form of obligation to make himself *accountable* (Stewart 1984). According to Roberts and Scapens (1985, p. 447), the nature of the accountability relationship is not only informative, but also justifies the "giving and demanding of reasons for conduct".

The concept of accountability presents clear points in common with that of *responsibility*. Some researchers (i.e.: Hoskin 1996) have highlighted how the notion of accountability is superordinate, all-encompassing and more systemic than that of responsibility. In particular, accountability involves a delegation of responsibility that requires formal verification, and entails the need for reporting (Guarini 2003). Other authors (i.e.: Lindkvist and Llewellyn 2003) claim that the concept of responsibility is endowed with ethical content, and is morally superior, since it may contain ideological and idealistic values. Conversely, accountability remains strictly procedural and operational by nature. The key point is that the activity of reporting is generally recognized as an essential requirement of being accountable.

The recent spread of approaches inspired by NPM and PG has impacted the idea of accountability,[1] resulting in:

- changes in codes of accountability;
- changes in the object of reporting;
- a more active role played by citizens, and a greater emphasis on external rather than internal accountability.

Gray and Jenkins (1993, p. 559) define an accountability code as a "system of signals, meanings and customs which binds the principal and steward in the establishment, execution and adjudication of their relationship".

The basis of each code of accountability would be a different combination of *rationalities*. The changes experienced in the public sector have reduced the importance of *financial codes* (traditionally prevailing and oriented to the pursuit of probity, compliance and efficiency) in favor of *managerial codes* (more focused on technical, economic rationality and responsibility for the efficiency of the services provided) and *professional codes* (more focused on social rationality, attention to quality and the appropriateness of services provided).

The spread of NPM has consequently promoted an evolution of the logic of accountability, while also affecting the contents of the accountability relationship itself. The concept of *managerial accountability* indicates the responsibility of public officials (typically in a managerial role) to make themselves accountable for their performance as well as for the levels of efficiency in their organization. In this way managerial accountability can be distinguished from the political dimension of accountability: a distinction can be made between elected policy-makers, responsible for achieving institutional goals, and managers, to which are delegated tasks regarding the administration and regulation of resources, in compliance with stated objectives.

More recently, the idea of accountability as a form of democratization and empowerment of communities has become more common, with the active (direct or indirect) involvement of citizens in the accountability process. Among the many terms used in this regard, one of the most common is *social accountability*. The distinctive element of this concept is the fact that the community is both recipient and active subject in processes of accountability. This involves an extension of the idea of accountability, oriented not only towards parameters of effectiveness and

---

[1] An overview of the main approaches taken in the public sector and their development is provided by Steccolini (2004, pp. 330–333).

efficiency, but also to compliance with socially shared values. As highlighted by Kickert (1997, p. 34):

> *"Without denying whatsoever the great importance of effectiveness and efficiency in the public sector, other norms and values play a role as well; values such as liberty, legality, legitimacy, equity and social justice".*

The emergence of the social dimension also implies a shift from a form of "vertical" structure to "horizontal" relations between the parties involved in the accountability relationship. There are intermediate bodies that allow communication and interaction between citizens and public administrations. In this way, power is more widespread and relations are more equal (Bovens 2005). This leads to a "flattening" and downward enlargement in relations, introducing a horizontal dimension of accountability.

These changes have also posed some questions regarding the capacity of the Annual Report to be the fundamental tool of accountability in public institutions. What is at stake, is not so much the centrality of the Annual Report within the process of communication and disclosure, but the opportunity to connect it with other documents that are different in terms of contents and preparation. The major criticism relates to the citizens' lack of interest for the information typically contained in annual financial reports. Some researchers (i.e.: Jones 1992) demonstrate that the number of people who actually make use of the information contained in public administration financial reports is very small compared to the potential audience. This is due both to the typology of published information, which excludes important informative profiles (Guthrie and Farneti 2008), and the high complexity and limited accessibility of these documents. The risk is that the Annual Report is of interest for internal users only (Brusca Alijarde 1997). Furthermore, the information requirements that are useful in decision making may not necessarily be the same as the requirements for accountability (Patton 1992).

Steccolini (2004) demonstrates how the Annual Report of Italian provinces and municipalities cannot be regarded as an effective medium of accountability. The author hypothesizes the existence of a vicious circle in the relationship between citizens and local government annual reports: citizens' lack of interest in the report would discourage those in charge of preparing the document to make the necessary improvements and introduce voluntary forms of disclosure. Therefore, it is possible to comment that the inertia of preparers, whose principal concern is the compliance with legal requirements, may further contribute to the disenfranchisement of citizens, who are not inclined to read and utilize the report. Other studies (i.e.: Ryan and Walsh 2004) argue that external stakeholders prefer other, less institutional, forms of information and reporting. From this perspective it would not seem sufficient to enrich financial reports with other qualitative information and non-financial indicators, but rather it may be necessary to find other "ad hoc" means to attract the attention of citizens and convey information more effectively. This is the road that many public institutions have embarked on in recent years.

12.3 New Trends in Reporting

The forms of non-financial reporting that have gradually developed over the last few years are numerous and varied. In many cases, these reports originated in the private sector, and were subsequently transposed into the public sphere; in other cases, however, they emerged from practices that have been developed to meet the reporting needs of public institutions. In general, these cases relate to voluntary disclosure, although in some countries national regulators have issued specific rules over time.[2]

While it is difficult to undertake a complete mapping of the phenomenon, it is possible to classify the non-financial reports adopted in the public sector in the following four categories:

- documents that arise from the logic of strategic monitoring and control, such as the *balanced scorecard* and *mission reports*;
- documents regarding social and environmental responsibility, such as *social reports*, *environmental reports* and *sustainability reports*;
- documents that report intangible assets, such as *intangibles reports* and *intellectual capital reports*;
- other documents associated with the completion of particular budgetary cycles, such as *gender reports* and *participatory reporting*.

The first category of these instruments deals with the activities of strategic monitoring and control of the performance of an organization. These are often "introductory" documents to more complex accountability practices. They include the balanced scorecard (BSC) and mission reports.

Introduced in the 1990s by Kaplan and Norton, the BSC aims at integrating traditional financial indicators with other kind of information, in order to translate mission and strategy into a coherent set of performance measures. The approach pursued is holistic by nature, allowing for the re-alignment of the strategic and operational levels of management (Kaplan and Norton 1992). The BSC represents the main dimensions of value creation in an integrated form, and constitutes one of the most effective approaches for guiding an organization (including public ones) in the definition of its strategic priorities. While not originally developed as an external communications tool, the use of the BSC has repeatedly been the stimulating factor for a multidimensional analysis of activity and the subsequent adoption of instruments of non-financial disclosure (Farneti and Guthrie 2009).

The mission report is an instrument developed in public and non-profit organizations to highlight and report on social result achieved, verify the mission and activities undertaken, and define objectives and actions consistent with institutional functions and their effectiveness and efficiency. It is a document of a political-institutional nature, which aims to communicate results to stakeholders to fulfill accountability requirements. The mission report is closely connected to

---

[2] As an example, a Directive of the Ministry of Public Administration on social accountability in public administrations was adopted in Italy in 2006.

documents of a financial nature, and re-interprets information consistently with the mission and the strategic plan (Hinna 2004; Propersi 2004).

The second group of documents concerns information provided to stakeholders on the social and environmental impact of activities. These documents are adapted, with appropriate modifications, from the experiences of for-profit organizations. They serve to clarify the relationship between public policy formulation and its implementation, and become a particular medium through which the activity of the organization is reinterpreted.

In particular, social reports are intended to highlight the impact on the community as broken down into categories of relevant social groups. This stands as an expression of a broader approach to social issues that, similarly to Corporate Social Responsibility (CSR), contributes to integrate ethical concerns within the strategic vision of the business. The preparation of the social report is conceived as a phase of the broader and more articulated management cycle. Various models of social responsibility management have been developed, such as the SA8000, AA1000, and ISO26000 standards. Essentially, the social report is a document which gives an account of the mission and strategies of the organization, its projects, actions taken and results produced with regard to different categories of stakeholders. In the public sphere the objective is to report value produced to citizens, especially in terms of services provided and citizens level of satisfaction.

The environmental report is an instrument that allows for the reporting of the environmental policies implemented across the organization, and accounts for spending related to environmental goals. It describes the main issues, the strategic approach of the organization, and the actions implemented for the protection of the environment. There have been numerous initiatives for the development of an accounting system capable of representing environmental issues. Among these, the CLEAR (*City and Local Environmental Accounting and Reporting*) project can be recalled as it is specifically intended for public administrations. Funded by the European Union for the implementation of environmental budgeting by a sample of local authorities, this method is based on the notion of environmental accounting as a governance process, involving a system of indicators to measure the commitments and targets set periodically by the institution, that will subsequently be summarized in a periodic report.

The extension of the concept of social and environmental responsibility to the protection of future generations has led to the development of the sustainability report. This report attempts to integrate financial, social and environmental activities, their results and their external impact. The sustainability report derives from the approach known as *triple bottom line* (Elkington 1997), according to which the annual financial result (*single bottom line*) appears in itself to be insufficient for an adequate measurement of business performance. For this reason, it is suggested to integrate financial data with social and environmental information. The sustainability report presents itself as a tool for strategic planning and control, through the analysis of the entire work of the institution and a subsequent evaluation which aims to confirm the ability to manage the balance between the variables considered. Among the various guidelines produced at the international level, the most commonly used are those issued by the Global Reporting Initiative (GRI), a project launched in 1997 in order to provide reference standards in the field of sustainability. The GRI Framework is now a universally accepted model, irrespective of size of operation, sector of activity or country of origin. Although these guidelines are applicable to all organizations, in 2005 the GRI released a pilot version of a supplement dedicated to public agencies, and in 2010 it published a specific document for government agencies (*GRI Reporting in Government Agencies*).

An independent stream of research attempts to assess, account and report the management of intangible resources (Cañibano et al. 2000). Also in this case the need to address this issue initially emerged in the for-profit sector, and in particular with regard to knowledge-based businesses. Subsequently the world of non-profit organizations has also been affected by similar problems and, more recently, the situation has spread to public institutions. In particular, the main focus of attention is the evaluation of intellectual capital. Models of representation of intellectual capital differ in terms of recognized constitutive elements (Bontis 2011). Typically these are identified in relational capital (attributable to existing relations with external parties and the reputation of the organization), human capital (regarding the knowledge and skills of personnel), and organizational capital (in terms of know-how and the ability to create a collaborative environment).

The final category of documents is the result of approaches aimed at innovating public administration budgeting and reporting according to the logic of gender and participation.

Gender reports provide an assessment of policies with respect to certain social groups, and highlights the actions taken in pursuit of equal opportunities. Although the first studies on the subject go back more than 20 years (Sharp and Broomhill 1990), it was only in the late 1990s that these ideas became widespread. This type of analysis consists in the reclassification of activities carried out, alongside items of revenue and expenditure, for areas directly and indirectly related to gender (the focus was initially on the female gender, but more recently consideration has been given to other "sensitive" categories such as the elderly, young people and immigrants). The theoretical basis of the report is the idea that economic policies are not neutral, but reflect the existing distribution of power in society.

Participatory budgeting is an tool that refers to the broader approach of "participatory democracy", i.e. the inclusion of various local actors in the decision-making processes of public institutions. The participation process can take several forms (public meetings, focus groups, technical committees, e-voting, etc.) to consult citizens or to achieve a form of shared deliberation regarding the use of a portion of the resources available in the budget. The inclusion of citizens has important political, social and technical significance, and is particularly emphasized in visions of PG. Citizen participation can also be extended to public services delivery, in mechanisms of evaluation and monitoring of activity, as well as reporting. Participatory practices have the potential to contribute to the enhancement of the accountability of an organization.

12.4 Bringing Integrated Reporting into the Public Sector: An Analysis of the IIRC Consultation Draft

The development of non-financial reporting has led to new means of integrating different forms of information content and the various instruments used. In 2010, 14 % of the initiatives registered in the GRI's publicly available Sustainability Disclosure Database was self-declared as "integrated".[3] This percentage reached 20 % in 2011. A survey sponsored by the GRI (2013), as conducted on a sample of 231 integrated reports published in 2012, demonstrates that IR is coming into use also in the public sector. In particular, at least seven reports published by public institutions qualified as integrated in 2012 (3 % of the total, as opposed to 1 % in the previous year).

The CD illustrates that the "Framework is intended primarily for application by private sector, for-profit companies of any size but it can also be applied, adapted as necessary, by public sector" (CD 2013, p. 8).

This is a document of a conceptual nature, which is intentionally limited to the expression of a set of principles intended to drive the process of integration, without entering into the merits of technical measures for its implementation. In light the potential extension to the public sphere of the model published in the CD, this section intends to offer some comments concerning the possible applications.

The CD is essentially written with a view to informing and promoting an understanding of the dynamics of value creation. In this sense the business model is of crucial importance. This can be understood as the system of organization and management of activities that produce or destroy value (CD 2013, p. 14). An additional concept introduced by the CD is that of the six capitals, which are conceived as instruments that enable the creation, accumulation and diffusion of new value.

The concept of value in the public sector was initially proposed and developed by Mark Moore (1995, p. 28), who suggested how *"the aim of managerial work in the public sector just as the aim of managerial work in the private sector is to create private value"*.

There is neither a precise agreed definition of public value, nor a specific method of evaluation. Moore (1995) identifies several standards for capturing public value. These standards are: the capacity to achieve mandated objectives efficiently and effectively; the capacity to defend the long-term general public interest against politicians that pursue short term consent; the analytical evaluation of single policies and programs; the satisfaction of citizens understood as customers. Therefore, it seems clear that public value is the result of several factors, in which the social environment, strategic choices and structure all play a role. From this point of view, the CD, with its division of assets in diverse capitals, can provide a considerable contribution to highlighting specific factors and processes in value creation. The basic idea is that the value created is calculated by taking into account the sum

---

[3] See http://www.database.globalreporting.org

of the variations in the individual capitals. For this reason, within IR it is necessary to analytically map the elements that constitute the different capitals, and highlight the interaction between them.

The business model could be described as an "activity model". This is clearly affected by the specific institutional arrangements of the public institution in question. In particular, there will be differences among forms of local government (some with legal powers and the ability to raise taxes), institutions of an instrumental nature, such as agencies (with functional tasks in the service of a superordinate institution), and other organizations (which provide services of general interest in particular sectors such as education and training, culture, research, etc. In general terms, three main areas of public institution activity can be recognized: traditional government activities, social service provision, and utility delivery. The latter two forms of responsibility may be exercised directly or through contracting solutions. Such decisions are relevant in the definition and description of an "activity model". In any case, a correct assessment can only be made in the light of the way in which the institution intends to interpret its mission and vision. As a result, it will be closely connected with the strategic plan.

With reference to the capitals, it can be said that the various concepts identified in the CD will also be of potential interest for the public administration. It should also be noted that the document explicitly recognizes that "not all capitals are equally relevant or applicable to all organizations" (CD 2013, p. 13), confirming the flexible nature intended to be conferred to the Framework.

The following observations intend to offer an analysis of the different capitals included in the CD, and speculate on their adoption in the public sphere. For the purposes of reporting on financial capital, funding should be particularly highlighted, providing guidance on taxation decisions, the degree of financial autonomy of the institution, and the extent of future constraints on the sources used. An important piece of information concern debts, and is capable of offering insights on duration, guarantees, amortization schedules, and the interest rate. In the same way, an appropriate information framework should be provided regarding the allocation of spending, highlighting decision making processes and the results achieved. This type of information calls for a close connection with the annual financial report.

The concept of manufactured capital might be reinterpreted. In doing so, it may be more accurate to make reference to "available assets". The assets of a public entity can take on different forms, and may also be subject to binding legal regimes. It follows that not all assets are inclined to release value and, more generally, not all assets can be used as an instrument for the strategic objectives of an institution. It is therefore important to have information systems available to provide details of the composition, value and manner in which assets can be used.

The analysis of intellectual capital is not yet widespread in the public sector. This appears to be the type of capital that has, up to now, been paid the least attention (Guthrie et al. 2012). Among the various points raised by the CD, it seems that special consideration should be given to the issue of organizational capital, while less weight might be given to information on intellectual property, as this is not yet widespread in the public sphere.

In contrast, human capital is of paramount importance, as it is the primary and fundamental resource of the public sector. A relevant question in this area of reporting is the focus on the ethical dimension and, therefore, the models of ethics management and certification that may be adopted. In this regard, aiming to contrast corruption, national legislation may combine specific disclosure and transparency requirements.

The theme of social capital is closely connected to the social function that public institutions perform. The CD provides a conceptualization of social capital that focuses on the relational skills of an entity, relationships that aim to improve the spirit of collaboration with stakeholders and the legitimacy of the organization in the community. The associated difficulties are well known, even in the public sphere, and the development of social responsibility management, social auditing and social reporting models has made great progress in recent years. The impact on natural capital is another profile to which many governments have been committed for some time. As a consequence, advanced and complex models of environmental reporting have now been developed. It should be noted that the CD does not expressly refer to sustainability, which it would appear beneficial to include.

The above comments highlight the importance of the interaction between the different information systems that underlie the specific reports on each form of capital. It can be asserted that the public institutions that develop an integrated report prepare the release of the document after having already put in place "ad hoc" reporting forms based on appropriate information systems.[4]

The underlying idea of the CD is not to create a system that necessarily replaces existing reporting documents, but to foster connections between them and enhance their informative capacity. The CD strikes an appropriate balance between relevant thoroughness and conciseness, meeting the specific and in-depth information needs of stakeholders with access to appropriate sources of information. This latter aspect is of particular importance today, and is in line with the evolution of the idea of public sector accountability. In this regard a particularly important role should be given to the possibilities provided by ICT (CD 2013, p. 35). One route that some governments are taking is the promotion of open data experiences, designed to increase the degree of transparency and communication. IR can represent a process capable of giving a special impetus to such practices.

With regard to the objectives of the CD, it should be noted that the document puts great emphasis on the internal, as well as external, benefits of "integrated thinking". This is of particular importance in public organizations, where the highly compartmentalized organization can lead to fragmentation and dispersion of the

---

[4] A brief analysis of the experiences available in the GRI database confirms that the experiences that define their own reports as "integrated" have been engaged in the adoption of forms of sustainability, environmental and social reporting for some years. In the GRI Sustainability Disclosure Database there are 529 sustainability reports published in 2013 by public institutions 85 out of whom are self-defined as integrated reports.

overall strategy. This problem is of particular importance during crisis, where difficulties in public finances suggest that activities be streamlined to save money.

In relation to the issue of the external users of IR, it can be noted that, following the typical perspective of companies operating in financial markets, the approach proposed in the CD is too focused on the interests of the shareholders. A related issue is the importance of mechanisms for citizen involvement, where forms of consultation and participation in decision making by citizens have been activated. (CD 2013, pp. 19–20).

The CD guiding principles and content elements are in line with those developed by other frameworks for "ad hoc" reporting. It is appropriate, however, to pose a question regarding the identification of the reporting boundary. The choice suggested in the CD is to make the financial reporting entity a central element of the reporting boundary (CD 2013, p. 33). This criterion may not necessarily be suitable for the public sector because entities that are not tied by control relationships or dominant influence may still provide information that is socially relevant and worthwhile for inclusion.

Conclusions

Recent calls for accountability in the public sector have led to the use of alternative forms of reporting, which typically focus on contents that go beyond the financial aspect. Sometimes organizations implement different reporting processes that end up being disconnected. This aspect can create confusion within the organization, and reduce the effectiveness of internal and external reporting.

The CD has the opportunity to make an important contribution to the public sector in the logic of more complete and effective communications. The analysis conducted in this chapter suggests that, although with some adjustments, the document also responds to the requirements of various forms of public administration.

The main strength of the IIRC approach is to promote integrated thinking, which can lead "to integrated decision-making and actions that consider the creation of value over the short, medium and long term" (CD 2013, p. 9). The need to counteract traditional "silo thinking" is particularly acute in the public sector.

From an external perspective the model should allow for the overcoming of barriers between different categories of stakeholders, thus encouraging their involvement in processes of accountability. Indeed, one of the major limitations of traditional financial reports is that they are generally intended for internal use. This limit has also been found in some cases of non-financial reporting (Farneti and Guthrie 2009). In the logic of the CD, reporting should provide information that can be easily assimilated by external stakeholders on "connectivity and interdependencies between the range of factors that have a material effect on an organization's ability to create value over time" (CD 2013, p. 9).

The theme of IR has already been promoted by the GRI and, as such, it is easy to imagine that it would be perceived as an evolution of the sustainability report, and used by organizations with many years of experience. In reality, the framework does not anticipate "barriers to entry", and leaves open the possibility that other forms of "ad hoc" reporting will persist. In general, IR can be portrayed as a system in which specific models of management, auditing and reporting interact, and may offer a database where stakeholders can extract information on specific aspects of interest.

One specific question concerns the nature of the document and the subject responsible for its preparation. Mission reports have become popular in some countries. These documents, although technical in their nature, perform a function of political accountability. "Ad hoc" forms of reporting are more focused on a particular object of accountability (relationships with certain categories of stakeholders, environmental impact, etc.), and despite having a profound political significance, have a more technical background. These are often promoted by management, in accordance with their political representative (for example, the commissioner of reference). IR requires an increased capacity for interaction between all organizational sectors of an institution and, above all, between the political and the managerial realm.

The preparation of an integrated report requires a close integration between information systems and planning and control systems in the institution concerned. In particular, internal control systems must be redesigned, evaluating their ability to provide elements that are useful towards integrated thinking and communication. In this sense, from an organizational point of view, it is the board of executives that acts as a driving force and supervises the management of information integration processes.

A further aspect concerns the theme of the assurance of reporting by the appropriate international bodies. Currently, the most renowned assurance standards of non-financial reporting are ISAE 3000 and AA1000AS specific for companies. However, in the public sector there is a lack of specific references, also due to the more limited scope of the phenomenon. In this case it is best not to accelerate the process. Non-financial reporting, and even more IR, constitutes a voluntary exercise that should not be so rigid that it becomes meaningless. Introducing obligatory rules of assurance in a premature fashion would most likely encourage formal and cerimonial adoption of the regulation. As pointed out by Ackerman (2005, p. 21), a "central element of the accountability equation is to understand that it is a process and not a state". Therefore, it is not a question of simply providing a report that respects certain formal guidelines, but of activating a process where becoming accountable is internalized. Farneti and Guthrie (2009), in their study about what motivates public and non-profit organizations to adopt sustainability reporting, demonstrate that the primary purpose is to improve the reputation of the organization and legitimize its activities. In order to guarantee that IR is not just a temporary fashion, or a simple communication exercise, it is essential that it affects the way in which an organization operates and its impact on the outside world. Overall, the ultimate question is not *whether* IR is useful, but rather *how* it will be operationalized.

References

Ackerman JM (2005) Social accountability in the public sector. A conceptual discussion. Social Development Papers, 82. Word Bank, Washington, DC

Behn RD (1998) The new public management paradigm and the search for democratic accountability. Int Publ Manag J 1(2):131–164

Bontis N (2011) Assessing knowledge assets: a review of the models used to measure intellectual capital. Int J Manag Rev 3(1):41–60

Bovens M (2005) Public accountability. In: Ferlie E, Lynne L, Pollitt C (eds) The Oxford handbook of public management. Oxford University Press, Oxford

Brusca Alijarde MI (1997) The usefulness of financial reporting in Spanish local governments. Financ Account Manag 13(1):17–34

Cañibano L, Garcia-Ayuso M, Sanchez P (2000) Accounting for intangibles: a literature review. J Account Lit 19:102–130

Elkington J (1997) Cannibals with forks: the triple bottom line of 21st century business. Capstone, Oxford

Farneti F, Guthrie J (2009) Sustainability reporting by Australian public sector organisations: why they report? Account Forum 33:89–98

Gray A, Jenkins W (1993) Codes of accountability in the new public sector. Account Audit Account J 6(3):52–67

GRI (2010) GRI reporting in government agencies. GRI, Amsterdam. https://www.globalreporting.org/resourcelibrary/GRI-Reporting-in-Government-Agencies.pdf. Accessed 9 Jul 2013

GRI (2013) The sustainability content of integrated reports. A survey of pioneers. GRI, Amsterdam. https://www.globalreport-ing.org/resourcelibrary/GRI-IR.pdf. Accessed 8 Jul 2013

Guarini E (2003) Un modello di riferimento per la progettazione dei meccanismi di accountability delle aziende pubbliche. In: Pezzani F (ed) L'accountability delle amministrazioni pubbliche. Egea, Milano

Guthrie J, Farneti F (2008) GRI sustainability reporting by Australian public sector organizations. Public Money Manag 28(6):361–366

Guthrie J, Ricceri F, Dumay J (2012) Reflections and projections: a decade of intellectual capital accounting research. Br Account Rev 44(2):68–92

Hinna L (2004) Il bilancio sociale nelle amministrazioni pubbliche: processi, strutture, valenze. Franco Angeli, Milano

Hoskin K (1996) The "awful idea of accountability": inscribing people into the measurement of objects. In: Munro R, Mouritsen J (eds) Accountability: power, ethos and the technologies of managing. International Thomson Business, London

IIRC (2013) Consultation draft of the international <IR> framework. IIRC, New York. http://www.theiirc.org/wp-content/uploads/Consultation-Draft/Consultation-Draft-of-the-InternationalIRFramework.pdf. Accessed 15 Jun 2013

Jones R (1992) The development of conceptual frameworks of accounting for the public sector. Financ Account Manag 8(4):249–264

Kaplan RS, Norton DP (1992) The balanced scorecard. Measures that drive performance. Harv Bus Rev 1–2:71–79

Kickert WJM (1997) Public management in the United States and Europe. In: Kickert WJM (ed) Public management and administrative reform in Western Europe. Edward Elgar, Cheltenham

Lindkvist L, Llewellyn S (2003) Accountability, responsibility and organization. Scand J Manag 19(2):251–273

Moore M (1995) Creating public value: strategic management in government. Harvard University Press, Cambridge, MA

Patton JM (1992) Accountability and governmental financial reporting. Financ Account Manag 8 (3):165–180

Propersi A (2004) Il sistema di rendicontazione degli enti non profit. Dal bilancio di esercizio al bilancio di missione. Vita & Pensiero, Milano

Radin BA, Cooper TL (1989) From public action to public administration: where does it lead? Public Admin Rev 49(2):167–169

Roberts J, Scapens R (1985) Accounting systems and systems of accountability: understanding accounting practices in their organizational. Account Org Soc 10(4):443–456

Ryan C, Walsh P (2004) Collaboration of public sector agencies: reporting and accountability challenges. Int J Public Sector Manage 17(7):621–631

Sharp R, Broomhill R (1990) Women and government budgets. Aust J Soc Issues 25:1–14

Steccolini I (2004) Is the annual report an accountability medium? An empirical investigation into Italian local governments. Financ Account Manag 20(3):327–350

Stewart JD (1984) The role of information in public accountability. In: Hopwood A, Tomkins C (eds) Issues in public sector accounting. Philip Allan, London

Vigoda E (2002) From responsiveness to collaboration: governance, citizens, and the next generation of public administration. Public Admin Rev 62(5):527–540

Part III

Towards Integrated Reporting: Cases and Best Practices

The Case of Eni

Domenica Di Donato, Raffaella Bordogna, and Cristiano Busco

Abstract

This chapter focuses on Eni, the sixth largest integrated energy company by market value in the world, characterised by a strong position on the oil and gas value chain from the upstream phase of hydrocarbon exploration to the downstream phase of product marketing. The purpose is to shed light on Eni's recent advances in corporate reporting. Therefore, after having briefly illustrated Eni's distinctive approach to sustainable value creation, the chapter focuses on the structure and the contents of Eni's 2012 Annual Report. Issued in May 2013, Eni's 2012 Annual Report is an Integrated Report, prepared in accordance with the principles included in the prototype Framework developed by the International Integrated Reporting Council. The analysis presented in the chapter highlights the most innovative contents and elements of the report, and focuses on the connections between issues such as the company's business model, the competitive environment and strategy, the integrated risk management model, and the corporate governance system. The review of the report continues with a brief illustration of the section regarding the Consolidated Sustainability Statement. In particular, sustainability represents one of the fundamental drivers of Eni's business model, to the point that sustainability has always been conceived as part of the company's strategy, rather than a separate and distinctive element. The illustration of Eni's 2012 Annual Report continues with a discussion of the ways in which Eni has interpreted and then operationalized the principle of connectivity of information. Some concluding comments are offered at the end of the chapter.

D. Di Donato (✉) • R. Bordogna
Eni, San Donato Milanese, Italy
e-mail: domenica.di_donato@eni.com; Raffaella.Bordogna@eni.com

C. Busco
School of Business and Economics, National University of Ireland, Galway, Ireland
e-mail: cristiano.busco@nuigalway.ie

C. Busco et al. (eds.), *Integrated Reporting*, DOI 10.1007/978-3-319-02168-3_13,
© Springer International Publishing Switzerland 2013

3.1 Introduction

The objective of this chapter is to illustrate and discuss the recent evolution of corporate reporting in Eni, a major corporation in the oil and gas industry.[1] In particular, the focus of the analysis is placed on how the company's distinctive approach to sustainable value creation has been affecting the structure and the content of the latest two Annual Reports. Significantly, Eni's Annual Report for 2012 is an Integrated Report (IR), prepared in accordance with the principles included in the prototype Framework developed by the International Integrated Reporting Council (IIRC).

According to the IIRC, an integrated report is a concise communication about how an organization's strategy, governance, performance, and prospects, in the context of its external environment, lead to the creation of value over the short, medium, and long term.[2] Although providers of financial capital are the primary intended IR users, an integrated report should be designed to benefit all stakeholders—including employees, customers, suppliers, business partners, local communities, regulators, and policy makers—interested in an organization's ability to create value over time. The key objective of Integrated Reporting (IR) is to enhance accountability and stewardship with respect to the broad base of six types of capital, or "capitals" (financial, manufactured, intellectual, human, social and relationship, and natural), and promote understanding of their interdependencies.[3] Through this approach, IR is designed to support integrated thinking, decision making, and actions that focus on sustainable value creation for stakeholders.

With these objectives in mind, the chapter is structured as follows. First, the company profile of Eni is briefly illustrated. Then, Sect. 13.3 presents the company's approach to sustainable value creation. Section 13.4 describes Eni's recent journey towards Integrated Reporting. Then, the chapter focuses on the most original features of the company's Annual Report for 2012 and, specifically, on issues such as the company's business model, the competitive environment and strategy, the integrated risk management model, as well as the Consolidated Sustainability Statement. Section 13.6 explains how Eni has dealt with the principle of connectivity of information. The chapter ends with some concluding comments in Sect. 13.7.

---

[1] The authors wish to acknowledge the fundamental guidance received from Dr. Sabina Ratti, Sustainability vice President at Eni.

[2] See p. 8 of the IIRC Consultation draft of the international IR framework, 2013.

[3] The IIRC Consultation Draft refers to "capitals" instead of "capital," so we continue that use here.

13.2 Company Profile

Eni is the 6th largest integrated energy company by market value, active in 90 countries in the world, with a staff of approximately 78,000 employees. It has net sales from operations of €127 billion. The company boasts a strong position in the oil and gas value chain, from the hydrocarbon exploration phase to product marketing. Its strong presence in the gas market and in the liquefaction of natural gas, its skills in power generation and refinery activities, strengthened by world class competences in engineering and project management, enables the company to catch opportunities in the market and to develop integrated projects. Eni has a significant position in some of the world's most attractive mining areas. It explores and produces hydrocarbons in Italy, Africa, the North Sea, the United States, Latin America, Australia and in a number of other areas of high potential, such as the Caspian Sea, the Middle and Far East, India and Russia. Africa is one of the core regions since, in 2012, it accounts for 55 % of total hydrocarbon production.

In the European gas market, Eni is involved in securing energy supplies through a unique and integrated business model. It operates in the supply, trading and marketing of natural gas and LNG, and in the generation and sale of electricity. In Italy, Eni is the first operator in the refining business, with five refineries, and is a leader in the distribution of petroleum products. Finally, through Saipem, Eni is leading contractor for the supply of engineering, procurement, project management and construction. Eni is one of the largest international engineering and construction companies, serving the onshore and offshore oil and gas markets.

13.3 Eni's Approach to Sustainable Value Creation

Being sustainable, for an energy company, means to achieve economic growth and to enhance reputation through a distinctive approach that is also a catalyst for external development, by promoting respect for individuals and for the environment and, in general, by creating opportunities for local people and businesses.

Sustainability in Eni is not a specific area of activity but represents a business approach in itself. This is not a new approach for the company. In the 1950s, Enrico Mattei, Eni's first chairman, adopted an innovative way to start oil and gas activities and guarantee access to resources. In particular, Mattei pioneered a way of managing relations between international oil companies and producing countries based on long term cooperation, on the transfer of knowledge and skills, and on mutual development.

Next, a series of examples concerning the way in which Eni operates, to create sustainable value, are illustrated. In particular, attention is placed on one of the main sectors of activity, i.e. exploration and production.

In the following examples we consider three of the main drivers which characterize Eni's distinctive business approach, which are as follows:

- *to be local*—this means working side by side with the host countries and communities to reach mutually beneficial objectives. The unique model of integration with host countries is the key to consolidating, protecting and expanding Eni's presence over time;

- to maintain and develop *in-house competences*—these competences have supported exceptional performance in exploration, and in reservoir management and maintenance;
- to *manage and mitigate risks* throughout the operation—this characterizes every aspect of Eni's business, starting from asset selection to the design and development of the projects.

13.3.1 To Be Local

To be local means "to fly a double flag", that of the host Country, with its opportunities, challenges and development aspirations, and that of an International Oil Company (IOC), with the managerial, technological expertise, and the standards of a major company. *To be local* means, first of all, hiring local staff, as well as offering them the opportunity to grow and progress in their carrier. In Africa, for example, 80 % of Eni's people are local, with responsibilities that range from operational to managerial. To support this approach, Eni invests heavily in training.

Additionally, *to be local* also means favouring the growth of local suppliers to support the economic development of the host countries. In 2012, Eni created opportunities through projects for almost 7,000 local suppliers in Africa and Asia for a total amount of nearly 10 billion euro. Finally, *to be local* suggests considering the possible business opportunities which, at the same time, will contribute to the development of local communities.

In Africa, for example, Eni has been the only IOC to make a unique and radical decision: to use produced gas for the domestic market, thus providing the local population with access to electricity. In Nigeria and Congo, Eni invested a total of about 300 million dollars (Eni share) in power generation projects, building, only in Nigeria, about 700 MW of capacity. Because of these projects, today Eni power stations in these countries account for 20 % and 60 % of domestic electricity production respectively, with a massive reduction of gas flaring in both Countries.

On one hand, this approach protects the interests of the stakeholders and shareholders, and on the other hand it preserves investments and production growth. Right from the outset, the implementation of this approach has lead to a number of successes in Africa, where Eni has achieved the leading position, among IOC, in terms of geographical footprint, production and reserves. Significantly, in this region, production growth has been around 5 % a year since the turn of the century, and is expected to be around 3 % over the next decade.

13.3.2 To Maintain and Develop In-house Competences

Aiming *to maintain and develop in-house competences*, Eni develops and further enhances the abilities and knowhow of its people. In doing so, first of all Eni is strongly focused on developing and adopting its own technologies and on maintaining in-house competencies. In exploration, this means centralizing the process of technical decision making, which leads to concentrating attention on the best opportunities for exploration on a worldwide basis, and increasing efficiency of the overall process. Turning to development, this leads to delivering new projects on time and on budget.

In addition, by leveraging a solid internal base of competences, Eni has reduced execution risks and delivered excellent results in terms of exploration and production. For example, over the past 5 years, around 7.5 billion barrels of oil equivalent (boe) of new resources have been discovered, which is more than double, compared to the company's 2012 cumulated production of 3.8 billion boe.

13.3.3 To Manage and Mitigate Risks

To manage and mitigate risks Eni is required to identify strategies, introduce procedures and opt for investments that are able to minimize the probability of accidents to people and reduce the impact on the environment. The operational risk poses the biggest potential threat to upstream activities, in environmental, financial and reputational terms. Because of this, Eni is committed to maintaining the industry-leading results on operation safety and, in particular, is strongly committed to achieving zero blow-outs.

The strategy for preventing major drilling accidents is based on strong competencies for improving processes, distinctive technologies and a performance-based contract approach. Regarding the safety of well operations, Eni's centralized control of all critical wells are monitored by the headquarters in real time. On technologies, Eni has developed a proprietary and distinctive portfolio, which allows the achievement of higher standards of safety and well performance. Eni is also working on the improvement of the HSE performance of its suppliers, introducing a new HSE incentive scheme in the contracts, promoting those contractors with outstanding HSE behaviour, measured through ad hoc KPIs.

The continuous efforts to mitigate operational risks to people, assets and the environment are a crucial part of activities, and have led to two important results: the decreasing trend of the injury frequency rate, and zero blow-outs during the last 9 years.

13.4 The Diffusion of Integrated Thinking

The prerequisite for a sustainable business is *integrated thinking*. As the IIRC framework states, integrated thinking is the consideration, by the company, of the relationship between its various operating and functional units and the capitals used and affected. This implies that all forms of capital, from financial to manufactural, human, environmental, intellectual and social, find a proper place in all decision processes and that their proper management plays a role in the creation of value over time.

Thanks to *integrated thinking*, people who work in the organization, are able to see things in a broader perspective, taking into account the achievement of economic and financial results as well as the impact of business activities on people, environment and society, or furthermore, by considering, new opportunities that can be generated in areas close to those specifically managed. This holistic view stems from different factors that affect or that can be affected by business decisions. Let's take into consideration, for example, the project of transforming the Porto Marghera refinery into a biorefinery. In 2012, the demand for oil and gas products suffered a strong slowdown, down by 10 % in Italy and by 3 % in Europe.

In 2009, 11 refineries were closed in Europe and another 15 risk closure in the next few years. The Green Refinery projects were encouraged by the European scenario for bio-fuels and strongly linked to the environmental policy of the European Union aimed at the reduction of greenhouse gases. This project derives from a very innovative idea that intends to substitute the traditional model of refinery with a green cycle for the production of high quality biofuels from biomass. Project development aims at employing state-of-the-art technologies and will reposition Eni in the refinery industry, while seizing the opportunities provided by the green inclusive economy. The biorefinery will also be a way of sustaining employment in the territory of Porto Marghera, giving people new and technologically advanced skills, and, at the same time, contributing to the reduction of environmental damage.

This project is the result of a process started during the last few years that is aimed at a viewpoint of operationalized sustainability in the principle business processes.

The most important is the planning process. At the beginning of every planning cycle all the company functions are asked to identify areas of improvement and new activities that could be realized in a future 4-year plan, in order to contribute to sustainable value creation over time. This process is derived from prior analysis of the external context and the evolution of sustainability issues in the international scenario, from the consideration of stakeholder expectations, from financial market request analysis, and last but not least, from the outputs of integrated risk assessment and related mitigation plans. At the end of this preliminary process, the Eni CEO issues specific operational and economic guidelines for sustainability, so that all functions reach their strategic targets. On the base of these guidelines, all managers have MBOs for the first year of the plan that contribute variable remuneration.

Another important process that is defined in an integrated way is risk assessment and management. Thanks to this integration, all risk events are considered and evaluated with impact metrics that do not concern only the financial and operating side but also the social, environmental and reputational side. In the past, the various risk factors were evaluated separately by each function; but now a unique monitoring and reporting system evaluates the overall risk level, highlighting the most relevant risks, independent from their financial or non financial nature.

13.5   Eni's Journey Towards Integrated Reporting

Eni began the process of integration in corporate reporting in 2010, when the publication of a stand-alone sustainability report (which was in its fourth edition) was discontinued. The primary reason for this decision was the opportunity offered by the IR to represent Eni's integrated thinking approach thoroughly. In addition, there were also external factors influencing the decision, such as the evolution of laws and regulations, both domestically and internationally (ESG directives on transparency of accounting practices in Europe, SEC guidelines and Dodd-Frank Act in the United States, Grenelle II in France) that required increased integration of non financial and financial information. Additionally, few events happened in 2010, which seriously strained the reputation of some big corporations. Among others, in the oil and gas industry the devastating accident of the Deepwater Horizon platform in the Gulf of Mexico, showed with great clarity the impacts generated by a non optimal management of non financial aspects on business results and definitely on the company's reputation. This highlighted how much the competitive level of a company resides in its ability to run a sustainable business.

Therefore, Eni realized that a new approach was needed for communicating its business model and performance to stakeholders. The idea was to develop a reporting tool in order to illustrate how integrated management of financial and non financial aspects helps manage risks, reduce costs, and seize new opportunities for attaining sustainable value. This was a big challenge for Eni at the time because, in that period, no framework on integrated reporting existed. Furthermore, many other companies around the world had not published an integrated report yet.

Faced with this need for change, in 2010 it was decided that the integrated report for Eni should be the actual Annual Report, considered the main document of the company primarily dedicated to the financial community. For this reason, the Annual Report was seen as the best tool for communicating Eni's integrated thinking, first to financial capital providers, and then to all other stakeholders.

Significantly, it was clear that Eni opted to achieve the integration into its Annual Report rather than into the Sustainability Report or, alternatively, through a third document. In the 2010 reporting year Eni started preparing its integrated report, abandoning the stand-alone sustainability report and exploring, within the Annual Report, the possibility for better illustrating the connections existing between financial and non financial information. In so doing, a selection of the main sustainability issues that drive Eni's value creation processes was complete.

step towards integration began internally. An analysis of the
ty data collection system was carried out in order to identify a series
rs that were relevant for operations to be included in the profile of the
year. In addition, a section describing specific sustainability outputs and projects
that were more relevant for economic and financial performance was also included.
The result of this first process led to the 2010 Annual Report, which can arguably be
considered a combined report.

13.5.1 The Participation in the IIRC Pilot Program

On August 2, 2010, The Prince's Accounting for Sustainability Project (A4S) and
the Global Reporting Initiative (GRI) announced the formation of the IIRC. The
IIRC's mission is "to create a globally accepted integrated reporting framework
which brings together financial, environmental, social and governance information
in a clear, concise, consistent and comparable format" in order to "help business to
take more sustainable decisions and enable investors and other stakeholders to
understand how an organization is really performing" (see the IIRC web site).
According to the IIRC, the IR process has the potential to shed light on these
critical issues as it "brings together material information about an organization's
strategy, governance, performance and prospects in a way that reflects the commercial, social and environmental context within which it operates. It provides a clear
and concise representation of how an organization demonstrates stewardship and
how it creates and sustains value".[4]

In 2011 Eni adhered to the Pilot Program launched by the IIRC. This choice was
based on the belief that this program could help Eni share the knowledge and best
practices on reporting that it had acquired in the previous year of experience. At the
same time, this choice offered Eni the opportunity to learn other companies' best
practices, as well as to participate in the process of defining new guidelines aiming
at redesigning corporate reporting. Thanks to the participation in the Pilot Program,
two of the main corporate departments involved in the integrated reporting process,
i.e. the Administrative and Sustainability departments, defined a common plan in
drafting the report, with milestones and activities to be performed in the following
2 years.

In these 2 years, specific changes to the structure of the Annual Report were
identified in order to redesign it and align its contents with the key elements and
guiding principles of the "Consultation Draft of the International IR framework"
recently finalized by the IIRC. To complete this task, a work group, composed of
people from different departments, was created. The functions involved were
strategic planning, administrative, sustainability, investor relations, corporate governance and integrated risk management. This led to an ongoing improvement and
refinement of the 2011 and 2012 Annual Reports. Thanks to the diverse

---

[4] Visit http://www.theiirc.org/, accessed on 28 June 2013.

competences of the different people involved in working group, Eni succeeded in summarising and combining three different components (strategy model, a structural model and sustainability model) in one single representation—the integrated Business Model (which will be illustrated later in the chapter).

The main changes featuring the last two editions of the Annual Report were the introduction of a strategic focus and a future orientation, the representation of the integrated Eni business model, the description of the integrated risk management systems as well as the connectivity of information. For the first time a section on strategies was included in the Annual Report. Thanks to this section, the Integrated Annual Report does not merely represent performances from the past but shows the relationship between past performances and future goals and perspectives, highlighting the main factors that might change such relationships. The future orientation was adopted to better explain the ability of the company to create value in the short, medium and long term. With respect to connectivity—as illustrated later in chapter—the Annual Report shows Eni's value creation story by focusing on the interdependences between capitals and processes. Finally, the new structure of the document was identified and approved. The main changes concerned the first 25 pages of the overall document that is represented in Fig. 13.1.

13.6   Eni's 2012 Integrated Annual Report

Approved by its board of directors in May 2013, Eni's Annual Report for 2012 is an IR prepared in accordance with the principles included in the prototype of the International IR Framework developed by the IIRC. Eni 2012 IR aims at representing financial and sustainability performance, as well as underlining the existing connections between competitive environment, group strategy, business model, integrated risk management, and the corporate governance system.

The integrated approach of the report is clear from the very beginning of the document, which opens with a section labelled "profile of the year". Significantly, within this section, financial as well as operating and sustainability aspects are blended to offer an integrated picture of the company. In doing so, financial highlights such as sales, profit or dividends, are disclosed and commented next to operating and sustainability data such as employees injury frequency rate, oil spills or percentage of female managers, to name only a few.

Interestingly, after the letter to the shareholders, the report offers an illustration of Eni's business model, which is arguably the fundamental content of any integrated report. As suggested early in this chapter, Eni claims that the company's market position and competitive advantages derive from its strategic decision-making process, which is consistent with the long-term nature of the business (see p. 11 of the 2012 Eni IR).

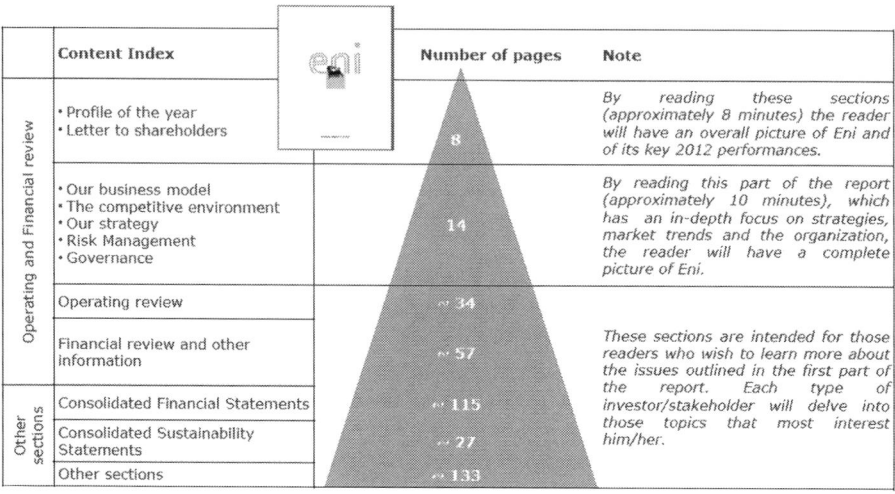

	Content Index	eni	Number of pages	Note
Operating and Financial review	• Profile of the year • Letter to shareholders		8	By reading these sections (approximately 8 minutes) the reader will have an overall picture of Eni and of its key 2012 performances.
	• Our business model • The competitive environment • Our strategy • Risk Management • Governance		14	By reading this part of the report (approximately 10 minutes), which has an in-depth focus on strategies, market trends and the organization, the reader will have a complete picture of Eni.
	Operating review		~ 34	These sections are intended for those readers who wish to learn more about the issues outlined in the first part of the report. Each type of investor/stakeholder will delve into those topics that most interest him/her.
	Financial review and other information		~ 57	
Other sections	Consolidated Financial Statements		~ 115	
	Consolidated Sustainability Statements		~ 27	
	Other sections		~ 133	

Fig. 13.1 The structure of Eni's 2012 Integrated Annual Report

13.6.1 Eni's Business Model

The creation of sustainable value is pursued through a business model focused on assets and strategic guidelines distributed along the entire value chain. The model is characterized by activities conducted within a framework of clear and rigorous governance rules complying with the highest ethical standards, with an integrated corporate risk management system, sustained by continuous interaction with all stakeholders. The combination of the above mentioned features with six distinctive drivers—integration, cooperation, innovation, excellence, inclusiveness and responsibility—guides investment choices and allows strategic targets to be pursued. Eni's Business Model is illustrated in Fig. 13.2.

Within the implementation of the Company mission and the running of day-to-day operations, Eni's efforts are inspired by these key drivers:

- *Cooperation* in the development of the territories where Eni works, expressing the ability to understand local needs and the willingness to contribute to their fulfilment;
- *Integration* of all activities along the energy supply chain, as a source of crucial synergies for facing market challenges and ensuring a competitive advantage;
- *Innovation* as key element for accessing new energy resources, improving recovery from the subsoil and the efficiency of its use, ensuring respect for and responsible use of natural resources;
- *Excellence* in running operations, which hinges on making use of best practices, quality systems, advanced technology and safety systems to ensure full respect for the community and the environment;

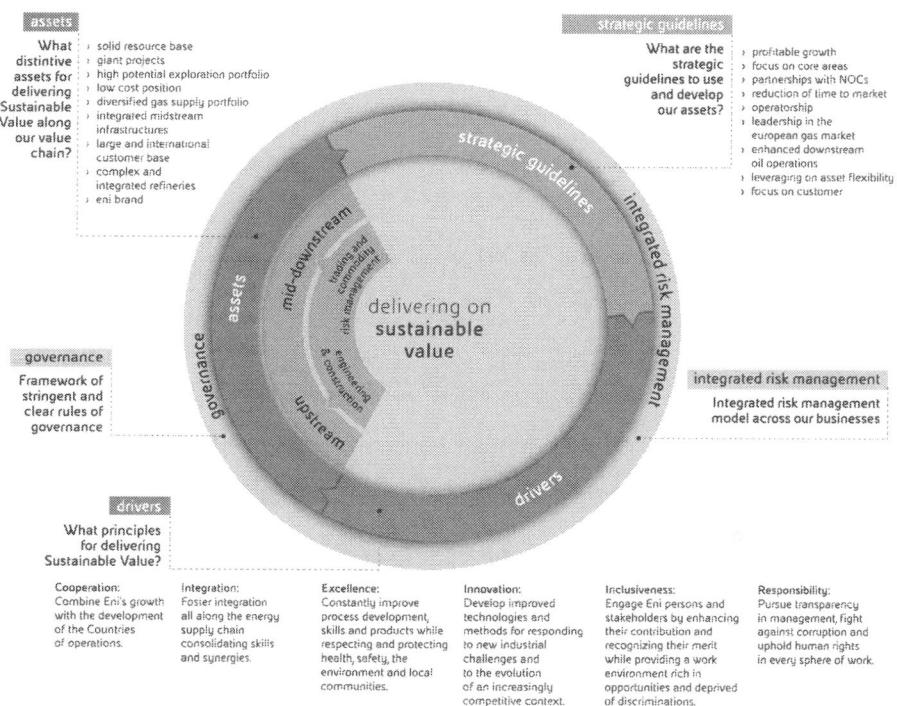

Fig. 13.2 The Eni business model

- *Inclusion* of all Eni's people, with their broadly expressed diversity, which combines with health and safety protection in the workplace, as well as their personal development and involvement in the company's goals;
- *Responsibility* in terms of commitment to transparency in the business management, in the fight against corruption, and in the respect for human rights in every sphere of our work, being requisites for effective contribution toward the development of countries and societies.

Leveraging on these distinctive drivers, as well as on its strategic assets, Eni has designed its strategies of growth along the following guidelines:

- increasing profitable oil and gas production in the upstream, also by capturing opportunities in high risk/high reward plays in frontier exploration basins, notably the recently acquired leases in Mozambique;
- strengthening its competitive position in core areas;
- establishing and consolidating strategic partnerships with key host Countries, leveraging the "Eni co-operation model" that integrates the traditional business of hydrocarbon exploration and production and sustainable activities;
- increasing the volume of operated production; operatorship will enable Eni to deliver on-time schedules and cost budgets and better manage the technical risk by deploying Eni standards and technologies in drilling and completion;

- consolidate the profitability of our downstream operations through network upgrading, expansion of non-oil activities and growing selectively outside Italy; in particular Eni intends on refocusing the chemical business, strengthening the product mix of the company by developing higher value-added products and effectively and efficiently managing operations in order to lower the break-even point;
- maximizing asset flexibility mainly in refinery activities; the flexibility of Eni's refinery plants will allow taking advantage of the availability of discounted crudes on the marketplace, also leveraging on the ability of the infrastructures to process heavy and extra-heavy crudes.

Eni believes that founding its way of operating on the key elements described above has reinforced its own business culture over recent decades. This can be considered the company's source of a long enduring competitive advantage.

13.6.2 Eni's Competitive Environment and Strategy

The illustration of the business model is followed by an analysis of the external competitive environment. In particular, the IR identifies a number of industrial challenges (in terms of both market dynamics and an increasing requirement to conduct operations in a sustainable manner) and describes the actions and initiatives that Eni implemented during the year to face those challenges, the performance for the year, and the performance outlook at the end of the 2013–2016 business plan (see pp. 14–15 of Eni's 2012 IR). For example, one of the most important challenges was the increasing competitive and regulatory pressure on the European energy market. The actions Eni implemented in 2012 were directed towards renegotiating long-term gas supply contracts in Europe, strengthening its position in the gas and liquefied natural gas (LNG) market outside Italy, re-launching efficiency programs at European industrial sites, selecting new initiatives in green refinery and bio-chemistry, and retaining and strengthening the customer base.

Eni's integrated report continues by illustrating the strategy for the 2013–2016 4-year period, highlighting the priorities of profitably increasing oil and gas production; recovering profitability in the downstream gas sector; improving efficiency in downstream oil, chemicals, and general services supporting business activities; and retaining global leadership in engineering and construction by focusing on the most technologically advanced and innovative segments. It is worthwhile to note that within Eni, sustainability is conceived as part of the strategy rather than a separate element. Therefore, sustainability represents one of the drivers that enable Eni to achieve its business goals. Next, the integrated report then offers additional details on the strategy at divisional levels across the oil and gas value chain: exploration and production, gas and power, refining and marketing, chemical, engineering and construction (see pp. 16–19 of Eni's 2012 IR).

For example, in Exploration and Production, Eni confirms its strategy of organic growth focused on exploration and reserve replacement as major drivers for value creation. Average production growth is expected at a rate of more than 4 % in the 2013–2016 period. The main driver for growth will be the start-up of new fields. A further driver of production growth is technological innovation, which is aimed at developing drilling techniques to be applied in complex environments and monetizing gas reserves. Over the next 4 years, Eni will make capital expenditure of approximately €1.1 billion, of which €400 million in the Exploration and Production Division. Among other things, to manage the risks of "project delivery" Eni intends to in-source critical engineering and project management activities, also by redeploying to other areas key competences, which will be freed with the start-up of certain strategic projects, and increase direct control and governance on construction activities.

From the above examples, it is evident that business goals are achieved through a set of different drivers that are both financial and non financial.

13.6.3 Eni's Integrated Risk Management Model and Process

The section on risk management follows that of strategies in order to give a deeper understanding of the effective ability of the company to manage the main risks related to the achievement of strategies and goals.

Eni has developed and adopted an Integrated Risk Management model that targets to reach a comprehensive and selective view of the company's main risks and a strengthening of company awareness, at any level, regarding the impact of risks on long term value creation.

In this section, there are two main aspects of Eni's integrated approach that should be highlighted.

The first one is about the very comprehensive nature of Eni's Risk Management System which includes all the different risks that can affect the business. The model entails an articulation of risks by country, regulatory development, environment, finance, strategy and operations. The basic feature of the IRM model is the integrated and cross-sectional assessment of risks according to rankings of probability (from remote to probable) and impact (from negligible to extreme). In assessing impact, management evaluates both quantitative parameters (i.e. reduction in results of operations and cash flows, and operating-productive impact) and qualitative aspects (impact on the company's reputation, on social, environmental, health and safety aspects).

The second aspect to be considered is risk governance that attributes a central role to the Board of Directors. The Board, with the support of the Control and Risk Committee, outlines the guidelines for risk management, so as to ensure that the main corporate risks are properly identified and adequately assessed, managed and monitored.

13.6.4 Eni's Corporate Governance and Remuneration Policy

This section describes how the organization's governance structure supports the company's ability to create value in the short, medium and long term.

Eni considers effective corporate governance to be a foundation stone of its business model. Corporate governance represents a prerequisite for pursuing Eni's mission while ensuring compliance with standards of fairness and cost effectiveness. The governance system is designed to support the relationship of trust between Eni and its stakeholders and, supplementing Eni's business strategy, to help achieve stable results and create sustainable value over a long-term period.

The section "Governance" opens with the description of Eni's Corporate Governance structure and the main roles and responsibilities held by the board members. In particular, responsibilities connected to strategic decision making and monitoring are illustrated, with a focus on those related to the most important strategic, operational and organisational activities. It describes how the Board has a central role in the areas of internal control and risk management, as well as in setting the key corporate governance guidelines. The Board has also retained the exclusive power to set sustainability policies and agree upon the results to be presented at the Shareholders' Meeting, demonstrating how sustainability is fully integrated within Eni's long-term value creation processes. This section shows how the implementation of best governance practices go beyond legal requirements. Some examples are the Board Induction as well as the Board and peer reviews. The way that remuneration and incentives are linked to value creation in the short, medium and long term is also described.

Consistently within the IIRC framework conciseness principle, this section contains a very brief overview of Eni's Corporate Governance System. Additional and broader information is available in the Corporate Governance Report 2012, published on the company website in the section on Governance. In addition, a specific Remuneration Report is also available on the company website with all the necessary information.

13.6.5 Eni's Consolidated Sustainability Statement

In order to have a full picture of the company and to prove that sustainability results play an important role, as well as the economic and financial results, starting from the 2011 annual report, Eni has introduced Consolidated Sustainability Statements that include tables and notes on sustainability performance, in accordance with the "Sustainability Reporting Guidelines, version 3.1" issued by the GRI (Global Reporting Initiative) and the related "Oil and Gas Sector Supplement", with particular reference to the principles of materiality, completeness, stakeholder inclusiveness and sustainability contexts.

This is not a specific requirement of the IIRC framework, but rather it is the company's decision to give an enhanced view of the company on all the different forms of capital that could be affected or managed by corporate activities.

The Consolidated Sustainability Statements collect all the sustainability performances for the last 3 years at group level which are representative of the effective integrated business model in action. For instance, there are environmental results that are compared to operational results, or the link is reported between financial and non financial performance. The reduction in energy consumption, for example, is quantified in terms of cost or CO_2 emission reductions. There is the effort to show how a sustainable business can lead to the reduction of impacts on different forms of capitals. It is also illustrated how a sustainable business is the prerequisite for seizing new opportunities. Finally, it is worthwhile to highlight how Eni calculates and reports value creation for stakeholders. The configuration chosen in Eni's integrated report is that of "overall added value net of amortization and depreciation". Net overall added value is divided among employees (direct remuneration consisting of wages, salaries, and provisions for termination benefits and indirect remuneration consisting of social welfare contributions); the public administration (income taxes); financial backers (medium/long-term interest paid for availability of borrowed capital); shareholders (dividends distributed); and the company (quota of reinvested earnings). The net added value distributed in 2012 was €22,475 million and was divided as follows: 52 % to the state and public administrations through taxes on the income of Italian and overseas businesses, 22 % to human resources, 18 % to shareholders, 4 % to the company system, and 4 % to financial backers (see p. 236 of the 2012 Eni Integrated Annual Report).

All the information included in this section has been certified by an independent auditing entity in order to report on the quality and level of performance.

13.6.6 Connectivity of Information

In line with the contents, elements and principles included in the IIRC Framework, in each of the sections included in the 2012 IR Eni has attempted to operationalize the principle of connectivity of information. In particular, the attention towards connectivity of information has gone beyond the need for showing how sustainability is embedded within the individual organizational processes, to include the integration mechanisms across the entire Eni management system.

Eni has interpreted the principle of connectivity by focusing on the broad picture of the company's value creation story. To achieve this goal, Eni's 2012 IR includes a detailed description of how the company strategy, governance, performance and prospects concur to create value over time. The interdependences between the industrial challenges featuring the external environment, the actions in place, the performance of the year, and future targets are illustrated and analysed in the IR. The fundamental purpose is to break down the established silos in accessing, measuring, managing and disclosing data and information. Overcoming information silos has allowed Eni to increase awareness and knowledge of the dynamic of value creation. This is useful for both the internal top management, in order to refine the decision-making process, and for the external stakeholders, including capital providers, in order to make better investment decisions.

An informative discussion of the performance of the year and the related targets for the future, can provide the intended report users with useful information for assessing the reliability of what has been reported concerning the present period, in relation to future trends. In addition, the connection between the external context and Eni strategy enables report users to understand how different factors affect the future of the organization and its capability for creating value over time. Eni's 2012 IR, as an example, shows how the increasing requirement to conduct sustainable operations lead the company to develop new technologies for minimizing the environmental footprint and water consumption in order to achieve leadership in the oil and gas sector.

Conclusions

Aiming to offer a fair understanding of Eni's journey towards IR, the chapter begins by discussing the Company's distinctive approach to sustainable value creation. Significantly, at the outset it is highlighted that in Eni sustainability is not a specific area of activity but represents a business approach in itself. It means managing risks: political, operational and financial. But more than that, it is a lever to support long term value creation . This approach has been embedded in the Company's culture since its foundation, when Eni's first chairman, Enrico Mattei, in order to be more competitive pioneered a way to manage relations between international oil companies and producing countries based on long term cooperation, on the transfer of knowledge and skills, and on mutual development.

Due to the complexity of the environment in which a company operates, to achieve a sustainable business, an approach based on the excellence of the sustainability management system is not sufficient. An integrated thinking is needed. This requires the existence of a holistic view capable to encompass the multiple factors that affect or that can be affected by business decisions. In particular, forms of capital such as financial, manufactured, human, environmental, intellectual and social have been identified as the main "stock of value" whose management plays a role in the creation of value over time. For this reason Eni adopts in its different processes an integrated thinking that starts from the two main processes: planning and integrated risk management. Thanks to those integrated processes, projects are defined taking into account all the capitals that could be affected by the organisation and different kind of risks are valuated considering all the impact generated.

The IR is the best opportunity to reinforce the sustainable value creation approach as well as reinforce an integrated thinking thoroughly. Thanks to this approach the established silos in accessing, measuring, managing and disclosing data and information are broken down and the company ability to create value in the long term is illustrated. This is a great opportunity to explain how sustainability is embedded in the business, and to offer capital providers a solid understanding for their decision of investments.

In light of these reasons Eni began the process of integration in corporate reporting in 2010, when the publication of a standalone sustainability report (which was at its fourth edition) was discontinued. The Annual Report was considered the main document to be integrated as it is the institutional document that addresses primarily the financial community with the goal of representing how the company creates value. It is the document that already adopts the right language to tell the story of the business.

To achieve the IR Eni adhered to the Pilot Program launched by the IIRC and in accordance to the IIRC framework restructured its Annual Report. The third edition the new Annual Report offers a discontinuity with the traditional financial reporting because it discloses on the future and not only on past performance, on financial and non financial results as well as on all the connection existing between issues such as the company's business model, the competitive environment and strategy, the integrated risk management model, and the corporate governance system.

The work done until now on IR offers a deeper knowledge on the dynamics of value creation, and improves not only the internal management system but also the external communication process. This work, which is still in progress, will lead Eni to further refine and improve the way to communicate with its stakeholders.

Reference

IIRC (2013) Consultation draft of the international <IR> framework. http://www.theiirc.org/consultationdraft2013. Accessed 10 Jul 2013

The Case of Enel

14

Chiara Mio and Marco Fasan

Abstract

The aim of this chapter is to provide a discussion of the business case of Enel, which is an International Integrated Reporting Council (IIRC) pilot program company currently evolving its corporate disclosure towards Integrated Reporting (IR). The relevance of pilot company business cases has been recognized by the IIRC, which defined their experience as "invaluable". On the one hand, Enel did modify its corporate reporting system coherently with the IIRC guiding principles by including considerable non-financial information in its annual report, reducing the length of its sustainability report and improving its materiality determination process and business model analysis. On the other hand, it will be interesting to see how the company applies other aspects of the IIRC framework, such as the six-capital structure and the way in which reporting boundaries are defined. The analysis done in this chapter may be of interest to companies, standard setters and scholars wishing to enhance their knowledge on how companies are currently evolving their corporate disclosure systems towards IR.

14.1 Introduction

Standard setters, academics, practitioners and also policymakers around the world are currently discussing and working towards the evolution of the Integrated Reporting (IR) framework. At the same time, companies are currently facing the challenges of actually implementing IR, experiencing difficulties and, sometimes, finding possible solutions to open issues. The International Integrated Reporting

The authors wish to thank Marina Migliorato, Csr manager of Enel S.p.a. for her valuable contribution.

C. Mio (✉) • M. Fasan
Department of Management, Ca' Foscari University of Venice, Venice, Italy
e-mail: mio@unive.it; marco.fasan@unive.it

Council (IIRC) pilot program currently includes over 90 companies around the world, which have decided to take the path towards integrated reporting. The experiences of these companies are invaluable elements that need to be capitalized, as recognized by the IIRC itself: "the IIRC Pilot Program is a major contribution to <IR> (...) their (pilot program companies') feedback on the application of the guiding principles and content elements outlined in the 2011 Discussion Paper is invaluable to inform the development of a practical Framework" (IIRC 2013b, p. 4).

This chapter aims to analyse the case of Enel, which is an IIRC pilot program company currently evolving its corporate disclosure towards IR. According to Enel (2013b), "the company is willing to integrate the various aspects of its report, in order to give all stakeholders a comprehensive assessment of the Group's activities and results. In this light, Enel is gradually including information on sustainability in its report on operations with the publication and discussion of the selected quantitative sustainability indicators provided below" (Enel 2013b, p. 103).

In particular, this analysis will focus on the sustainability strategy of the company and on the evolution of its main disclosure documents (the Annual Report—AR—and the Sustainability Report—SR—in particular), with an IR perspective. The analysis confirms that Enel's reporting system, although still based on the SR in 2012, has to a certain extent already changed according to IIRC guidelines. For instance, the number of pages in the 2012 SR was drastically reduced compared to 2011 (-37%), in coherence with the IIRC focus on conciseness. The materiality determination process, which is one of the main pillars of the IIRC framework, requires "those charged with governance" to determine the impact of the issues on the ability of the company to create value. The approach employed by Enel in its 2012 SR presents some differences compared to the IIRC framework, but nevertheless the company involves functions and people with a high degree of responsibility in the process, in coherence with IIRC indications. The 2012 Enel SR also significantly improved the definition of the business model compared to 2011, in coherence with the IIRC framework, which sees the business model as one of the main elements (see IIRC 2013c).

In some other cases, the evolution towards IR is still unfolding, and it will be interesting to see how the company reacts to the new guidelines expressed in the IIRC Consultation Draft (CD) and to the upcoming international IR framework version 1.0. For instance, Enel is already disclosing information about IIRC capitals. Such information is embedded in different reports and it is not organized by capitals, as in the IIRC approach, although the IIRC itself does not require a strict adoption of the language and classification proposed in its documents. Some significant efforts towards the engagement with the supply chain have been made.

The chapter is organized as follows: the second section provides a brief overview of Enel's history, identity and governance; the third section describes the evolution and the current situation of Enel's sustainable strategies; the fourth section focuses on corporate disclosure and in particular on AR and SR, pointing out similarities and challenges as compared to the IIRC framework; the fifth section, finally, discusses the materiality determination process and stakeholder engagement process of Enel, which represent two of the main strengths of its corporate disclosure system.

14.2 Enel Group: History and Identity

Enel is a multinational group based in Italy and one of the main integrated players in the power and gas markets of Europe and Latin America, operating in 40 countries across four continents and serving 61 million customers overall. In 2012, the company earned 84,889 million euros in revenues, with an increase of 6.8 % as compared to 2011 and the net profit of the group was 2,075 million euros. The net capital employed amounted to 96,106 million euros as of December 31, 2012, and was financed by a total shareholders' equity of 53,158 million euros and net financial debt of 42,948 million euros. As of December 31, 2012, Enel Group employees totaled 73,702 (see Enel 2013b).

Enel S.p.a. was established in 1962, and its objective was to perform electricity production, import and export, transportation, processing, distribution and sale in the Italian market. In 1976, as a consequence of the oil crisis, Enel planned to build both new power plants and hydroelectric pumping plants, in order to reduce dependence on oil. During the 1980s, the growing interest in public opinion towards environmental issues led Enel to start the production of renewable energies and at the same time determined the abandonment of nuclear energy, as a consequence of the 1987 referendum on nuclear power. In 1992, Enel became a joint-stock company, and this operation represented the first step towards the upcoming privatization. 1999 represents a fundamental year in the history of Enel, as the 1999 Bersani Decree liberalized the electricity sector. Thus, Enel had to separate production, transmission and distribution, creating three different legal entities in the Italian market: Enel Produzione, Enel Distribuzione and Terna respectively. 1999 was also the year of Enel's privatization and stock market debut on the Italian Stock Exchange and the New York Stock Exchange. Since 2001, Enel has increased its propensity towards foreign investment, with the acquisition of Spanish and US-based electricity companies. The implementation of a more comprehensive sustainable strategy started in 2002, through the issuance of the Enel code of ethics. The following year, Enel was admitted to the list FTSE4Good Europe 50, and in 2004, it was included in the Dow Jones Sustainability Index (DJSI). In recent years, Enel's attention to sustainability issues has been confirmed by its increased focus on the renewable energy and zero emission objectives. Enel Green Power, leader in the renewable energy field, has been listed since 2010. In the same year, the first ever industrial hydrogen plant and the thermodynamic power plant Archimede were opened, together with a few plants for carbon capture and storage technology.

Enel has about 1.3 million retail and institutional investors. Enel's most important institutional shareholder is the Italian Ministry of Economy and Finance, which holds 31.24 % of the company's shares. On the one hand, although the company is subject to the de facto control of the Ministry of the Economy and Finance, the above-mentioned Ministry is not in any way involved in managing or coordinating the company, since the company makes its management decisions on a fully independent basis. On the other hand, in implementing the provisions of the legal framework on privatizations, the company's bylaws assign certain special powers to the Italian government (represented for this purpose by the Ministry of the Economy and Finance), which are exercisable regardless of the number of shares owned by the aforementioned Ministry. The company board of directors is divided into several different committees: the control and risk committee, the compensation committee, the related parties committee and the nomination and corporate governance committee.

14.3 Enel's Journey Towards Sustainability

The core business of the company is relevant both from an environmental and a social perspective so, as was briefly discussed in the previous paragraph, Enel has always devoted a considerable amount of attention to such ESG issues, especially in the last few years.

The sustainability policy of Enel relies on an ethical system, which is composed by four main pillars (see Enel 2013a, b). The first one is the code of ethics, which was adopted in 2002. It expresses the ethical commitments and responsibility in conducting business and corporate activities. The code is not only valid for Enel, but also for all the companies in which Enel has an equity interest and that are for this reason required to comply with it. The second pillar is the Compliance Model that meets the requirements of the Legislative Decree 231 of June 8, 2001, which introduced into Italian law a system of liability for companies for certain types of offences committed by its directors, managers or employees on behalf of or to the benefit of the company. Similarly to the Code of Ethics, in 2010 Enel also approved specific guidelines in order to apply the principles of the Compliance Model to all the other foreign subsidiaries of the group. The third pillar is a zero tolerance of corruption plan, which is a move marking Enel's participation in the Global Compact (a 2000 UN program of action) and the PACI—Partnering Against Corruption Initiative (an initiative promoted by the World Economic Forum in Davos in 2005). Finally, the fourth pillar is a human rights policy, which requires appropriate due diligence processes such as, for example, the Human Rights Compliance Assessment (HRCA) in all the countries in which the Group is present and the integration of ESG issues in the risk management process.

The Enel sustainability plan focuses on the issues that the materiality analysis has defined as most important, and it identifies the specific objectives and/or targets which Enel will take on for each commitment. The main commitments of the company deal both with financial performance and with environmental and social performance. From an IIRC perspective, such commitments will have an impact on financial capital as well as the other five kinds of capital. The first commitment is the creation of economic-financial value, to be reached through, among other things, protection of margins and cash flows, growth on expanding markets and in renewables, increased efficiency and debt reduction. Other commitments include: growth in renewables, energy efficiency (also through investments in smart grids, smart cities and electric transportation), access to electricity, governance (also through an increase of female presence on the boards), ESG risk management (also through the development of methodology and processes for the assessment of ESG risks at the group level), correctness and transparency (also through the development of a dedicated software system to collect and monitor qualitative and quantitative data on sustainability at Group level, from a One Report viewpoint); mitigation of emissions; efficient use of water; biodiversity; global environmental management; responsible relations with communities; respect for human rights; quality for customers; people development; diversity and equal opportunities; occupational health and safety; responsible supply chain.

14.4   The Corporate Disclosure System

The following table summarizes the main documents constituting Enel's overall corporate disclosure, from an IR perspective. The six capitals (the term "capitals" refers to any store of value that an organization can use in the production of goods and services) the IIRC framework proposes are the following: financial; manufactured; intellectual; social and relationship; human; natural. According to the framework, it is fundamental to possess all the capitals for the company to operate, as the capitals are ultimately the input of an organization's business model (Table 14.1).

The financial capital is analyzed and discussed in detail in the Annual Report, where the report reader can find much information on the stock and financial performance of the company in particular. Over the years, Enel has included more and more sustainability information in its Annual Report (more specifically, in the "Relazione sulla gestione—Management Commentary"). This process of integration is due to the fact that the firm is following the Modernisation Directive but also due to its willingness to move towards the IR framework. The AR therefore includes also a great deal of information on human capital, its organizational structure and on the policies for human resources management (from selection to training). It is also possible to find a focus on the compensation policy of the firm, with particular reference to stock incentives plans and stock options plans.

Issues related to human resources and to remuneration, despite being disclosed in the AR, are more carefully tackled in the corporate governance report attached to the AR and in the sustainability report. Also, social capital is analyzed in the AR, but it is described in more detail in the sustainability reports and in the environmental report. In particular, the environmental report describes more carefully the environmental issues included in the SR, in terms of environmental governance and results. The report also includes information about Enel personnel who have responsibilities in the environmental field and about assets constituting the manufactured capital of the company (such as plants), their environmental impact and their certifications. The environmental report follows the GRI indicators. Enel's disclosure on the capitals does not employ the six-capital terminology proposed by

Table 14.1 Enel corporate disclosure system and the IIRC framework

IIRC capitals	Enel denomination	Enel documents
Financial capital	Synthesis of the financial performance of the Group	Annual report
	2012 results	Sustainability report
Manufactured capital	Annual report	Annual report
	Processes and products	Environmental report
Environmental capital	Sustainability in Enel	Annual report
	Environmental strategy	Sustainability report
	Environment	Environmental report
Human capital	People	Annual report
	People and community	Sustainability report
	Human resources dedicated to the environment	Environmental report
Social capital	Industrial relations	Annual report
	Community	Sustainability report
	People and community	Environmental report
Intellectual capital	–	–

the IIRC yet, but, even if it is not organized by capitals, the information is available. It should be underlined that IIRC does not require a strict adoption of language and classification proposed in its documents: IIRC pushes companies to deal with their own specific approach. And Enel successfully selects its own way.

14.4.1 Enel 2012 Annual Report

As pointed out above, the Enel AR includes some non-financial information, both because it is required to do so by the Modernisation Directive and because it represents a step towards IR. For instance, Enel's AR provides a summary of results, including both financial and non-financial information, including indicators such as: average efficiency of thermal plants, injury frequency rate and verified violations of the code of ethics (Enel 2013a, b, p. 18). Besides this, there is a whole section of the AR, starting at page 99, discussing the Enel sustainability policy. The section is divided into several chapters: human resources and organization, customer, society, climate strategy and environment, research and innovation.

The main risks and uncertainties that have been identified are the following: risks connected with market liberalization and regulatory developments, risks connected with CO_2 emissions, market risks (risks connected with commodity prices and supply continuity, exchange rate risks, interest rate risks), credit risks, liquidity risks, country risks and, finally, industrial and environmental risks.

The AR was audited by Reconta Ernst and Young, which relied on the auditing standards recommended by CONSOB (the Italian Stock Exchange regulatory agency). In accordance with such standards, Reconta obtained the information necessary to determine whether the consolidated financial statements were materially misstated and whether such financial statements could be relied upon. The auditing process included the examination, on a test basis, of evidence supporting the amounts and disclosures in the financial statements, as well as assessing the appropriateness of the accounting principles applied and the reasonableness of the estimates made by directors. In the opinion of Reconta, the consolidated financial statements of the Enel Group were prepared in accordance with international financial reporting standards and give a true and fair view of its financial position. Also the non-financial sustainability information included in the AR is therefore fully verified.

14.4.2 Enel 2012 Sustainability Report

Sustainability reporting plays a central role for Enel, given the primary role of the company in the global market. Enel, as many the other international corporations, is subject to scrutiny from investors, institutional investors and other organizations rating its ESG activity. In particular, the ability of the company to raise capital from institutional investors considering ESG aspects in their investment decisions is greatly influenced by its social disclosure. Socially Responsible Investing (SRI), defined as "(. . .) the practice of directing investment funds in ways that combine investors' financial objectives with their commitment to social concerns such as social justice, economic development, peace or a healthy environment" (Haigh and Hazelton 2004, p. 59), currently holds a significant portion of the company's shares (14.6 %, according to the 2012 Enel SR). Because of these reasons, SR plays a central role in a company's disclosure and management, as shown by previous literature (see Berthelot et al. 2003; Brammer and Pavelin 2004; Healy and Palepu 2001).

   Although Enel is part of the IIRC pilot company program, it has issued, since 2002, its own SR. This coheres with the indications by the IIRC, which view the SR and IR as complementary (see IIRC 2013a, b, c, p. 2). In other words, Enel chose to implement the innovation in its reporting to the greatest extent in its SR, despite working on the AR as well by increasing the non-financial information included in it. The SR requires a constant commitment to measuring and reporting on corporate responsibility from a company, following the famous motto by Peter Drucker "if you can't measure something, you can't manage it".

   In drafting the SR, since 2006, Enel has followed the guidelines of the GRI-G3 international standard of the Global Reporting Initiative (GRI), coupled since 2008 with the EUSS (Electric Utility Sector Supplement) for the electricity industry, and since 2011, with G3.1. Ever since their adoption, Enel has applied the guidelines at the highest level recognized by the GRI (A+). Besides following the GRI guidelines, the 2012 SR also conforms to the principles of inclusiveness, materiality and responsiveness indicated in AA1000APS (AccountAbility Principles Standard) issued in 2008 by AccountAbility (see Enel 2013a, b).

The process leading to the issuance of the SR is structured in different phases, as it is analysed and assessed by the Control and Risks Committee and the Appointments and Corporate Governance Committee which, with the support of the Audit Department, verify the completeness and reliability of the report; the SR is then approved by the Board of Directors and finally presented at the Annual General Meeting, together with the Group Annual Report.

It is interesting to note that the 2012 Enel SR, in coherence with indications from the IIRC, is significantly shorter as compared to the 2011 Enel SR, as the total number of pages decreased from 306 to 194 (-37%). Such reduction is particularly relevant because it has involved the financial data as well. Also, this reduction is aligned with is one of the guiding principles of the IIRC, i.e. conciseness. This principle states that: "an integrated report includes concise information that provides sufficient context to make it understandable, and avoids redundant information. The organization seeks a balance between conciseness and the other Guiding Principles, in particular completeness and comparability. In achieving conciseness, an integrated report can be linked to additional detailed information that is provided separately" (see IIRC 2013a, b, c, paragraph 3.29). Coherently with this increased conciseness of the report, the SR discloses the highlights of the sustainability performance at the beginning of the report, pointing out: total net production, net renewable production, electricity volumes sold, gas volumes sold, electricity transported, average number of electricity and gas customers, number of employees, workforce of contractors, EBITDA, EBIT, revenues and SRI funds in institutional shareholdings.

The scope of the SR includes these "companies included on a line-by-line basis in the scope of consolidation of the Annual Report at December 31, 2012. The associated companies (which in the Annual Report are valued using the equity method) and the other entities over which Enel exercises significant influence (including joint ventures) are included in the calculation of the data, where available, in proportion to Enel's equity interest and are mentioned in the text where they produce significant impacts" (Enel 2013a, b, p. 121). According to the IIRC, "an integrated report identifies its reporting boundaries and explains how it has been determined. Determining the boundaries for an integrated report involves two aspects: the boundaries used for financial reporting purposes (i.e., the financial reporting entity); and opportunities, risks and outcomes attributable to or associated with other entities/ stakeholders beyond the financial reporting entity that have a material effect on the ability of the financial reporting entity to create value over time" (see IIRC 2013a, b, c, paragraph 5.25). Even if some significant efforts have already been made by Enel in the sense of framing the report's boundaries according to the IIRC framework, this is a crucial challenge both for Enel and for other entities involved in the IR pilot program.

A particularly important piece of information in the IR context is the information about the business model. In the 2011 Enel SR this information was not present, even if it did contain some information about the organizational model of the company. The 2012 Management commentary includes a detailed description of the business model, which is a central element in the IR framework. According to the IIRC: "An organization's business model is its chosen system of inputs, business activities, outputs and outcomes that aims to create value over the short, medium and long term" (see IIRC 2013a, b, c, paragraph 2.26). A clear understanding of the business model is fundamental for the company to be able to define material issues and to coherently frame its strategy from an IR perspective. Even in this case, the evolution of the Enel reporting has been coherent with the principles of the IIRC.

One of the main shortcomings of Sustainability Reporting is its (perceived) low reliability, which requires companies to provide the market with some form of control of the SR in order for it to be value-relevant. At Enel, the Internal Audit and an independent auditor review the SR for completeness and accuracy. Besides this, since 2012, the SR is checked not only by the Risk and Control Committee but also by the Corporate Governance Committee and is submitted to Enel Spa's Board of Directors for its approval before being presented at the Shareholders' Meeting.

Besides this "internal" form of control of the process leading to the issuance of the SR, the 2012 Enel SR was also assured by Reconta Ernst and Young, which carried out a limited assurance (see Enel 2013a, b, p. 191). The directors of Enel Spa are responsible for the preparation of the report in accordance with the inclusivity, materiality, and responsiveness principles set out in the AA1000APS and for the data on sustainability performance. The guidelines and principles employed by E&Y are those provided by the ISAE3000 framework and are in accordance with the criteria established by the AA1000AS, Type 2, concerning both the nature and adherence to the AA1000APS and the evaluation on the reliability of data on sustainability performance. The procedures employed in order to assure the report were: interviews with the departments responsible for the topic reported in the sustainability report; on-site verification of data and interviews with personnel involved in the data collection and management process for production sites selected; and analysis, on a sample basis, of the documentation supporting the preparation of data and information on the sustainability performance.

14.5   Materiality Analysis and Stakeholder Engagement

Two of the most advanced aspects of the 2012 Enel SR refer to the materiality analysis and to the description of stakeholder engagement. The 2012 Enel SR devotes a whole section to the discussion of the analysis of materiality (see Enel 2013a, b, p. 23), which aims at mapping and calibrating the issues and expectations of stakeholders, and the means and processes with which the company responds to such expectations. The analysis of materiality was conducted on the basis of AA1000SES guidelines for the stages of mapping and prioritizing stakeholders and analysing the results, and of the criteria of AccountAbility and of the GRI G3.1 for the definition of key issues and the application of the principle of materiality.

The materiality matrix has, on the horizontal axis, the "priority of intervention according to stakeholders" and, on the vertical axis, the "impact on sustainability

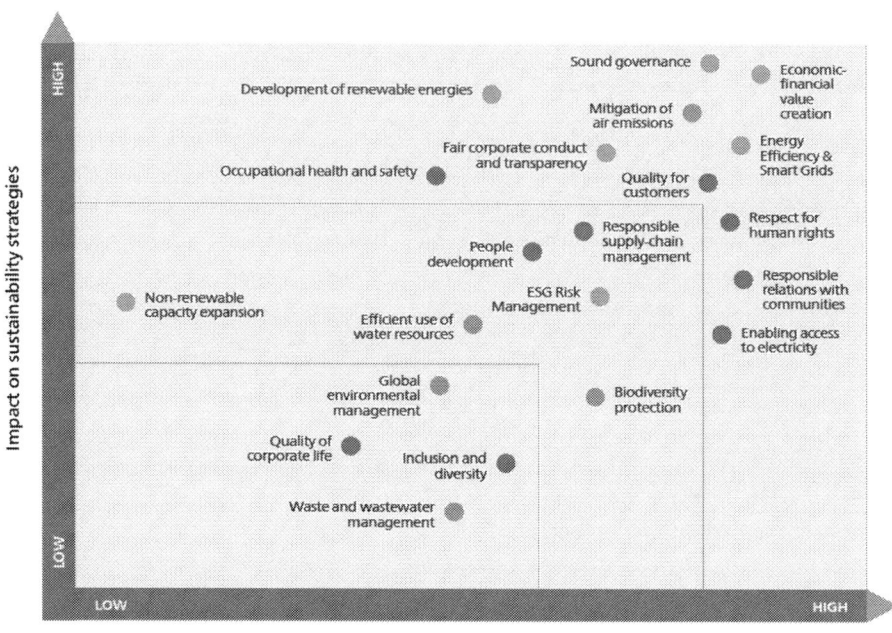

Fig 14.1 Enel materiality matrix 2012

strategies". Therefore, looking at the horizontal axis, the issues for which stakeholders request more commitment from the Group in terms of investments or formalization of commitments and policies are placed on the right hand side of the matrix, while the issues on the left-hand side are those to which stakeholders give a low priority. On the vertical axis, there are the issues with the potential to significantly impact, both immediately and in the near future, Enel's sustainability strategies.

In the upper part of the matrix are, therefore, the issues on which, as part of the Group's strategic objectives, a high level of investment is planned for coming years, while those in the bottom part are significant at divisional/departmental level (Fig. 14.1).

An analysis of the issues represented in the matrix allows us to point out that the governance issues are considered among the most relevant, both in terms of creation of financial value and in terms of improvement of the transparency standards and stakeholder engagement. The environmental issues, on the other hand, are issues that Enel has been tackling for many years, and therefore they are of great importance in the long-term sustainable strategy and in the definition of the business model itself.

According to the IIRC, the materiality determination process ought to be carried out by "those charged with governance": "those charged with governance have ultimate responsibility for how the organization's strategy, governance, performance and prospects lead to value creation over time. They are responsible for ensuring that there is effective leadership and decision-making regarding <IR>, including the identification and oversight of the employees actively involved in the <IR> process (e.g., those involved in identifying material matters, and in collecting, accumulating, measuring and reporting material information)" (see IIRC 2013a, b, c, paragraph 5.17). According to the Enel 2012 SR, "the impact of the issues on Enel's sustainability strategies was determined by involving the Strategic Planning Unit and other company departments for analyses on specific issues, and reflects the strategic guidelines defined by the 2013–2017 Industrial Plan, the objectives of the departments/divisions and the commitments taken on by the Group through policies and conduct criteria." (Enel 2013a, b, p. 119). Therefore, from this perspective, Enel is already involving the subjects that will ultimately be responsible for the strategy of the company in the materiality determination process, and this is another aspect that moves towards the IR framework.

The IIRC also makes clear "to whom" the issue ought to be material, that is, the providers of financial capital. From this perspective, the Enel SR has a different approach, as it considers the materiality for the stakeholders themselves and according to its impact on the sustainable strategy.

Connected to the materiality determination process is the stakeholder engagement process, which is fundamental in order to point out the main issues the company ought to look at. According to the IIRC CD: "engagement with stakeholders occurs regularly in the ordinary course of business (e.g., day-to-day liaison with customers and suppliers or broader ongoing engagement as part of strategic planning and risk assessment). It may also be undertaken for a particular purpose (e.g., engagement with a local community when planning a factory extension). The more integrated thinking is embedded in the business, the more likely it is that a fuller consideration of stakeholders' legitimate needs, interests and expectations is incorporated as an ordinary part of conducting business" (IIRC 2013a, b, c, paragraph 3.18). According to the SR, Enel did organize numerous initiatives to listen to, involve and talk to key stakeholders. Besides this, a structured analysis of the positions independently expressed by 'authoritative' stakeholders was undertaken, such as national and transnational institutions, authorities, stakeholder associations, and multilateral bodies on sustainability issues. Enel cites among the examples of sources considered in the stakeholder engagement process: customer satisfaction and customer complaints, climate surveys and internal communication, dealings with analysts and investors, questionnaires from sustainability rating agencies, dealings with representative and category associations, institutional relations at national and local level, union relations, media monitoring and surveys.

Conclusions

The aim of this chapter was to analyze how one of the IIRC pilot program companies (Enel) is evolving its corporate disclosure system, from an IR perspective. The company states, in its 2012 AR, its willingness to integrate the various aspects of its report, in order to give all stakeholders a comprehensive assessment of the Group's activities and results. This is confirmed by the fact that the AR includes substantial non-financial information, both because of the Modernization Directive but also because of the willingness of the company to integrate different dimensions of the report.

Some evidence indicates that Enel has already taken some steps towards the IR framework. The number of pages of the 2012 SR was drastically reduced as compared to 2011 (-37 %), in coherence with the IIRC focus on conciseness. The materiality determination process (despite relying on different criteria, as compared to those proposed by the IIRC) involves functions and people with a high degree of responsibility in the process, in coherence with IIRC indications. Also, compared to 2011, the business model is defined much more clearly, this being one of the main pillars of the IIRC framework.

In other cases, the evolution is still in process, and it will be interesting to see how the company reacts to the new guidelines expressed in the IIRC Consultation Draft (CD) and to the upcoming international IR framework version 1.0. Enel is already disclosing information about the IIRC capitals, although such information is embedded in different reports and not organized by capitals, as in the IIRC approach. How will the company frame its IR, in coherence with this capital approach? Enel did try to go beyond the boundaries of the legal entity, in order to include in the reporting process also the supply chain. The company made a significant effort in order to provide information and to educate the supply chain, thus assuming a role of leadership in engaging with its suppliers in a sustainability perspective. The future challenge will be to employ such full range of information in the whole corporate reporting.

References

Berthelot S, Cormier D, Magnam M (2003) Environmental disclosure research: review and synthesis. J Account Lit 22:1–44

Brammer S, Pavelin S (2004) Voluntary social disclosures by large UK companies. Bus Ethics A Eur Rev 13(2/3):86–99

Enel (2013a) Sustainability report. http://www.enel.com/en-GB/doc/report_2012/enel_sustainability_report_2012.pdf. Accessed 22 Jul 2013

Enel (2013b) Annual report. http://www.enel.com/en-GB/doc/report_2012/annual_report_enel_2012.pdf. Accessed 22 Jul 2013

Haigh M, Hazelton J (2004) Financial markets: a tool for social responsibility? J Bus Eth 52

Healy P, Palepu K (2001) Information asymmetry, corporate disclosure, and the capital markets: a review of the empirical disclosure literature. J Account Econ 31(1/3):405–440

IIRC (2013a) Consultation draft of the international <IR> framework. IIRC, New York. http://www.theiirc.org/consultationdraft2013. Accessed 22 Jul 2013

IIRC (2013b) Pilot Program (2012), Yearbook. IIRC, New York. http://www.theiirc.org/wp-content/uploads/Yearbook_2012/sources/indexPop.htm. Accessed 22 Jul 2013

IIRC (2013c) Business model—background paper for <IR>. IIRC, New York. http://www.theiirc.org/wp-content/uploads/2013/03/Business_Model.pdf. Accessed 22 Jul 2013

The Case of Vodacom Group

15

Fabrizio Granà and Libero Mario Mari

Abstract

In 2009, the King Report on Corporate Governance in South Africa provided local companies with guidelines on how to develop an Integrated Report. Since 2010, Integrated Reporting has become compulsory for all companies listed on the Johannesburg Stock Exchange Limited. Given the diffusion of Integrated Reporting in South Africa, this chapter aims to illustrate the structure of the 2013 Integrated Report of Vodacom Group, a South African private telecommunications company. The analysis is based on the content elements and guiding principles proposed by the Consultation Draft released by the International Integrated Reporting Council in April 2013. In doing so, this chapter compares the Integrated Report of Vodacom with the international recommendations on Integrated Reporting in order to explore their adaptability to a private company in the telecommunications industry.

15.1 Introduction[1]

Integrated Reporting guidelines were first proposed in 2009 by the King Report on Corporate Governance in South Africa (King III), which provided principles for preparing an Integrated Report (IR). Since 2010, Integrated Reporting is

---

[1] Although this chapter is the result of a joint effort, Sects. 15.1 and 15.2 can be assigned to Libero Mario Mari. The following sections related to the description of the Content Elements (15.3,

F. Granà (✉)
School of Business and Economics, National University of Ireland, Galway, Ireland
e-mail: f.grana1@nuigalway.ie

L.M. Mari
University of Perugia, Perugia, Italy
e-mail: liberomario.mari@unipg.it

C. Busco et al. (eds.), *Integrated Reporting*, DOI 10.1007/978-3-319-02168-3_15,
© Springer International Publishing Switzerland 2013

compulsory for all South African companies listed on the Johannesburg Stock Exchange (JSE) Limited (KPMG 2012). King III is a key step of the regulating process in corporate governance in South Africa, which started in 1994 (King I) and was improved in 2002 (King II), in accordance with standards agreed at the United Nations World Summit on Sustainable Development in Johannesburg. Importantly, King III provides a series of principles and recommendations based on the so called "apply or explain"[2] approach, and describes the IR as a way to present quantitative and qualitative information about the positive and negative impacts of business activities in the social, environmental and economic contexts in which companies operate (Institute of Directors Southern Africa 2009, p. 4). In compliance with King III, South African companies are obliged to disclose qualitative and quantitative information about their short, medium and long term value creation process in order to "enable stakeholders to make a more informed assessment of the economic value of a company" (Institute of Directors Southern Africa 2009, p. 12).

In parallel with the publication of King III, in 2011, the International Integrated Reporting Council in the UK (IIRC) published a discussion paper aimed at proposing shared guidelines for the development of IR (Abeysekera 2013; IIRC 2011). In accordance with the principles proposed in the discussion paper of the IIRC, an IR "brings together the material information about an organization's strategy, governance, performance and prospects, and ... reflects the commercial, social and environmental context within which it operates" (Abeysekera 2013, p. 3; IIRC 2011, p. 6). Two years later, on April 16th 2013, the IIRC presented the Consultation Draft (CD) of the International IR Framework, with the aim to provide an international guide of principles and content elements to develop a successful IR (IIRC 2013).

Given the importance of the Integrated Reporting concepts in South Africa and abroad, this chapter illustrates the structure of the 2013 Integrated Report of Vodacom Group, a South African private telecommunications company. After providing a brief description of the company's business history and the socio-economic landscape in which it operates (Sect. 15.2), Sects. 15.3 and 15.4 describe in detail the structure of the 2013 IR of Vodacom, analysing its development in the light of the content elements and guiding principles proposed in the CD of the IIRC.

15.3.1, 15.3.2, etc.), the Guiding Principles of the IR of Vodacom (15.4, 15.4.1, 15.4.2, etc.) and Discussion and Conclusions can be assigned to Fabrizio Granà.

[2] "Apply or Explain"—King III provides corporate governance standards in the form of recommendations and principles rather than compulsory rules ("Comply or explain" approach used in King II). This means that companies are advised to structure a statement whether they comply with the standards or not (KPMG 2009).

15.2 The Case of Vodacom: Company Profile

Vodacom Group Ltd (Vodacom) is a mobile communications and investment holding company, located in Johannesburg and listed on the JSE. Vodacom was established in 1993 as a joint venture between three multinational firms Telkom, Vodafone and VenFin. Respectively they owned shares of 50 %, 35 % and 15 % of the subscribed capital. In 2006, Vodafone, one of the world's largest mobile communications companies by revenue and Information Systems listed on the JSE,[3] acquired VenFin holding. In 2009, Vodafone had a majority shareholding (65 % of shares), obtaining part of the stakes owned by Telkom, which decided to sell its remaining holding by listing it on the JSE.

After its establishment in 1993, Vodacom provided GSM Mobile services in South Africa, introducing the first pre-paid SIM-card in Africa. Thanks to its quality-oriented vision, Vodacom was one of the first mobile communications companies in South Africa, and now provides mobile network connections to 51.7 million clients (private and public). Since 1995, Vodacom has extended its operations from South Africa to Lesotho,[4] Tanzania,[5] Democratic Republic of Congo (DRC),[6] and Mozambique. Vodacom also offers business managed services to enterprises in over 40 countries across Africa.

Two main innovative services differentiate Vodacom from its competitors:
1. The launch of its pre-paid SIM-card service in 1996.
2. The reduction price plan on mobile phones and calling tariffs, which opened the market to low income customers.

Today, Vodacom embraces all mobile communications segments offering a wide range of telecommunications services and products.[7]

Sections 15.3 and 15.4 define the main content elements and guiding principles of the 2013 IR of Vodacom, analysing in detail the IR in light of the guiding principles and content elements proposed within the CD of the IIRC.

15.3 The 2013 IR of Vodacom: Content Elements

When Vodacom published an IR for the first time in 2011, it was placed in the top ten telecommunications sector's IRs of the "Nkonki Top 100 Integrated Reporting Awards". In 2012, Vodacom's IR was awarded first place in the telecommunications sector "Nkonki Top 100 Integrated Reporting Awards" and was also ranked in the top ten Ernst and Young's "Excellence in Integrated Reporting

---

[3] JSE Limited is the largest stock exchange in Africa.

[4] Joint venture with Lesotho Telecommunications Corporation in 1995.

[5] Vodacom acquired a 10-year GSM mobile service licence in collaboration with the telecommunications company Planet Communication Ltd in 1999.

[6] Joint venture with three DRC wireless web networks service providers in 2001.

[7] http://www.in.reuters.com/finance/stocks/companyProfile?symbol=VODJ.J

awards" (Vodacom 2013, p. 2). The 2013 IR is the third such report published by Vodacom.

In accordance with the 2011 discussion paper of the IIRC and G3.1 guidelines of the Global Reporting Initiative (GRI), Vodacom's IR provides information about the past, present and future strategic priorities of the company and its ability to create value. Interestingly, the IR contents page is structured in two parts, illustrating the link between the contents of the IR (Overview; Our business; Strategic Review; Financial Review; Corporate Governance and Administration) and those described in the online version of the IR. In order to provide a complete description of the information disclosed in the IR and facilitate stakeholders' interpretation of financial and non-financial data, the IR of Vodacom indicates links to the company's website, which gives access to annual financial statements since 2003. Online statements include stakeholders' engagement reports and additional video-interviews with top Vodacom executives.[8] Furthermore, the IR contents page illustrates the icons used throughout the report to connect the information reported and to help the reader in finding new documents and identifying the most relevant positive and negative performances achieved during the year.

The IR of Vodacom is divided into six sections:

1. The "Overview" section provides an introduction to the relevant matters illustrated throughout the report, some premises on the financial and non-financial performances achieved during the year and interviews with the Chairman, CFO and CEO of the company.
2. The "Our Business" section gives information about the external environment, business activities and strategic objectives of Vodacom, and illustrates in brief the company's value, culture and governance structure.
3. The "Strategic Review" section describes the strategic objectives of Vodacom analysing its performance during the year, the most relevant financial and non-financial KPIs and future expectations of the company.
4. The "Financial Review" section contains a summary of the financial situation of the company, its income and cash-flow statements for 2012–2013.
5. The "Corporate Governance" section describes the company's risk management and remuneration policies.
6. The "Administration" section provides external assurance statements and corporate information. The glossary and notice of the annual general meeting are also parts of the administration section.

The next part analyses the content elements presented in the IR of Vodacom in light of the 2013 CD.

---

[8] http://www.vodacom.onlinereport.co.za/vodacom_ir_2013/

15.3.1 Organizational Overview and the External Environment

Information about "Organizational Overview and External Environment" content element is spread throughout the first two sections of the IR ("Overview" and "Our Business" sections) and provides a comprehensive description of Vodacom's main external environment relationships, ownership and operating structure.

In line with the "Organizational Overview" content element described in the CD (IIRC 2013, p. 24), the "Overview" section of Vodacom's IR provides some introductory information about the development of the telecommunications market in Africa and highlights future opportunities. In the "Chairman's statement" in the "Overview" section of the IR, Vodacom's Chairman, Peter Moyo, affirms that the increasing mobile usage throughout the African countries in which the company operates led Vodacom to improve the quality of its network connections and supply more voice and data services at a lower price (Vodacom 2013, p. 8).

In line with section 4A/4.7 of the CD (IIRC 2013, p. 24), the "Our Business" section of the IR describes the company's competitive landscape and market position. The "Our Business" section highlights how the continuous growth of smartphones and tablets in the global market is expected to increase the number of new mobile customers to 3 billion in 2017 (Africa counts for 20 % of this growth). The "Our Business" section also gives information about the company's competitive landscape, underlining how the competition among device manufacturers and operating system developers has increased (Vodacom 2013, p. 9). Vodacom's competitors have differentiated their services delivering "non-traditional" services such as mobile financial services.[9] The "Our Business" section of the IR also illustrates the principal activities, products and services offered by Vodacom to private and public customers. Customer oriented services are mainly voice (mobile and fixed), messaging (SMS, MMS) and data (mobile internet access) available in contract, top up or prepaid form[10] (Vodacom 2013, p. 18). The IR describes Vodacom's "non-traditional" services, such as mobile payment services (M-Pesa) and long-term insurances products and services, which are supplied both in South Africa and internationally.[11] Furthermore, Vodacom provides customized network and cloud facilities to private and public firms. In line with the "Organizational Overview" content element of the CD, the "Our Business" section of the IR

---

[9] Mobile financial services are financial services delivered using a mobile phone. Two categories can be distinguished: (1) Mobile Banking services; (2) Mobile Payment services. Mobile Banking services enable bank clients to connect to their bank accounts using a mobile phone. Mobile Payment services offer a broad set of services that are not provided by a bank, but in which a bank is always involved. http://www.microfinancegateway.org/gm/document-1.9.48603/AFI_Policynote_%20Mobile%20Financial%20Service_EN.pdf

[10] Contract services give customers the opportunity to pay via monthly debit order; prepaid services enable customers to exploit the service paying whenever they need to, without being locked into a contract, and the top up is a combination of contract and prepaid benefits (Vodacom 2013, p. 18).

[11] http://www.itweb.co.za/index.php?option=com_content&view=article&id=54823

provides information about Vodacom's governance and leadership structure, which consists of a unitary Board with 12 directors, ten of whom are non-executive directors (five dependent non-executive directors and five independent non-executive directors).

Some premises about key developments made to sustain the cultural, social, governance and risk management aspects of the company are also summarised in the IR's "Our Business". Following the recommendations given in the "Organizational Overview" section of the CD, Vodacom's IR emphasises the importance of building trustful relationships between employees, customers, industry players, business partners, regulators and governmental authorities, to drive the business to success (Vodacom 2013, p. 22). In accordance with section 4A/4.7 of the CD, the "Overview" section of Vodacom's IR contains charts of the most relevant KPIs in 2012–2013, highlighting how Vodacom "creates value for company's stakeholders" (employees, Governments, financial providers).

In line with the "External Environment" content element of the CD (IIRC 2013, p. 25), the "Our Business" section of the 2013 IR gives information about Vodacom's external environment, international investment and relationships with international Governments, describing where the company operates and which countries are the most profitable. Although South Africa still retains the most profitable market with more than 30.3 million customers and a mobile penetration growth of 144 % in 2012, over the last few years, increasing mobile market competition has led Vodacom to improve its network investments in high performing international markets (Mozambique, Tanzania, DRC and Lesotho), differentiating the products and services it offers (Vodacom 2013, pp. 20–21). In line with section 4A/4.9 of the CD (IIRC 2013, p. 25), Vodacom's IR stresses the necessity to build reliable and continuative relationships with local (South African) and international governments in order to increase its network connection spectrum, roll out the Long Term Evolution (LTE)[12] programme and better comply with the BBBEE[13] code and licenses fees regulations.

After a brief description of the internal and external context in which the company operates, the IR of Vodacom describes strategic activities and objectives of the firm.

15.3.2 Business Model

In line with section 4E/4.23 of the CD (IIRC 2013, p. 27), the "Our Business" section of the IR describes Vodacom's business model using a chart of the vision,

---

[12] Long Term Evolution (LTE) is commonly referred to as 4G, providing a faster and more efficient data transfer speed than 3G/HSPA and increased network capacity (Vodacom 2013, p. 94).

[13] Broad-based Black Economic Empowerment ('BBBEE') is a programme launched by the South African Government to redress the employment inequalities by giving disadvantaged groups opportunities previously not available to them (Vodacom 2013, p. 93).

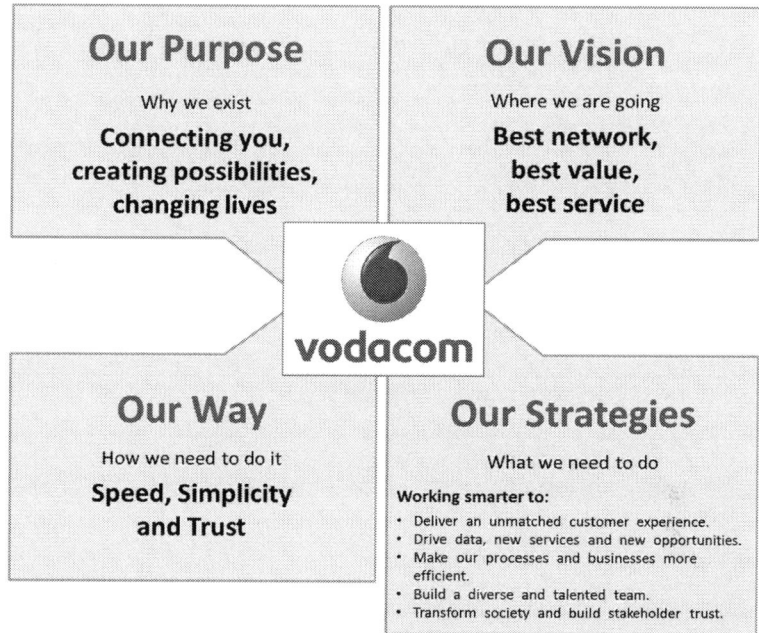

Fig. 15.1   Vodacom's business model (*Source*: adapted from Vodacom's IR, 2013, p. 16)

purpose, direction and strategic objectives that the company aims to achieve. This chart communicates both internally and externally "what Vodacom lives for". Since its establishment, Vodacom's mission is to maintain its position as market leader of the telecommunications sector in South Africa, improving the quality of the services it offers and providing better customer experiences. The "reason to get up in the morning" (how Vodacom defines its vision) is based on the necessity to continually increase the number of new network connections. Furthermore, Vodacom aims to improve customer service and product experience (Vision), provide high quality services and network connections (Purpose), and build trusting and reliable relationships among the group's stakeholders (Way), in order to (Fig. 15.1):

- Deliver unmatched customer experience.
- Drive data, new services and new opportunities.
- Make processes and businesses more efficient.
- Build a diverse and talented team.
- Transform society and build stakeholder trust.

Regarding section 4E of the CD (IIRC 2013, p. 27), Vodacom's IR provides an overall picture of the company's business model. The "Strategy Review" section specifies the inputs employed, activities performed to achieve listed strategic objectives and outputs and outcomes during 2012. The IR explains how Vodacom's profitability growth over time depends on its ability to diversify the services provided, improve the company's competitive position and operate efficiently through simplified and standardised processes and smarter distribution (Vodacom 2013, p. 32). In line with the "Business model" section of the CD, the IR of Vodacom gives some information about the company's ability to adapt to change (section 4E/4.22) (IIRC 2013, p. 27). For instance, the "Strategic Review" section of the IR highlights how Vodacom and local and foreign governments are investing in rolling out the broadband services to all customers (local and foreign) in order to reduce socio-economic imbalances and increase countries' GDP (Vodacom 2013, p. 37).

In accordance with section 4E/4.22 of the CD, the "Strategic Review" section of Vodacom's IR provides information about the results achieved throughout the year disclosing financial and non-financial data. This "Strategic Review" section highlights that, in 2012, 40 % of Vodacom's non-South African revenues were generated from financial and assurance services, which have impacted on the company's reputation and communities' and the broader society's perception of the value delivered (Vodacom 2013, p. 30).

15.3.3 Strategy and Resource Allocation

In line with the "Strategy and Resource allocation" section of the CD (IIRC 2013, p. 26), the "Overview Section" of the IR provides a general description of Vodacom's strategic focus. The "Overview section" of the IR describes the main "material issues" defined by Vodacom's top management as the "most likely to affect the company stakeholders' assessments of Vodacom's ability to create value over time" (Vodacom 2013, p. 5). Five material issues have been identified:

1. Network quality: improving the quality of network infrastructure to differentiate customer experience and to comply with Government and regulatory quality standards.
2. Reliance on the South African Market: increasing investment in existing markets, exploiting unknown opportunities outside current markets and developing new profitable products and services.
3. Competition: maintaining leadership in the South African telecommunications market and beating the competition by delivering a differentiated service experience.
4. Relationships with Governments and Regulators: aligning strategic decisions to the government and regulator requests in order to acquire new licences in the markets in which Vodacom operates.
5. Talent and Succession: developing employees' technical skills necessary to differentiate Vodacom's expertise and local knowledge.

The company's ability to create value in the short, medium and long term is based upon the achievement of five strategic objectives as described in Sect. 15.3.2. The "Strategic Review" section of the IR illustrates step by step each strategic objective describing the activities performed during the 2012–3. In accordance with section 4D/4.20 of the CD (IIRC 2013, p. 26), the IR highlights the external opportunities, organizational capitals employed, financial and non-financial performances and the short, medium and long term orientation of Vodacom.

In line with the CD, the "Strategic Review" section of the IR provides detailed information about what differentiates Vodacom from other competitors, how it fosters innovation and which capitals have been employed. It also explains that in order to deliver "unmatched customer experience" (Vodacom's first strategic objective), Vodacom created new service approaches, investing in IT systems to support all possible customer interactions (stores, call centres, Twitter, Facebook and e-mail) (Vodacom 2013, p. 27). Due to the limited presence of financial services in Africa, increased foreign Small and Medium Enterprises (SMEs) and Multi-National Companies (MNCs) integration in the African market, large investments have been made in the provision of financial and assurance services for customers and customized Information Communication Technology (ICT) services for companies (Vodacom 2013, p. 31). Furthermore, substantial investments in network infrastructure (R9.5 billion in 2012 alone) and network capacity expansions (adding 1,752 3G and 1,406 2G sites across the group) have been made at a local and international level, especially in markets in which mobile penetration is slightly below 40 % and with a good 0 GDP (Vodacom 2013, p. 30). Significant improvements have also been made in Vodacom IT and billing systems to increase their efficiency and effectiveness (Vodacom 2013, p. 33).

Section 4D/4.20 of the CD (IIRC 2013, p. 26) recommends that international IRs provide information about the external environment's response to company's strategies. In doing so, the "Strategic Review" section of the IR of Vodacom describes the company's sustainability policies to invest in efficient technologies, minimising the company's environmental footprint and network maintenance in comparison to the previous years (Vodacom 2013, p. 33). Furthermore, this section also gives insights into the company's social responsibility to "promote safe and fair working conditions and the responsible management of environmental and social matters" (Vodacom 2013, p. 37). In line with the "Strategy and Resource allocation" content element of the CD, the "Strategic Review" section of the IR of Vodacom highlights the importance of fostering employee engagement and motivation in order to develop internal wealth and careers. Workforce skills development is considered relevant to improve the company's innovation process and to offer differentiated services and products (Vodacom 2013, p. 35).

The IR's "Strategic Review" section also identifies the company's outcomes and performances in 2012–3 and highlights the most significant KPIs for each strategic objective described.

15.3.4 Performance

In line with the "Performance" content element of the CD, the IR highlights quantitative financial and non-financial indicators and compares them to past performance (IIRC 2013, p. 28). Furthermore, the contextualization of quantitative performances offered in the IR provides an overall representation of the value creation of Vodacom. The "Overview" section of the IR illustrates the performance achieved in the past 3 years through the use of charts that show the company's most relevant KPIs (Financial, Economic, Social-Employees, Social—Communities, and Environment). Furthermore, in line with section 4 F/4.28 of the CD (IIRC 2013, p. 28), the "Overview" section of the IR describes the relationships with the company's stakeholders highlighting the value distributed during the year (Vodacom 2013, pp. 3–6).

The interview with the CFO presented in the "Overview" section of Vodacom's IR gives some insights into the company's financial position. Vodacom's CFO, Ivan Dittrich, affirms that positive financial performances registered in 2012 (10.9 % EBITDA growth for Vodacom South Africa and 2 % expansion in the Group's EBITDA margin), are the result of investments made in renewing the company's radio access network, transforming IT and billing systems to extract additional process efficiencies, improving the business intelligence system, standardizing and simplifying processes to support cost management and strategic achievements (Vodacom 2013, p. 13). The "Financial review" section of the IR also provides a summarized description of the operating results of Vodacom over the last 3 years, distinguishing between South African and international performance.

In line with the "Performance" content element of the CD, the "Strategic Review" section of Vodacom's IR also highlights non-financial indicators. For instance, considering Vodacom's first strategic objective, the company's brand reputation is measured through annual reputation surveys and analysis of the Net Promoter Score (NPS)[14] (Vodacom 2013, p. 27).

15.3.5 Governance

The IR of Vodacom provides information about the company's leadership structure, top management responsibilities, remuneration and incentive policies. In accordance with the "Governance" content element of the CD (IIRC 2013, p. 25), the "Overview" section of Vodacom's IR contains two charts which show the board of directors and the leadership structure of the company. In line with section 4B/4.11 of the CD, the "Corporate Governance" section of the IR contains a chart of the main responsibilities of the board of directors of Vodacom, describing in particular the actions taken to drive and monitor the company's strategic direction, ensuring the effectiveness of internal control and improving relationships with company shareholders (Fig. 15.2).

Vodacom's board of directors fosters shareholders' relationships, communicating strategies and activities performed during the year. A planned investor programme is described in the "Corporate Governance" section of the IR of Vodacom and includes (Vodacom 2013, p. 72):

---

[14] The NPS measures the level of customer satisfaction by how likely customers are to recommend Vodacom's brand to people around them. (Vodacom 2013, p. 27).

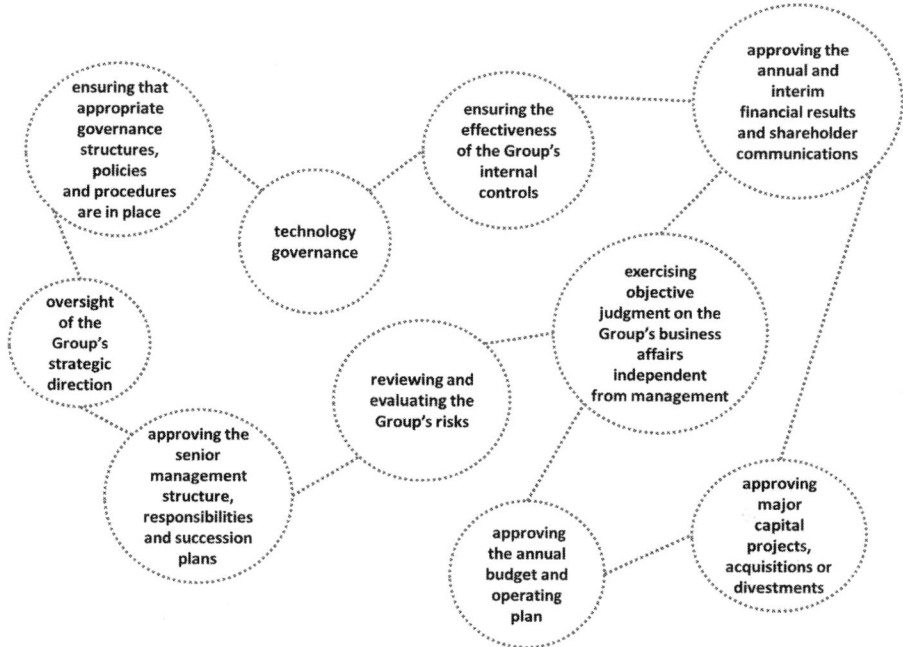

Fig. 15.2 Responsibilities of Vodacom's Board of Directors (*Source*: adapted from Vodacom's IR, 2013, p. 69)

- Formal presentations of annual and interim results.
- Briefing meetings with major institutional shareholders after the release of results.
- Hosting investor and analyst sessions.

The stakeholder engagement report is not included in the IR and it is instead provided online.

Following section 4.12 of the CD, the "Corporate Governance" section of the IR provides detailed information about Vodacom's remuneration policies. The description of the remuneration policies is divided in two parts:

1. The remuneration policy for executive directors and prescribed officers, delineating the short term and long term incentives plan.
2. Quantitative information about payment accruals and awards for the year ended 31 March 2013 (Vodacom 2013, p. 65).

The "Corporate Governance" section of the IR of Vodacom also provides quantitative and qualitative information to describe policies used for short-term and long-term remunerations and incentives, including a table with the remuneration of executive directors and prescribed officers.

15.3.6 Opportunities and Risks

The "Corporate Governance" section Vodacom's IR provides information about the company's risk management, describing the actions taken to detect and minimize the recurrence of risks (Vodacom 2013, pp. 66–67). In accordance with the "Opportunities and Risks" content element of the CD, the "Corporate Governance" section of the IR provides precise information about the major risks encountered during the year, circumstances of recurrence of the risks and counter-attack actions taken to minimize their impact. In line with section 4C/4.17 of the CD (IIRC 2013, p. 26), the "Corporate Governance" section of the IR explains how Vodacom manages its risks, appointing a specific Group Risk Management Committee (GRMC) which is responsible for two main functions (Vodacom 2013, p. 65):

1. Filtering and approving the list of strategic, high and critical risks.
2. Overseeing and monitoring various projects and structures designed to manage specific identified risks.

Furthermore, the IR describes Vodacom's risk management on three different levels (the Line Manager at operational level, the Risk Group and the Risk Management Committees within each operation). A chart shows the specific steps taken by the GRMC to define, assess, classify and monitor the risks incurred (Fig. 15.3).

As different from Vodacom's risk management description, the company's opportunities are not disclosed in the "Corporate Governance" section of the IR, but instead are described in the IR's "Strategic Review". In light of point 4C of the CD, the IR of Vodacom identifies specific opportunities for the company through the description of the company's strategic objectives. In line with the "Opportunities and Risks" section of the CD (IIRC 2013, p. 26), the IR's "Strategic Review" analyses the activities performed and capitals (financial, intellectual, human, social and natural) employed in the company's value creation process, highlighting opportunities associated with the achievement of its strategic objectives (IIRC 2013, p. 26). For instance, in line with section 4C/4.15 of the CD, the "Strategic Review" section of Vodacom's IR describes how the company's relationships with the South African government have an impact on its ability to create value over time. In compliance with South African Government targets, Vodacom is still improving its spectrum of connectivity with the aim to deliver broadband access to the entire South African population by 2020 (Vodacom 2013, p. 37).

Sources of opportunities are also briefly summarized in the "Chairman's statement" in the IR's "Overview" section.

15.3.7 Future Outlook

Even though Vodacom's future outlook is not explicitly described in a specific section of the IR, information about the company's short, medium and long term orientations are described in the "Overview" and "Strategic Review" sections of the report. The Chairman's statement in the "Overview" section of the IR, describes

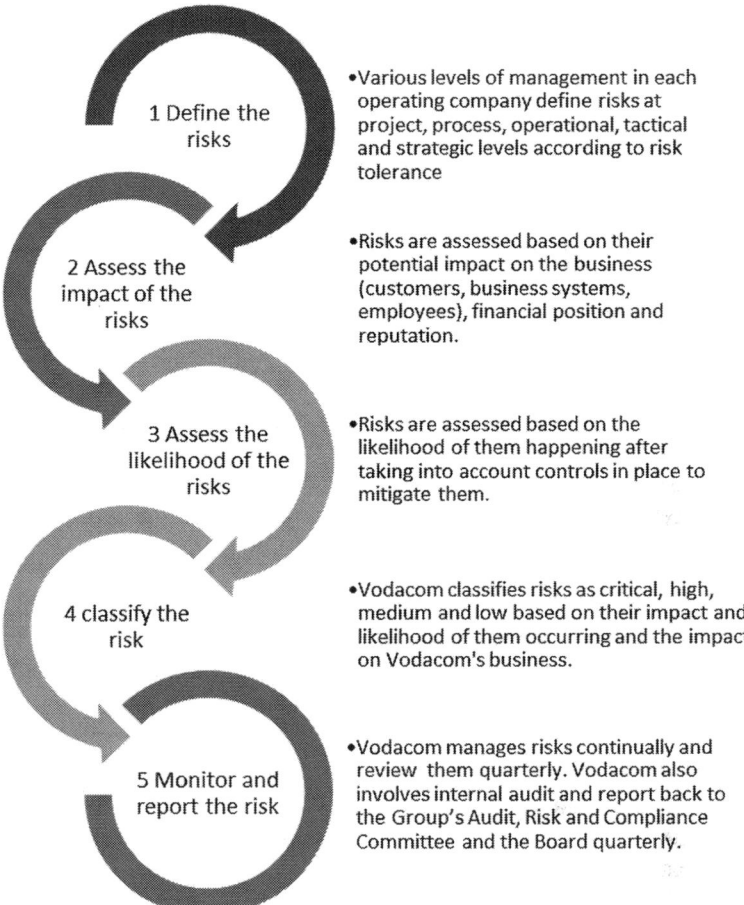

1 Define the risks
• Various levels of management in each operating company define risks at project, process, operational, tactical and strategic levels according to risk tolerance

2 Assess the impact of the risks
• Risks are assessed based on their potential impact on the business (customers, business systems, employees), financial position and reputation.

3 Assess the likelihood of the risks
• Risks are assessed based on the likelihood of them happening after taking into account controls in place to mitigate them.

4 classify the risk
• Vodacom classifies risks as critical, high, medium and low based on their impact and likelihood of them occurring and the impact on Vodacom's business.

5 Monitor and report the risk
• Vodacom manages risks continually and review them quarterly. Vodacom also involves internal audit and report back to the Group's Audit, Risk and Compliance Committee and the Board quarterly.

Fig. 15.3 Vodacom's risk management process (*Source*: adapted from Vodacom's IR, 2013, p. 65)

Vodacom's African mobile and internet service as a "watershed" and one of the present and future objectives for the company.

Having described the main content elements of the IR of Vodacom, the next part analyses the 2013 IR on the basis of the six guiding principles proposed by the CD.

15.4   Analysis of the CD's Guiding Principles in Vodacom's IR

Following the guiding principles presented within the CD, the IR of Vodacom attempts to provide a "total picture of the company's value creation story" (IIRC 2013, p. 18), connecting the content elements analysed in the previous parts.

This section analyses the main guiding principles that underpin the preparation of Vodacom's IR.

15.4.1 Connectivity of Information

Throughout the IR of Vodacom qualitative and quantitative information are connected together tracing the storyline of the company's value creation process. In line with the "Connectivity of information" principle proposed in the CD (IIRC 2013, p. 18), the "Overview" section of Vodacom's IR integrates in a single chart the most relevant KPIs of the factors that have affected and will affect the company's value creation (financial, economic, social-employees, social-communities, environment) (Vodacom 2013, p. 3). In accordance with section 3B/3.8 of the CD, the IR's contents page illustrates the icons used to facilitate users in understanding the most relevant information. The icons are used to highlight additional documents and to "quickly spot" the company's positive and negative performances during the year. In line with section 3B/3.10 (IIRC 2013, p. 18), the "Strategic Review" section of Vodacom's IR integrates quantitative and qualitative information describing the capitals employed to achieve the company's strategic objectives and the most significant KPIs for each of the strategies illustrated. The connection between financial and non-financial information is also highlighted in the "Overview" section of the report. The interview with the Vodacom's CFO provides insights into the relationships between the increased EBITDA margin and the activities performed to improve the efficiency of the connections provided, standardize the company's production processes and transform the company's IT and billing systems.

15.4.2 Materiality and Conciseness

In line with the "Materiality and conciseness" principle (IIRC 2013, p. 21), the IR's "Overview" pays great attention to material matters that Vodacom's stakeholders want to know. Five material issues are identified (Network quality, Reliance on the South African market, Competition, Relationships with governments and regulators, Talent and succession), and are briefly described highlighting market opportunities and risks that affect the organization's strategic path. In accordance with section 3D/3.25 (IIRC 2013, p. 21), the most relevant matters for Vodacom's stakeholders are identified by the company's top management, the Audit committee and the Risk and Compliance committee, to be those material factors that "are most likely to affect stakeholders' assessment of the company's ability to create value over time" (Vodacom 2013, pp. 4–5). Interestingly, Vodacom's Board and Executive Committee and its stakeholders meet annually to summarize the material issues relevant to the strategic objectives of the company. As explained in the IR's "Overview" the material issues "create the storyline of the report of Vodacom".

The IR's "Overview" highlights the necessity to provide even more concise information by focusing on issues considered significant to company's stakeholders. Furthermore, the "Overview" and the "Corporate Governance" sections of Vodacom's IR underline that the stakeholder engagement table is available online (Vodacom 2013, p. 2; Vodacom 2013, p. 72). In accordance with the "Conciseness" principle of the CD, the use of bullet points and numbering lists facilitates the reader in understanding the most relevant data reported.

15.4.3 Stakeholder Responsiveness

In line with the "Stakeholder responsiveness" principle of the CD (IIRC 2013, p. 19), Vodacom's IR gives great importance to the relationships with its stakeholders. The IR's "Overview" section describes the main material issues for the company as "those that are most likely to affect stakeholders' assessments of Vodacom's ability to create value over time" (Vodacom 2013, p. 5). Regarding section 3C/3.18 of the CD, the "Overview" section gives information about the annual meeting with the company's stakeholders. The IR's "Overview" also provides information about the value created and the value distributed during the year to all company's stakeholders (employees, investors, governments, customers). In the "Strategic Review" section of the report, information is provided about how the company uses its capitals to satisfy the expectations of customers, shareholders, social (employees and communities), and environmental stakeholders, clearly describing the past performances and the company's future orientation. In accordance with section 3D/3.15 of the CD, the IR's "Strategic Review" gives information about the most significant actions taken to renew telecommunications networks and supply a service which, as much as possible, meets customer expectations (Vodacom 2013, pp. 27–28).

Furthermore, the "Strategic Review" section of Vodacom's IR provides detailed information about the decisions and actions taken to meet strategic objectives and stakeholders' requests. In particular the company operates to:
1. Promote innovative IT systems to support customer interaction with the company (Vodacom 2013, p. 27), and to reduce its environmental footprint (Vodacom 2013, p. 33).
2. Engage with tax regulation authorities and reduce the import costs of the devices sold (Vodacom 2013, p. 35).
3. Provide training and development programmes for employees at all levels of the business (Vodacom 2013, p. 34).
4. Comply with local and international Government regulations and restrictions to be successful in commercial operations (Vodacom 2013, p. 15).
5. Sustain health and education programmes by exploiting the company's technological resources in the countries in which it operates (Vodacom 2013, p. 37).

However, the IR's "Overview" underlines that "given that the legitimate concerns of Vodacom's stakeholders define the content boundary for the IR and that they inform strategic decision-making as a matter of course at Vodacom", the stakeholder engagement report is not provided in the printed version of the IR, but is available online (Vodacom 2013, p. 2).

15.4.4 Consistency and Comparability

In line with the "Consistency and comparability" principle of the CD, results are compared over time. The "Financial review" section of the IR gives a summary of Vodacom's operating results, financial and cash-flow statements, briefly illustrating the most relevant financial results of the past 3 years. Furthermore, in light of the "Comparability" principle of the CD (IIRC 2013, p. 23), the IR of Vodacom provides a 5 year overview of the company's income statement, financial position and cash-flow statement, and benchmarks operating results and the financial statement on the basis of the South African and International contexts in which it operates.

15.4.5 Reliability and Completeness

In line with section 3E/3.31 of the CD, Vodacom's IR provides information about the company's external assurance and robust internal reporting systems (IIRC 2013, p. 21). The IR of Vodacom also provides forward-looking statements which have not been reviewed by the company's external auditors.

Regarding the "Completeness" principle of the CD (IIRC 2013, p. 22), the IR of Vodacom includes material information and highlights both positive and negative performances during the year.

15.4.6 Strategic Focus and Future Orientation

The IR of Vodacom gives great emphasis to the strategic focus of the company. In accordance with the "Strategic focus and future orientation" principle of the CD, the IR's "Overview" section provides a general description of Vodacom's strategic objectives, which are also illustrated in detail in the "Strategic Review" section of the report. A complete analysis of the company's market opportunities, strengths and weaknesses of its business activities is illustrated in the "Strategic Review" section, also giving information about past performances achieved and future oriented actions. However, Vodacom's IR does not reserve a specific section of the report for the description of the future outlook of the company.

Discussion and Conclusions

This chapter analyses the IR of Vodacom in light of the content elements and guiding principles proposed within the CD of the IIRC. In compliance with King III, Vodacom's IR aims at disclosing relevant information about the company's material issues and strategies that influence the financial (shareholders and investors), social (communities and employees) and environmental landscapes in which the company operates. The integration of financial, social and environmental information provides a retrospective and prospective overview of the company's performance. In particular, the chapter describes how Vodacom's IR adapts South African and international recommendations on Integrated Reporting to provide a comprehensive overview of the company's value creation process and business model disclosing relevant, concise and connected qualitative and quantitative information. Following the narration of the value creation story, the IR of Vodacom describes the company's past, present and future strategic priorities, providing information considered relevant to meet social, financial and environmental stakeholders' requests (IIRC 2012). Moreover, additional references to interlinked reports, notes and communications, which accompany the reader throughout the report and make the data clearly understandable, demonstrate the IR's ability to provide a comprehensive vision of the company.

References

Abeysekera I (2013) A template for integrated reporting. J Intellect Cap 14(2):227–245

IIRC (2011) Towards integrated reporting: communicating value in the 21st century, discussion paper. IIRC, New York. http://theiirc.org/wp-content/uploads/2011/09/IR-Discussion-Paper-2011_spreads.pdf. Accessed 12 Jun 2013

IIRC (2012) Understanding transformation: building the business case for integrated reporting. http://www.theiirc.org/resources-2/other-publications/building-the-business-case-for-integrated-reporting/. Accessed 12 Jun 2013

IIRC (2013) Consultation draft of the international <IR> framework. http://www.theiirc.org/wp-content/uploads/Consultation-Draft/Consultation-Draft-of-the-InternationalIRFramework.pdf. Accessed 12 Jun 2013

Institute of Directors Southern Africa (2009) King code of governance for South Africa. http://www.ecgi.org/codes/code.php?code_id=262. Accessed 10 Jul 2013

KPMG (2009) Corporate governance and king 3. http://www.kpmg.com/ZA/en/IssuesAndInsights/ArticlesPublications/Tax-and-Legal-Publications/Documents/Corporate%20Governance%20and%20King%203.pdf. Accessed 23 Jun 2013

KPMG (2012) Integrated reporting: performance inside through better business reporting. Issue 2. http://www.kpmg.com/Global/en/IssuesAndInsights/ArticlesPublications/integrated-reporting/Documents/integrated-reporting-issue-2.pdf. Accessed 23 Jun 2013

Vodacom (2013) Integrated report. http://www.vodacom.co.za/cs/groups/public/documents/vodacom.co.za_portal_webassets/vodacomir2013.pdf. Accessed 25 Jun 2013

The Case of Smithfield Foods

16

Loredana G. Smaldore and Christian Cavazzoni

Abstract

This chapter analyses the Integrated Report of Smithfield Foods, a North American company operating in the food industry. The purpose is to examine the content elements and principles of this company's Integrated Report in light of the guidelines provided by the Consultation Draft issued by the International Integrated Reporting Council. The aim is to compare the structure of this report with the guidelines of the Consultation Draft, in order to discuss their applicability and adaptability to companies operating in the food industry.

16.1 Introduction[1]

The "buzz around integrated reporting" (GreenBiz Group and Ernst and Young 2013, p. 29) has been gradually increasing over the last few years, particularly attracting the attention of regulators, investors, companies, NGOs, the accounting profession and standard setters. As a result, the International Integrated Reporting Council (IIRC) was established and issued a Consultation Draft[2] (CD) for the

---

[1] Although this chapter is the result of a joint effort, the paragraph 1 (Introduction) can be assigned to Christian Cavazzoni. The paragraph 2 (Smithfield Foods, Inc.: Company Background) and the paragraph 4 (Smithfield IR vs. the IIRC Consultation Draft) can be assigned to Loredana G. Smaldore. The paragraph 3 (Smithfield's Integrated Report) is the joint work of both authors.

[2] The Consultation Draft was published by the IIRC in April 2013. It was developed following the analysis of responses to the 2011 Discussion Paper "Towards Integrated

L.G. Smaldore (✉)
School of Business and Economics, National University of Ireland, Galway, Ireland
e-mail: l.smaldore2@nuigalway.ie

C. Cavazzoni
University of Perugia, Perugia, Italy
e-mail: christian.cavazzoni@unipg.it

C. Busco et al. (eds.), *Integrated Reporting*, DOI 10.1007/978-3-319-02168-3_16,   255
© Springer International Publishing Switzerland 2013

international Integrated Report (IR) framework, whose initial version is due to be published in December 2013. The guidelines proposed by the CD are not supposed to follow a strict "rules-based" approach. Rather, they leave room for adaptation and personalization, to allow "businesses to tell their story on their own terms" (KPMG 2013, p. 2). These guidelines are structured into fundamental concepts, guiding principles and content elements. In addition, the CD outlines specific topics to take into account during the preparation and presentation of the IR.

The fundamental concepts are mainly related to the various capitals (financial, manufactured, intellectual, human, social and relationship, and natural) of the organization, the business model and the process of value creation over time (IIRC 2013, p. 6). The capitals constitute the resources used by an organization within its process of value creation according to its strategies and business model.

Moreover, the IR has to disclose information on value creation in the short, medium and long term according to the following content elements: Organizational overview and external environment, Governance, Opportunities and risks, Strategy and resource allocation, Business model, Performance, and Future outlook (IIRC 2013). In so doing, the IR should follow the guiding principles of Strategic focus and future orientation, Connectivity of information, Stakeholder responsiveness, Materiality and conciseness, Reliability and completeness, and Consistency and comparability (IIRC 2013). The CD also suggests the following topics during IR preparation and presentation: Frequency of reporting, The materiality determination process, Disclosure of material matters, Involvement of those charged with governance, Credibility, Time frames for short, medium and long term, Reporting boundary, Aggregation and disaggregation, and Use of technology (IIRC 2013). The alignment with these principles should stimulate organizations to recognize and integrate the fundamental concepts of capitals, business model and value creation within their IR.

The present chapter aims to illustrate and analyze the 2012 IR of Smithfield Foods Inc,. a multinational company operating in the food sector. The purpose is to explore the extent to which the guidelines of the CD are applicable and can be eventually adapted to the context of the food industry and to a multinational company.[3]

The following section illustrates the background of Smithfield Foods Inc., and its business. Next, the contents of the report are described and compared with the concepts, principles and elements of the CD issued by the IIRC. Finally, the last section summarizes the key features of the 2012 IR of Smithfield Foods Inc.

Reporting—Communicating Value in the 21st Century", the publication of a draft outline in July 2012 and a prototype framework in November 2012.

[3] The IR of Smithfield Foods, Inc. is publically available at http://www.smithfieldfoods.com/our-company/our-mission-values/download-integrated-report/.

16.2   Smithfield Foods, Inc.: Company Background

Smithfield Foods Inc.[4] (hereafter Smithfield), a global food company founded in 1936, began its business as a pork processing operation called The Smithfield Packing Company (Smithfield 2012). Through a series of acquisitions starting in 1981, it has become the world's largest pork and hog producer, as well as the market leader in numerous packaged meats categories in the United States (Smithfield 2012). The company's principal executive offices are located in the United States but the company also operates in Poland, Romania, the United Kingdom and Mexico. Smithfield operates in four segments: Pork, Hog Production, International and Corporate, comprised of diverse subsidiaries, joint ventures and other investments. In particular, the fourth segment provides management and administrative services that support the others (Smithfield 2012).

The mission statement of the company is as follows: "Smithfield Foods is determined to be an ethical food industry leader that excels every day at bringing delicious and nutritious meat products to millions of people around the world in a manner that sets industry benchmarks for sustainability" (Smithfield 2012, p. 10).

The company boasts twelve core brands (Smithfield, Farmland, John Morrell, Gwaltney, Armour, Eckrich, Margherita, Carando, Kretschmar, Cook's, Curly's and Healthy Ones), a workforce of approximately 46,050 employees worldwide (Smithfield 2012, p. 25) and annual revenues of about $13 billion (Smithfield 2012, p. 10). Smithfield is also publicly traded on the NYSE under the ticker symbol SFD. Interestingly, in the year 2012 Smithfield published its first IR.

16.3   Smithfield's Integrated Report

The purpose of this paragraph is to describe how Smithfield creates and sustains value in the short, medium and long term, as it is disclosed in the company's IR. In doing so, we illustrate the factors that provide information that is material to assess the organization's ability to create value over time (IIRC 2013, p. 21) and we also compare Smithfield's IR with the concepts, principles, elements of the CD issued by IIRC. Therefore, subsequently we illustrate all sections of the IR in the sequence that they appear in the report. Then, we analyse these sections in light of the concepts, principles and elements of the CD (the principles, elements and the other topics of the CD which illustrate the fundamental concepts of the report are indicated in italics).

---

[4] The information and data about the company in this chapter have been extracted from the official website of Smithfield Foods, Inc. (http://www.smithfieldfoods.com) and from its 2012 Integrated Report.

16.3.1 Overview of the Report

The cover page of Smithfield's IR states the following: "We combine Leading Brands and a Commitment to Sustainability to produce Good Food. Responsibly®". (Smithfield 2012). From this first message, some concepts behind the IR may be identified. "Leading brand" refers to one of Smithfield's capitals, in particular, intellectual capital. A "commitment to sustainability" reveals the intent and engagement of the company to sustain value creation over time. "Food" refers to the core business of the company. Finally, the adverb "responsibly" communicates the sustainable approach to value creation. This claim already sets out to convey Smithfield's integrated thinking, which involves capitals, value creation, and the business model illustrated in the IR.

Smithfield's 2012 IR is structured as follows. The first three pages (of which only the page that illustrates the Map of Operations is included in the Table of Contents) present an overview of the IR. They illustrate the countries in which Smithfield's operations are located, some financial highlights and information about the preparation of the report, along with a section made up of forward-looking statements. The Table of Contents of Smithfield's 2012 IR lists the sections that compose the report, as follows: Chief Executive Officer Letter, Ask the Chief Sustainability Officer, Our Business Journey, Value Creation, Governance and Management, Animal Care, Employees, Environment, Food Safety and Quality, Helping Communities, International Operations, and Our Family of Companies. Information about Management and the Corporate (common stock data, holders, dividends etc.) is also reported at the end of the report. A separate part of the Table of Contents lists the maps, diagrams, and the tables included in the IR. In this respect, it is interesting to note that between the sections Ask the Chief Sustainability Officer and Our Business Journey the report illustrates a recap of some of its key performance indicators, the Key Data Summary, and a recap of the Key Commitments in Smithfield. The last section, Our Family of Company, is followed by tables and graphs which report the 10-Year Financial Summary and the Cumulative Total Return Comparisons.

The first three pages of the report give a snapshot of the *organizational overview*, graphically reporting the geographical extent of its operations, over 12 countries in America and Europe. This is followed by a table which illustrates a *concise* overview of the financial *performance* achieved by the company during the previous 3 years. This element is reported by drawing upon the principles of *conciseness* and *consistency*, and conveying *reliability* of information.

The first few pages also reveal the report's aim, though it is not to couple the annual and sustainability reports (Dobkowsky-Joy and Brockland 2013), rather it is to combine the financial results with company's sustainability reporting (Smithfield 2012). Within Smithfield, this integration relies on six elements called "pillars". The first five pillars concern the strategy for sustainability. They are: animal care, employees, environment, food safety and quality, and helping communities, which also identify the capitals that the business uses and that are affected. The sixth pillar, value creation, interconnects the sustainability strategy with Smithfield's business results.

The *future outlook* is communicated from the beginning of the report through "forward-looking information and statements" which relate to the company's plans and strategies. Smithfield's *risks* and uncertainties are also identified, including live hogs, raw materials, fuel and supplies, food safety, livestock disease, live hog production costs, product prices, competitive environment and related market conditions, indebtedness, etc. (Smithfield 2012). The content elements *future outlook* and *risks* are illustrated, therefore, through the principle *strategic focus and future orientation*.

Moreover, the third page of the report states the following: "this report contains "forward-looking" statements within the meaning of the federal security laws" (Smithfield 2012). This quote from the report reveals Smithfield's consideration of the topic *disclosure of material matters* while preparing the IR.

The *reporting boundary*, that consists of the company units in which Smithfield has a majority (51 % or more) interest (Smithfield 2012), is also communicated on the third page of the report. Furthermore, the recall of external links and sources of further information defines the level of *aggregation and disaggregation* of information within the report. The report focuses on elements that are deemed *material* in order to explain the sustainability strategy of the company and value creation over time. Smithfield suggests that for further information the reader should visit its website, which highlights the company's dedication to sustainability commitments[5] and u*se of technology*.

16.3.2 Chief Executive Officer Letter

The report opens with a letter written by Smithfield's President and CEO that addresses some of the topics included within the IR. The company's 2012 financial *performance*, innovation *strategy*, *opportunities and risks* and the *future outlook* for growth are illustrated here, in line with the principles of *strategic focus and future orientation*, *conciseness* and drawing upon a narrative approach.

In this letter, the CEO describes value creation within the company as the creation of jobs; tax payments; educational programs; the donation of food to communities in need; the conversion of waste into energy; the good health of animals raised for products; and financial performance (Smithfield 2012). The CEO's letter conveys the idea of *governance* in support of the IR, as well as the *reliability* and *credibility* of the data within the IR.

---

[5] See http://www.smithfieldcommitments.com

16.3.3 Ask the Chief Sustainability Officer

This section reports an interview with the Chief Sustainability Officer (hereafter CSO), who is also the Executive Vice President, about sustainability in Smithfield. In line with the principle of *completeness* of information, the CSO illustrates the relationships between sustainability and business *performance* measurement systems to ensure *stakeholder responsiveness*. The CSO also mentions the sustainability commitments of the company, such as worker safety, environmental compliance, antibiotics policy, greenhouse gas (GHG) emission reductions, packaging reduction projects, and sow gestation conversion (Smithfield 2012). Similar to the letter by the CEO, the interview with the CSO conveys the *reliability* and *credibility* of information within the IR, as well as the support offered by the *governance* system.

16.3.4 Key Data Summary and Key Commitments

The interview with the CSO is followed by a recap of the pillars of sustainability (animal care, employees, environment, food safety and quality, and helping communities). In particular, the quantitative *performance* (and the related KPIs— Key Performance Indicators) of the previous 5 years (2008–2012) is illustrated in the table, Key Data Summary (Smithfield 2012, p. 6), illustrated in Fig. 16.1.

The table also identifies the pages of the report where indicators are explained in more detail. By summarizing the key elements of the company's sustainability performance, the table is aligned with the principles of *materiality* and *conciseness* of information.

As already mentioned, Smithfield's simultaneous achievement of (social and environmental) sustainability and business performance is built on six pillars. The first five pillars of sustainability, along with the company's capitals, are interconnected with the sixth pillar, value creation, which aims to "drive growth and improve shareholder and stakeholder value" (Smithfield 2012, p. 9).

The five pillars, along with the pillar of value creation, are organized in Key Commitments synthesized in a scorecard with their qualitative and quantitative goals, targets and results. A snapshot of this scorecard is illustrated in Fig. 16.2 which shows two of the six key commitments, specifically, animal care and employees.

By identifying the goals and targets of the Key Commitments (see the first two columns of Fig. 16.2), the scorecard incorporates the company's *strategy and resource allocation* and *future outlook* through the principle of *strategic focus and future orientation*. Finally, by concentrating and organizing the Key Commitments within a table, the *materiality* and *conciseness* principles are fulfilled.

Moreover, symbols outlined in the target columns (see Fig. 16.2) express the status of goal achievement in relation to the targets (achieved, on track, needs

ANIMAL CARE					
	FY 2012	FY 2011	FY 2010	FY 2009	FY 2008
Market Hog Transportation Accidents[1]	4	4	9	6	6
Market Hog Transportation Fatalities[1]	261	208	466	356	243
Feed-Grade Antibiotics Used (lbs per cwt²)—page 23	0.157	0.147	0.124	0.106	0.116
	CY 2011	CY 2010	CY 2009	CY 2008	CY 2007
Sows in Company-Owned Group Housing (%)—page 21	30.4	6.6	4.8	3.8	2.6

EMPLOYEES					
	CY 2011	CY 2010	CY 2009	CY 2008	CY 2007
Total Case Rate—page 26	3.93	4.66	6.17	6.58	6.76
Days Away, Restricted, Transferred Rate—page 26	2.80	3.24	4.26	4.40	4.04
Days Away from Work Illness and Injury Rate—page 26	0.74	0.82	1.12	1.29	1.27
OSHA Notices of Violation—page 26	74	34	20	40	12
OSHA Penalties—page 26	$117,449	$33,323	$23,725	$38,787	$11,037

ENVIRONMENT[3]					
	FY 2012	FY 2011	FY 2010	FY 2009	FY 2008
Water Use (gallons per cwt)—page 28	79.8	80.1	78.1	78.6	88.9
Energy Use (decatherms per cwt)—page 29	0.117	0.122	0.124	0.121	0.123
GHG Emissions (metric tons CO_2e per cwt)—page 30	0.0143	0.0149	0.0150	0.0159	0.0161
Solid Waste to Landfill[4] (lbs per cwt)—page 30	2.33	2.70	2.71	2.90	2.66
	CY 2011	CY 2010	CY 2009	CY 2008	CY 2007
NOx Emissions (tons)[1]	414	414	403	434	301
SOx Emissions (tons)[1]	62	59	179	273	455
Notices of Violation—page 31	38	63	36	40	50
Significant Fines—page 31	$407,779	$164,184	$81,726	$69,616	$266,446

FOOD SAFETY & QUALITY					
	FY 2012	FY 2011	FY 2010	FY 2009	FY 2008
Food Safety Expenditures[5]—page 33	$5.6 million	$5 million	$4.2 million	$2.3 million	$1.9 million
Recalls—page 33	1	0	1	1	0

HELPING COMMUNITIES					
	FY 2012	FY 2011	FY 2010	FY 2009	FY 2008
Smithfield-Luter Foundation Scholarships—page 35	$256,000	$377,500	$196,500	$290,000	$349,979
Learners to Leaders® Contributions—page 35	$355,779	$288,388	$369,710	$319,415	$383,385
Total Food Donations (servings)[6]—page 34	6.9 million	8.4 million	11.6 million	16.4 million	13.2 million

Fig. 16.1 Performance of the five sustainability pillars over the past 5 years. (*Source*: Smithfield's 2012 integrated report, p. 6)

improvement), conveying a sense of *reliability* of information as they track the current status of the goals. These symbols are illustrated in Fig. 16.3.

16.3.5 Our Business Journey

This section describes the company's *organizational overview and external environment, strategy and resource allocation, opportunities and risks*, and *future outlook*, all corresponding to the content elements suggested by the CD. These elements contribute to illustrating the Smithfield's *business model* through the

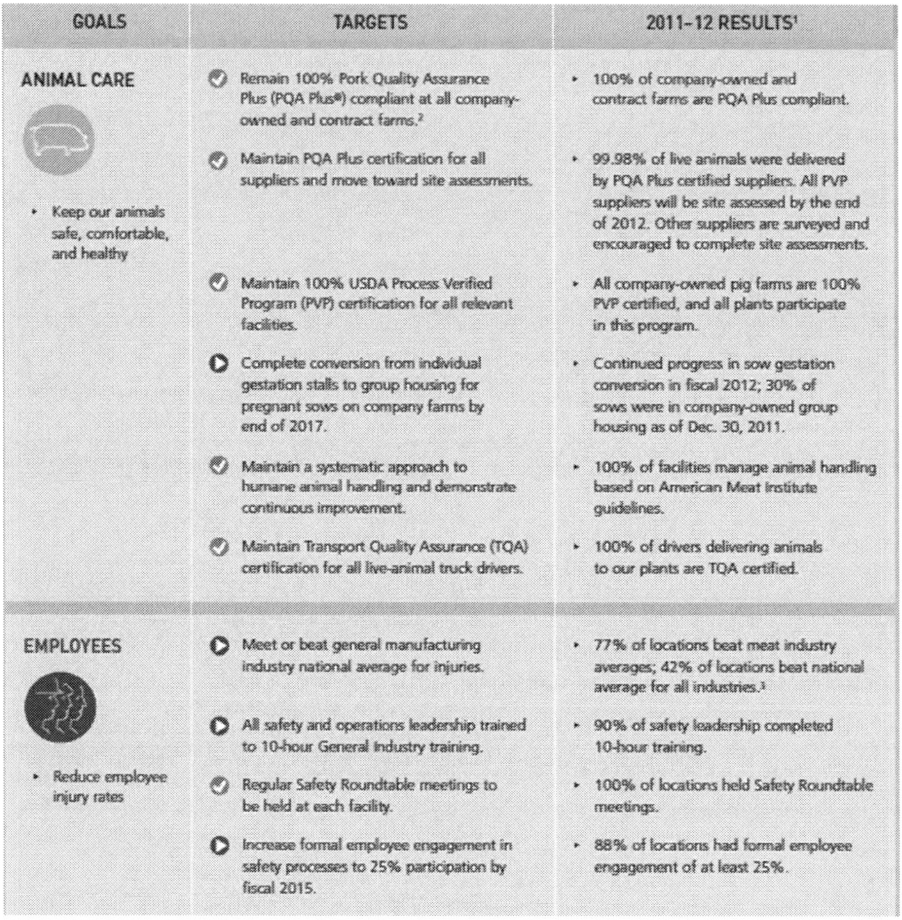

GOALS	TARGETS	2011–12 RESULTS[1]
ANIMAL CARE • Keep our animals safe, comfortable, and healthy	✅ Remain 100% Pork Quality Assurance Plus (PQA Plus®) compliant at all company-owned and contract farms.[2]	• 100% of company-owned and contract farms are PQA Plus compliant.
	✅ Maintain PQA Plus certification for all suppliers and move toward site assessments.	• 99.98% of live animals were delivered by PQA Plus certified suppliers. All PVP suppliers will be site assessed by the end of 2012. Other suppliers are surveyed and encouraged to complete site assessments.
	✅ Maintain 100% USDA Process Verified Program (PVP) certification for all relevant facilities.	• All company-owned pig farms are 100% PVP certified, and all plants participate in this program.
	▶ Complete conversion from individual gestation stalls to group housing for pregnant sows on company farms by end of 2017.	• Continued progress in sow gestation conversion in fiscal 2012; 30% of sows were in company-owned group housing as of Dec. 30, 2011.
	✅ Maintain a systematic approach to humane animal handling and demonstrate continuous improvement.	• 100% of facilities manage animal handling based on American Meat Institute guidelines.
	✅ Maintain Transport Quality Assurance (TQA) certification for all live-animal truck drivers.	• 100% of drivers delivering animals to our plants are TQA certified.
EMPLOYEES • Reduce employee injury rates	▶ Meet or beat general manufacturing industry national average for injuries.	• 77% of locations beat meat industry averages; 42% of locations beat national average for all industries.[3]
	▶ All safety and operations leadership trained to 10-hour General Industry training.	• 90% of safety leadership completed 10-hour training.
	✅ Regular Safety Roundtable meetings to be held at each facility.	• 100% of locations held Safety Roundtable meetings.
	▶ Increase formal employee engagement in safety processes to 25% participation by fiscal 2015.	• 88% of locations had formal employee engagement of at least 25%.

Fig. 16.2 Smithfield's goals and targets, 2011–2012 results of animal care and employees commitments. (*Source*: Smithfield's 2012 integrated report, p. 7)

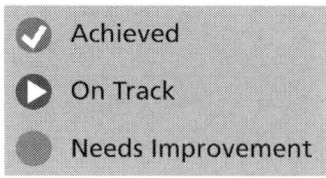

Fig. 16.3 Symbols used to show the status of goal achievement in relation to the targets of the Key Commitments. (*Source*: Smithfield's 2012 integrated report, p. 7)

guiding principles of *materiality, conciseness* and *strategic focus and future orientation*. The historical context of the company is also illustrated here, including its mission statement (see paragraph 2) and core values, such as producing safe, high quality and nutritious food, creating value for stakeholders, being an employer of choice, leading in animal care, protecting and reinvigorating the environment, making positive impact on communities, etc. This section also deals with the company's principal activities and current brands, acknowledging the pork segment as being the heart of the business. The company's success in executing growth strategies is summarized in chart form (see Smithfield 2012, p. 11).

16.3.6 Value Creation

The description of the business provided by the section *Our business journey* is followed by an in-depth analysis of value creation in Smithfield. This concept not only gives the title to a section of the report, but it also constitutes the background of the following sections, as they deal with the driver elements for value creation and sustainability in Smithfield. The report illustrates the sustainability elements which drive the value creation process, and how this process identifies, uses and affects the capitals of the company. Value creation in Smithfield is the result of a continuous enactment of six programs that may be considered the drivers of value creation for internal and external stakeholders. As illustrated in Fig. 16.4, these programs are: "Encourage competitiveness and innovation, Integrate business into the community, Mitigate operational impacts and risks, Create access to the growing influential consumer segment, Develop human capital, Promote sustainable business model" (Smithfield 2012, p. 14). Interestingly, the interconnections between these programs and value creation show how "an authentic commitment to sustainability enhances financial performance in the long-term, both through savings, risk mitigation and adding value" (CIMA 2011, p. 1).

The report further investigates the sustainable programs that are considered *material* for value creation, listing the elements in which Smithfield works for the enactment of each program. As shown in Fig. 16.5, the elements that influence the programs of value creation are "Governance and Management, Animal Care, Employees, Environment, Food Safety and Quality, Helping communities, and International Operations" (Smithfield 2012, pp. 14–15). It is interesting that these elements include the five pillars of sustainability.

The information in the table in Fig. 16.5 is aligned with the principles of *reliability and completeness, consistency and comparability, materiality and conciseness*. It is also worthy to note how this table illustrates the *connectivity* between value creation and value drivers, activities, capitals and stakeholders of the company.

Finally, this section also suggests visiting the YouTube website where videos showing the sustainability initiatives implemented in Smithfield can be viewed, which shows an innovative approach to reporting through the *use of technology* that also allows the *connectivity* of the report information with that on the YouTube website.

After this section, the report illustrates each of the elements that are considered crucial to value creation, namely Governance and Management, Animal Care,

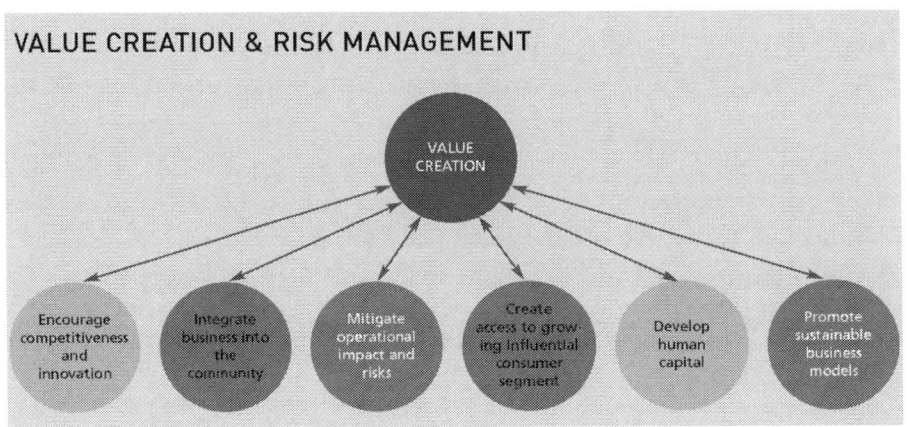

Fig. 16.4 Smithfield's programs for value creation. (*Source*: Smithfield's 2012 integrated report, p. 14)

Employees, Environment, Food Safety and Quality, Helping Communities and International Operations.

16.3.7 Governance and Management

This part of the report deals with the role of *governance* and management in Smithfield, as "foundations for trust, transparency and progress" (Smithfield 2012, p. 16). It is interesting to note that, in order to monitor and manage sustainability, the company has established sustainability committees (one for the board of directors and one for top executives across the company) and a new position of responsibility, the Chief Sustainability Officer.

Figure 16.6, an extract from the report, illustrates the organization of sustainability governance within the company.

This section also deals with the management of sustainability issues, identified after a *materiality determination process* and inspired by *stakeholder responsiveness*. This section also refers to one of the capitals used for value creation, the social and relationship capital, which involves the management of relationships with suppliers. This capital is reinforced through sharing norms, common values and behaviours with the suppliers. In that respect, Smithfield has also implemented the Suppliers Code of Conduct.

Despite the *risks* mentioned in previous sections, the organization's tangible and intangible, existing and emerging *risks* are further dealt with in this section of the report after a *materiality determination process*, based on the likelihood and impact of each risk. In particular, the *risks* may involve fluctuations in the commodity prices for hogs and grains; outbreaks of disease among, or attributed to, livestock; health risks related to products of the food industry in general; and environmental regulations and related litigation (Smithfield 2012, p. 17).

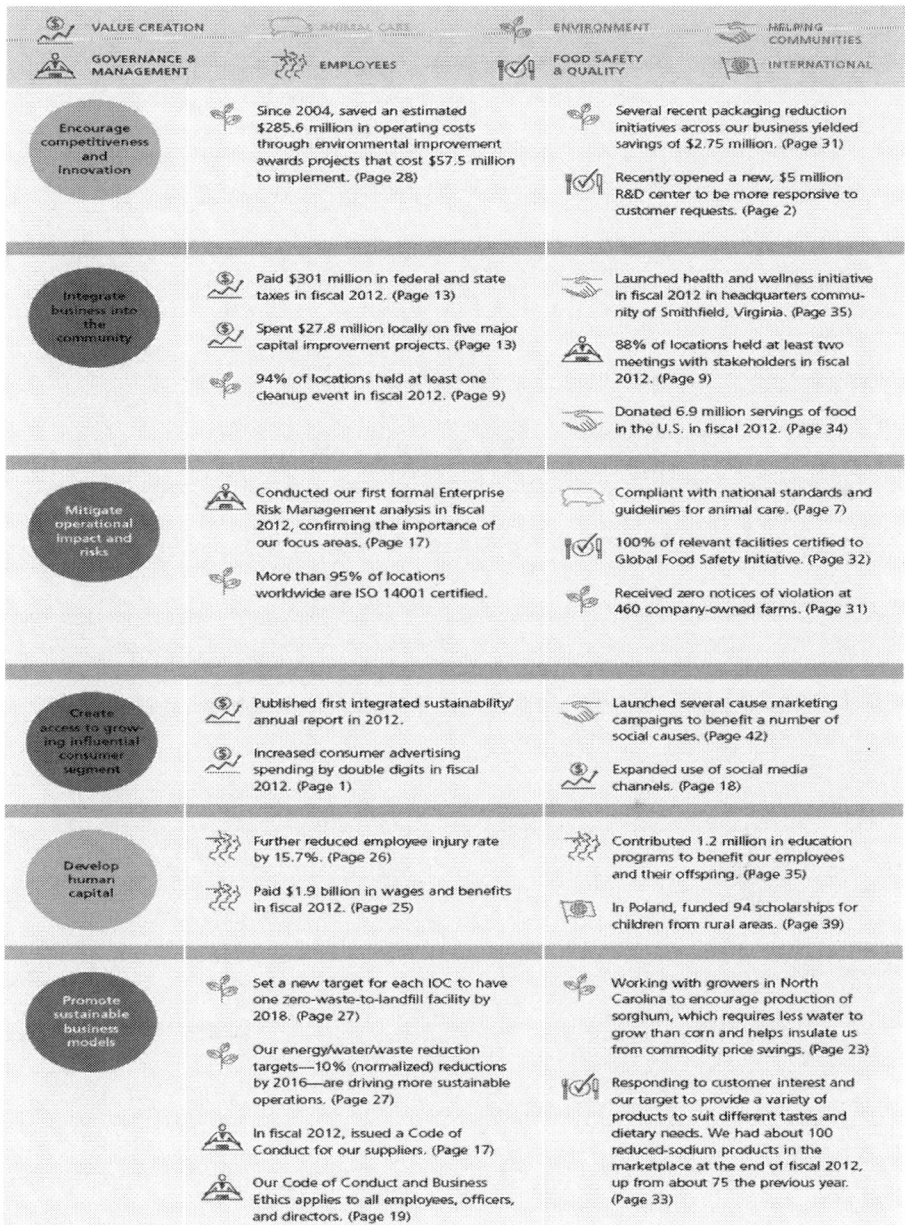

Fig. 16.5 Smithfield's programs for value creation. (*Source*: Smithfield's 2012 integrated report, pp. 14–15)

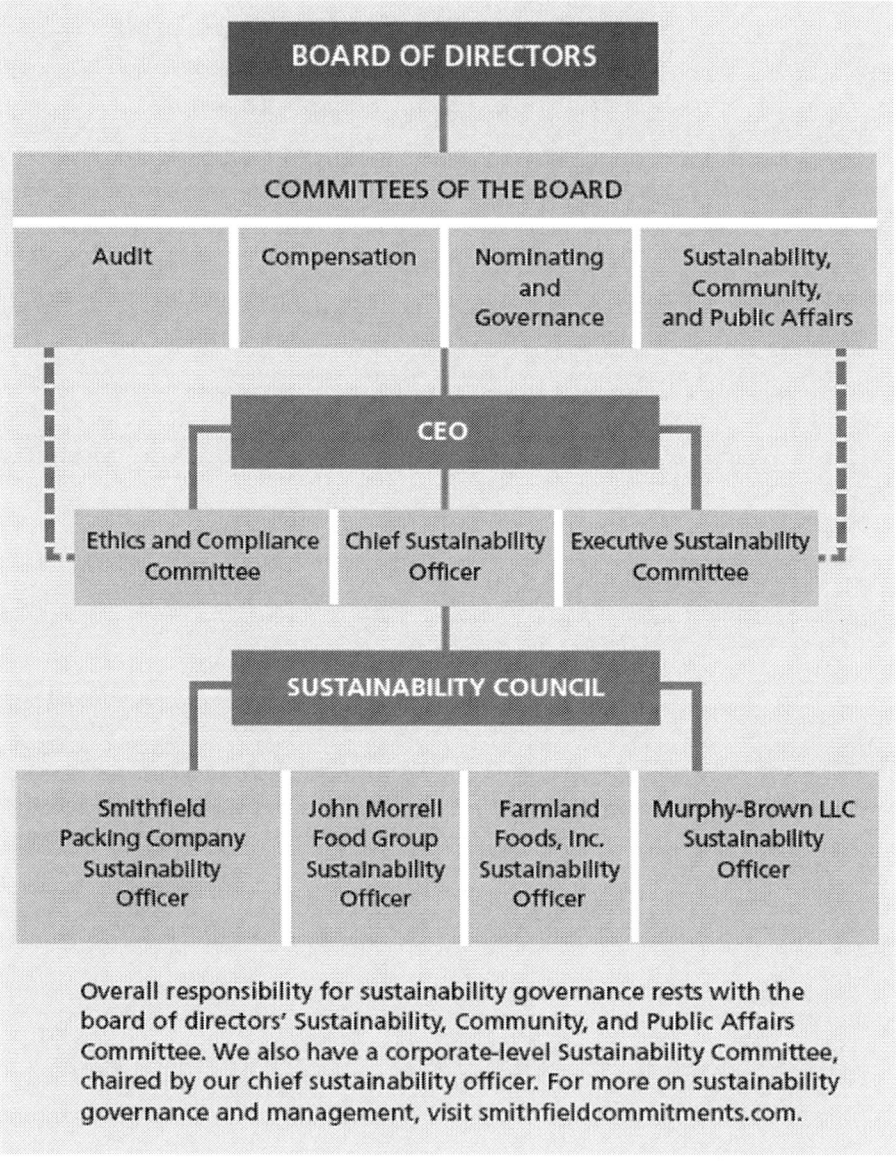

Overall responsibility for sustainability governance rests with the board of directors' Sustainability, Community, and Public Affairs Committee. We also have a corporate-level Sustainability Committee, chaired by our chief sustainability officer. For more on sustainability governance and management, visit smithfieldcommitments.com.

Fig. 16.6 Sustainability governance in Smithfield. (*Source*: Smithfield's 2012 integrated report, p. 17)

Additionally, the section on *Governance and Management* also deals with Smithfield's stakeholders, listing who they are and how they are related to the company.

16.3.8 Animal Care

The *Animal Care* section communicates the main targets and goals for animal care in Smithfield, such as eliminating the use of gestation stalls for pregnant sows on company owned farms; improving transportation for hogs; and developing markets for alternative feed grains and animal care targets (Smithfield 2012). Smithfield's *future outlook* concerning animal care is addressed through the principles of *strategic focus and future orientation*.

Drawing upon the *connectivity* between animal care and value creation, the section illustrates how animal care may have effects on the capitals of the company. The capitals that are identified in this section are influenced by reputation (intellectual capital), relationships with customers and consumers (social and relationship capital), and production levels (manufactured and financial capital). Further *connectivity* of capitals occurs when talking about sorghum, a new grain crop used to feed hogs. Specifically, the report highlights the positive relationship between this newly available natural capital and the financial capital, due to the lower cost of the new crop. Moreover, the latter aids environmental sustainability, affecting—again in a positive way—natural capital, with lower water demand and reduction of water and soil pollution. Business growth and positive financial capital performance also imply further value creation of social and relationship capital, as grain suppliers increase their levels of production.

Animal care and well-being are described as great *opportunities* for the growth of the company and its stakeholders, through the creation of markets for thousands of grain farmers across the US and internationally. The external and internal assessments of animal care and quality are also illustrated in this section, thereby adding *credibility* and *reliability* to Smithfield's business and value creation process. *Credibility* is also reinforced by including a perspective from a consultant in charge of evaluating Smithfield's overall systems of animal care (see Smithfield 2012, p. 22).

To fulfil *stakeholder* (restaurant customers) *responsiveness* regarding animal care, programs and actions have been undertaken concerning the housing of pregnant sows. This part of the report also refers to the *external environment*, by mentioning Smithfield's compliance with the U.S. Food and Drug Administration's new regulatory guidance relating to the use of antibiotics in food production.

16.3.9 Employees

The report dedicates a full section to employees—a pillar of sustainability and human capital. As illustrated in the IR, Smithfield pays constant attention to protecting their safety, health and their ethical workplace environment. In order to increase the value of human capital, Smithfield applies competitive wages, robust benefit packages, with tuition reimbursement and educational scholarships. The report also refers to its Human Rights Policy and Employee Injury Prevention Management System in order to increase the *credibility* of the company's *responsiveness* to employees' needs and expectations. This section also illustrates how the encouragement of safety training as well as employee health and wellness both lead to a reduction in the number of work-related injuries.

To be *complete* and *reliable*, the IR has to 'tell the true story', with its negative and positive outcomes. In this respect, it is worth noting that also negative facts are included in the report, such as the occurrence of one employee fatality in 2011. Nevertheless, a serious commitment to avoiding similar events in the future has been declared by the company, again communicating its *future outlook*.

This section demonstrates the *connectivity* and interrelatedness between the employees and value creation, in particular, between human and financial capitals. It translates the value of employees into monetary terms (salaries, wages, and benefits), as well as the actions undertaken for their safety training. This information communicates to the report's users, especially shareholders, how financial capital has been employed and invested in initiatives aimed at increasing the value of employees.

Finally, the result of a study conducted by the University of Missouri Extension states that Smithfield operations help to sustain more than 5,200 jobs in Missouri (Smithfield 2012). This illustrates how Smithfield increases social and relationship capital through its *stakeholder responsiveness*.

16.3.10 Environment

The environment is a pillar of sustainability in Smithfield. The section *Environment* opens with a presentation of *future outlook* in this field, reporting in a *concise* way the several environmental goals and targets concerning water and energy use, GHG emissions, and solid waste to landfill. The environment is one of the external stakeholders of Smithfield, as well as the source of its natural capital.

In this section, environmental *performance* is linked to financial *performance* in several way (*connectivity* of information). In particular, it is shown that investments in the management of natural capital (water, energy etc.) result in lower operating costs (impact on financial capital) and in stakeholder value creation (impact on social and relationship capital). Moreover, the effective management of natural resources allows the identification of *opportunities* for increasing the value of intellectual capital (in terms of increased reputation), as well as converting elements of manufactured capital (hog manure, solid waste, and bacon grease) and natural capital (land not used for crop production or hog raising) into renewable energy (natural capital).

Moreover, this section provides tables with the key objectives for environmental *performance* by 2016 (to the benefit of *consistency and comparability*, and *reliability* of information). An example of a table referring to water use is reported in Fig. 16.7.

Fig. 16.7 Water use performance from 2008 to 2012 vs. the goal by fiscal 2016. (*Source*: Smithfield's 2012 integrated report, p. 28)

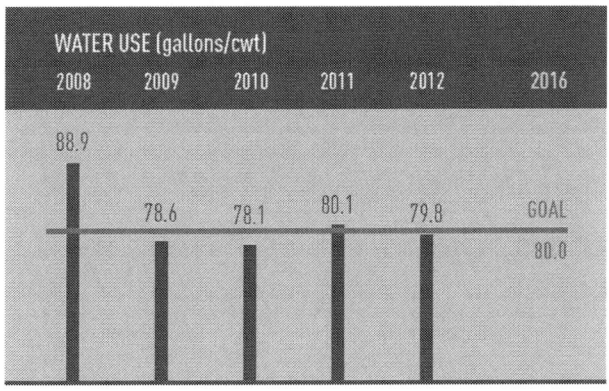

All values reported by fiscal year.

16.3.11 Food Safety and Quality

Food Safety and Quality constitute another pillar of sustainability for Smithfield and also a source of its value creation. The culture of food safety and quality is continuously conveyed to the employees in Smithfield. The section *Food Safety and Quality* mentions some episodes of success, such as the achievement of certification by all relevant facilities, as well as an unpleasant event, the Portobello mushroom-flavoured pork loins that were recalled from the market because some of the product may have contained an undeclared allergen, conveying a sense of *reliability and completeness* of information (Smithfield 2012, p. 33). The *connectivity* between the sustainability pillar of food safety and quality and value creation is also detailed in this part. Furthermore, the following statement: "producing safe, high-quality food builds value for our business, our investors, and our customers, including the restaurants and retail chains that sell our products" (Smithfield 2012, p. 33), summarizes and reinforces the sense of *connectivity* in Smithfield. In addition, this claim shows how the company deals with *stakeholder responsiveness*.

16.3.12 Helping Communities

Smithfield sustains value creation within the environment and society, producing positive impacts in the areas where employees work and live. The related goals and targets (following the element *future outlook*) are clearly illustrated in the section *Helping Communities*. Drawing upon integrated thinking and the *connectivity* principle, this section recognizes relationships between the capitals and the support provided to communities. In particular, helping communities increases human capital (through assistance to the communities that the employees belong to), social and relationship capital (through assistance to local communities and families which cannot afford food), intellectual capital (good reputation), and financial capital. Moreover, initiatives undertaken in hunger relief, education, health and wellness all have the potential to improve the social and relationship capital between the company and local government, community groups, and corporate partners.

Finally, the section *Helping Communities* also reports the financial capital employed to sustain some initiatives aimed at supporting communities, such as food and cash donations. This approach shows how part of the available financial capital of Smithfield has been invested into social capital.

16.3.13 International Operations

The company owns six international operations and aims to transfer its sustainability principles to them. The section *International Operations* mainly refers to operations conducted in Europe where Smithfield has about 10,000 employees (*reporting boundary* and *level of aggregation*). How international operations deal with the five pillars of sustainability along with the pillar of value creation is also illustrated in this section.

Moreover, value creation processes within the international operations and their effect on (financial, social and relationship) capitals in Romania and Poland, as well as their past environmental *performance* are illustrated.

16.3.14 Our Family of Companies

Finally, Smithfield's IR illustrates its 'family of companies', both graphically and in a narrative way. In particular, a description of the *business model* is provided in this section. The three segments named Pork, Hog Production, and International in Smithfield are illustrated by following the elements of *organizational overview and external environment*. Some of the companies belonging to those segments are also described here, reporting information about their headquarters, president, number of employees, fiscal 2012 sales, core brands, supporting brands and facilities. Their recent sustainability achievements are reported, conveying *reliability* about sustainability plans.

16.3.15 10-Year Financial Summary and the Cumulative Total Return Comparisons

A 10-year financial summary (2003–2012) of the company's *performance* (Smithfield 2012, pp. 48–49) is contained within the report. Moreover, data and graphs, provided by Zacks Investment Research, regarding both the 5-year and 10-year cumulative total return of Smithfield stocks are reported (fulfilling the principles of *credibility, consistency, comparability, reliability*).

Throughout the report, the *time frame* of plans is often indicated. In relation to the *frequency of reporting*, this is the first annual IR that Smithfield has released but, on the third page of its IR, Smithfield states: "We expect our reporting will continue to progress over time, and we welcome feedback on how we might improve our approach" (Smithfield 2012).

16.4   Smithfield IR vs. the IIRC Consultation Draft

All companies need better business reporting which should illustrate a more comprehensive picture of the organization that goes beyond mere financial performance (KPMG 2013) and that stimulates integrated thinking, decision-making and actions when creating value in the short, medium and long term (IIRC 2013). Therefore, an IR is a document that sets out to fulfil these expectations and that gives shareholders the opportunity to assess not only the quality of the results achieved in the past, but also the validity of corporate future strategies.

In preparing the report, Smithfield has been inspired by recommendations made by the IIRC published in 2011. The alignment with the content elements and guidelines is shown on the inside back cover of the report where a map of the report with the elements recommended in 2011 is provided. A snapshot of this map is shown in Fig. 16.8.

Also, the comprehensive picture of the company provided by Smithfield's IR is in line with the CD and shows how the guiding principles and content elements of the CD are applicable within, and can be adapted to, a company operating in the food industry sector. Next, in Table 16.1, we summarise the main results of the analysis undertaken in this chapter. More specifically, the table maps the sections where the content elements of the CD are addressed within the report, along with the guiding principles that characterize their exposure. Also, the last column in Table 16.1 reports what capitals Smithfield uses and in which section of the report they are dealt with.

From the analysis undertaken in this chapter, it is evident that the report is aligned with the IIRC guidelines, which are also flexibly adapted to the company's characteristics. In so doing, it conveys a sound interconnection between the fundamental concepts of IR, such as capitals, business model and value creation in the specific context of a company operating in the food industry. In particular, when presenting the value creation process through sustainability pillars, Smithfield's IR discloses the company's capitals, its stakeholders and the features of its business model. In doing so, the Smithfield IR also communicates the capacity of the company to recognize the interconnections between its capitals through the process of value creation. Moreover, the connectivity between capitals, how they are invested or increased, along with their performances, is enriched with examples throughout the report.

Smithfield's IR also shows the factors that serve as material for the company's value creation, as well as the interconnections and interdependences among them. It is also interesting to note how the sustainability elements and business initiatives are often translated into value creation in financial terms.

IIRC REPORTING CONTENT ELEMENT	MAJOR REPORT SECTIONS ADDRESSING	PAGES
Organizational overview and business model	Our Business Journey	10
	Our Family of Companies	40
Operating context, including risks and opportunities	Chief Executive Officer Letter	1
	Our Business Journey	10
	Governance & Management	16
	Value Creation	12–15, 21, 25, 28, 33, 35, 37
Strategic objectives	Our Business Journey	10
	Key Commitments	7
Governance and remuneration	Governance & Management	16
Performance	Key Data Summary	6
	Core Reporting Areas	12, 20, 24, 27, 32, 34
Future outlook	Chief Executive Officer Letter	1
	Our Business Journey	10

Fig. 16.8 Mapping of Smithfield's 2012 Integrated Report compared with the content elements recommended by the IIRC in 2011. (*Source*: Smithfield's 2012 integrated report, on inside back cover)

Several images enrich the report. The portrait of the CEO, as well as the portrait of, and the interview with, the CSO convey the idea of how governance is closely related to sustainability issues. The photographs of their faces also gives a sense of credibility and reliability to what is reported throughout the document. Furthermore, the tables and graphs showing both qualitative and quantitative performance support the text and make its content more reliable. This reliability is also reinforced through quotes from the people who work for, collaborate with and are involved in Smithfield's business.

Also, the exposure of various KPIs and future targets across the report, provide an easy, visual understanding of the key issues, facilitating users' comprehension (Dobkowsky-Joy and Brockland 2013). It is also worth noting the modalities for aggregation and disaggregation of information within the report, which address both the completeness and conciseness of information.

Finally, Smithfield's IR tells the story about its business, value creation and sustainability process, in line with the information requirements expressed in the CD, while also maintaining the company's peculiarities. It manages to do so by continuously focusing "on what is strategically important and material to understanding an organization's capacity to create and sustain value in the short, medium and long term" (PWC 2012, p. 5). The overall result is a continuous balance between following prescription and flexible adaptation to the company's particular characteristics.

Table 16.1 Mapping of Smithfield's 2012 integrated report with the content elements and guiding principles of the consultation draft, issued by the IIRC in April, 2013

Section within Smithfield's IR	Content elements	Guiding principles	Capitals
(First three pages of the report) Sect. 16.3.1	Organizational overview, performance, future outlook, risks	Conciseness, consistency, reliability, strategic focus and future orientation, materiality	
Sect. 16.3.2	Performance, strategy, opportunities and risks, future outlook, governance	Strategic focus and future orientation, conciseness, reliability	
Sect. 16.3.3	Performance, governance	Completeness, stakeholder responsiveness, reliability	
Sect. 16.3.4	Performance, strategy and resource allocation, future outlook	Materiality and conciseness, strategic focus and future orientation, reliability	
Sect. 16.3.5	Organizational overview and external environment, strategy and resource allocation, opportunities and risks, future outlook, business model	Materiality and conciseness, strategic focus and future orientation	
Sect. 16.3.6	Business model	Reliability and completeness, consistency and comparability, materiality and conciseness, connectivity	
Sect. 16.3.7	Governance, risks	Stakeholder responsiveness, materiality	Social and relationship
Sect. 16.3.8	Future outlook, opportunities, external environment, business model	Strategic focus and future orientation, connectivity, reliability, stakeholder responsiveness	Intellectual, social and relationship, manufactured, financial, natural
Sect. 16.3.9	Future outlook, business model	Stakeholder responsiveness, reliability and completeness, connectivity	Human, financial, social and relationship
Sect. 16.3.10	Future outlook, performance, opportunities, business model	Conciseness, connectivity, consistency and, comparability, reliability	Natural, financial, social and relationship, intellectual, manufactured
Sect. 16.3.11	Business model	Reliability and completeness, connectivity, stakeholder responsiveness	
Sect. 16.3.12	Future outlook, business model	Connectivity	Human, social and relationship,

(continued)

Table 16.1 (continued)

Section within Smithfield's IR	Content elements	Guiding principles	Capitals
			intellectual, financial
Sect. 16.3.13	Performance, business model		Social and relationship, financial
Sect. 16.3.14	Organizational overview and external environment, business model	Reliability, connectivity	
Sect. 16.3.15	Performance	Consistency and comparability, reliability	

References

CIMA (2011) Tomorrow's balance sheet. http://www.cimaglobal.com/Documents/Thought_leadership_docs/balance-sheet-final-report.pdf. Accessed 08 Jul 2013

Dobkowsky-Joy A, Brockland B (2013) The state of integrated reporting. Innovation and experimentation in the merging of ESG and financial disclosures. http://framework-llc.com/wp-content/uploads/2013/03/FrameworkLLC_StateOfIR_Rev0313.pdf. Accessed 07 Jul 2013

GreenBiz Group and Ernst and Young (2013) 2013 six growing trends in corporate sustainability. An Ernst and Young survey in cooperation with GreenBiz Group. http://www.ey.com/Publication/vwLUAssets/Six_growing_trends_in_corporate_sustainability_2013/$FILE/Six_growing_trends_in_corporate_sustainability_2013.pdf. Accessed 25 Jun 2013

International Integrated Reporting Council (2013) Consultation draft of the international < IR > framework. http://www.theiirc.org/wp-content/uploads/Consultation-Draft/Consultation-Draft-of-the-InternationalIRFramework.pdf. Accessed 02 Jun 2013

KPMG (2013) Integrated Reporting The Journey to better business reporting. http://www.kpmg.com/Global/en/IssuesAndInsights/ArticlesPublications/In-the-Headlines/Documents/ITH-2013-06.pdf. Accessed 25 Jun 2013

PWC (2012) Integrated Reporting The Future of Corporate Reporting. http://www.pwc.de/de_DE/de/rechnungslegung/assets/integrated_reporting.pdf. Accessed 02 Jul 2013

Smithfield Foods, Inc. (2012) Smithfield 2012 integrated report. http://www.smithfieldfoods.com/media/12902/smithfield-integrated-report-2012.pdf. Accessed 2 Jun 2013

The Case of Monnalisa

17

Cristiano Busco, Maria Pia Maraghini, and Sara Tommasiello

Abstract

This chapter focuses on Monnalisa, a medium-sized Italian company that operates in the fashion industry. The purpose is to illustrate the way in which Monnalisa has gradually redesigned its Annual Report. To do this, after having introduced the company's background information, the evolution of corporate reporting in Monnalisa is briefly reviewed. During the last decade Monnalisa has progressively engaged with its key stakeholders in order to develop an Integrated Report that now combines the European Union format of an Annual Report with the triple bottom line reporting that characterises sustainability reports. In particular, since 2009 the information and the key performance indicators presented within Monnalisa's annual Integrated Report reflect a combination of the requirements of the key stakeholders together with the main strategic objectives of the company. The current structure and some insights into Monnalisa's Integrated Report are illustrated and discussed in the chapter.

C. Busco (✉)
School of Business and Economics, National University of Ireland, Galway, Ireland
e-mail: cristiano.busco@nuigalway.ie

M.P. Maraghini
Department of Business Studies and Law, University of Siena, Siena, Italy
e-mail: maraghini@unisi.it

S. Tommasiello
Jafin – Monnalisa, Arezzo, Italy
e-mail: s.tommasiello@jafin.it

C. Busco et al. (eds.), *Integrated Reporting*, DOI 10.1007/978-3-319-02168-3_17,
© Springer International Publishing Switzerland 2013

17.1   Introduction: Monnalisa's Background Information

Monnalisa is a medium-sized company located in Arezzo, Italy. Founded in 1968 by Mr. Piero Iacomoni, Monnalisa designs and sells garments and accessories for children.[1] The clothing sector has always played an important role in the economy of the region surrounding Arezzo. This has provided significant opportunities for the company in terms of networking and available know-how. To distinguish his company from the competitors, Mr. Iacomoni decided to focus on a high-quality segment of the market, offering coordinated articles of clothing (the so-called *total look* concept).

Since its foundation, each line of products developed by Monnalisa has been characterized by the search for a high level of style, creativity, differentiation and production quality. Despite the increasing turbulence of the market environment, during the past 10 years, Monnalisa has experienced considerable growth in turnover (revenues—from 2000 to 2010 Monnalisa's turnover has tripled), which reached about 36 million euros in 2010. Significantly, 90 % of Monnalisa's customers come from Europe (54 % from Italy). In 2013, the company employed about 65 people.

Monnalisa's traditional and core business is to create and sell high-end fashion garments and accessories for girls from new-borns right through to teenagers. Monnalisa bases its business on four main brands: *Monnalisa Bebé*, suitable for ages 3–6 months; *Monnalisa Girls*, for ages 2–12 years; *Chic Monnalisa*, for those 4–16 years of age; *Jakioo*, a trendy brand for 6–16 years and two newer brands, *Ny&lon*, a sportive brand for 3 months to 16 years of age, and *Hitch-Hiker* for boys 3 months to 12 years of age. Recently, Monnalisa has diversified its business by partnering with furniture and accessories manufacturers to market products for little girls' bedrooms, such as white-washed bed frames and furniture with a vintage flavour, cabinets with soft spirals, sinuous chairs and lamps.[2]

The *mission* of Monnalisa is to create value and values over time by offering a fashionable, high quality, high identity product for both clients (the retailers) and consumers. According to the company's Annual Report this mission should be fulfilled through a flexible, reliable and customized service; a dynamic and challenging work environment; an ongoing and profitable relationship with suppliers; and a sustainable company policy for the territory. The *vision* to be accomplished by Monnalisa embraces (1) to excel in innovation, creativity and practicality to gain new markets; (2) to drive a diffused *managership* inside the company to take on the challenges of the small and medium family enterprises successfully; and (3) to expand worldwide, both productively and commercially, while maintaining the company values and identity, to spread a culture of social responsibility. The fulfilment of the mission and the achievement of the vision should be sought by adhering to the four company *values*:

---

[1] Monnalisa is both the name of the company and the brand name of clothes designed and sold by the company. For the web site of the company please see http://www.monnalisa.eu

[2] This work extends previous contributions on Monnalisa. Please see Busco et al. 2012a, b; and Giovannoni and Maraghini 2013. See also Giovannoni et al. 2011.

- *Respect*: for skills and competencies, diversity, pace of life and work;
- *Dialogue and participation*: meaning a stimulating work environment, connection with the territory, and growth together with the related industries and services;
- *Fairness*: meaning the acknowledgement of everyone's dedication to their relationship with Monnalisa, and also transparent decisions;
- *Responsibility*: towards customer satisfaction, efficient and effective use of all resources as well as transparent reporting of policies and strategies.

The purpose of this chapter is to explore how Monnalisa has gradually redesigned its Annual Report throughout the last decade to develop an Integrated Report (IR). To do this, after the second section where the company's organizational structure and value chain is introduced, Sect. 17.3 focuses on the evolution of corporate reporting in Monnalisa. Next, Sect. 17.4 summarizes Monnalisa's journey towards Integrated Reporting where the role of stakeholder engagement is emphasised. The current structure and some insights into Monnalisa's Integrated Report are illustrated and discussed in Sect. 17.5. The chapter ends with some concluding thoughts.

17.2   Value Chain and Organizational Chart

Similar to the majority of the companies operating in the *fashion industry*, Monnalisa's business and value chain is structured and managed around two collections of clothes per year, one for the autumn–winter season, and the other for the spring–summer. Each collection kicks-off with a *collection briefing*, a meeting where the heads of the Design, Sales and Marketing, Production, and Finance Departments identify and finalize the broad plan for the collection by listing the number of lines, as well as the categories of products (for example shirts, skirts or shoes) that will be featured in the forthcoming collection. Next, within Monnalisa, research and design of the collections, preparation of the prototypes and development of the samples are carried out by the Design Department (see the organizational chart represented in Fig. 17.1). The collections are then presented to retailers through show rooms and fashion shows, as well as a network of independent sales agents who sell for Monnalisa during the two main sales campaigns, allowing the collection of orders and the first feedback on the creations.[3] In this context, a key role is played by the Sales and Marketing Department, which is responsible for providing accurate sales forecasts for the sales campaigns, and for collecting feedback and comments from retailers and consumers on the style of the clothes. This information is communicated by the Sales and Marketing Department to the Design Department (for style projects), as well as to the Production Department for production planning.[4]

---

[3] Traditionally Monnalisa sold its products through independently owned single brand and multi-brand shops, and department stores. Only recently has Monnalisa started to sell its products directly to the final consumer through its web-site and the first company-store in Arezzo.

[4] Production is planned according to the orders collected during the sales campaigns.

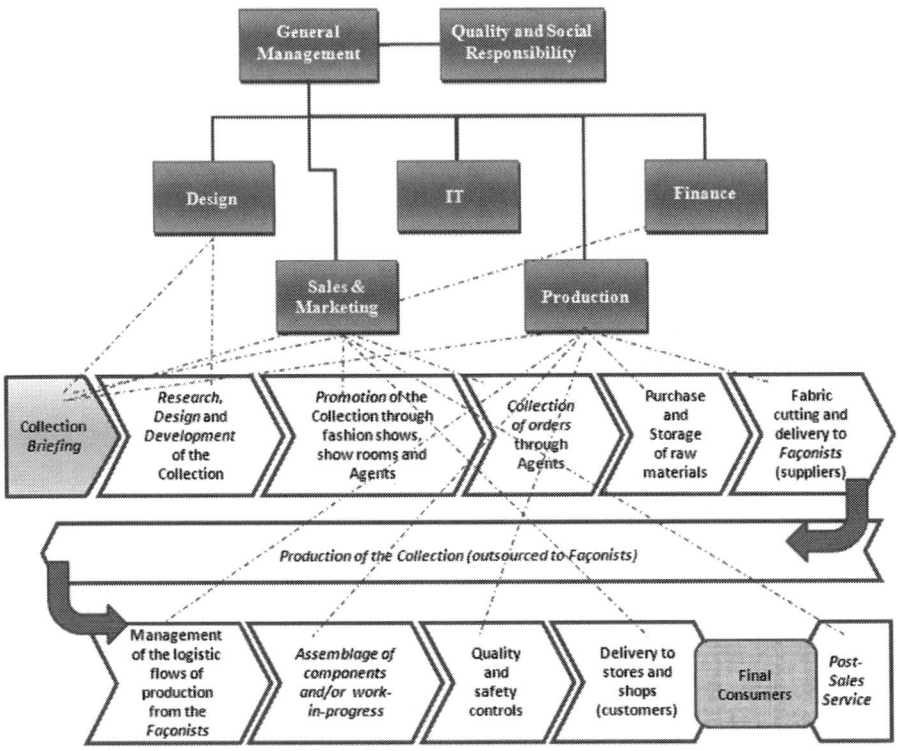

Fig. 17.1 Monnalisa's organizational structure and value chain

Like a number of other companies of a comparable size operating in the fashion industry, Monnalisa has a flexible production structure. The purchases of raw materials, as well as their storage and fabric cutting are carried out internally by the Production Department. In contrast, all the transformation phases from raw materials to work-in-progress, and sometimes to finished products, are outsourced to small suppliers (named Façonists[5]) mostly located in central Italy. Components, work-in-progress and finished products are then delivered to Monnalisa's premises in Arezzo, where the Production Department is responsible for the control and management of the logistic flow, the assembly of components and work-in-progress, the quality and safety control of the garments, and their storage and distribution to national and international markets. All post-sales activities are carried out by the Sales and Marketing Department.

---

[5] The relationship with Suppliers (of fabric and accessories) and Façonists is managed by the Production Department (although suppliers and Façonists are not involved in cross-functional teams). Around 50 % of the suppliers have a long-term relationship with Monnalisa, which is renewed collection by collection. This percentage increases up to 90 % for the Façonists.

Next, we describe the recent evolution of Monnalisa's annual reporting activities both in terms of content and structure, and highlight the choices of the company in terms of communicating results, as well as the process of value creation to its stakeholders. In particular, to explore Monnalisa's journey towards IR, we focus our analysis on reports after 2005, the year in which Monnalisa decided to discontinue the traditional reporting format that separated, into two different documents, the financial and social-environmental results.

17.3   The Evolution of Corporate Reporting in Monnalisa

Published for the first time in 2003, the social and environmental report released by Monnalisa was originally divided into three main sections: corporate identity, financial performance, and social performance (offering information related to the relationships with the key stakeholders of the company, i.e. employees, customers, suppliers, shareholders, lenders, local institutions, local community, and the environment). However, it is with the 2005 report that Monnalisa introduced a substantial innovation in its way of communicating annual results to its stakeholders. In particular, in the 2005 report the company integrates, for the first time, the disclosure of financial and social-environmental performances. Within this report financial, social and environmental information are strongly integrated with each other on the assumption that the company's financial performance depends directly on the social responsibility policies that are implemented, and vice versa.

Due to this innovation, Monnalisa was awarded with the Italian annual report Oscar in 2006, a prize that is given to companies that distinguish themselves for excelling in corporate reporting.[6] Building on this acknowledgement, the 2006 annual report suggested that Monnalisa focus on intangibles. At the time, Monnalisa felt the need to communicate, and make evident to stakeholders, what is an invisible and not always fully perceived and acknowledged value. As a result of this need to unveil and discover the intangible, the company accompanied the

---

[6] Since 1954, the Annual Report Oscar has been assigned to companies that have carried out the best economic, social responsibility and environmental communication. The award has been created and administered by FERPI—The Italian Federation of Public Relations—under the Patronage of the President of the Italian Republic. This prize is the only national award recognised by the Italian economic-financial community as promoting a culture of transparent and exhaustive reporting. In particular, the motivations that were released by the jury in 2006 in support of awarding Monnalisa were the following: "*The report is* clear, *complete, transparent and well structured. The integration of documentation providing all the necessary information both of an economic-patrimonial and socio-environmental nature was particularly appreciated. In this latter area, proposed objectives and results obtained have been clearly highlighted with an interesting focus carried out with suppliers that has permitted both dialogue with subcontractors and a complete control of the entire production. The document is exhaustive and proportioned, with clear graphics, preceded by an index which facilitates easy consultation. The successful effort put into improving the communicative and informative impact of the report from year to year emerges clearly*".

financial statement with a narrative that offered an account of the people, the ideas, the values, and the resources of trust, which distinguish and make Monnalisa unique in comparison to any other company.

On its 40th anniversary since its inception, Monnalisa presented the 2008 Annual Report by giving its employees the opportunity to have their say. This was possible through the adoption of a double method: interviewing and, by means of a suggestion box, gathering ideas that each employee had regarding the past and future of the company. Additionally, with its suppliers, Monnalisa decided to discuss a shared topic which could be summarized with the question "What can we do together (we, at Monnalisa and you, the suppliers) about environmental issues?". The company's commitment to reporting its environmental performance was confirmed and strengthened. Impact analysis of every production process stage has been maintained, turning subsequently to field experts for a third-party evaluation of this impact on the surrounding environment. Finally, the 2008 Annual Report presented an extended analysis of corporate risks, divided into "remote/possible" and "external/internal".

The 2009 annual report was characterised by a very innovative layout. In this document, for the first time, the economic, social and environmental performance were reported and illustrated by using a particular lens: the areas of interest and the perspectives of the stakeholders. The identification of these interests and perspectives started in 2003 as Monnalisa began a process of engagement and dialogue with stakeholders. During meetings and open sessions with the key stakeholders, some major issues and areas to be monitored emerged. This also led to a clearer identification of the objectives to be achieved in order to satisfy the needs of the stakeholders. This process, which unfolded over the last 10 years, was realised on the basis of the principles of materiality and correspondence of the AA1000 international standards. These standards suggest combining the stakeholder's requests with the mission and the values of the involving company. Overall, seven issues were identified. They currently represent the chapters of the IR, as well as its key of interpretation. These seven issues are: maintain a strong identity, guarantee economic sustainability, guarantee a high quality, excel in innovation, promote valorisation, communicate and involve in a transparent and effective way, and contribute to the development of the territory.

In 2011, for the second time, Monnalisa was awarded the Italian annual report Oscar. In this case, the process of integration was considered a fundamental element for awarding Monnalisa's annual report.[7] As the jury commented, Monnalisa's 2010 IR is an "excellent example of integrated reporting in which economic and sustainability information exist together and find the right space. The document is complete, analytic and integrated with all the elements of corporate social

---

[7] "A success that honors me, and the combination of talent working in Monnalisa at all corporate levels. This award represents a recognition for the commitment we pursue in communicating to stakeholder our results and values with transparency and correctness" commented Piero Jacomoni, President of the CDA and founder of Monnalisa, when he received the Annual Report Oscar in 2011.

responsibility. The document is also complete relating to the relationship with all the stakeholders . . . The innovation section is particularly interesting as a means for creating value".

As discussed above, since 2009 the information and the key performance indicators presented in Monnalisa's IR reflect a combination of the areas of interest and the perspectives of the key stakeholders within the main strategic themes and objectives of the company. This is an IR that includes the EU format of the Annual Report as well as the triple bottom line reporting that characterises sustainability Reports. However, integration goes beyond the simultaneous publication of these two documents, as it includes the real connectivity of all information related to the issues identified. This allows an understanding of the relationships between strategic objectives and the capacity for creating and maintaining value over time, keeping in mind external factors that influence the company, including risks as well as relations the organisation has with its multiple stakeholders.

The structure and insights of Monnalisa IR are illustrated in the next section.[8]

17.4   Monnalisa's Integrated Report

As illustrated in the previous section, it seems possible to affirm that the current structure of Monnalisa's IR has been jointly created during the last decade through conversations and engagement with its key stakeholders. As emphasized by the President and founder of the company, "the Integrated Report is driven by our mission, values, vision and strategic agenda and complemented by the expectations of our stakeholders". In particular, as highlighted above, conversations and engagement with stakeholders lead to the identification of seven issues and areas of interests that currently represent the chapters of the IR, as well as its key of interpretation.

In the following pages we illustrate some of the insights into these key issues as they are presented and discussed within Monnalisa's IR. In particular, we will be focusing on: maintain a strong identity; guarantee economic sustainability; excel in innovation and promote valorisation of human and relational capital; communicate and involve in a transparent and effective way; contribute to the development of the territory.

17.4.1 Maintain a Strong Identity

According to Monnalisa's IR, the identity of a company is what makes it stand out in comparison to others. In particular, Monnalisa wishes to stand out and be a leader in its field of business thanks to the strong identity of its products. Maintaining this identity is the result of an approach, which stems from a strong set of values seen as the guide for the decisions and choices the company makes. In particular, the identity is strengthened within the company by:

---

[8] For a better understanding on the idea and logic of Integrated Reporting see KPMG 2013; PWC 2012; International Integrated Reporting 2013.

Fig. 17.2 Monnalisa's group structure

- carrying out the entrepreneurial activity coherently with the mission and the values;
- operating to guarantee a transparent, clear and effective corporate governance system;
- developing and improving the structure and process of production, for better and more efficient results;
- consolidating the approach to sustainability as the key element on which company choices and activities lie.

Monnalisa sits at the centre of a group of five companies (see Fig. 17.2): *Babalai* is responsible for and carries out style, creation and design of prototypes and collections. *Penta Service* carries out fabric control, storage of raw materials and fabric cutting. *Monnalisa & Co.* manages single brand stores (Arezzo, Florence, Milan and Forte dei Marmi). *Jafin* is the financial company of the group, responsible for all financial and administrative services, as well as human resources for the group. *P.J.* manages the company real estate. Fifty-one percent of the shareholder's equity of Monnalisa S.p.A. is held by the Iacomoni family and forty-nine percent by the holding company of the group, Jafin. Since February 2010, when the founder, Mr. Piero Iacomoni, formally retired, the company has been managed through a Management Committee, chaired by the Managing Director, and includes the heads of every function. The purpose of the Management Committee is to execute the strategy formulated by the Board of Directors (chaired by Mr Iacomoni). The Board of Directors' main task is to determine the strategies and development policies for Monnalisa.

The distribution of Monnalisa products is carried out as follows:
- wholesale: independent multi brand stores;
- wholesale/retail: single brand in partnership;
- corporate/retail: direct single brand;
- e-business retail: on-line sales aimed at the end consumer.

Overall, the retail distribution channels counts for approximately 32 % of the company turnover, with 42 single brand stores, to which is added the on-line store and the shop in shop that can be found in the best department stores (Harrods, La Rinascente, Galeries Lafayette, etc.). These distribution channels, for which a "concept store" has been developed that is more in line with the company identity, requires ongoing personnel training and the presence of systems capable to collect and analyse data, enabling the company to understand in a deeper and faster way the dynamics of supply and demand, in order to steer company policy. However, now the strong point in distribution is the wholesale channel, which is very widespread and exclusive. As of today, there are about 1,000 retail customers, and in the extra EU area they count for approximately 43 %. Several customer-oriented services have been implemented to strengthen this relationship and to encourage a shift from a supplier-customer to a supplier-partner mentality. This is the spirit behind the "Monnalisa space" contracts, through which a number of services to clients are provided, such as, for example, internet access to a specific warehouse for re-assortment.

As for the production process, Monnalisa's business and value chain is structured and managed around two collections of clothes per year, one for the autumn–winter season, and the other for spring–summer. The sales projections based on the outcome of the sales campaign enable the company to plan purchases in advance, and then to schedule production according to sales agreements. Aiming to satisfy the clientele's requests at its best, Monnalisa has set up an extremely flexible production structure, which allows the effective control of the organization's critical areas in terms of production and delivery. All the transformation phases from raw material to finished product are outsourced to small laboratories, primarily located in central Italy. Creation and design of the collection, preparation of the prototypes and development of the stylistic project are carried out by Babalai. Support and control of the marketing and sales network remain internal, as does the purchase of raw materials and marketed items, control and management of the logistic flow of the external production and quality control, storage, shipment and post sales activities of finished goods. Penta Srl uses innovative technology to guarantee high quality workmanship, and carries out fabric control, storage of raw materials and fabric cutting. Fabric that has been cut, together with trimmings and accessories, is then sent to the sewing, embroidery, printing and dyeing stations for the following

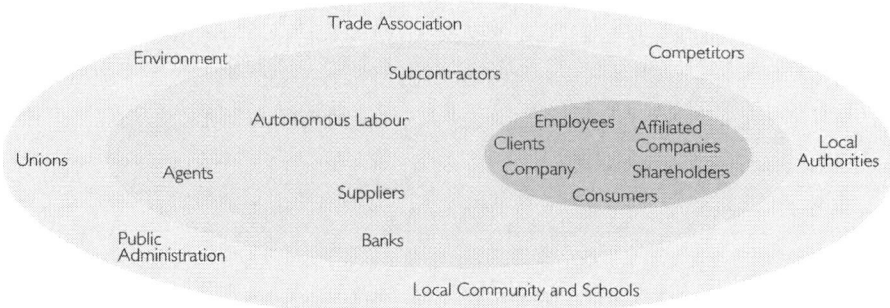

Fig. 17.3 Monnalisa's stakeholder map

production phases. Finally, the finished product goes back to Monnalisa where it is stored for the client.

While carrying out its activities, Monnalisa engages with multiple entities and organizations who connect with the company for a variety of reasons, and therefore contribute interest together with the company for pursuing its mission and for achieving its vision. Monnalisa has various types of relationships with its stakeholders, which are graphically presented in a "stakeholder map" (see Fig. 17.3). In this map, the stakeholders are arranged in concentric circles in relation to their greater (inner circle) or lesser (outer circle, the largest) level of partnership with the company itself. As anticipated above, in 2003 Monnalisa began a process of engagement and dialogue with many of these stakeholders. This process has led to the identification of the current structure of the IR. During meetings and open sessions with key stakeholders, major issues and areas to be monitored have emerged. This has led Monnalisa towards a clearer identification of the objectives to be achieved to satisfy the needs of the stakeholders, as well as its planned economic, social and environmental objectives.

17.4.2 Guarantee Economic Sustainability

Within this section of the Integrated Report, a detailed presentation and analysis of the economic, financial and patrimonial situation of Monnalisa is offered. In addition, the calculation and distribution of added value, as well as the "risk per stakeholder map" is illustrated. The statement of added value produced is generated by following the Guidelines of the Italian Study Group on Company Reports. The purpose is to highlight the added value created and distributed among the various company stakeholders. However, in developing this statement, it was decided to consider affiliated companies, subcontractors and agents as recipients of the added value created by the Company, rather than as a source of internal costs. Figure 17.4 illustrates the way in which Monnalisa distributes the added value that is produced.

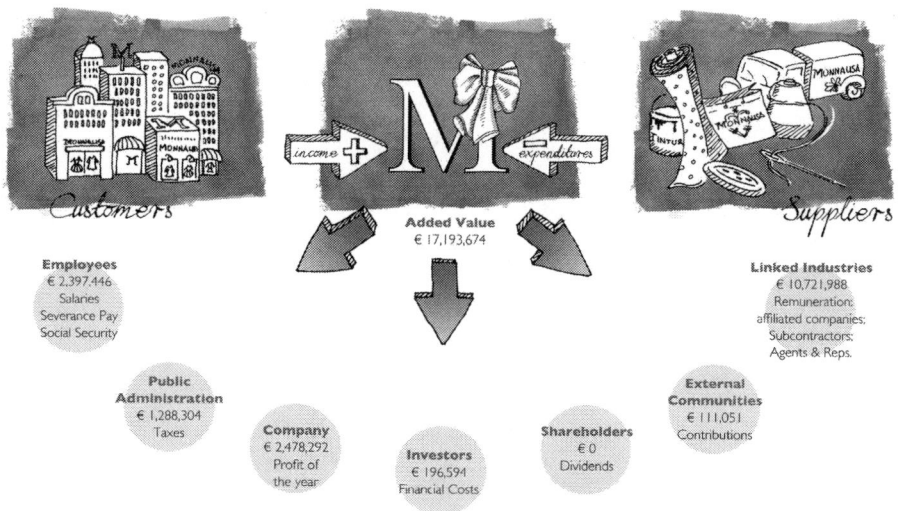

Fig. 17.4 Distribution of added value

Stakeholder	Risk	Possibility	Actions to contain the risk	Effectiveness indicator
SHAREHOLDERS	stability in composition	remote	Family pact and appointment of a Board of Directors open to members that are not related to the family	In 2008 a family Pact between the shareholders was signed, in 2010 the Board of Directors included all family members and one external member, expect its financial matters.
COMPANY	Difference in views among affiliated companies	Possible	Subsidiary companies are similarly composed and organized; Jafin S.p.A. financial and services	Company structures are homogeneous; Jafin offers administrative services to subsidiary companies
	Lack of economic and financial balance	remote	Increase of share capital	Structure Q is 2.14
			Growth perspectives	Orders for A/W 2012 show the same value in volumes as the corresponding previous season.
			Liquidity management	The availability ratio is equals to 1.70
			Maintaining Margins	The ROI is 21.83% and the ROS is 10.29%
	Risk on import currencies	remote	Controlling exchange rates	Covering fixed Exchange rate when compiling the price sheets for the price lists by activating the "flexible forward" tool
	Loss of data due to technical problems	Remote	Back up procedures, control of DB	Although the obligation to draw up and update the data in the security document is no longer needed, Monnalisa has inserted back up and management procedures in the ISO9001 manual instructions. There have never been complaints on violation or loss of privacy data.
	Obsolescence of IT instruments	possible	Constant updating	One of the three persons in this dept. is assigned to this activity
			Technology development	The Management Committee is also responsible for this area
	Incorrect accounting management	remote	Board of auditors as auditing body	During the annual audits there have been no significant events; there have been no monetary fines for non conformities to laws and regulations.
			Jafin-experienced employees	Jafin employees have worked for about 18 years in the same role
	Warehouse obsolescence	Possible	Prudent valuation of the unsold stock	Only 1.9% of finished products in stock as of 31/12/2011 are previous to 2011
			Production to customers	98% of confirmed orders is dispatched on average
BANKS	Rating decrease	remote	Capitalization, liquidity and marginality management	The average rating confirmed is AA
			Ample disclosure to banks	Drawing up of integrated annual report, distributed and presented to banks in dedicated meetings. The Annual Report is on the company website from where it can be viewed and downloaded;

Fig. 17.5 Risk analysis regarding shareholders, company and banks

Additionally, within this section, a risk analysis that Monnalisa underwent was developed by using the stakeholder approach. Once the eight main interest bearers were chosen, the relationship with Monnalisa was analysed for each of them, with the result of outlining the risks to which each one was subjected. The risks were then classified according to nature (internal or external) and possibility of occurrence (probable, possible, remote). For each risk, the management levers (the areas where it is important to act in order to limit the risk and its consequences), the measures to contain the risk (concrete actions that diminish the risk and/or its consequences) and the indicators to measure the effectiveness of the actions taken, are highlighted (see Fig. 17.5 for a risk analysis regarding shareholders, company and banks).

The risks that are estimated as probable are internal and refer to the excessive reliance on specific suppliers and to the absorption of liquidity for the expansion of credit as turnover increases. In order to reduce these risks, on one hand Monnalisa carries out an intense activity of worldwide scouting for new suppliers and creates long-lasting partnerships with its traditional suppliers. On the other hand, it constantly monitors its working capital, trying to keep a balance between its various components (credits, debts and inventory) in terms of volume and turnover.

However, the main risk, in terms of significance of the possible consequences of the risk, is external and is represented by reputational risk. That is, the possibility that the Monnalisa collections may not satisfy the client's tastes (the retailer or/and of the final consumer) before or after the purchase. It is evident how the market is the real test-bed for a company which bases its raison d'être on innovation, research and creativity. Even more so in the fashion market, which is characterised by a short shelf-life and by frenetic and continuous offers of new products and brands. In order to monitor, manage and limit the reputation risk, Monnalisa operates as follows:

– careful management of the product and company image (brand, product and company communication). For these reasons, public relations has been internalised in the attempt to enhance control over communication and deliver more effective messages when communicating externally;
– scrupulous quality control of the product (internally and at the suppliers' premises);
– attention to the safety of the product and of the materials used.

17.4.3 Excel in Innovation and Promote Valorisation of Human and Relational Capital

Monnalisa considers innovation as an important source of competitive advantage. The ability to innovate should be preserved and improved as one of the key elements of the company's intangible assets. Monnalisa perceives innovation as both the ability to design and develop new products that will bring to light the knowhow and creativity of its employees, and as a means for finding sustainable solutions while respecting the social and environmental context. For these reasons, the Integrated Report illustrates performance as it relates to innovation and style, as well as innovative actions regarding some of the production and relational process phases.

However, to fully appreciate the contents of the "excel in innovation" section of the report, it is worth illustrating the way in which creativity and innovation within Monnalisa are carried out within the Design Department. The research, design and development process includes a number of activities generally structured around the following five phases: (*1*) *research*, (*2*) *design*, (*3*) *paper pattern drafting*, (*4*) *prototyping, and* (*5*) *sampling* (see Fig. 17.6).

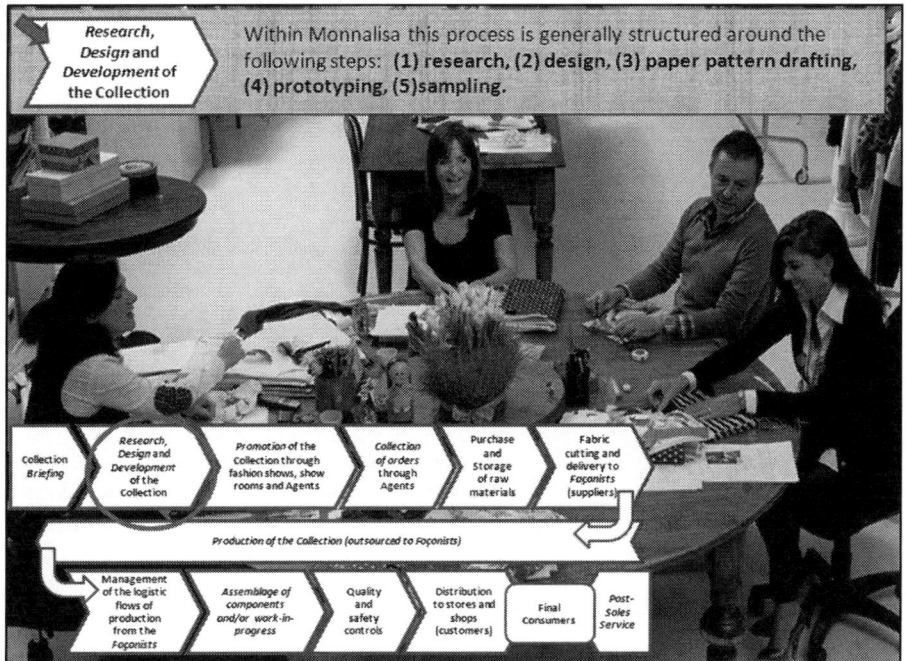

Fig. 17.6 The research, design and development process in Monnalisa

(1) *The research phase*: here the stylists try to become familiarized with markets and trends, trying to sense where fashion will be going during the next season. The sources of information can vary, ranging from their own feelings to inspirations coming from the market based on trade shows; from their own contacts and networks in society to the industry trend reports that try to anticipate the styles, colours, and fabrics that are likely to be popular in the coming seasons; and finally, from their visits to textile and accessories manufacturers (raw material suppliers) to see and evaluate the possible fabrics, colours and patterns to be eventually included in the design of the collection.

(2) *The design phase*: once stylists have selected fabrics, colours and patterns, the actual design phase starts. In this phase, the stylists sketch preliminary designs. Initially, designers use pencils for their sketches, but then translate it into digital blueprints with CAD (Computer-Aided Design) systems. Digital blueprints allows stylists to see sketched designs of clothing on virtual models and in different colours and shapes, thus reducing the time for possible refinements and adjustments in the later phases of prototyping and sampling.

(3) *The paper pattern drafting phase*: the technical aspects of the designs, which are extremely important in preparing for the production stage and for instructing the

third-party Façonists, are addressed in this phase. The paper pattern is the drawing on paper of the basic silhouette, indicating all the different parts and features of a garment (for example, in a teen-age girl's shirt, the neckline, the sleeves, the pockets, the cuts, the lengths, the draperies). The paper pattern is then cut to shape and placed on the fabric to guide the cutting.

(4) *The prototyping phase*: a number of prototypes are built using different materials or with small changes to the original pattern in order to experiment with various alternatives and styles. These prototypes are then tried on a human model for the first time to see how they fit and look, and decide whether adjustments are needed. This process leads to the selection of the models that will actually be listed and offered for sale.

(5) *The sampling phase*: once the final adjustments and selections of the models have been made, the design phase ends with the development of multiple sizes of samples for the same article. This activity is complex in that not all the elements of an article become larger in the same proportion and in a predetermined manner for developing the different sizes. Finally, the various samples of the articles, using the actual materials, are produced and marketed to retailers directly through fashion and trade shows, as well as through independent sales agents.

Even if described as linear, the fashion research, design and development process is iterative in its nature. Fabrics, colours and patterns can be re-assessed in light of new information generated throughout the various phases of the process or collected from other internal and external sources. Notably, as the creative process unfolds, the Design Department is expected to interact constantly with other functions such as Sales and Marketing, Production, and Finance, which participate in the development of the collection, offering their support and evaluation on the implications of the company's performance for the products being developed.

Within Monnalisa, stylists are free to interact and explore their perceptions of social trends and moods. The aesthetic conception of the product, applied research, and the creation of the garments represent the creative engine of the company. In particular, the research and development activities, consisting of a steady formal and informal exchange between the design and the other departments (especially marketing), include spotting fashion trends, colours and themes to be developed in every line; researching, selecting and creating materials, fabrics and appliqués; creating sketches for prints, embroidery, appliqués on printed fabrics; researching, selecting and realizing specific accessories for each item and its packaging.

The adoption of the intellectual capital framework in 2005 has helped Monnalisa to develop and systematize a set of performance indicators concerning creativity and the capacity to innovate, but also individual abilities, motivation, and collaboration within the company (a sample of these performance indicators are illustrated in Fig. 17.7). Although, at present, these indicators are not formally tied to compensation, the aim of the Company is to refine this system of control and performance evaluation to be in a position to implement a structured scheme of incentives in the

Key factor	Key factor (*second level*)	Performance indicator
Training	Training investment	- Training investment *per-employee* - Training investment/Total revenues
	Specialized training	- number of trained employees - # of training sessions
Attractiveness	Opening to new resources	- # of new employees younger than 30
Internal climate	Employees satisfaction	- % of employees who consider the system of performance measurement useful
Professionalization	Variety of skills	- # of employees who have accomplished different tasks within the company
Visibility	New customers	- # of visitors to the stand at fashion weeks
	Brand	- # of countries where the brand is registered
Reliability	Shipments quality	- # of shipments by order
	Post-sales service	- # of employees in the marketing department devoted to post-sales activities
Technologies development	E-commerce	- # web-orders
Creativity	Turnover of the stylists	- Average age of the stylists
	Design R&D	- Design R&D investment/Total Revenue

Fig. 17.7   A sample of KPIs Used to Monitor the Human Capital in Monnalisa

foreseeable future. For example, Monnalisa has recently developed software that allows HR to feed the indicator "number of employees who have accomplished different tasks" by tracking the length and the specific duties of job rotation processes.

17.4.4 Communicate and Involve in a Transparent and Effective Way

As illustrated throughout this chapter, stakeholder engagement plays an important role in Monnalisa's development process and communication strategies. Dialogue with and participation of stakeholders enables Monnalisa to communicate information in a different way (i.e., through a new and integrated structure of the annual report), and to identify the content that is relevant—i.e. "material"—to the needs of both the company and the stakeholders themselves. Among the mechanisms of engagement, are inter-functional workgroups and focus groups, with relevant external stakeholders playing a significant role.

Since 2009, inter-functional workgroup meetings are organized every week to discuss coordination all across the value chain. Together with an internal bimonthly newsletter that updates Monnalisa's employees as to the status of the business and of the main projects, these meetings prove to be extremely important for sharing and communicating information within the organization. As argued by a stylist, "it is important for us to be educated about the cost implications of our creations, to be aware of the financial consequences that could be dictated by design". The inter-functional workgroups allow managers to spot early warning signals. As emphasized by a production manager, "last week during one of our weekly meeting the creative director talked about the most appropriate combinations of straps, colours and accessories for the next collection... it is always fascinating to listen to stylists sharing their ideas and discussing their sources of inspiration, however, after few minutes, I could not stop thinking about the production challenges associated with those new creations".

Within Monnalisa, *ad hoc* focus groups with the relevant stakeholders represent additional ways to manage the interplay between sources of innovation, and systems of performance management and measurement. In 2009, for instance, following the outcome of a workshop with suppliers and the local community on environmental issues, the company launched an innovative research project on the theme of ecological t-shirts. "The idea is to produce a t-shirt made of organic cotton on which four endangered animals are printed: a panda, a Siberian tiger, a sea horse and an arctic fox. The organic cotton used for the t-shirt would come from land farmed according to the principles of organic agriculture, without using either genetically modified seeds or synthetic pesticides, which are generally used (according to industry surveys confirmed by meetings with key suppliers) in conventional cultivation with negative consequences for the environment. Packaging would be entirely made of recycled materials and come with an educational game which gives more information on the four animals and their habitats.

To reduce the impact on the company, the game would not be printed in colour but children can have fun completing it with an included set of ecological crayons", suggests one of the stylists. This project was co-created with suppliers, customers, as well as the local community (namely the Florence *Polimoda* Fashion Institute). Interestingly enough, creative exploration was facilitated and guaranteed throughout the project, but all the stakeholders had also the environmental, social and financial conditions that should have characterized the production of the new t-shirt clearly in mind. Focus groups enabled creativity and control to be reconciled in practice through ongoing social interaction that stimulated innovation, as well as monitored the other performance dimensions concerning the various interests at stake.

In 2010, with the aim of improving the alignment among performance indicators in the Integrated Report, Monnalisa's employees were asked to gather informally and express their understanding of certain strategic objectives through a series of pictures, which were included in the report. The "photo-stories" workout proved to be extremely important for capturing and representing the main objectives of the company, especially those related to intellectual capital and to relations with stakeholders. These objectives are generally the most difficult to digest, since their practical consequences may be distant and not immediate. Additionally, not every individual within the organization has the experience or the background knowledge to understand the interplays across functions and their consequences for the company as a whole and its stakeholders. The effort of trying to convey individual perceptions through a photo story helped Monnalisa's employees to shed light on a number of critical issues characterizing the cause-and-effect relationship among the performance indicators used to monitor the result across the internal value chain. Again, from creative design to production and distribution, all functions were called upon for increasing their awareness of the overall integrated management system of the company.

17.4.5 Contribute to the Development of the Territory

Monnalisa wishes to be a sustainable enterprise contributing to the economic and social development of the territories in which it operates. Additionally, Monnalisa aims at reducing the environmental impact derived from its activities. Contributing to the growth and well-being of individuals and society depends on the capacity of enterprises to offer long-term employment within the area they operate. For this reason, the section of the IR titled "Contribute to the development of the territory" presents a picture of the composition and solidity of the work force employed by Monnalisa, as well as of the suppliers that work with and for the company.

Moreover, although the type of production process and the location of the company do not involve specific physical risks linked to the change in climate, Monnalisa is actively involved in limiting its environmental impact that is directly linked to climate change. In particular, in order to reduce the environmental impact derived from its activities to a minimum, Monnalisa has developed a system to monitor its main areas of consumption. This will enable the company to take action when the data exceed the parameters considered appropriate. Among others, the following aspects are monitored and reported in the Integrated Report: business trips and deliveries (people mobility and goods mobility); fuel, water and power consumption; raw material consumption for packaging; and green house gas emissions (direct and indirect). A full list of GRI-G3 indicators is offered in Appendix A.

Conclusions

This chapter has focussed on Monnalisa, a medium-sized Italian company that operates in the fashion industry. The chapter aimed at exploring Monnalisa's recent trajectory towards Integrated Reporting. To do this, after a brief illustration of the company's organizational structure and value chain, we offered a review of the evolution of corporate reporting in Monnalisa.

The purpose has been to illustrate the way in which Monnalisa has gradually redesigned its Annual Report. We have highlighted how during the last decade Monnalisa has progressively engaged with its key stakeholders in order to develop an Integrated Report that now combines the European Union format of an Annual Report with the triple bottom line reporting that characterises sustainability reports. In particular, we stressed how since 2009 the information and the key performance indicators presented within Monnalisa's annual IR reflect a combination of the requirements of the key stakeholders together with the main strategic objectives of the company.

We have illustrated and discussed a number of key issues that were generated by stakeholder engagement, and that today represent chapters of Monnalisa IR. In particular, we focused on the following: maintain a strong identity; guarantee economic sustainability; excel in innovation and promote valorisation of human and relational capital; communicate and involve in a transparent and effective way; contribute to the development of the territory. These issues represent a distinctive feature of Monnalisa's approach to Integrated Reporting, as well as the ground for its future development.

Appendix A: GRI-G3 Indicators adopted by Monnalisa (2011 Annual Report)

GRI	Description
1. Strategy and Analysis	
2. Organisation profile	
3. Report parameters	
4. Governance, commitmens, stakeholder involvement	

FINANCIAL PERFORMANCE INDICATORS

		Management style
ASPECT: FINANCIAL PERFORMANCE		
CORE	EC1	Directly generated and distributed financial value
CORE	EC2	Financial implications and other risks and opportunities for the activities carried out by the organisation due to climate change
CORE	EC4	Significant funds received by Public Institutions
ASPECT: PRESENCE IN THE MARKET		
ADD	EC5	Ratio between the standard salary for newly hired and the minimum local salary in the most significant operative venues
CORE	EC6	Policies, practices and percentage of expense concentrated on local suppliers in relation to the most significant operating venues
CORE	EC7	Recruiting procedures for persons residing where the activity mainly takes place and percentage of senior managers hired locally
ASPECT: INDIRECT FINANCIAL IMPACT		
CORE	EC8	Development and impact of investments on infrastructures and services mainly supplied for "public needs"
ADD	EC9	Analysis and description of the main indirect financial impact considering generated externalities

ENVIRONMENTAL PERFORMANCE INDICATORS

		Management style
ASPECT: RAW MATERIALS		
CORE	EN1	Raw materials used per weight and volume
ASPECT: POWER		
CORE	EN3	Direct consumption of power per primary energy source
CORE	EN4	Indirect consumption of power per primary energy source
ASPECT: WATER		
ADD	EN7	Initiatives aimed at reducing consumption of indirect energy and reductions obtained
CORE	EN8	Total water intake per source
ASPECT: BIODIVERSITY		
ASPECT: EMISSIONS, DRAINS, WASTE		
CORE	EN16	Total direct and indirect greenhouse effect gas emissions
CORE	EN17	Other indirect greenhouse or gas emissions
ADD	EN18	Intitiative to reduce greenhouse effect gas emissions and results achieved
CORE	EN22	Total weight of waste per type and method of disposal
ASPECT: PRODUCTS AND SERVICES		
CORE	EN26	Initiatives to reduce environmental impact of products and services
CORE	EN27	Percentage of items sold and relative recycled or re-used packaging material

ASPECT: FREEDOM OF ASSEMBLY AND COLLECTIVE NEGOTIATION

CORE	HR5	Activities that may pose serious risks on freedom of assembly and collective negotiation and the actions undertaken to defend those rights

ASPECT: CHILD LABOUR

CORE	HR6	Identification of those operations with a high risk of child labour and measures taken to help eliminate it.

ASPECT: HARD LABOUR

CORE	HR7	Activities with a high risk of mandatory or hard labour and measures taken to help eliminate them

ASPECT: SAFETY PRACTICES

ADD	HR8	% of the staff assigned to safety who have been trained on human rights

RIGHTS OF NATIVE POPULATIONS

ADD	HR9	Number of violations of local community rights and actions taken

PERFORMANCE INDICATORS ON THE COMPANY

		Management style

ASPECT: COMMUNITY

CORE	SO1	Impact of operations on the community

ASPECT: CORRUPTION

ASPECT: POLITICAL CONTRIBUTIONS

CORE	SO4	Actions taken following a corruption episode
CORE	SO5	Position in public policies, participation in the development of public policies
ADD	SO6	Total financial contributions and benefits given to parties, politicians and relative institutions per country.

ASPECT: ANTI COLLUSION BEHAVIOUR

ASPECT: CONFORMITY (COMPLIANCE)

CORE	SO8	Monetary value of significant sanctions and number of non monetary sanctions for non-compliance to laws and provisions

PERFORMANCE INDICATORS ON PRODUCT RESPONSIBILITY

ASPECT: CONSUMER HEALTH AND SAFETY

CORE	PR1	Analysis of the life cycle stages of products/services to improve impact on health and safety
ADD	PR2	Non-compliance cases in regards to regulations and voluntary codes concerning impact on the health and safety of products and services

ASPECT: LABELING PRODUCTS AND SERVICES

CORE	PR3	Information on products and services
ADD	PR4	Non-compliance cases in regards to regulations and voluntary codes concerning information and labelling of products and services
ADD	PR5	Customer satisfaction practices

ASPECT: MARKETING AND COMMUNICATION

ADD	PR7	Non-compliance cases in regards to regulations and voluntary codes referred to marketing activities including advertisement, promotion and sponsorship

ASPECT: PRIVACY

ADD	PR8	Complaints on privacy violations and loss of consumer data

ASPECT: CONSUMER HEALTH AND SAFETY

CORE	PR9	Monetary value of sanctions for non compliance to laws or regulations concerning the supply and use of products and services

ASPECT: FREEDOM OF ASSEMBLY AND COLLECTIVE NEGOTIATION		
CORE	HR5	Activities that may pose serious risks on freedom of assembly and collective negotiation and the actions undertaken to defend those rights

ASPECT: CHILD LABOUR		
CORE	HR6	Identification of those operations with a high risk of child labour and measures taken to help eliminate it.

ASPECT: HARD LABOUR		
CORE	HR7	Activities with a high risk of mandatory or hard labour and measures taken to help eliminate them

ASPECT: SAFETY PRACTICES		
ADD	HR8	% of the staff assigned to safety who have been trained on human rights

RIGHTS OF NATIVE POPULATIONS		
ADD	HR9	Number of violations of local community rights and actions taken

PERFORMANCE INDICATORS ON THE COMPANY

		Management style

ASPECT: COMMUNITY		
CORE	SO1	Impact of operations on the community

ASPECT: CORRUPTION		

ASPECT: POLITICAL CONTRIBUTIONS		
CORE	SO4	Actions taken following a corruption episode
CORE	SO5	Position in public policies, participation in the development of public policies
ADD	SO6	Total financial contributions and benefits given to parties, politicians and relative institutions per country.

ASPECT: ANTI COLLUSION BEHAVIOUR		

ASPECT: CONFORMITY (COMPLIANCE)		
CORE	SO8	Monetary value of significant sanctions and number of non monetary sanctions for non-compliance to laws and provisions

PERFORMANCE INDICATORS ON PRODUCT RESPONSIBILITY

ASPECT: CONSUMER HEALTH AND SAFETY		
CORE	PR1	Analysis of the life cycle stages of products/services to improve impact on health and safety
ADD	PR2	Non-compliance cases in regards to regulations and voluntary codes concerning impact on the health and safety of products and services

ASPECT: LABELING PRODUCTS AND SERVICES		
CORE	PR3	Information on products and services
ADD	PR4	Non-compliance cases in regards to regulations and voluntary codes concerning information and labelling of products and services
ADD	PR5	Customer satisfaction practices

ASPECT: MARKETING AND COMMUNICATION		
ADD	PR7	Non-compliance cases in regards to regulations and voluntary codes referred to marketing activities including advertisement, promotion and sponsorship

ASPECT: PRIVACY		
ADD	PR8	Complaints on privacy violations and loss of consumer data

ASPECT: CONSUMER HEALTH AND SAFETY		
CORE	PR9	Monetary value of sanctions for non compliance to laws or regulations concerning the supply and use of products and services

References

Busco C, Frigo ML, Giovannoni E, Maraghini MP (2012a) Control vs. creativity. In: *Strategic Finance*, n.8, August, pp 29–36

Busco C, Frigo ML, Giovannoni E, Maraghini MP (2012b) When creativity meets control: a fashion industry case study. J Corporate Account Finance 23(6):61–72

Giovannoni E, Maraghini MP (2013) The challenges of integrated performance measurement systems: integrating mechanisms for integrated measures. Account Audit Account J 26(6): 978–1008

Giovannoni E, Maraghini MP, Riccaboni A (2011) Transmitting knowledge across generations: the role of management accounting practices. Family Bus Rev 24(2):126–150

International Integrated Reporting Council (2013) Consultation draft of international <IR> framework. http://www.theiirc.org/wp-content/uploads/Consultation-Draft/Consultation-Draft-of-the-InternationalIRFramework.pdf. Accessed 02 June 2013

KPMG (2013) Integrated reporting the journey to better business reporting. http://www.kpmg.com/Global/en/IssuesAndInsights/ArticlesPublications/In-the-Headlines/Documents/ITH-2013-06.pdf. Accessed 25 June 2013

PWC (2012) Integrated reporting the future of corporate reporting. http://www.pwc.de/de_DE/de/rechnungslegung/assets/integrated_reporting.pdf. Accessed 02 July 2013

The Case of Eskom

18

Fabrizio Granà and Francesca Ceccacci

Abstract

From 2010, South African companies listed on the Johannesburg Stock Exchange Limited have been required to prepare and present the Integrated Report (IR). Given the increasing relevance of integrated reporting in the South African context, in which the preparation of the IR is compulsory for many companies, this chapter examines the experience of Eskom, a South African electricity supply company. The aim is to analyse the IR of the company during the period 2011–2012 in light of the content elements and guiding principles presented in the Consultation Draft published by the International Integrated Reporting Council. Therefore, this chapter sheds light on the applicability and/or adaptability of international recommendations on IR within a public company in the electric power industry.

18.1 Introduction[1]

On the first of March, 2010, the King Report on Corporate Governance in South Africa (the so called King III) provided local companies with indications on how to prepare an Integrated Report (IR). Since then, South African companies listed on the Johannesburg Stock Exchange Limited (JSE) have been required to prepare and

---

[1] Although this chapter is the result of a joint effort, the Sect. 18.1, paragraphs related to the description of the Content Elements of the IR of Eskom (Sects. 18.3, 18.3.1–18.3.6) and Discussion and Conclusions can be assigned to Fabrizio Granà. The Sect. 18.2 (The case of Eskom:

F. Granà (✉)
School of Business and Economics, National University of Ireland, Galway, Ireland
e-mail: f.grana1@nuigalway.ie

F. Ceccacci
University of Perugia, Perugia, Italy
e-mail: francesca.ceccacci@unipg.it

C. Busco et al. (eds.), *Integrated Reporting*, DOI 10.1007/978-3-319-02168-3_18,
© Springer International Publishing Switzerland 2013

present the IR (Abeysekera 2013; KPMG 2012). The King III describes Integrated Reporting as "a holistic and integrated representation of the company's performance in terms of both its finance and its sustainability" (Institute of Directors Southern Africa 2009, p. 54). The IR has also been defined as an innovative way of examining and presenting the company's financial results by illustrating how business activities have had a positive or negative impact on the social, environmental and economic contexts in which the company operates (Institute of Directors Southern Africa 2009, p. 11). In so doing, the IR should give information on both short term needs and long term value creation (Institute of Directors Southern Africa 2009, p. 12). Rather than strict rules, the King III provides guidelines on how to prepare an IR based on the "apply or explain approach" (KPMG 2009).

At an international level, the importance of shared standards for integrated reporting has been also discussed by international standard setters, companies and accounting bodies. In 2011, the International Integrated Reporting Council (IIRC) published a discussion paper specifying the main principles that a successful IR should apply (Abeysekera 2013; IIRC 2011). According to this discussion paper, IR should communicate how companies achieve their strategic objectives integrating financial, environmental and social information, and giving a retrospective and prospective vision of the company's performance as a whole (Piermattei and Ventoruzzo 2011). Importantly, in April 2013, the IIRC presented the Consultation Draft (CD) of the IR Framework, the first official international guide of principles and content elements necessary for drawing up an IR (IIRC 2013).

Given the increasing relevance of integrated reporting in the South African context, where the IR is compulsory for many companies, this chapter analyses the experience of Eskom, a South African electricity supply company. The aim is to analyse the IR of the company during the period 2011–2012 on the light of the guiding principles and content elements presented within the CD, published by the IIRC.[2]

After a brief overview of the environmental, social and economic contexts in which Eskom operates, Sects. 18.3 and 18.4 analyse in detail the main content elements and guiding principles of the 2011–2012 IR in light of the guidelines provided by the CD. The aim is to explore whether, and how, these guidelines can be applied and eventually adapted to the specific context of a public electric power company.

Company Profile) and paragraphs related to the description of the Guiding Principles of the IR of Eskom (Sects. 18.4, 18.4.1–18.4.6) can be assigned to Francesca Ceccacci.

[2] The 2011–2012 Integrated Report of Eskom analysed in this chapter is publicly available on the company website: http://financialresults.co.za/2012/eskom_ar2012/integrated-report/index.php

18.2   The Case of Eskom: Company Profile

Eskom was established in 1923 and is currently the main electricity supplier in South Africa. Wholly owned by the South African government since 2002, Eskom generates and transmits electricity to various customer companies, which in turn redistribute electricity to businesses and households. Eskom generates and transmits electricity to about 3,000 industrial customers, 1,000 mining customers, 50,000 commercial customers and 84,000 agricultural customers.[3]

Being a South African public company, Eskom must comply with the regulations issued by the National Energy Regulation of South Africa (NERSA) and the National Nuclear Regulator. Eskom also operates under the jurisdiction of the Department of Environmental Affairs, provincial and local governments, which take care of the South African public and environmental interests.[4] Furthermore, Eskom is subject to the NERSA electricity tariffs plan and to the Government's Integrated Resource Plan 2010. The latter established the future electricity generation priorities in South Africa.[5]

Over the last few years Eskom has reorganized the functional structure of its businesses, identifying three main functional divisions (Fig. 18.1—see Eskom 2012, pp. 24):

- Line functions that run the business and the value creation process (Generation, Transmission, Distribution, and Group Customer services).
- Service functions which manage Eskom's assets and optimise value chain activities (Human Resources, Technology and Commercial, Finance and Group Capital).
- Strategic functions that provide broader strategic support to the group (Enterprise Development and Sustainability).

The head office of Eskom is in Johannesburg and operates through its brand offices located all over South Africa. In December 2008, Eskom established an office in London to control the quality of the equipment manufactured for the "Capital Expansion Program"[6] . Even though a large part of the business activities are performed in South Africa, Eskom has invested beyond South African boundaries (within the so called Southern African Development Communities),

---

[3] Ranked among the top twenty utilities in the world by generation capacity, Eskom generates enough electricity to provide 95 % of the electricity requirements in South Africa and 45 % of the overall electricity consumption in Africa. Eskom sells electricity directly to approximately 138,000 business customers and supplies electricity to 4.7 million residential customers, equal to 40 % of all residential customers (including prepaid customers) in the country. http://www.eskom.co.za/c/article/223/company-information/

[4] http://www.globalelectricity.org/en/index.jsp?p=256

[5] http://www.globalelectricity.org/en/index.jsp?p=256

[6] By 2018, Eskom's Capital Expansion Program aims to increase electricity demand and diversify Eskom's energy sources. Through the exploitation of new power plants, Eskom is planning to increase its generation capacity by 17,120 MW and its transmission lines by 4,700 km. See http://www.eskom.co.za/c/article/223/company-information/

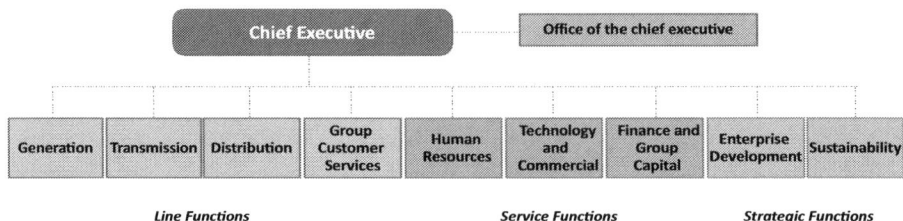

Fig. 18.1 Eskom's line, service and strategic functions (*Source*: adapted from Eskom 2012, pp. 24)

building additional power stations and power lines to meet the increased demand for electricity and to diversify the energy sources of the company.[7] Among the different Eskom subsidiaries it is worthwhile to acknowledge the following:

- the Eskom Enterprises group which provides support for the capital expansion programme for all Eskom Holding SOC Limited divisions;
- Escap SOC Limited which manages and insures Eskom's business risk;
- Eskom Finance Company SOC Limited grants home loans to Eskom employees;
- The Eskom Development Foundation NPC, a non-profit company that manages Eskom's corporate social investment.

Following the prescriptions of GRI and King III, Eskom published its first IR in 2012 (Eskom 2012). The following two sections (3–4) analyse the structures of Eskom's IR in 2011–2012 in light of the content elements and guiding principles of the CD.

18.3   Eskom's IR in 2011–2012: Content Elements Analysis

Recently, the reporting system of Eskom combined sustainability and financial information in the attempt to meet the information needs of a wide number of stakeholders. Being a member of the IIRC pilot programme (Eskom 2012, pp. 9) and publishing its first IR for 2011–2012 (from April 2011 to March 2012), Eskom adopted the main guiding principles and content elements described in the IIRC 2011 discussion paper. Moreover, Eskom formed an "Integrated Reporting Steering Committee" which is responsible for removing barriers to inter-departmental collaboration and for ensuring coherence in the IR system (Eskom 2012, pp. 8). In line with the IIRC content elements, Eskom's 2011–2012 IR is divided into the following nine sections:

1. *"Leadership Overview"* describes the top management view of the environment in which Eskom operates, the achievements for the year and the strategic objectives;

---

[7] http://www.eskom.co.za/c/article/223/company-information/

2. *"About the company"* illustrates the nature of the company's business and legal structure, strategic objectives and values;
3. *"Corporate Governance"* describes the composition of the board and the executive management committees, and specifies the board of directors' responsibilities and remuneration policies;
4. *"Operating Context"* details the principal material issues, opportunities and risks encountered throughout the year;
5. *"Value Chain Performance"* describes the value creation process and the main results achieved, as well as the impact of material issues;
6. *"Service and Strategic Functions"* provides information about the management and the monitoring of financial performance, safety, quality management, skills, transformation and employment equity, regulation and legal, supplier development and localisation, group IT, delivery unit, research and technology, environmental management, climate change and corporate social investment;
7. *"Financial Performance"* summarises the financial results of Eskom for 2011–2012;
8. *"Future outlook"* describes the future strategic priorities of Eskom over the next 5 years;
9. *"Appendices"* shows charts of the key non-financial indicators for each material issue described throughout the report, and the stakeholders' engagement matrix. Furthermore, information about the sustainability responsiveness of the company is provided.

Subsequently, we analyse the sections mentioned above in light of the content elements proposed by the CD (i.e. organizational overview and external environment, governance, opportunities and risks, strategy and resource allocation, business model, performance and future outlook).

18.3.1 Organizational Overview and External Environment

In line with the CD, Eskom's IR gives a brief overview of the mission and vision of the company, as well as of the external environment in which it operates. Particularly, the IR provides an analysis of the most relevant issues determined in accordance with company stakeholders' requests, including the company's core objectives and strategic activities at the base of the value creation process of the firm (Eskom 2012, pp. 8–9).[8]

Before describing the organizational context in which the company operates, the introductory section of the IR introduces Eskom's value chain activities and discloses the performance achieved during the year in terms of volume of electricity

---

[8] Because of the public nature of the company, Eskom's IR speaks to a wide range of stakeholders, which include employees and unions; the government and parliament; lenders, analysts and investors; customers and regulators; industry experts, academics and the media; business groups, civil society and non-governmental organizations (NGOs); and suppliers and contractors (Eskom 2012, pp. 10).

generated (GW/h). To make the report easier to read, the introductory section of the IR shows a navigation panel in which icons are used to indicate the material issues—the most relevant issues relating to stakeholders—(Eskom 2012, table of contents).

In addition to the information provided in the introductory section of the report, a large part of the information relating to the culture, competitive landscape and external environment of the company is briefly introduced in the "letter from the Chairman" and in the "report of the CEO" (the leadership overview section). In the "letter from the Chairman", Zola Tsotsi, (Eskom's Chairman) has acknowledged that, being a state owned company, Eskom cannot merely rely on commercial objectives and needs to take care of the "overall value added to the lives of the public" (Eskom 2012, pp. 12). From this point of view, Eskom's main goal is to "provide sustainable electricity solutions to stimulate the economy and improve the quality of life of the people of South Africa and of the foreign regions" (Eskom 2012, pp. 12).

In particular, the "report of the CEO", describes the financial, sustainable, social and human capital investments made from 2011 to 2012 and introduces the main operational challenges for the company in the short, medium and long term. In this context, the social and environmental investments made in promoting the government's "New Growth Path"[9] are highlighted, together with the strategies for improving the company's competitive advantage and increasing the efficiency of human and operational skills (Eskom 2012, pp. 17). Similar to the "letter from the Chairman", the "report of the CEO" gives information about organization's strategic activities in 2011–2012 and also the 2012–2013 strategic priorities.

Finally, the section "About the company" completes the overview of the company and of its external environment by describing the company's divisional structure, culture, ethics, values and strategic objectives.

18.3.2 Governance

Within Eskom IR, an ad hoc section (titled "Corporate Governance") is devoted to the description of the content element "Governance". Based on the concept of "Effective Ethical Leadership" (Eskom 2012, pp. 28), the corporate governance section of the IR provides an insight into the responsibilities and actions taken by the company's board of directors to monitor its strategic direction, governance and sustainability. After a description of the appointed committees (Executive

---

[9] In 2010 the South African Government released the Framework of the New Economic Growth Path with the aim of enhancing growth, employment creation and equity (http://www.info.gov.za/aboutgovt/programmes/new-growth-path/).

Eskom contributes to this by supplying reliable, sustainable and cost effective energy to fuel South Africa's power-intensive core industries (Eskom 2012, pp. 54,)

management committee, Audit and risk committee, Investment and finance committee, Tender committee, Social ethics and sustainability committee and People and governance committee), the IR gives concise information about the board's responsibilities to comply with government regulations, manage the risks that could hinder the company's assets integrity, promote innovation and guide the value creation process (Eskom 2012, pp. 30–33).

In accordance with section 4B/4.11 of the Governance content element of the CD, Eskom's IR gives information about the relationship with the South African Government (Eskom's sole shareholder) and how it influences the strategic orientation of the company. Every year, Eskom and the Minister of Public Enterprises (Government Representative) meet together in order to establish the performances and targets to achieve in accordance with the Public Finance Management Act of South Africa[10] (Eskom 2012, pp. 35). Furthermore, the IR describes Eskom's compliance with local and international regulations.

Taking into account point 4B of the CD, Eskom's IR discloses quantitative and qualitative information about the remuneration policies of the company (IIRC 2013, pp. 25; Eskom 2012, pp. 38–40). Remuneration policies of Eskom aim at attracting and retaining skilled and high-performing employees. To be able to engage the most qualified workforce, Eskom has established a series of remuneration principles by which the company strives to:

- keep its market position stable;
- provide market related remuneration structures;
- maintain external competitiveness to attract and retain key skills;
- follow the lead-lag market approach;
- ensure internal equity through defensible differentials in pay and benefits;
- remunerate employees in accordance with their employment level.

Further detailed information is also provided about the non-executive, executive, management and employee total remuneration for 2011 (Eskom 2012, pp. 40).

18.3.3 Strategy and Resource Allocation, the Opportunities and Risks

In the "Operating Context" section of the IR, Eskom provides detailed information about the strategic objectives of the firm, agreed on in September 2011, highlighting the resource allocation plans and the main risks encountered. In line with the content elements "Strategy and resource allocation" and "Opportunities and risks" outlined in the CD (IIRC 2013, pp. 26), the "Operating Context" section of Eskom's IR illustrates the material issues and risks that in the view of the top management and stakeholders of Eskom "can potentially affect the company's

---

[10] The Public Finance Management Act (PFMA) is one of the most relevant legislations in South Africa and encourages good financial management to maximize service delivery, efficiently and effectively exploit the limited resources employed. http://www.treasury.gov.za/legislation/PFMA/

achievement of its strategic objectives" (Eskom 2012, pp. 42). A table on page 42 of Eskom's IR links "the strategic objectives of the firm and the issues considered material to the value chain, key performance indicators and the company's stakeholder engagement" (Eskom 2012, pp. 42).

The eight "material issues" relevant to the company's value creation, correspond to the strategic objectives that the company aims to pursue. The following three main "material issues" are at the base of value creation in Eskom and for this reason are called "building blocks" (Eskom 2012, pp. 26):

1. set up the company for success;
2. ensure the company's financial sustainability;
3. become a high performance utility.

Directly linked to the "building blocks" listed above, the other five material issues are as follows:

1. leading and partnering to keep the lights on;
2. reducing the company's carbon footprint and pursuing low-carbon growth opportunities;
3. securing future resource requirements, mandates and the required enabling environment;
4. implementing coal haulage and the road-to-rail migration plan;
5. pursuing private sector participation.

In the "About the company" section, Eskom's IR illustrates the company's purpose, values and material issues through the picture of a Greek temple façade. The top of the temple (the pediment) represents the purpose of the firm and the columns represent the material issues. These issues are built upon the three building blocks and the company's culture and values, which are represented by the base of the temple (Fig. 18.2).

"ZIICSE"—Zero Harm, Integrity, Innovation, Sinobuntu (i.e. caring), Customer satisfaction, Excellence—is the acronym used to describe the most relevant values for top management, which support the key strategic initiatives (i.e. to provide safe and innovative electricity solutions, to maintain the integrity of the electricity infrastructures and to improve the quality of the services delivered in the socio-economic environment in which Eskom operates).

In line with the request of section 4D/4.20 of the CD to disclose how strategies "are influenced by/respond to the external environment" (IIRC 2013, pp. 26), the "Value Chain Performance" section of Eskom's IR describes the performance achieved throughout the generation, transmission and distribution of electricity in South Africa and highlights its impact on the environment and the social community in which the company operates.

In line with the "Opportunities and risks" content element of the CD, the "Operating Context" section of the IR highlights the likelihood of opportunities and risks for each material issue. After having explained the main causes of risk, the IR describes the actions taken to minimise and mitigate them (e.g. "A project to coordinate a comprehensive, synchronised maintenance and refurbishment plan is under way. . . to improve plant and grid efficiency while reducing the possibility of plant failure") (Eskom 2012, pp. 48). In compliance with the global and South

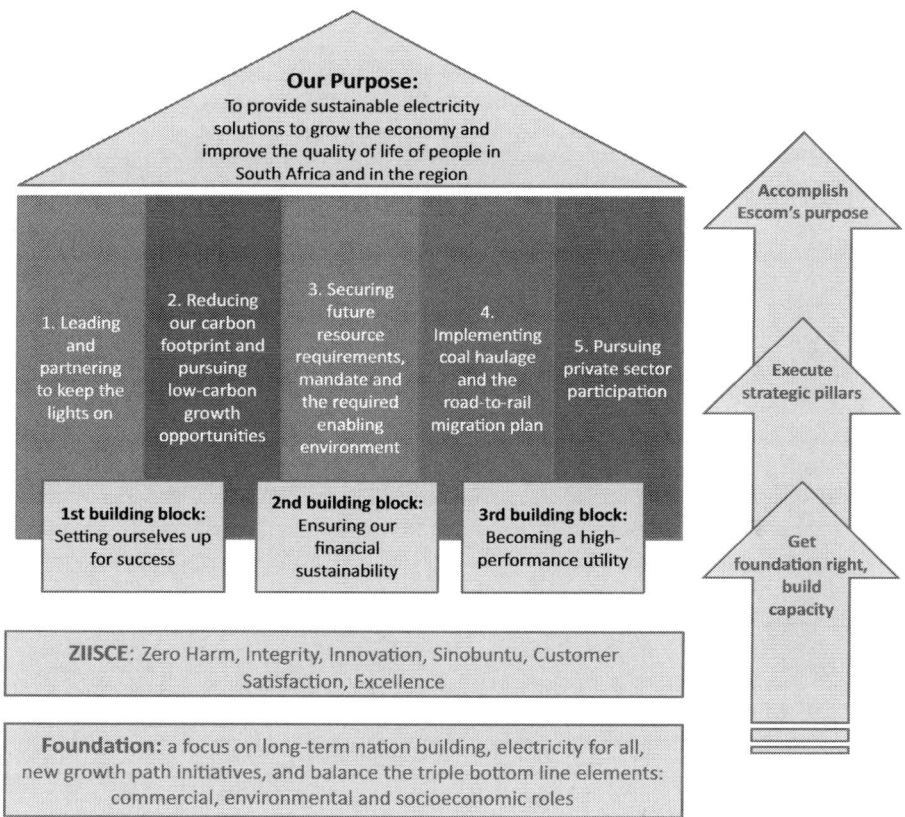

Fig. 18.2 Eskom's purpose, strategic objectives and values (*Source*: adapted from Eskom 2012, pp. 26)

African best governance practices, Eskom's IR highlights the importance of providing adequate and timely plant maintenance controls in order to reduce safety risks. In this context, considering for example nuclear electricity generation, Eskom adopts the following three-tier system of nuclear safety governance (Eskom 2012, pp. 34):

- top tier: social, ethics and sustainability committee;
- middle tier: nuclear management sub-tier, which gives recommendations on nuclear policies, standards and benchmarks;
- safety review committees, which evaluate the nuclear safety issues with the help of company experts.

18.3.4 Business Model

Eskom's IR does not reserve a specific section to the description of the company's business model, but focuses on the value chain activities in the section "Value Chain Performance". The main activities described in this section as follows (Eskom 2012, pp. 58):

- construction (managed by the service functions);
- primary energy consumption (managed by the service functions);
- generating electricity;
- transmitting and distributing;
- customer service;
- service and strategic function key issues (health, safety, environmental and quality issues are addressed in this section);
- financial performance.

The section "Value Chain Performance" accurately describes each activity of the value chain, identifying the company's key resources employed, the outputs produced and outcomes achieved (operational highlights), the most significant challenges and opportunities for each activity (operational challenges), and the company's future focus (future focus areas). In line with section 4E/4.22 of the CD, Eskom's IR gives high attention to the internal and external key outcomes of the value chain activities of the company.

The "Value Chain Performance" also provides information about costs and revenues from the transmission, distribution and sale of electricity from 2010. Further non-financial data are also provided about the company's infrastructure and technical performance, comparing the actual achievements to the targets budgeted for 2012 and to the results of the previous year.

18.3.5 Performance

In line with the "Performance" content element (section 4F) of the CD, IR discloses financial and non-financial indicators to provide information on how positive and negative performances impact on the value creation activities of the firm (IIRC 2013, pp. 28). Particularly, the "Value Chain Performance" section combines financial and non-financial indicators on the basis of the value chain activities performed and the main future opportunities for the company. In this context financial and non-financial information is provided through three different charts (Eskom 2012, pp. 59–61):

- The capital expenditures chart, describing the capital expenditures per value chain division (Construction, Generation, Transmission and Distribution) excluding capitalised borrowing costs (Eskom 2012, pp. 59).
- The capital expansion projects progress, explaining the resources employed in each of the South African region in which the company operates (Eskom 2012, pp. 60).

- The projected power station completion schedule, illustrating the timeline of the project accomplished on the basis of the regions and the source of energy exploited (Eskom 2012, pp. 61).

In compliance with the requests of the Minister of Public Enterprise, Eskom's IR also provides a table of the yearly performance objectives, measures and indicators agreed with South African Government (Eskom 2012, pp. 36). To clearly illustrate and recap the most relevant non-financial KPIs, Appendix A shows a table of the KPIs listed according to each material issue described throughout the report. The appendix shows a concise analysis of results of the past 5 years and reports the targets to be achieved by the end of the 6-year corporate strategic plan (2016–2017) (Eskom 2012, pp. 144–151).

Also, the "Financial Performance" section of the IR briefly summarizes the company's financial situation giving information about sales and revenues for the year, operating costs and the Group's cash-flow statements (Eskom 2012, pp. 100).

18.3.6 Future Outlook

Eskom's IR also describes the company's future priorities by presenting a chart of the future orientation approved by the top management and the company's stakeholders. In the section "Financial Outlook", a five-year plan shows the objectives to be achieved by 2016–2017. The main strategic objectives are classified according to the capitals involved in the company value chain (Fig. 18.3).

Based on the 2011–2012 material issues described throughout the report, Eskom's IR also identifies five main material issues to be accomplished for the year 2012–2013 (Eskom 2012, pp. 142), as follows:

1. ensure that employees have a safe working environment;
2. ensure a constant power supply by cutting down on unplanned closures of power stations;
3. ensure financial sustainability;
4. deliver high quality capacity expansion programmes;
5. foster the firm's innovation process to achieve operational excellence.

The five year plan shows the strategic orientation of Eskom, which focuses on fostering intellectual and human resource skills, socio-economic performance and environmental sustainability of the operations through the value creation processes.

After having described the most relevant content elements within the 2011–2012 Eskom's IR, next we analyse the report in light of the CD's guiding principles.

18.4   Analysis of the Guiding Principles in Eskom's IR

As discussed in the previous sections, the CD proposes a series of guiding principles necessary for the organization of the content elements and the information disclosed within an IR.

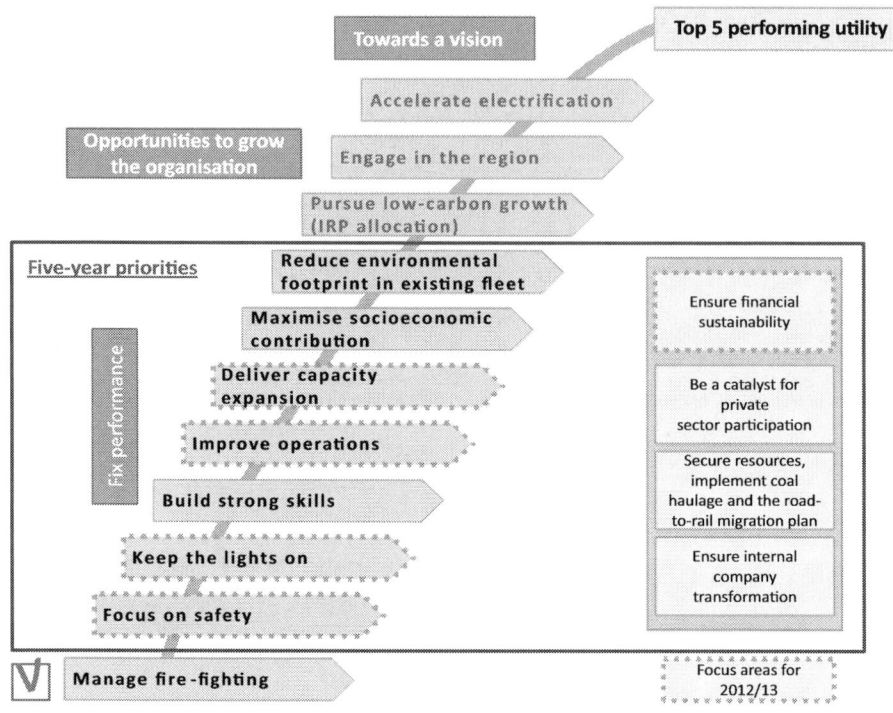

Fig. 18.3 Eskom's future outlook (*Source*: adapted from Eskom 2012, pp. 141)

18.4.1 Connectivity of Information

In line with the connectivity of information principles of the CD, Eskom's IR provides an overall understanding of the content elements and of their interconnections throughout the value creation process of the firm (IIRC 2013, pp. 18). The connectivity of the information is continuous, linking together qualitative and quantitative information and highlighting the interactions between the different capitals involved in the value creation process. This interaction is supported by a navigation panel, presented on the contents page of the IR, which illustrates the icons used throughout the report and symbolizes each of the material issues discussed. Furthermore, the navigation panel links the data contained in the various sections of the IR, facilitating understanding, conciseness and reliability of the information provided.

According to section 3B/3.11 of the connectivity principle, the "Value Chain Performance" section of the IR illustrates financial and non-financial indicators integrating them with the description of the most relevant activities in the value chain and giving a comprehensive picture of company's value creation over time. Furthermore, on the basis of the connectivity principle of the CD (Section 3B/3.10), the section "Value Chain Performance" combines data of past (operational highlights), present (operational opportunities) and future (future focus areas) activities for each part of the company's value chain. This structure facilitates IR users in understanding the performance achieved in the past and during the year, having an accurate picture of the company's future actions for each value chain activity (Eskom 2012, pp. 58–83).

18.4.2 Stakeholder Responsiveness

The IR highlights the need to build "extensive, on-going stakeholder" relationships (Stakeholder responsiveness principle) with a wide range of stakeholders (Eskom 2012, pp. 16). Owned by the South African government, Eskom maintains regular contact with government departments (including the Department of Public Enterprises, the Department of Energy, the Department of Water Affairs and the National Treasury) local governments and trade unions (Eskom 2012, pp. 16).

The stakeholders' engagement in the IR is crucial for determining which issues are considered "material" for the top management of Eskom and its stakeholders. In line with section 3C/3.18 of the CD (IIRC 2013, pp. 20), Appendix B of the IR gives information about the material issues discussed with the company's stakeholders (Eskom 2012, pp. 152).

18.4.3 Materiality and Conciseness

Eskom's IR gives great attention to the materiality and conciseness of information disclosed, dedicating a specific section (Operating Context) to the description of material issues. Throughout Eskom's IR, qualitative and quantitative issues relating to business operations and strategic objectives of the company are linked together to enhance the comparability and the conciseness of the information provided.

Also, the section "Value Chain Performance" summarises the past activities (operational highlights), present (operational opportunities) and future actions (future focus areas) indicated in a bullet point list. The bullet points facilitate the reader in understanding and visualizing the most relevant information about the outcomes achieved throughout the year, the resources employed and the future expectations of the company (Eskom 2012, pp. 58–83). The conciseness of the report is also highlighted by the continuous reference to information available on the company's website.

18.4.4 Reliability and Completeness

In line with the guiding principle of completeness of the CD (section 3E), the "Value Chain Performance" section of Eskom's IR provides positive and negative information about company's activities. For example, the IR gives detailed information about the employees' mortality rate and about the actions taken to reduce the possibility for further accidents to occur (Zero Harm value).

The idea of reliability of information is enhanced by the external independent assurance statements reported in the Appendices, as well as by the stakeholders' engagement matrix which shows the level of involvement of stakeholders in the preparation of the IR.

18.4.5 Consistency and Comparability

The consistency and comparability of the information provided is one of the guiding principles of the report, which links indicators of different natures (financial and non-financial) and compares the results achieved throughout the years. The "Financial Performance" section of the IR reports the key figures of the firm's balance sheet, income statement and cash-flow statement, comparing results with the previous year's achievements. The consistency of the non-financial data provided in the IR is visible in Appendix A, which compares non-financial KPIs of the past 5 years (Eskom 2012, pp. 144–151).

The comparability of the information is notable in the sections "Value Chain Performance" and "Service and Strategic Functions", which analyse financial and non-financial indicators in the form of ratios over the years. The comparability principle proposed in the CD is also visible in the description of the construction activity of the Eskom's value chain, in which a chart compares the power stations' performance throughout the regions of South African.

18.4.6 Strategic Focus and Future Orientation

Eskom's IR discloses significant strategic information, illustrating in detail the opportunities and risks of each strategic objective (Eskom 2012, pp. 42–56). The "Value Chain Performance" section gives information about the availability and quality of the capitals employed, presenting the results achieved during the year 2011–2012.

Furthermore, considering point 3A/3.4 of the CD, the section "Future Priorities" of Eskom's IR provides information about the firm's future orientation, unveiling Eskom's strategic priorities that are to be achieved by 2016 and describes the activities and the capitals involved for achieving strategic objectives (2012–2013).

Discussion and Conclusions

This chapter analyses Eskom's IR in light of the content elements and the guiding principles suggested in the 2013 CD of the IIRC. It is interesting to note that Eskom's IR gives particular attention to the description of the organization's material issues and strategic objectives, which are annually decided in accordance with the principal stakeholders of the company. Eskom's past and present performance and future strategic priorities are continuously described throughout the report, highlighting positive and negative information. The use of the interlinking navigation panel contributes to connect data and to transform the IR into a fluent narration of the most relevant elements that have affected the company's value creation process. This process is explained, disclosing financial and non-financial KPIs and comparing them with the previous year's achievements. Qualitative and quantitative information are both illustrated, tracing the storyline of the firm's value creation.

Furthermore, the IR clearly shows the values and culture (ZIICSE) which inform the strategic orientation of the company. In the achievement of the strategic purpose, the values underpin the material issues which are relevant "to provide sustainable electricity solutions to stimulate the economy and improve the quality of life of people in South Africa and in the region" (Eskom 2012, pp. 16).

References

Abeysekera I (2013) A template for integrated reporting. J Intellect Capital 14(2):227–245

Eskom (2012) Shift performance, grow sustainably: integrated report. Available at http://financialresults.co.za/2012/eskom_ar2012/integrated-report/index.php. Accessed 27 June 2013

Institute of Directors Southern Africa (2009) King code of governance for South Africa. Available: http://www.ecgi.org/codes/code.php?code_id=262. Accessed 10 July 2013

IIRC (2011) Towards integrated reporting – communicating value in the 21st century, discussion paper. New York: IIRC. Available at http://theiirc.org/wp-content/uploads/2011/09/IR-Discussion-Paper-2011_spreads.pdf. Accessed 12 June 2013.

IIRC (2013) Consultation draft of the international <IR> framework. Available: http://www.theiirc.org/wp-content/uploads/Consultation-Draft/Consultation-Draft-of-the-InternationalIRFramework.pdf. Accessed 12 June 2013

KPMG (2009) Corporate governance & King 3. Available at http://www.kpmg.com/ZA/en/IssuesAndInsights/ArticlesPublications/Tax-and-Legal-Publications/Documents/Corporate%20Governance%20and%20King%203.pdf. Accessed 23 June 2013

KPMG (2012) Integrated reporting: performance inside through better business reporting. Issue 2. http://www.kpmg.com/Global/en/IssuesAndInsights/ArticlesPublications/integrated-reporting/Documents/integrated-reporting-issue-2.pdf. Accessed 23 June 2013

Piermattei L, Ventoruzzo F (2011) Dall'Integrated reporting all'Integrated management. Harv Bus Rev 11:62–66

The Case of HERA

Pasquale Ruggiero and Patrizio Monfardini

Abstract

In the raising complexity of the environment within which companies have to currently operate, the drawing up of integrated reporting seems to be one of the most challenging and demanding tasks for any company, which have to deal both with an increasing number of powerful stakeholders and provide its managers with increasingly complex and useful information. The present chapter analyses the approach and the experience of the HERA Group. We will outline the business features, its evolution since operations began and the similarities and differences of the HERA Sustainability Report with the Integrated Reporting framework. This case study is an important and informative example of how integrated reporting is a useful tool for governing particular kind of firm such as HERA. It is owned by both private investors and public administrations whilst operating in the public services sector.

P. Ruggiero (✉)
Brighton Business School, University of Brighton,
Brighton, UK

Department of Business and Law, University of Siena, Siena, Italy
e-mail: p.ruggiero@brighton.ac.uk; ruggiero@unisi.it

P. Monfardini
Department of Economic and Business Sciences, University of Cagliari, Cagliari, Italy
e-mail: monfardini@unica.it

C. Busco et al. (eds.), *Integrated Reporting*, DOI 10.1007/978-3-319-02168-3_19,
© Springer International Publishing Switzerland 2013

19.1 Introduction[1]

"Today, there are growing expectations that businesses do more than simply turn a profit. They must operate (and be perceived to operate) in a manner that is responsible, ethical and sustainable, that minimises negative impacts on the environment, that takes into consideration the varied needs of a spectrum of stakeholders, and that positively contributes to the communities in which they operate and the planet generally". These words have been used by Brendan Sheridan (2012: p. 1), Director of the Financial Reporting Technical Services in Deloitte, to define the growing complexity that organisations have to face when they operate. In the accounting and management field, integrated reports are increasingly considered as one of the most important instruments through which the aforesaid objective can be accomplished. All the information contained in an integrated report can be useful within the organisation for managerial purposes at the different organisational levels as well as outside the organisation for various key stakeholders. For decision-making purposes, it seems important to provide managers with tools that enable them to see the whole simplified "picture" of all the different results an organisation is achieving. Similarly, any external stakeholder needs to know the overall results of the organisation in order to better invest resources and to be able to assess organisational performance (Monfardini et al. 2013).

Looking at the flow of information, Schaltegger and Wagner (2006) have classified organisations' performance management, measurement and reporting systems as 'outside-inward' and/or 'inside-outward' driven. The former are based on issues stemming from the public debate and define measurement and management activities on these issues; the latter starts from the business strategy and the analysis of the relevant issues for the effective implementation of the strategy. According to this classification, it seems possible to clearly define a boundary between an organisation and the environment within which it operates and by which is influenced. Furthermore, both the aforesaid approaches seems to assign to performance management, measurement and reporting systems a functionalistic role aiming at representing the reality outside or inside the organisation in order to carry out more efficient and effective decision making. Despite these interpretations, the actual situation is much more complex. A first problem is related to the nature of an organisation. Until a recent past, an organisation has been considered the way through which people act together in order to be able to produce goods and services at a lower cost level (Williamson 1985). Differently nowadays, single organisations are no more considered as being able to produce goods and services suitable to satisfy the increasing complexity of customers' needs and demand. Organizations are called on to work in a more cooperative than competitive way (Nahapiet and Ghoshal 1998). Both in the public and the private sector, networks are considered the new organisational model suitable for implementing more efficient and effective value production processes (Powell 1990).

---

[1] The authors are very grateful to the HERA company, especially to Dott. Filippo Bocchi—Director of the Corporate Social Responsibility Department—for the support provided during the drawing up of the case study.

The growing number of interacting actors and the possible adoption of moral hazard behaviours by them could increase the transaction costs instead of decreasing them. In this context, accounting systems, especially management accounting ones, are increasingly considered a tool able to foster and facilitate the relationships at the inter-organisational level between two or more actors having a positive impact on transaction costs (Barretta and Busco 2011; Mouritsen and Thrane 2006; Hakansson and Lind 2004; Dekker 2004). Therefore, management accounting systems have to play a multitude of roles in an ever increasingly complex situation. The boundaries between an organisation and its environment of reference become difficult to be defined. Relationships among actors are more and more different in nature and variable in time (Birnberg 1998).

In the public sector the aforesaid environmental complexity is clearly highly present. The increasing collaboration between private and public sector organisations in producing and providing public services makes the environment highly variable and unpredictable (Goldsmith and Eggers 2004). Many are the reasons of such variability and unpredictability, as well as the difficulties in defining the concept of value being produced (Moore 1995) and the potentially contrasting interests of the different organisations involved in public services production and provision processes (Barretta and Ruggiero 2008; Barretta et al. 2008). Furthermore, organisations with a private legal status owned by public administrations and private investors are in charge of producing and providing public services. In these kinds of organisations, even two different value systems could clash within the same organisational structure. In front of this complexity and of the different roles management accounting systems are called to play in the aforesaid reality, many scholars and professionals consider the integrated reporting as a new tool able to cope with the potential problems that could derive from the increasing complexity within which public organisation or public owned organisations have to live.

Because of all these features, the aims of this chapter are to present, analyse and discuss the integrated reporting system that an Italian multi-utility has developed along the last 11 years. To this end, in the next sections after a brief overview of the company, the structure and the contents of the Sustainability Report are presented, discussed and compared with the provisions contained in the Consultation Draft (CD) of the international Integrated Reporting Framework (IR). Successively a discussion of the case proposed and some final remarks are presented.

19.2 The Integrated Reporting System in HERA

19.2.1 The HERA Group: An Overview

Hera is one of the main multi-utility operating in Italy providing services to about three million of customers dwelling in 240 municipalities located in ten Provinces (Ancona, Bologna, Ferrara, Firenze, Forlì-Cesena, Modena, Ravenna, Rimini, Pesaro and Urbino) in the Centre-North-East of the Italian peninsula. In particular, the HERA group operates in different service sectors: energy, water and waste management.

Fig. 19.1 HERA reference territory. *Source*: HERA business plan 2012–2016

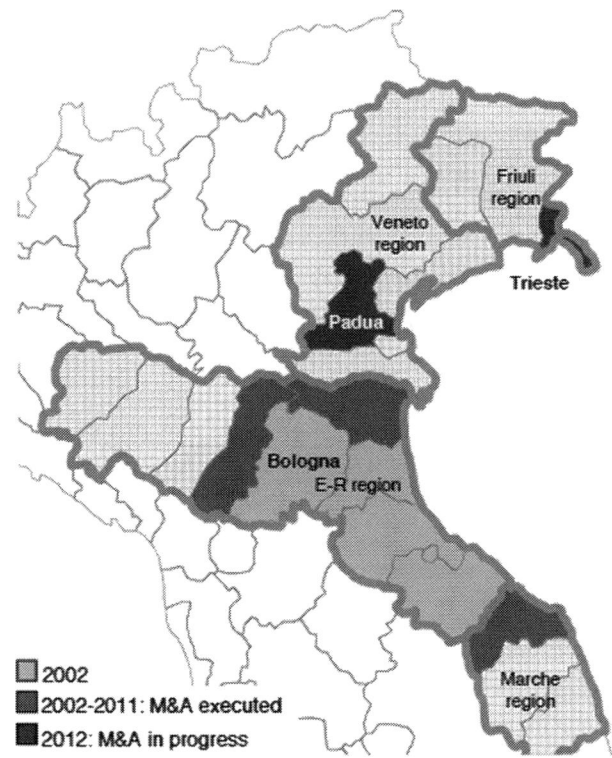

The group was established at the end of 2002 through one of the most important business combination operation ever realised within the Italian public utilities sector. The business combination involved 11 local public service concerns. After its establishment, the company was partly privatised by placing the 44.5 % of the share capital on the Milan Stock Exchange. During the following years, the group has continued to grow by incorporating other companies, operating in the energy, water and waste management sectors, located in the territorial area where the group provides the public services (Fig. 19.1).

Coherently with its strategic planning 2012–2016, in 2013 the HERA group has concluded the incorporation of the AcegasAps Holding (the largest multi-utility in North-Eastern Italy) becoming the second multi-utility in Italy. In 2012 the whole group has 6,629 employees and it generates 4,223 of indirect employment.

The HERA organisational structure is different from other multi-utilities. The HERA group is characterised by the existence of a financial holding at the top of the organisational structure. This choice aims at achieving a more efficient and effective business and operational integration. The Holding is structured in Central Divisions to set-up, support and control the activities carried out by the different organisations that are part of the group. The divisional structure should guarantee an integrated group perspective and favours the exploitation of synergies. The holding also has General Divisions which steer and coordinate the strategic areas of relevant

Table 19.1   HERA main financial results

Financial data (*mln* €)	2002–2012	2012	2011	2010	2009	2008	2007	2006
Revenues	+15.5 %	4,492.7	4,105.7	3,666.9	4,204.2	3,716.3	2,863.3	2,311.5
Ebitda	+13.2 %	662.0	644.8	607.3	567.3	528.3	453.4	426.7
Ebit	+15.8 %	335.4	334.5	315.4	291.3	280.7	220.6	231.3
Profit before tax	+11.0 %	213.4	221.2	205.6	162.6	188.9	142.5	179.2
Income taxes	+7.4 %	(79.1)	(94.5)	(63.6)	(77.6)	(78.6)	(32.6)	(79.0)
Net profit	+13.9 %	134.4	126.8	142.1	85.0	110.3	109.9	100.2
Minority profit	+16.2 %	15.7	22.2	24.8	13.9	15.5	13.7	10.1
Hera net profit	+13.6 %	118.7	104.6	117.2	71.1	94.8	96.2	90.1

Source: HERA website, accessed July 2013

businesses and also guarantee the operational management of the Group's activities through dedicated business lines. To this end within the Operations General Management area three divisions were established, each of them focused on one of the HERA's core activity sectors.

In addition, the Customer Technical Division has been established, aiming at offering a unified view of the technical service provided to final customers. Finally, because of the strong linkage of the group with the territories within which the activities are carried out, seven local areas have been established to ensure the strengthening and the development of relationships with local stakeholders.

Two committees have been set up for managerial purposes at the holding level:

- the Management Committee: responsible for analysing and sharing policies, strategies and operational planning decisions, while fostering integration between the various functions;
- the Steering Committee: responsible for monitoring the business performance and the level of accomplishment of the different projects planned within the Balanced Scorecard (BSC) system.

The group has shown an increasing positive trend in its economic and financial results during the last years.

Since 2006, as a result of the strategy carried out the HERA's revenues are almost doubled. The Ebitda has raised by approximately 50 %, the Ebit has increased by approximately 40 % and the net profit has increased by approximately 30 %.

Because of the results shown in the Table 19.1, the HERA group has also had a very important performance on the Stock Exchange in 2012. Differently from the trend of the utility sector companies showing a negative performance of approximately 10 %, the HERA group has had a performance of approximately 12 %, exceeding the stock market performance (8.4 %).

The HERA group is composed of various firms operating in different public service sectors and it is owned by public administrations for the majority of the share capital

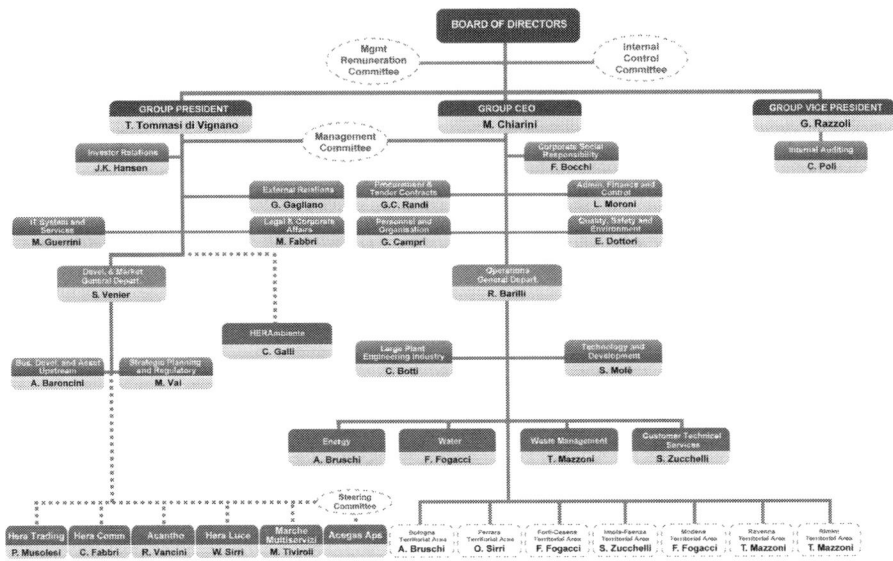

Fig. 19.2 The Hera holding organizational structure. *Source*: HERA website (accessed July 2013)

(189 municipalities own the 61.8 % of the share capital, made up of 1,340,383,538 ordinary shares) but also by private investors who account for approximately 40 % of the share capital. Because of the economic sector within which the group operates and the structure of the ownership, the HERA's top management have to meet the requests coming from groups of interest characterised by different values and objectives. This situation is complex not only for managerial work, but also for the definition of an information system suitable to satisfy the various information needs of the different actors involved in or affected by the HERA group activity.

Since its establishment in 2002, the HERA group decided to disclose more information than those necessary to be complaint with the current legislation. A report able to give more information than the financial-based ones was considered the best way in order to produce more suitable information for the managerial decision-making process, and also to better communicate with the different stakeholders. As written in the 2010 Sustainability Report (p. 5), this report "is a primary tool for reporting on its activities and results in the economic, environmental and social fields, as well as a fundamental tool for providing information to and dialoguing with stakeholders. [...] provides the principles which guide our actions, the performance achieved, the objectives reached compared to stated and future objectives, the results of our dialogue with stakeholders and projects in the field".

19.2.2 The Organisational Aspects of the Sustainability Report

The production of the Sustainability Report has been so pervasive in HERA to produce a deep impact on the organisation. In particular, the publication of the

Sustainability Report has had an impact on the organisational structure of the firm at the holding level and in the producing and disclosing process of the information contained in the report.

From the first point of view a specific organisational structure of the HERA holding has been devoted to the drawing up and to the issuing of the Sustainability Report. Only after 3 years from its establishment and the disclosing of two reports, in May the CSR Organisational Unit was established in a staff position to the Chief Executive Officer. From 2010 the Organisational Unit has been transformed in a Department aiming to ensure that the social responsibility principles are an integral part of corporate planning and management processes. Specifically, the CSR Department is in charge of defining and proposing corporate guidelines concerning corporate social responsibility, reporting on sustainability, ensuring the continued development of the integrated balanced scorecard system with sustainability strategies, and proposing and managing the execution of social responsibility projects. Since the end of 2010, the department has been structured in three different units: the BSC System Management, Sustainability Reporting and CSR Projects.

From the procedural viewpoint, it is worthwhile to highlight that the Sustainability Report is not the mere ex-post result of the combining process of all the information collected by the organisational structure in charge of producing the report. In HERA it seems more correct to speak of an integrating reporting process than a mere document containing integrated information. As showed in the report and on the company website, the Sustainability Report is the final result of a process that starts from the stakeholders and finishes by providing them with the integrated information. As written in the 2012 Sustainability Report (pp. 20–21), "the Mission and Charter of Values expressed in the Code of Ethics dictate the guidelines for corporate conduct and underlie each corporate action and relationship. A shared Mission, Charter of Values and Conduct established in the Code of Ethics is the strategic and cultural framework in which the Business Plan takes shape, results are reported in a transparent way through the Sustainability Report, and economic planning is carried out annually. The Balanced Scorecard system makes it possible to differentiate the corporate strategy and social responsibility policies into specific operational projects managed by managers and middle managers and periodically monitored. These projects are an integral part of the management bonus system. This virtuous cycle of social responsibility within Hera is characterized by numerous initiatives of stakeholder involvement that allow for the examination of legitimate claims and their opportune insertion as part of the corporate policies and the relative implementation instruments" (Fig. 19.3).

In order to soundly integrate the financial and non-financial aspects related with the implementation of the different projects and the company sustainability strategy, some indicators relative to the sustainability strategy have been included in all the different documents. These are part of the planning system such as the strategic plan, the budget and the Balanced Scorecard and, at the same time, the same indicators are included in the pay for performance system of the HERA's managers. In particular, the remuneration policy of the company is based on three main principles. According to the first principle, managers' remunerations are defined according to the level of

Fig. 19.3 The strategy-
operation management cycle
in HERA. *Source*: HERA
sustainability report (2012:
p. 21)

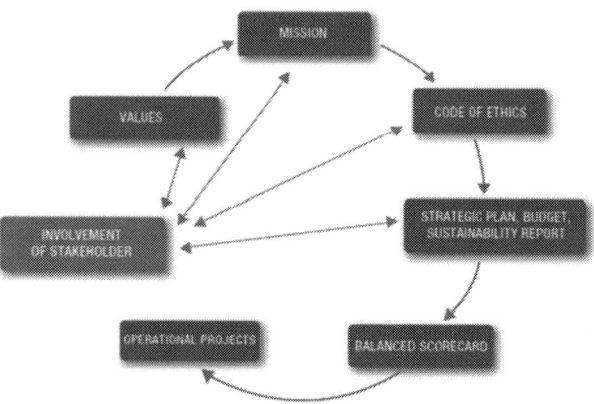

remuneration in the external market, with the aim of ensuring that the company has a comparable remuneration package, but always taking into consideration the objective of both retaining executives and keeping costs down. The second principle is to ensure that the pay grade matches the difficulty of the job. The third principle is to provide constant updates of job evaluation methods, with a view to ensuring uniform and consistent salary analysis and comparisons. Specifically, the implementation of these principles resulted in a series of concrete decisions being taken to:

- link the annual executives' and managers' bonus plan with the Balanced Score-card system, being approved annually by a specific committee;
- limit the maximum bonus at a maximum 30 % of the gross fixed annual salary for general managers and 48 % for executive directors;
- limit upside the difference between the maximum bonus and the performance-related bonus at a maximum of 20 %.

Also a specific committee was established in order to apply and control the implementation of the aforesaid principles and decisions: the Remuneration Committee. This committee is in charge of making proposals to the Board of Directors regarding both the remunerations of the Chairman, the CEO, General managers and the adoption of general criteria for determining fees for management (without prejudice to the fact that the CEO is tasked with defining policies and levels for remuneration of management).

To define and compute the remuneration of managers holding specific offices, the committee has set a maximum limit in order to discourage the taking on of burdensome commitments and to further strengthen the independence of the management. The committee is composed of four independent, non-executive members, including one representing the minority shareholders.

Finally, the document has included the accounts of all the companies in the Hera Group, consolidated using the line-by-line method in the Group's consolidated financial statement. A specific paragraph is dedicated to this issue in order to show all the differences in the scope of the document compared with those of the previous years.

19.2.3 The Content of the Sustainability Report

Even if the Sustainability Report is drawn up by 2002, this paragraph presents the structure and the content of the Sustainability Report published for the 2012 financial year. The 2012 report is the last published and its content is very similar to those published in the previous years. At the beginning of the 2012 report there is an additional section that shows the HERA's results achieved during the last 10 years. As stated by the CEO during the presentation of the report at the public meeting in Modena on the 27 of June 2013, the inclusion of this additional section aims to give stakeholders an overview of the projects and results carried out during that period. Furthermore, this additional section aims at assuring the public administrations that own the majority of the HERA share capital about the linkage of the group with the territory that the public administrations are in charge of governing.

The rest of the document has a structure that is near similar from previous years. This unchanged structure has not to be interpreted as a fault because it results from the adoption of a specific standard of reference: the AA1000. The main aim of this standard is to make any company transparent about the effects of its policies, decisions, actions, products and performances by involving "stakeholders in identifying, understanding and responding to sustainability issues and concerns, and to report, explain and be answerable to stakeholders for decisions, actions and performance" (Accountability UK 2008: p. 6). To reach these objectives, any company has to define a strategy that is contemporarily based on a "comprehensive and balanced understanding of and" able to "response to material issues and stakeholder issues and concerns"; fix goals and standards suitable for evaluation purposes to be compared with the strategy implemented; disclose reliable information to all those subjects have based their activity on the aforesaid corporate strategy and actions. According with this standard, all the information disclosed in the document should respect three principles: inclusivity, materiality and responsiveness. The first principle states "the participation of stakeholders in developing and achieving an accountable and strategic response to sustainability" through "collaborating at all levels, including governance, to achieve better outcomes". The materiality principle specifies that reporting information regards "issue that will influence the decisions, actions and performance of an organization or its stakeholders". The third principle is relative to "how an organization demonstrates it responds to its stakeholders and is accountable to them" (Accountability UK 2008: pp. 10–14).

Other standards have been used to draw up the 2012 Sustainability Report. The standard G3.1 of the Global Reporting Initiative and the GBS Guidelines, have been used to specifically define the content of the report. The first standard defines the principle and the content a sustainability report should apply and disclose. The principles of the GRI standard adopted are similar to those declared in the AA1000 (materiality, stakeholder inclusiveness, completeness, balance, etc.). In terms of the content of the report, the GRI refers to issues more strictly related with the concept of sustainability. According with the standard, "a sustainability report should provide a balanced and reasonable representation of the sustainability performance of a reporting organization—including both positive and negative contributions"

(GRI 3.1, 2011: p. 3). To reach this objective, any sustainability report should give information on an organisation's economic, environmental, and social performance. The GBS standard focuses on the principle for drawing up the social balance sheet. In particular, after having defined an organisation's identity and mission and stakeholders, the standard stresses the necessity to disclose the value added produced by the organisation and its distribution among the different stakeholders. Compared to the other two, this standard is more accounting based (Gruppo Bilancio Sociale 2013).

Coherently with the aforesaid standards, the HERA Sustainability Report is structured in five sections. In summary, "the first two sections of the report provide an account of how the company was created, its identity, mission, corporate strategies, sustainability policies and the key indicators for assessing economic, environmental and social sustainability. The third section describes the methods applied for the dialogue with stakeholders. The fourth section highlights corporate economic returns by means of the methodology based on value added allocated to stakeholders proposed by the GBS. The next sections provide an account of the results achieved for each class of stakeholder, given as performance ratings of a qualitative and quantitative nature and related to the objectives set forth in the previous report and achievement of these. In each section, the stakeholder listening, dialogue and involvement initiatives are indicated" (HERA Sustainability Report 2012: p. 6).

After a brief presentation of the whole document and the principles and guidelines adopted for drawing it up, in the first and second section of the document the history of the company and its mission and values are depicted. Mission and values are then made more practical by singling out some operational principles. These principles are very important because they have been created with the participation of the HERA group's entire workforce, were approved by the Board of Directors of HERA and are taken into consideration when the other document of the planning and budgeting system are drawn up, i.e. Business Plan, Budget, BSC. In particular, with reference to the last above mentioned document, a specific subsection is devoted to disclose the sustainability strategy of the company and its operationalisation through the BSC (Fig. 19.4).

As stated in the HERA Sustainability Report, "each year, the strategic map, updated based on the contents of the business plan, provides a summary of the strategic objectives of the Group and its commitments to stakeholders set forth in the Sustainability Report. To achieve the 29 strategic objectives for the purpose of increasing the company's long term value, 42 priority projects were selected during the 2012 budgeting process. These were assigned to members of the Executive Committee. Of these projects, four fell within the strategic macro-area of 'Involvement of personnel, professional development, dialogue with stakeholders,' six within the strategic macro-area of 'Optimisation of organizational model and software,' five within 'Commercial and tariff policy development', six within 'Improvement of quality, environmental impact and company image', nine within 'Development of plants, raw materials and complementary business activities,' and, lastly, 12 projects within 'Efficiency and rationalization'" (HERA Sustainability Report 2012: p. 16).

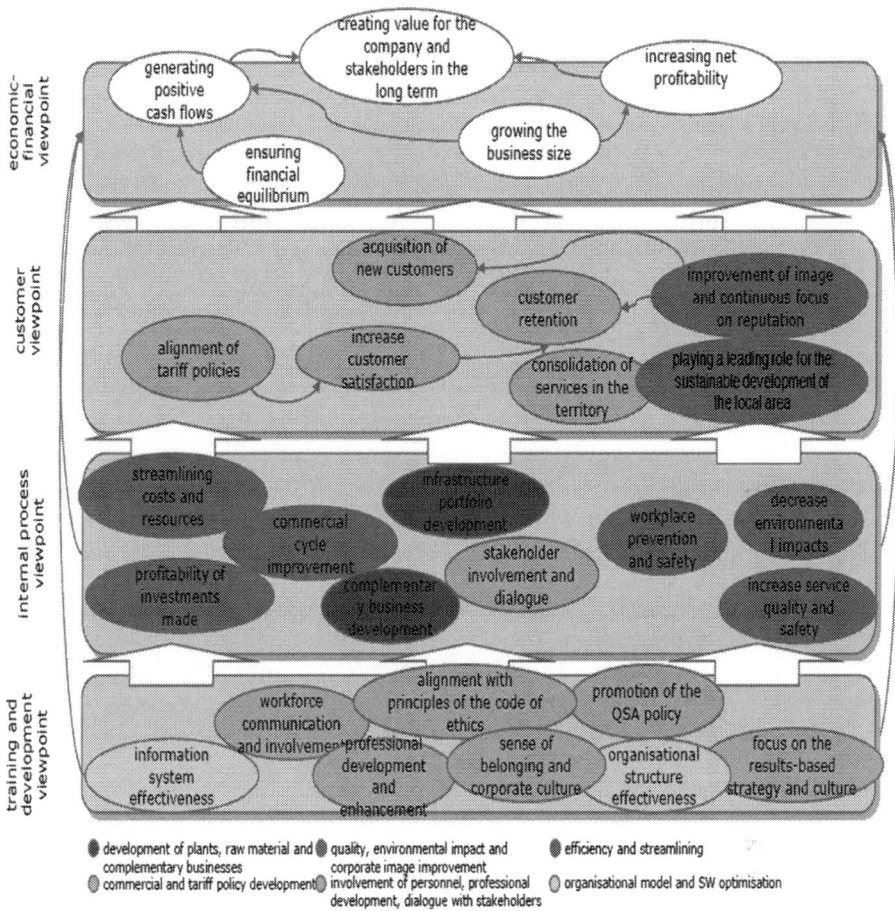

Fig. 19.4 Strategic map of the Hera Group 2013–2016. *Source*: HERA sustainability report (2012: p. 21)

After having shown the strategy map of the whole company, a paragraph is dedicated to specifically single out and discuss the strategic objectives that have the greatest impact on sustainability. All the information provided in the first two sections of the document result in a table containing the KPI from the economic, social and environmental perspective. These indicators refer to a time span of 8 years in order to give the reader of the document more fruitful information about the trend of those indicators and summarise their value at the end of the reporting year.

The third section of the document describes the corporate governance system of the company, highlighting the different boards and commissions operating within the company and describing their members and responsibilities. A wider analysis is dedicated to the company risk management system. In particular, the Quality, Safety

Stakeholder	Main categories	Key issues	Main dialogue and consultation initiatives
Workforce	- Employees - Non-employee workforce - Trade unions	Stability, internal climate, training, career advancement, bonuses, remuneration, life/work balance, equal opportunities, safety, internal communication	- Biennial internal climate survey: following the survey carried out in 2011, 22 improvement actions were defined, 12 of which were developed in 2012, 2 only for the part related to 2012 and 8 are under way. The fifth survey will be carried out in 2013 - Satisfaction survey on the main internal communication tools: all Group workforce involved, around 1,600 questionnaires filled in (around 1,200 of which online), focus groups with around 70 employees, 10 in-depth interviews - Meetings of the Chairman and Chief Executive Officer to illustrate the business plan to all staff (16 meetings held in March 2012, with all staff) - "Passaparola" ("Word of mouth") project: approximately 180 meetings and 1,600 employees involved in at least one meeting - Meetings to present the Sustainability Report 2011 (involving approx. 500 workers) - Application of the Group's Supplementary Collective Labour Agreement signed on 24 March 2010: LaborHERA (technical study for organisational and work quality innovation) met four times in 2012 - 11 workers appointed by the corporate trade unions for the position of SA8000 workers' representative; the first two meetings with the SA8000 management representative were held in December 2012

Fig. 19.5 Example of HERA stakeholders and relative dialogue and consultation initiatives. *Source*: HERA sustainability report (2012: p. 41)

and Environmental Management System and Major regulatory developments most impacting sustainability and the businesses managed are presented.

The fourth section is entirely dedicated to single out who the company's stakeholders are and what the main issues each of them have. This initiative has been carried out in order to create dialogue with stakeholders and consult them (see Fig. 19.5).

In the next section of the report, accounting information is disclosed. The first piece of information sets out the Consolidate Income Statement and the Balance Sheet. In addition, information of interest for the territories of reference of the company is showed. In particular, the following information is disclosed:

• operating investments (non-financial) per sector of activity;
• financial equity investments and acquisitions;
• environmental costs and investments.

In the last part of this section, the value added and its distribution among the company's stakeholders singled out previously are displayed. The information about the value added and its distribution are important because "firstly it enables quantification of the wealth generated by the company, and accounts for how this wealth was generated and how it is allocated to stakeholders; it is therefore useful for comprehending the economic impacts the company produces. Secondly, through this report it connects the Sustainability Report with the Financial Statements. In this sense, production and allocation of value added provides an instrument by means of which we can reconsider the corporate Financial Statements from the vantage point of stakeholders" (HERA Sustainability Report 2012: p. 52).

in millions of Euro	2010		2011		2012	
Workforce	361.9	35.8%	370.0	35.4%	382.1	35.5%
Shareholders	125.2	12.4%	122.6	11.8%	135.1	12.6%
Company	241.1	23.9%	238.1	22.8%	239.0	22.2%
Financial institutions/Banks	115.6	11.4%	119.5	11.5%	134.1	12.5%
Public Administration	164.8	16.3%	190.4	18.3%	183.3	17.0%
Local community	1.8	0.2%	2.0	0.2%	2.0	0.2%
Gross overall value added	**1,010.4**	**100.0%**	**1,042.6**	**100.0%**	**1,075.6**	**100.0%**

Fig. 19.6 Distribution of value added to stakeholders. *Source*: HERA sustainability report (2012: p. 41)

Finally, in this accounting based section some information about the distribution of the value added to the stakeholders localised in the company's territory of reference are provided (Fig. 19.6).

The next seven sections provide information regarding the different stakeholders singled out in section four. In particular, in the different sections the following stakeholders are considered: the workforce, the customers, the shareholders, the financial institutions, the public administrations, the local communities, the environment and the future generations. For each typology of stakeholder are provided information about the communication tools used and the activities carried out in order to communicate with them. This information also outlines the effects on stakeholders stemming from company strategies and activities. For example, in the workforce section, information is provided on the turnover, the diversity and equal opportunities, the training and professional development, the rewards and bonuses, the health and safety, the industrial relations, the internal communication, the recreational associations and the staff morale.

Information tailored on the typology of stakeholder is provided at the beginning of all sections, except those dedicated to the financial institutions and the public administrations. These sections are drawn up using a common content structure consisting of information about the objectives and performance and the breakdown of the stakeholders.

In order to be more informative about the group's future activities and objectives and to provide an evaluation on the activities carried out during the last financial year a specific visual disclosure frame is adopted. In particular, a three cells table is displayed, each cell respectively titled: "What we said we would do...", "What we have done..." and "We shall...". The first cell shows the objectives of the company defined in the previous financial year as objectives to be reached by the end of the year which the report refers to. The second cell contains the description of all the activities the company has carried out during the year to reach the aforesaid objectives and the results achieved. In the third cell, information about the future activities to be met in order to fill the gap between the objectives to be reached and the performance obtained are displayed (Fig. 19.7).

In addition to all the information contained in the Sustainability Report, much more information is provided through the company website. In particular, a specific web address has been devoted to the presentation of the Sustainability Report. On the

What we said we would do...	What we have done...
• Implement the regular production of reports on the use of the waste collected separately, making the contents more extensive along with the sphere of the external audit.	• In October 2012, the 3rd edition of "Tracking waste" was published. The divulgation of the document and the sphere of the external audit were extended. (see page 188)
• Give continuity to environmental education activities in schools.	• The students involved in environmental education initiatives rose from 41,306 in 2010 to 51,906 in 2012. (see page 192)
• Promote additional corporate voluntary ventures throughout the local area via the "VolontariHeraPer" project. • Complete construction of the renewable energies laboratory in Forlì.	• During 2012, an initiative was furthered in all the areas: food collection day in favour of the Onlus Food Bank. (see page 90) • The conclusion of the work for creating the laboratory on renewable energies was postponed until the first half of 2013. (see page 181)
• Complete the tour of the Rimini waste-to-energy plant and create the tour of the Ravenna sludge dehydration plant.	• The tour of the Rimini waste-to-energy plant was opened in March 2012 while that related to the Ravenna sludge dehydration plant was opened in April 2012. (see page 189)

We shall...

- Plan and launch in two areas during 2013 a new governance model for the involvement of the stakeholders in sustainability aspects aimed at strengthening the protection of the area: set up two local multi stakeholder committees by the end of the year.
- "Gift a tree to your city" campaign: launch the first municipal replanting measures for the achievement of the objectives in terms of compliance with the on-line bill.
- Open the renewable energies laboratory in Forlì during 2013.
- Give continuity to environmental education activities in schools and continue to promote visits to the plants run by the Group.
- Carry out a communications campaign against the abandonment of waste.
- Launch the "Decoro urbano" project aimed at improving the quality of waste collection in the historic centres of the main towns and cities.
- Define and implement disclosure and involvement initiatives for local communities in relation to the "Polo Energie Rinnovabili" project in Ferrara.
- Design the new Group website in 2013 and launch the creation thereof.

Fig. 19.7 Hera's objectives and performance relative to local communities. *Source*: HERA sustainability report (2012: p. 187)

website it is possible to find all the information contained in the printed version of the document and links to the different sections of the company website, especially the social responsibility, investor relations and the corporate governance sections. In these sections of the company website, more detailed information about the different topics showed in the report are provided. HERA's efforts have been awarded as the best company in Italy for online corporate social responsibility (CSR) communications (see the websites http://www.gruppohera.it and bs.gruppohera.it—accessed on July 2013).

19.3 Discussion

In this section an analysis and discussion of the HERA Sustainability Report is proposed by comparing the document with the provisions contained in the IR, especially those contained in the Sect. 19.4 (content elements) of the framework.

From a general point of view, the HERA Sustainability Report is very similar to an integrated report. In fact, the HERA Sustainability Report outlines different viewpoints (economic, social and environmental), the company's strategy and results. But because of the particularity of the economic sector where the company operates in and the strong presence of public organisations as shareholders of its share capital, the report is particularly focused on showing information about issues that could affect or have already affected its stakeholders. This feature is not in contrast with the provision contained in the IR. All the company's stakeholders are equally considered and accounted for whereas the IR states that "an integrated report should be prepared primarily for provider of financial capital in order to support their financial capital allocation assessments" (IICR 2013: p. 8). Because of the aforesaid peculiarities, the accounting information showed in the report is focused on the value added and its distribution among the stakeholders instead of stressing the production of profit or the increase in the shares value. In general, always because of the aforesaid peculiarities, the report is less concentrated on the financial information and more on the quantitative but non-financial information relative to the effects that the company activity produces on its stakeholders. These are the reasons why the report has been nominated Sustainability Report and not Integrated Report although it can be assimilated to an integrated report from many points of view. Beside the report's name, the importance in HERA in providing integrated information is testified by the board of directors' approval of the document contemporaneously with the approval of the Financial Statements.

Moreover, the way through which the comparability principle is respected in drawing up the report deserves to be highlighted. Even if along the years the information contained in the report could refer to different and not fully comparable issues, in the second section of the report, a table containing 28 consistent KPIs is provided. This makes the report not only integrated as containing information about different aspects, but also flexible and stable at the same time. In fact, these consistent KPIs are: relative to the economic, social and environmental aspects of the company activity; used as indicators also in the other documents of the planning and control system; made more informative through the disclosure of all the information contained in the other sections of the report.

Moving to the comparison of the fourth paragraph of the IR with the content of the HERA's report, it is possible to assess the wide compliance of the report with the framework of reference. As provided by the framework, at the beginning of the HERA's report, the following information is provided: the organisation's materiality determination process, the governance body with oversight responsibility for the reporting and the reporting boundary and how it has been determined. After this information, coherently with the IR, an organisational overview and the governance structure of the company are displayed. The information about the external environment is not displayed in a specific paragraph, but are disseminated along all the sections dedicated to the different company stakeholders. In these sections, it is also possible to find the information about many of the different capitals and the business model the IR analytically refers to respectively in the sections 2B and 2C. Even if not in a specific section of the document, the business model, especially its outputs and outcomes, is many times explicated because it has to be implemented in different business sectors that are regulated by national and supra-national laws. A shortage in the information provided on the business model is about the interconnections and potential synergies stemming from the company operating in different public service sectors. Similarly to the business model, the information about the different HERA's capitals are disclosed in the specific sections dedicated to each stakeholder. With reference to the HERA's capitals, an important aspect to highlight is internal structure of the perspectives utilised in the BSC strategy map. As showed in the Fig. 19.4, all the typologies of actions to be carried out in order to implement the company strategy and reach the planned objectives have been classified in a way that recall the different capitals the organisation has at disposal. For example, the action named "infrastructure portfolio development" is related with the "Manufactured capital", the other action, "Improvement of image and continuous focus on reputation", is related with the intellectual capital while the action "increase customer satisfaction" is related with the social and relation capital. This structure of the BSC strategy map could be a good starting point for a better and more structured presentation of the information about the HERA's capitals as required by the IR.

To be more compliant with the IR, two issues need to be better disclosed: the opportunity and risks and the future outlook. With reference to the former, in the HERA Sustainability Report, some information about the risks the company has to face are disclosed. A section dedicated to the risks of the company is provided on the company website but it should also be included in the HERA Sustainability Report. The future outlook section is the one that needs more development. At the moment, as declared during the meeting in Modena where the report was presented to the public, this aspect of the document has not been fully developed mainly because it is contained in the 5-year strategic planning document that is updated on a rolling based procedure.

Finally, it is particularly interesting that the company website is used in order to integrate and disclose complementary information to those contained in the report. In order to make the consultation of the website easier, a specific web address has been use in order to provide a web environment within which only the information contained in the report are displayed and only the links to other specific information are made available. In this way the company has been able to be selective in providing information and to avoid to any potential web-reader of the report to face the overload of information generates by the openness of the web technology.

19.4   Final Remarks

In the raising complexity of the environment within which companies have to operate and the increasing typologies and amount of stakeholders involved by a company, the drawing up of an integrated reporting is one of the most challenging and demanding tasks for any company. Stakeholders need more and more information to make any decision and companies are called to meet this information need. Drawing up an integrated report pulls many problems to the surface. Some of these problems concern the integration of the information contained in the integrated report with those contained in the other documents used by a company as part of its planning and control system and the consistency, materiality and completeness of the information disclosed. These aspects are even more important in a company providing public services in regulated sectors and owned by both public and private subjects.

The case presented in this chapter demonstrates the possibility to make convergent all the potentially contrasting interests involved in a company as that analysed. An integrated report could be a useful tool through which reach the aforesaid objective. To this end some suggestions may be drawn from the HERA case-study:

- Insert some measures to be used also in the top management remuneration system in order to create a strong involvement of the management in caring about the aspects disclosed in the report. To this end is also important to use some of the indicators contained in the integrated report in the other documents that are part of the company's planning and control system. This linkage among many documents make the integrated report more a final result of a continuing process than an assemblage of information at the end of the financial year (Durden 2008);
- Insert a set of information consistent along the years in order to make possible comparisons without reducing the flexibility of the integrated report in giving different information according with the contingency;
- Provide a strong top management support to the integrated reporting process. In the case study presented in the chapter a specific department has been established in the organisational structure of the parent organisation and the report is approved by the board of directors together with the Financial Statements.

These are the main aspects that seem to have fostered the adoption and wide spreading of the integrated report within and outside the company. Besides all this aspects, it is necessary to remember that an integrated report, as any other accounting document, cannot be considered as a simple tool that is unable to influence the development of the reality within which a company operates. The information provided by an integrated report and the structure of power stemming from its existence impact the way through which a company and its stakeholders operate. Therefore, in the future, researchers will certainly have to analyse the different roles played by the integrated report(ing).

References

Accountability UK (2008) AA1000 accountability principles. http://www.accountability.org. Accessed Jul 2013

Barretta A, Busco C (2011) Technologies of government in public sector's networks: in search of cooperation through management control innovations. Manag Account Res 22(4):211–219

Barretta A, Ruggiero P (2008) Ex-ante evaluation of PFIs within the Italian health-care sector: what is the basis for this PPP? Health Policy 88(1):15–24

Barretta A, Busco C, Ruggiero P (2008) The role of trust in the PFI: an explorative analysis on the Italian health-care sector. Public Money Manage 28(3):179–184

Birnberg J (1998) Control in interfirm co-operative relationships. J Manag Stud 35(4):421–428

Dekker HC (2004) Control of inter-organizational relationships: evidence on appropriation concerns and coordination requirements. Acc Organ Soc 29(1):27–49

Durden C (2008) Towards a socially responsible management control system. Account Audit Account J 21(5):671–694

Goldsmith S, Eggers WD (2004) Governing by network. The new shape of the public sector. Brookings Institution Press, Washington, DC

GRI (2011) Sustainability Reporting Guidelines, 3.1 version. https://www.globalreporting.org. Accessed Jul 2013

Gruppo Bilancio Sociale (2013) Il Bilancio Sociale. Giuffrè, Milano

Hakansson H, Lind J (2004) Accounting and network coordination. Acc Organ Soc 29(1):51–72

Hera (2012) HERA sustainability report at. http://bs.gruppohera.it/index.php?lang=1#start. Accessed Jul 2013

IICR (2013) Integrated reporting consultation draft downloadable at. http://www.theiirc.org/wp-content/uploads/Consultation-Draft/Consultation-Draft-of-the-InternationalIRFramework.pdf

Monfardini P, Barretta AD, Ruggiero P (2013) Seeking legitimacy: social reporting in healthcare sector. Account Forum 37(1):54–66

Moore MH (1995) Creating public value. Strategic Management for Government Harvard University Press, Cambridge, MA

Mouritsen J, Thrane S (2006) Accounting, network complementarities and the development of inter-organisational relations. Acc Organ Soc 31(3):241–275

Nahapiet J, Ghoshal S (1998) Social capital, intellectual capital, and the organizational advantage. Acad Manag Rev 23(2):242–266

Powell WW (1990) Neither market nor hierarchy: network forms of organization. Res Organ Behav 12:295–336

Schaltegger S, Wagner M (2006) Integrative management of sustainability performance, measurement and reporting. Int J Account Audit Perform Eval 3(1):1–19

Sheridan B (2012) Integrated reporting—dream or reality? In: *Accountancy Plus*, N. 1, March, pp 29–30

Williamson OE (1985) The economic institutions of capitalism. Free, New York, NY

Luca Bartocci and Francesca Picciaia

Abstract

Recent social, political and economic changes have led to an evolution of the concept of public sector accountability. Greater awareness among citizens and the demand for greater transparency among public officers have led to new forms of reporting. Practices in use among private companies have been adapted to public organizations, leading to the spread of social, environmental, sustainability, intellectual capital reports, and more recently integrated reports. In this context, whereas the Consultation Draft of the International Integrated Reporting Framework (2013) was designed to provide guidelines on integrated reporting mainly to for-profit enterprises, it is also extendable to the public sector. This chapter examines the case of the Auditor-General of South Africa (AGSA), a public institution which published its first integrated report in 2012. The aim is to explore the integrated report of AGSA in light of the guiding principles and content elements provided by the Consultation Draft.

20.1 Introduction

Over the past 20 years, social, political and economic changes have led to an evolution of the concept of accountability in the public sector. Initially, this concept was focused on managerial accountability, with a particular emphasis on results, followed by a subsequent extension of the application of performance measures to non-financial profiles (Parker and Gould 1999). At the same time, forms of direct citizen involvement in decision-making and reporting were activated, fore-shadowing a horizontal dimension of accountability (O'Donnell 1999). Greater awareness among citizens, and the demand for greater transparency among public officers led to new forms of reporting. Practices already in use in the private sector

L. Bartocci (✉) • F. Picciaia
Faculty of Economics, University of Perugia, Perugia, Italy
e-mail: luca.bartocci@unipg.it; francesca.picciaia@unipg.it

C. Busco et al. (eds.), *Integrated Reporting*, DOI 10.1007/978-3-319-02168-3_20,
© Springer International Publishing Switzerland 2013

were adapted, and this led to the spread of social, environmental, and intellectual capital reports (int. al.: Ball and Grubnic 2007; Campedelli 2005).

A noteworthy contribution to the spread of new reporting practices was made by the Global Reporting Initiative (GRI) which released a pilot version of a supplement dedicated to public agencies in 2005 and published a document for government agency reporting in 2010. The approach promoted by the GRI is a development of the *triple bottom line*, an approach which supports the integration of activities, results and effects, from an economic, social and environmental perspective (Elkington 1997). The underlying idea is that global reporting should be carried out with particular emphasis on sustainability, in terms of the balanced use of available resources, compatible with the ability of future generations to meet their own needs (Farneti and Guthrie 2009). In the public sector this approach is based on three different levels of disclosure: organizational performance, public policies and implementation measures, and context or state of the environment (GRI 2010).

The spread of a plurality of reporting practices has the potential to create both internal and external critical issues within the public sector. From an internal point of view, the most critical element is the traditional "silo thinking", in which various activity profiles, and also individual reporting initiatives, are conceived separately, and often managed by different administrators that do not interact. In terms of external accountability, the proliferation of multiple reporting instruments, often complex and difficult to read, is likely to further disenfranchise citizens that lack specific technical expertise, and are not motivated to take a close interest in such reports.

The proliferation of reporting procedures has also impacted the private sector, with negative consequences for the accountability of companies and their relationship with stakeholders. It is on this basis that the International Integrated Reporting Council (IIRC) has, since 2011, promoted a process for the development of a Framework for the preparation and presentation of integrated reports. The Consultation Draft on the International Integrated Reporting Framework (CD) was published on April 15, 2013, with 3 months set aside to solicit comments. The basic concept of this model, designed for for-profit enterprises, but also expressly extendable to other sectors, is that stakeholders need to have access to information on the value-generating factors. In this sense six *capitals* are identified, which constitute instruments for both the creation and depositing of value (CD 2013, pp. 11–14). The total value created or destroyed over a period is provided by the sum of (positive or negative) changes for each capital considered (CD 2013, p. 16). In this context, the *business model* assumes a central role, in terms of the organization and management of inputs, activities, outputs, and results. Another fundamental idea is the concept of *integrated thinking*, a global approach that allows for the understanding and traceability of interactions between all factors and processes of an organization, geared towards the creation of value (CD 2013, p. 9). The CD provides a series of guiding principles, identifies relevant contents, and sets out certain requirements concerning the preparation and presentation of integrated reports. Not all capitals need to be represented, and adaptations and modifications may be made to the guidelines, in view of the specific characteristics of an organiza-tion (CD 2013, p. 11).

To facilitate the preparation of the CD, a pilot program was launched involving a number of companies. GRI was one of the promoters of the creation of the IIRC. The document *"The Sustainability Content of Integrated Reports – a Survey of Pioneers"* was published by GRI in 2013, and contains a first survey of integrated reporting, albeit concentrating on the theme of sustainability. The GRI database[1] has collected 1,730 reports, over several years. 46 of these reports, self-declared as integrated reports, are published by public agencies.

This fact demonstrates a potential interest in integrated reporting (IR) in the public sphere. This chapter examines the case of the Auditor-General of South Africa (AGSA), which published its first integrated report in 2012. The AGSA is a public institution not included in the pilot cases promoted by the IIRC, which initially consisted entirely of for-profit enterprises. As the AGSA did not participate in the preparatory phase of the CD, it was unable to benefit from the related guidelines in the preparation of its report[2]. The GRI guidelines were, however, followed in preparing part of the AGSA report. Moreover, the King Code of Governance Principles (King III Code), issued by the King Committee on Corpo-rate Governance in 2009, set out certain obligations for South African listed companies in terms of disclosure and the integration of information. The AGSA IR was intended to comply with the indications of the King III Code, although this was not a formal requirement.

This chapter analyzes the AGSA Integrated Annual Report 2011–2012 (AGSA IR) through a comparison with the guidelines of the CD. The aim is to verify the applicability of the CD to the public sector. After describing the institutional and organizational aspects of the AGSA, and presenting a general outline of the report, this chapter explores the underlying logic and structure of the integrated report in light of the guiding principles and contents of the CD.

20.2   AGSA Profile

The Auditor-General (AG) was established on 31 May 1910, as a result of the South Africa Act of 1909. It came into operation on 12 May 1911, with the passing of the Exchequer and Audit Act 1911 (Act No. 21 of 1911). In 1992 the Amendment Act (Act No. 123 of 1992) granted the AG full independence from government, giving the organisation the requisite autonomy to execute its mandate, without favour or prejudice.

AGSA functions were later redefined in the 1996 Constitution. Chapter 9, Section 188, of the Constitution of the Republic of South Africa, establishes that

---

[1] See http://www.database.globalreporting.org

[2] The CD was published in April 2013, while the AGSA IR was presented to the South African Parliament on 30 September 2012.

Table 20.1 AGSA's organization

Auditor-General T. Nombembe							

(Planning, Monitoring, Evaluation and Risk; Strategic Organisational Development and Leadership; Change & Transformation)

Deputy Auditor-General T. Makwetu

Ethics

Chief Operations Officer	Audit Support	Specialised Services	Audit Portfolio 1	Audit Portfolio 2	Audit Portfolio 3	Audit Portfolio 4	Audit Portfolio 5
Human Capital	Finance	Performance Auditing	Free State	Northern Cape	Gauteng	Mpumalanga	Eastern Cape
Communication	Audit Research & Development	Investigations	Limpopo	Western Cape	North West	KwaZulu-Natal	National E
Information & Communications Technology	Quality Control	Information Systems Auditing	National D	National B	National A	National C	National F
Information & Knowledge Management	International Auditing	Institutional Cooperation					
Business Process Re-engineering	Learning & Development						

"the Auditor-General must audit and report on the accounts, financial statements and financial management of:

a) all national and provincial state departments and administrations;

b) all municipalities, and

c) any other institution or accounting entity required by national or provincial legislation to be audited by the Auditor-General".

In addition, the AGSA may audit and report on the accounts, financial statements and financial management of any institution funded by the National Revenue Fund, or a Provincial Revenue Fund, or by a municipality, or any institution authorised to receive money for public purposes.

The AGSA is a state institution that supports constitutional democracy and, according to the Public Audit Act (PAA, Act No. 25 of 2004), it is the supreme audit institution, with full legal capacity, is independent and impartial, and must exercise its powers and functions without fear, favour or prejudice (PAA, Section 3).

From an organisational standpoint, the AGSA can be seen as a line and staff organization (*see the* Table 20.1).

The AGSA is headed by the AG, who is appointed for a period of not less than 5 years, and no more than 10, and shall not thereafter be eligible for re-appointment[3]. Beneath the AG is the Deputy Auditor-General, assisted by three staff offices, and working with an independent ethics office and eight operational branches. These are divided into two different categories: three of these are distinguished by function

---

[3] The incumbent AG, Mr. Terence Nombembe, was appointed with effect from 1 December 2006. He served as Deputy Auditor-General for 5 years prior to his appointment, and his contract runs until 1 December 2013.

(Chief Operations Officer; Audit Support; Specialised Services), while the others have territorial responsibilities.

The AGSA is accountable by law to the National Assembly, according to section 181 of the Constitution and section 3 of the PAA. In particular, the AG must submit an annual report to the National Assembly on their activities and the performance of their functions, their overall regulation of the administration, the annual report, financial statements, and an audit report on these statements.

20.3 Outline of the Integrated Annual Report 2011–2012

The AGSA published its integrated report for the first time in 2012. The period covered by the document runs from 1 April 2011 to 31 March 2012. The integrated report constitutes a unique and comprehensive document that has replaced the traditional Annual Report. The fundamental aim of the IR is to improve the quality of accountability "in a manner that enhances and refines our story of institutional sustainability" (AGSA IR, p. 12). As declared by the AG, Mr. Terence Nombembe: "we are therefore proud to demonstrate that we indeed lead by example in practising what we preach to our auditees" (AGSA IR, p. 11).

The principal idea underlying the IR is to present information beyond merely financial information. While the concept of "capitals", as proposed in the CD, is yet to be clearly defined in the AGSA IR, financial data is accompanied in the report by information concerning other aspects, such as: the management of human resources; the results of the corporate social investment program; and the economic, social and environmental impact of AGSA activities.

Another relevant aspect of the AGSA IR is the implementation of a logic of strategic evaluation and monitoring, with the aim of highlighting the organization's aptitude to generate value in the medium to long term. As stated in the document: "performance reported in this report is measured against the objectives and target set in the Strategic plan and budget 2011–2014" (AGSA IR, p. 15), and "all business units remain focused on the imperative of long-term sustainable value creation for our stakeholder" (AGSA IR, p. 23). The description of the business model of the organization is also highlighted in the document, as required by the CD.

Another key point declared in the report is the attention of AGSA towards stakeholders. The document lists and illustrates the interactions with institutional stakeholders during the year (AGSA IR, p. 16). Nevertheless, the IR focuses mainly on institutional stakeholders (primarily the Parliament to which the report is addressed by law), while a greater consideration of other stakeholders, in particular citizens, would be desirable.

As regards the reporting boundary, the document "reflects the performance, financial, social and environmental information for the entire organisation of the AGSA, including its head office in Pretoria, its provincial offices in Western Cape, Gauteng, Free State, Limpopo, Eastern Cape, Mpumalanga, KwaZulu-Natal, North West and Northern Cape, as well as our United Nations office in New York. No specific limitations were imposed on the scope and boundary of this report" (AGSA IR, p. 23).

The document is divided into seven sections. The main contents are as follows:

- Report of the Auditor-General and Deputy Auditor-General's review;
- Organisational overview, business model and operating context;
- Performance review for 2011–2012;
- Sustainability performance review;
- Key strategic priorities for 2012–2013;
- Governance, remuneration policies and auditing reports;
- Annual financial statements and GRI index.

An independent external auditor certified key information relating to the sustainability performance of the AGSA. The auditor also reviewed the financial statements and the organization's performance information. This was undertaken in accordance with ISAE 3000, issued by the International Auditing and Assurance Standards Board. The related independent assurance report can be found in Section 6 of the AGSA IR.

20.4 Analysis of Content Elements

The CD identifies the content elements to be described in the integrated report. These are defined as relevant and necessary elements, in order to ensure adequate information and the satisfaction of stated objectives. These are: organizational overview and operating context; governance; strategy and resource allocation; opportunities and risks; business model; performance; future outlook. These elements are closely interrelated, and must be presented in a manner that highlights their connections and interconnections. The aim of this section is to examine the contents of the AGSA IR in light of the relevant elements referred to by the CD.

20.4.1 Organisational Overview and External Environment

Among the important elements that should be contained in an integrated report, the CD suggests the description of organizational profiles and the external environment in which the company operates. The main purpose of this information is to describe the organizational structure, its culture, the core values, the mission and vision (internal profile), alongside the factors that can affect the organization's ability to create value by interacting with the external environment (external profile). This information is largely contained in Section 2 of the AGSA IR, which illustrates the purpose and functions of the institution, its independent nature, and its regulation by the Constitution and the PAA. The purpose of the AGSA is to achieve the best results, in terms of efficiency and effectiveness. A description of operations follows, highlighting that the institution is present in the entire territory of the State, and that the organizational structure is characterized by a "line and staff" structure, with operational tasks divided by function and geographical areas.

Furthermore, the introduction to the document describes the mission, vision and value system of the AGSA. The mission of the organization is "to strengthen our country's democracy by enabling oversight, accountability and governance in the public sector through auditing, thereby building public confidence", while the vision is "to be recognised by all our stakeholder as a relevant Supreme Audit Institution that enhances public sector accountability" (AGSA IR, p. 3).

The introduction also contains a reference to the values of the institution; in other sections, these values are related to concrete actions, primarily oriented to the promotion of social integration and equal opportunities. The attention given to social integration and equal opportunities is also motivated by the unique history of South Africa and its vicissitudes with regard to the struggle for racial integration.

There is a special focus in the AGSA IR on the operating context, which regards the different environments in which the institution operates, and its ability to influence them. A distinction is made between external and internal environments. In particular, this section illustrates the key material issues in depth, in the following areas:

- *political context*, in terms of the government's goals and objectives for the country;
- *economic context*, in terms of the implications of the new public infrastructure drive; continued application of the AGSA funding model; improved collection of municipal debt; effective retention strategies and competitive remuneration packages; continued focus on fruitless and wasteful expenditure in South Africa; continued implementation of the trainee auditor scheme;
- *social context*, in terms of continued application of B-BBEE[4] initiatives; continued display of good citizenship and support to the auditing profession; analysis of the social context of external and internal stakeholders; effective engagement and surveying of both the internal and external environment;
- *environmental context*, in terms of further development of skills for environmental auditing and reduction of the environmental footprint.

The description of the operating context of the AGSA IR is aligned with the CD, allowing for an adequate assessment of the environmental factors that may affect the organization's activities.

20.4.2 Governance

The governance framework of AGSA is defined by the Constitution, which establishes the institution's structure, principles, and key functions (*see the* Table 20.2).

Unlike a for-profit company, which is free to establish the most suitable form of governance in support of the creation of value, in the case of AGSA the structure, guiding principles and key functions are predetermined by the Constitution, and

---

[4] Broad-Based Black Economic Empowerment (B-BBEE) is a form of economic empowerment initiated by the South African government, with the aim of distributing wealth across a broad a spectrum of South African society.

Table 20.2 AGSA's framework

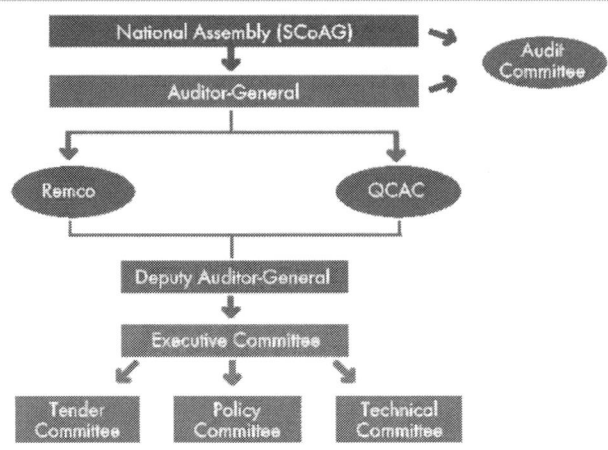

cannot be modified. Still, the integrated report provides details on the governance system of AGSA. Particularly, the document describes the functions of each office, the calendar of their meetings, the issues addressed during these meetings, and the attendance of individual members, so as to show the degree of effective participation, and the manner in which decisions were made. To complete the information on the governance system, this section contains a report on remuneration policies, which states that "the AGSA's approach to the remuneration of employees and senior manager is similar in that remuneration in both cases is informed by comprehensive salary market benchmarks" (AGSA IR, p. 117). In this context, the crucial factors for the level of remuneration are:

• "paying for performance and, where applicable, scarcity of skills;
• cost-to-company offers that are competitive;
• affordability;
• observing governance requirements applicable to reward and recognition" (AGSA IR, p. 117).

20.4.3 Opportunities and Risks

In line with the provisions of the CD, the AGSA IR must contain information on the opportunities and risks that may affect the ability to create value over time and, in particular, on the origins of these opportunities and risks, the manner in which the organization evaluates their emergence, and the extent of their effects on performance. The "Report Profile" section declares that "a start was made to identify material sustainability issues, in addition to those already covered in the five commitments, focusing on the risks and opportunities in the operating context of the AGSA. This was done by means of structured meetings and workshops with relevant senior management" (AGSA IR, p. 23).

These elements, however, appear to be only hinted at, and there is a lack of real analysis of their relationship with the performance of AGSA. One reason for this marginalization can be attributed to the nature of the institution that, as a public body that is strictly regulated by law, is particularly "constrained" in its administration, and thus unlikely to be influenced by opportunities and risks.

20.4.4 Strategy and Resource Allocation

Strategic goals are well described in the integrated report. In particular, five objectives that "guide all our actions" (AGSA IR, p. 33) are reported. These are:
- Simplicity, clarity and relevance of messages in all communication with internal and external stakeholders;
- Visibility of leadership to all internal and external stakeholders;
- Strengthening human resources to achieve a skilled, high-performing and diverse workforce;
- Leading by example in all internal processes;
- Funding operations in an economical, efficient and effective manner.

The first objective complies with the institutional objectives of the AGSA, and refers to improving auditing. A series of initiatives during the financial year improved the quality of communications, such as the introduction of an AGSA "house style" for the production of simple, clear, and relevant documents.

The strategic goals No. 3 and 4 concern human resources management and engagement with stakeholders. In this respect, the integrated report describes the activities oriented to the management and improvement of human capital, such as training, wellness programs and health issue awareness. Support for young students through the provision of scholarships and training courses are also described.

Another important strategic goal is to "lead by example", in continually improving the quality and timeliness of all reports, adhering to standards of clean administration.

The final strategic goal regards funding activities. The report offers a reasonably accurate analysis of the results for the period, and a comparison between what was achieved and budget estimates (*see the* Table 20.3).

The strategies adopted by the organization, while described in a rather complex fashion, do not clearly correlate with the plans adopted for the allocation of resources. The description is qualitative, and lacks quantitative indicators.

20.4.5 Business Model

The business model is defined by the CD as the system adopted by the organisation to manage inputs, business activities, outputs and results, to create value over time. It represents the heart of an organization. This element should be described in the integrated report in a manner that highlights the principal types of input, significant business activities, outputs, and key results obtained, both internally and externally.

Table 20.3 Comparison between performance measures and targets

AGSA's commitment	Performance measure	Target 2011–2012	Actual performance	Comments
Simplicity of our reports	Percentage clarity of message on root causes in all our reports	100 %	100 %	Achieved
Visibility of leadership	High-quality, value-adding stakeholder interactions are conducted and escalated, where necessary	100 %	100 %	Achieved
Strengthen human resources	Culture index	Industry norm: 3.2	3.71	Exceeded
	Leadership index	Industry norm: 3.2	3.76	Exceeded
	Staff engagement index	Industry norm: 3.2	4.01	Exceeded
Funding	% net surplus	3.76 %	4.79 %	Exceeded
	% debt collected within 30 days (Nat. A to F, Gauteng & WC)	75–80 %	67 %	Partially achieved
	% debt collected within 30 days (Limpopo, KZN)	65–70 %	45 %	Partially achieved
	% debt collected within 30 days (NW, FS, NC, EC & MP)	55–60 %	37 %	Partially achieved
	Creditors payment terms	45 days	31 days	Exceeded
Lead by example	Achieve dean audit report on the AGSA	Clean audit report	Clean audit report	Achieved
	Achievement of identified B-BBEE	Level 4 rating	Level 3	Exceeded
	% adherence to quality standards	Regularity audits: 86 %	70 %	Partially achieved
		Non-audit: 3 rating	100 %	Achieved
	% compliance with statutory and legislative deadlines	PFMA reports: 90 %	94 %	Exceeded
		MFMA reports: 90 %	96 %	Exceeded
		Annual report: 100 %	100 %	Achieved
		Strategic plan: 100 %	100 %	Achieved
		Investigation reports: 95 %	66 %	Partially achieved
		Performance audit reports: 95 %	100 %	Exceeded

In the integrated report, the AGSA declares that it is a "self-funding organisation that bills its auditees (clients) based on time worked at published tariffs. This business model allows us to pay for our indirect expenditure and achieve a minimal surplus of 4 % to finance our human capital resources and capital expenditure" (AGSA IR, p. 27).

As already noted with regard to governance, the lack of any further specification on the business model may be accounted for by an extreme rigidity in organizational structure, which is laid down by law and, therefore, cannot be modified by top management.

20.4.6 Performance

In addition to financial capital, a focus on human capital and investment directed towards its improvement emerges from the reading of the IR, alongside natural and social capital in a wider sense. This fact confirms the sensitivity of the AGSA towards issues regarding integration, support projects for education, vocational qualifications, and environmental protection.

As regards performance during the period, economic and financial results are illustrated in Section 7, which reports the annual financial statement, prepared in line with the requirements of the International Financial Reporting Standards and the PAA 2004. The reports and statements set out in this section comprise the annual financial statement:

- Deputy AG's responsibilities and approval (according to PAA, the Deputy AG is responsible for the preparation and fair presentation of the annual report);
- Report on independent auditor;
- Statement of financial position;
- Statement of comprehensive income;
- Statement of changes in equity;
- Statement of cash flows;
- Accounting policies;
- Notes to the annual financial statements.

The "imbalance" in favour of financial reporting is motivated by the fact that the integrated report replaces the traditional Annual Report, making it necessary to concentrate on the mandatory information required by the applicable standards.

Non-financial information is described in Section 4 ("Sustainability Performance Review"), which analyzes the social and environmental impacts of the activities of the institution. Interestingly, the document states that "integrated reporting is not just about combining financial and non-financial information on one report, but reflects the manner in which the management of sustainability issues is embedded in the fabric of organisation" (AGSA IR, p. 91). The aim is to provide information on the direct and indirect impact of institutional activities on the social and environmental context, through the description of the activities carried out and the measurement of value created through an analysis of the value added (*see the* Table 20.4).

Information about other areas of non-financial reporting can also be found in Section 4, with regard to social, environmental and sustainability issues in a broader sense. Again, the information is mainly qualitative, including descriptions of energy-savings initiatives (*see the* Table 20.5), rather than in the form of KPIs.

Table 20.4 Value added analysis

	2012		2011		2010	
	%	Rmil	%	Rmil	%	Rmil
Revenue	–	2,074	–	1,850	–	1,645
Paid to suppliers	–	(891)	–	(757)	–	(699)
Value added by operation	–	**1,183**	–	**1,093**	–	**946**
Interest income	–	71	–	57	–	42
Total value added	–	**1,254**	–	**1,150**	–	**988**
Applied as follows:						
Paid on internal and external empowerment	**1.12 %**	**14**	**1.13 %**	**13**	**1.32 %**	**13**
Corporate social investment	0.16 %	2	0.09 %	1	0.10 %	1
Bursaries—external	0.96 %	12	1.04 %	12	1.22 %	12
Paid on employees and internal empowerment	**87.88 %**	**1,102**	**84.26 %**	**969**	**85.22 %**	**842**
Salaries, wages and benefits	85.33 %	1,070	82.09 %	944	82.19 %	812
Employee wellness	0.24 %	3	0.09 %	1	0.20 %	2
Study assistance—internal	0.72 %	9	0.69 %	8	0.61 %	6
Training	1.59 %	20	1.39 %	16	2.22 %	22
To pay providers of capital	**0.80 %**	**10**	**0.87 %**	**10**	**0.81 %**	**8**
Finance cost	0.80 %	10	0.87 %	10	0.81 %	8
Re-invested in the business	**10.20 %**	**128**	**13.74 %**	**158**	**12.65 %**	**125**
Depreciation	2.31 %	29	2.17 %	25	2.63 %	26
Retained income	7.89 %	99	11.57 %	133	10.02 %	99
Total value added	**100 %**	**1,254**	**100 %**	**1,150**	**100 %**	**988**

Part of the information on sustainability performance is set out in the section on strategic goals. The GRI index (level C+) at the end of the IR is of particular interest, as it "guides the reader to the page(s) where information relating to GRI parameters and performance indicators can be found [...] and also indicates whether the level of detail on a parameter or performance indicator is partial or more or less complete with reference to the requirements of the GRI guidelines and performance indicator protocols" (AGSA IR, p. 191).

20.4.7 Future Outlook

The CD includes a section regarding future prospects. This section should highlight the problems and uncertainties that may have to be dealt with in the implementation of strategic guidelines, and analyzes the potential applications for the business model and future performance. An attempt in this direction is presented in Section 5 of the AGSA IR, in which future prospects are illustrated, so as to facilitate a comparison between what has been done and how much remains to be done in the following period. This analysis, however, is short-term oriented,

Table 20.5 Energy saving's initiatives

Initiative	Description	Benefit
Virtual servers	Standardisation of server environments to virtual server technology in its regional and head office data centres; through virtualisation a single server is used for several applications	Increased efficiency of server usage and considerable reduction of the total energy consumption
Chillers for cooling on the roof of the Head Office building with fresh air-dampers	Compressors switch off when the outside temperature is lower than the required office room temperature of 23 °C. The water pumps and air-handling units keep running and outside colder air is used to decrease the water temperature	Energy savings because the compressors do not run
Timers and low-energy globes to control lights	Timers are set so that office lights switch off between 18:00 and 21:00 at night and switch on at 06:00 the next morning. The lights have an override switch to keep power on for another hour after it has been pressed	Energy savings as a result of the lights being switched off during the night
Light sensors and motion detectors in offices	Light sensors and motion detectors were installed in some of our offices. The motion detectors ensure that the lights are switched on when a person enters the office and lights will switch off automatically after a set period of time after the person has left	Expected significant savings on electricity usage is the long run

addressing only the financial year 2012–2013. The description of these actions is rather general, and ignores the implications for the performance of the institution.

As regards the process of reporting and accountability, the willingness of the organization to continue on the path of IR is highlighted.

20.5   Guiding Principles Analysis

The AGSA IR is structured according to the IR approach, in order to highlight the creation of value over time. Although there is no explicit indication of guiding principles, different standards have been followed in the preparation of this document. These can be differentiated in terms of their objectives:

• IR guidelines (King Report III, GRI Guidelines);
• Standards for financial reporting (IFRS, PAA indications);
• Standards for the assurance process (ISAE 3000).

With regard to the first category, a central role is played by the King Report III. This standard adapts an "*apply or explain*" approach[5]. The King III comprises nine chapters, which give emphasis to three key elements of leadership, sustainability, and good corporate citizenship (*ubuntu*). In chapter nine, the Code also recommends that organisations produce an integrated report in place of an annual financial report, along with a separate sustainability report, and that companies produce these sustainability reports according to the GRI Guidelines. In the case of the AGSA IR, the application of the GRI Guidelines (version 3.1) (GRI 2011) is self declared, as part of a process of gradual implementation of non-financial reporting.

The financial information is prepared in accordance with the IFRS and the indications of the PAA. The latter, in section 41, establishes that "the financial statements must be in accordance with South African Statements of Generally Accepted Accounting Practice or other international best practice approved by the oversight mechanism". In this case, IFRS is considered appropriate for the representation of the financial and economic performance of the institution.

The AGSA IR is also subjected to a process of assurance by an independent body, in order to safeguard the credibility of sustainability and performance information. The adopted standard is ISAE 3000, which also supports the reliability of non-financial information.

According to the CD, the preparation of the integrated report must be based on certain guiding principles that guide the content of the report and how the information is presented. These are: a strategic focus and future orientation; connectivity of information; stakeholder responsiveness; materiality and conciseness, reliability and completeness, consistency and comparability.

With regard to the first principle (strategic focus and future orientation), the most significant strategic areas are illustrated in the AGSA IR. Section 4 ("Sustainability Performance Review") opens with the most relevant non-financial issues, and indicates the pages that deal with these issues. This principle, however, is applied only partially, as the integrated report lacks a description of the correlations and interdependencies between the components necessary to create value over time.

The principle of "stakeholder responsiveness", which concerns the presence of detailed information on the quality of relationships with stakeholders, and the description of the manner in which the organization understands, considers, and meets their expectations and needs, is only partly followed. While relationships and activities with different stakeholders are described in several sections, little is said about the involvement and participation of citizens.

The last three principles (materiality and conciseness, reliability and completeness, consistency and comparability) pertain to the more formal aspects of the

---

[5] The "*apply or explain*" approach is characterized by a focus on the ratio of principles and the way in which principles and recommendations can be applied, rather than compliance with precise dictates drawn up on the basis of the principles. This means that, in following this approach, the Board of Directors might opt in its decision making—in particular cases and in order to protect the interests of the institution—not to comply with a recommendation, or to apply it in a different way, while still maintaining the underlying principle behind the same recommendation

presentation of information, in order to allow the user to make informed value judgments with regard to the organization. In this context, the AGSA IR suffers some limitations that arise from the fact that this is the first year of application. The scarcity of quantitative data may explain the number of descriptive sections, and this fact does not facilitate understanding of the document, and renders some information redundant. With regard to the reliability of information, the presence of an external independent certifying body allows for a certain degree of security regarding the absence of material errors, and the reliability of the data reported.

Conclusions

The 2011–2012 Annual Report represents not the first IR experience of AGSA, but also one of the first in the public sphere. Undoubtedly, the initiative has been influenced by the environmental context in which the institution operates. In fact, South Africa has paid particular attention to themes of non-financial reporting. With the introduction of the new King III Code, government requires a multidimensional and integrated assessment and communication of company performance.

In general, the analysis of the AGSA IR demonstrates a high degree of consistency with the approach proposed in CD. Most requirements and instructions contained in the IIRC Consultation Draft are, at least formally, present in the AGSA IR. This alignment with the CD can be explained in light of the close cultural proximity between the proponents of the renewal of the South African Governance Principles Code and the IIRC[6].

Despite this alignment, a clearer definition of capitals and the business model, as outlined in the CD, would be appropriate, along with the use of more quantitative information and KPIs. Also, the concept of "integrated thinking" seems restricted to the display of cross-references between the various parts of the report; there is a lack of a real mapping of stakeholders and of an in-depth analysis of the opportunities and risks faced by the institution, as required by the CD. Finally, the methodology for developing the IR could be described in more detail (AGSA IR, p. 23). Overall, the CD shows potential to make a valuable contribution to further improving the IR process within AGSA.

More in general, the analysis done in this chapter confirms the great potential of IR in the public sphere, as well as the important contribution that could be provided by the CD for public administrations that wish to implement.

---

[6] As is widely known, Professor Mervyn King, as well as being the Chair of the Committee that promoted the famous South African Corporate Governance Code, is also the Chairman of the IIRC and the Chairman Emeritus of the GRI.

References

AGSA (2012) AGSA annual report 2012. AGSA, Pretoria. http://www.agsa.co.za/AboutUs/AGSAsannualreports.aspx. Accessed 18 Jun 2013

Ball A, Grubnic S (2007) Sustainability accounting and accountability in the public sector. In: Unerman J, Bebbington J, O'Dwyer B (eds) Sustainability accounting and accountability. Routledge, London

Campedelli B (2005) Il governo della responsabilità sociale tra consapevolezza aziendale e qualità relazionale. In: Campedelli B (ed) Reporting aziendale e sostenibilità. I nuovi orizzonti del bilancio sociale. Franco Angeli, Milano

Elkington J (1997) Cannibals with forks: the triple bottom line of 21st century business. Capstone, Oxford

Farneti F, Guthrie J (2009) Sustainability reporting by Australian public sector organisations: why they report? Account Forum 33:89–98

GRI (2010) GRI reporting in government agencies. GRI, Amsterdam. https://www.globalreporting.org/resourcelibrary/GRI-Reporting-in-Government-Agencies.pdf. Accessed 9 Jul 2013

GRI (2011) Sustainability reporting guidelines. Version 3.1. GRI, Amsterdam. https://www.globalreporting.org/resourcelibrary/ G3.1-Guidelines-Incl-Technical-Protocol.pdf. Accessed 5 Jul 2013

GRI (2013) The sustainability content of integrated reports. A survey of pioneers. GRI, Amsterdam. https://www.globalreport-ing.org/ resourcelibrary/GRI-IR.pdf. Accessed 8 Jul 2013

IIRC (2013) Consultation draft of the international <IR> framework. IIRC, New York. http://www.theiirc.org/wp-content/uploads/Consultation-Draft/Consultation-Draft-of-the-InternationalIRFramework.pdf. Accessed 15 Jun 2013

Institute of Directors of South Africa (2009) Code of governance principles for South Africa (King III). Parklands. http://www.african.ipapercms.dk/ IOD/KINGIII/kingiiireport. Accessed 30 Jun 2013

O'Donnell G (1999) Horizontal accountability in new democracies. In: Schedler A, Diamond L, Plattner MF (eds) The self restraining state. Power and accountability in new democracies. Lynne Rienner, Boulder

Parker L, Gould G (1999) Changing public sector accountability: critiquing new directions. Account Forum 23(2):109–135

List of Contributors

Federico Barnabè, Ph.D is Associate Professor in Business Administration at the Department of Business Studies and Law, University of Siena (Italy). Previously, Federico has been visiting scholar at the University of Bergen (Norway). You can reach Federico at federico.barnabe@unisi.it

Luca Bartocci, Ph.D is Associate Professor of Public Sector Accounting and Management at the University of Perugia (Italy). He got his Ph.D. degree at the University of Pisa (Italy). You can reach Luca at luca.bartocci@unipg.it

Monica Bartolini, Ph.D is Assistant Professor at the Department of Management Sciences at the University of Bologna (Italy) and lecturer in Financial Accounting and in Management Accounting in several master programs. During the Ph.D. period, she was visiting scholar at the Cardiff University (UK). You can reach Monica at monica.bartolini4@unibo.it

Raffaella Bordogna is Sustanabily Reporting manager in Eni. You can reach Raffaella at Raffaella.Bordogna@eni.com

Cristiano Busco, Ph.D is Established Professor and Chair of Accounting at the School of Business and Economics of the National University of Ireland, in Galway. Previously, Cristiano has hold positions at Babson College, the Manchester Business School (U.K.), University of Southern California and the University of Siena, Italy. You can reach Cristiano at cristiano.busco@nuigalway.ie

Christian Cavazzoni, Ph.D is Associate Professor of Accounting and Business Administration at the Department of Accounting, Business and Law of the University of Perugia (Italy). You can reach Christian at christian.cavazzoni@unipg.it

Francesca Ceccacci, Ph.D is Assistant Professor of Economics and Business Management at the Department of Accounting Business and Law at the University of Perugia (Italy). She attended the Ph.D. in Marketing at University of Roma "La Sapienza" (Italy). You can reach Francesca at francesca.ceccacci@unipg.it

C. Busco et al. (eds.), *Integrated Reporting*, DOI 10.1007/978-3-319-02168-3,
© Springer International Publishing Switzerland 2013

Domenica di Donato is Sustainability Planning, Reporting and Professional Community manager in Eni. You can reach Domenica at domenica.di_donato@eni.com

Giacomo Fabietti is Ph.D.student in Business Administration and Management at the University of Siena (Italy). You can reach Giacomo at giacomo.fabietti@unisi.it

Marco Fasan, Ph.D is Assistant Professor at the Ca' Foscari University of Venice. Marco has obtained his Ph.D. at LUISS Guido Carli University of Rome with a thesis on CSR and Performance Measurement and he has also been a visiting scholar at The University of Miami (FL). You can reach Marco at marco.fasan@unive.it

Mark L. Frigo, C.M.A., C.P.A., Ph.D is director of the Center for Strategy, Execution and Valuation and the Strategic Risk Management Lab in the Kellstadt Graduate School of Business and Ledger and Quill Foundation Distinguished Professor in the Driehaus College of Business at DePaul University in Chicago, Ill. You can reach Mark at mfrigo@depaul.edu

Maria Cleofe Giorgino, Ph.D is Lecturer of Business Administration at the University of Milano-Bicocca (Italy), where she teaches Financial accounting. Previously, Maria Cleofe has hold a research grant from the University of Siena (Italy). You can reach Maria Cleofe at maria.giorgino@unimib.it

Elena Giovannoni is Assistant Professor in Business Administration at the University of Siena (Italy). In the past, she was visiting lecturer and Marie Curie visiting fellow at the Manchester Business School (UK) and visiting lecturer at NUI Galway (Ireland). You can reach Elena at elena.giovannoni@unisi.it

Fabrizio Granà is a Ph.D. student in Management Accounting at the School of Business and Economics of the National University of Ireland, in Galway. You can reach Fabrizio at f.grana1@nuigalway.ie

Maria Pia Maraghini is Assistant Professor in Business Administration at the University of Siena (Italy). You can reach Maria Pia at maraghini@unisi.it

Libero Mario Mari, Ph.D is Full Professor of Business Administration and International Financial Accounting and Director of the Department of Accounting Business and Law at the University of Perugia (Italy). You can reach Mario at liberomario.mari@unipg.it

Carol J. McNair-Connolly is an internationally recognized expert in cost management. She has authored nine trade books and numerous articles on various aspects of the relationship and development of cost management and the new technologies that define modern management practice. Holding a MBA and Ph.D. from Columbia University, Dr. McNair-Connolly currently is an Honorary

Principal Fellow at the University of Wollongong. You can reach CJ at cjconnolly126@gmail.com

Chiara Mio is Full Professor at the Ca' Foscari University of Venice, where she teaches Management Control, Business Planning and Sustainability Performance Measurement and Environmental Accounting and Corporate Social Responsibility. Chiara is Deputy Chairman of the Sustainability Party at FEE—Fédération des Experts Comptables Europeens in Brussel and since 2009 she is the delegated to "Sustainability and Csr" at Ca' Foscari University. You can reach Chiara at mio@unive.it

Patrizio Monfardini, Ph.D is Lecturer of Business Administration at the University of Cagliari (Italy). Previously, Patrizio has hold a research grant from the University of Siena (Italy) and has been visiting scholar at the University of Kristianstad (Sweden) and Zeppelin (Germany). You can reach Patrizio at monfardini@unica.it

Francesco Orlandi is a Ph.D. student in Business Administration and Management at the Department of Accounting, Business and Law of the University of Perugia. You can reach Francesco at francesco.orlandi1@studenti.unipg.it

Sergio Paternostro, Ph.D is research fellow at the University of Palermo, Italy. Previously, he has been research fellow at the University of Siena (Italy), visiting research scholar at the University of Castilla La Mancha (Spain), and visiting research student at the IESE Business School, Barcelona. You can reach Sergio at sergio.paternostro@unipa.it

Francesca Picciaia, Ph.D is Assistant Professor of Financial Accounting at the Department of Accounting, Business and Law, University of Perugia (Italy). You can reach Francesca at francesca.picciaia@unipg.it

Sonia Quarchioni, Ph.D is a research fellow at the University of Siena, Italy. Previously, she has been visiting research student at the London School of Economics and Political Science, UK. You can reach Sonia at quarchioni@unisi.it

Paolo Quattrone, Ph.D is Professor and Chair of Accounting, Governance and Social innovation at the University of Edinburgh Business School. Before joining Edinburgh, he was Professor of Accounting and Management Control at IE Business School, Madrid, Reader in Accounting at the Saïd Business School, and Official Student (i.e. Fellow) of Christ Church, at the University of Oxford. You can reach Paolo at Paolo.Quattrone@ed.ac.uk.

Angelo Riccaboni, Ph.D is the Rector of the University of Siena and Professor of Management Control Systems. He was Visiting Scholar at USC (Los Angeles), INSEAD, LSE, University of Wales at Bangor (UK), Columbia Business School and DePaul University Chicago. Angelo is member of the Leadership Council of the UN Sustainable Development Solutions Network and Chair of Med Solutions, the UN SDSN Regional Center for the Mediterranean. You can reach Angelo at angelo.riccaboni@unisi.it

Leonardo Rinaldi, Ph.D is Lecturer in Accounting at the School of Management at Royal Holloway University of London and a member of the Centre for Research Into Sustainability (CRIS). Before joining Royal Holloway's School of Management in September 2006, he worked at the University of Florence, Italy. You can reach Leonardo at leonardo.rinaldi@rhul.ac.uk.

Pasquale Ruggiero, Ph.D is Senior Lecturer in Management Accounting at the Brighton Business School (UK) and Assistant Professor in Business Administration at the University of Siena (Italy). Previously, Pasquale has been visiting scholar at the London School of Economics and Political Science (UK). You can reach Pasquale at p.ruggiero@brighton.ac.uk and ruggiero@unisi.it

Fabio Santini, Ph.D is Assistant Professor of Management Accounting at the Department of Accounting, Business and Law, University of Perugia (Italy). You can reach Fabio at fabio.santini@unipg.it

Riccardo Silvi is Associate Professor of Management Accounting at the School of Economics, Management and Statistics of the University of Bologna (Italy) and member of the Department of Management of the same University. You can reach Riccardo at riccardo.silvi@unibo.it

Loredana G. Smaldore is a Ph.D. student in Management Accounting at the School of Business and Economics of the National University of Ireland, in Galway. You can reach Loredana G. at l.smaldore2@nuigalway.ie

Sara Tommasiello is Chief Financial Officer and CSR Manager in Jafin—Monnalisa. You can reach Sara at s.tommasiello@jafin.it

Francesca Trovarelli, Ph.D student in Business Administration and Governance, is a research fellow at the University of Siena, Italy. You can reach Francesca at trovarelli@unisi.it

23220443R00208

Printed in Great Britain
by Amazon